D0378913

CRYSTAL METH

THEY CALL IT *ICE*
BY: MARY F. HOLLEY MD

God is with you

TATE PUBLISHING, LLC

DEDICATION

This book is dedicated to the memory of
my brother Jim 1975–2000

ACKNOWLEDGMENTS

I would like to recognize the assistance of the Marshall County Drug Enforcement Unit, the University of Missouri Columbia Fire and Rescue Training Institute, Ronald V Mullins, National Drug Endangered Children's Coordinator, and the vast army of scientists cited in the references, especially Drs. Feng Zhou, Paul Thompson, Nora Volkow, and George Hatzidimitriou whose medical images are used in the fourth and fifth chapters and in the photo section. Dr. Eric Voth contributed the second appendix, and his work is greatly appreciated.

Special thanks go to the participants in the Koch Crime Institute internet discussion board, inmates at the Marshall County Correctional Institute, Guntersville City Jail, Albertville City Jail, Arab City Jail, and clients at the Cedar Lodge Rehabilitation Center, who offered valuable insight into the reality of addiction.

I am grateful to David K. DeWolf, Steven C. Meyer, and Mark E. DeForrest, authors of "Intelligent Design in Public School Science Curricula–A Legal Guidebook," for their permission to use the article as an appendix for this book.

I would like to thank Sam Huffstutler, Kathy Dahlke, Gail Pinegar, and Barbara Traylor for reviewing the manuscript, and my partner Dr. David Billue for allowing me the time and freedom to pursue my passion.

I would also like to thank my husband Clay. He has wondered about my sanity at times, but has supported me in every conceivable way as I have written this book and built Mothers Against Methamphetamine from scratch. With three small children at home and a medical practice to run, there is no way this book would exist without him.

CONTENTS

OKLAHOMA COUNTY
SEVENTH DISTRICT
STATE OF OKLAHOMA

320 ROBERT S. KERR AVE., SUITE 505
OKLAHOMA CITY, OKLAHOMA 73102
(405) 713–1600
FAX (405) 235–1567

C. WESLEY LANE II
DISTRICT ATTORNEY

JOHN M. JACOBSEN
FIRST ASSISTANT DISTRICT ATTORNEY

April 21, 2005

Tate Publishing, LLC
Attn: Rita Tate
127 E. Trade Center Terrace
Mustang, Oklahoma   73064

Dear Ms. Tate:

"Crystal Meth" is an excellent desk side reference that will be of tremendous use for those in the law enforcement, health care, treatment and education communities.

Dr. Holley has done extensive research into the history of methamphetamine use and abuse, the result of which is at once both captivating and informative.

Especially significant, Dr Holley speaks out in wonderfully politically incorrect detail what only a few years ago was dared to be mentioned in a national family and juvenile court magazine - that studies reflect that important sources of strength for children who have successfully resisted criminal conduct (like drug abuse) are the simple, old-fashioned pillars of living with their married parents and engaging in the worship of God. How far we have come to require studies to prove the once obvious.

Dr. Holley reminds the reader of the existence of a real God Who really stands willing to guide us in the choices we make in life and to strengthen us in our effort to survive the continuing bombardment of an MTV culture summoning our children to worship at the alter of self-indulgent self-gratification. An assault which threatens the very foundation of our national character.

Overall this is a chilling overview of a narcotic that continues to effect us all and that is what makes this a poignant "must read" book. I expect to have several copies available for prosecutors in my office.

Sincerely,

C. Wesley Lane II
District Attorney

Author's Foreword

For twenty years I have brought new life into this world on a daily basis. I am an Obstetrician/Gynecologist practicing in rural North Alabama. But this story is about suffering and death. It is about the death of individual people, real people with mothers and fathers and children. It is about the death of security in the family, acceptance and belonging, nurture and guidance. It is about the death of a society, a nation that has forgotten its heritage, has lost its bearings, and is adrift at sea.

The subject matter is methamphetamine, an illegal drug which is destroying the lives of our children. But the drug is not the disease. The drug is a symptom of a much more serious disease pervading our nation, our culture and our world. As you read this you will learn a great deal about methamphetamine, perhaps more than you wanted to know. You will also learn a great deal about yourself, your family, your neighborhood, and your nation, again, perhaps more than you wanted to know.

Drug addiction is not just an individual tragedy. It is not just a problem for the families involved. Drug addiction is a cultural failure. We, as a culture, have so neglected our basic responsibility to provide a moral framework for our lives and families that drug addiction is the natural and inevitable result.

But there is hope. As a nation, we can change the direction in which we are moving. As families, we can heal and renew our relationships. As individuals, we can stand up for what we know is true and right. As a community, we can join together and bring hope to our nation. It will take courage, emotional energy, commitment, and perseverance to pull it off, but is it not impossible for us, you and me, to heal our nation. We do it one person at a time.

~ Mary F Holley MD

SECTION 1:
THE PROBLEM

.1.

JIM'S STORY

I am a Gynecologist by trade; I have been delivering babies in rural North Alabama for the past fourteen years. I got involved with the methamphetamine problem when it affected *my* family. My youngest brother Jim was sixteen years younger than me and he lived in a different world than I had known. My parents divorced when he was five years old. In the first grade, he came home from school to an empty house, not enough money, and a tired and depressed mother getting by on minimum wage.

Jim started smoking, drinking, and sniffing glue in junior high, followed by marijuana and a little cocaine. He dropped out of school when he was seventeen. He got his GED and tried his hand at college. His girlfriend turned him on to crystal methamphetamine when he was twenty-two. He told me he thought it must have damaged his "blood-brain barrier." He said something was bad wrong with his brain after using that drug. He wondered if I had a medicine to fix it.

I thought that sounded ridiculous. Drugs are bad, but they don't cause *that* kind of damage. After the stuff wears off, you should be okay. Besides, if anything really happened to your "blood-brain barrier" you would be dead. Your brain would completely shut down and you would die.

Jim told me he would never do that stuff again, but he did. He started using heavily, not just on weekends. He couldn't concentrate on his school work and flunked out of the junior college he was attending. He didn't show up for work when he was supposed to and made a lot of mistakes. He lost his job and had to move back in with our mother in Missouri.

One night Jim was getting high at a party, when a man next to him got sick. His chest was hurting. He got all sweaty and couldn't stand up. The man told them to call an ambulance, but nobody did. They were doing drugs and they didn't want the ambulance people to know it. Then, the man vomited and passed out. The guy had a heart attack and died, right in front of Jim—from injecting methamphetamine.

The party was over. Everybody went wild trying to hide the lab, flush the drugs, and get rid of the evidence. They knew the police would eventually find out, and everybody would get nailed. Jim thought his handprints were on the flask in this guy's lab, and he would be framed for the murder of the man who had died. He was terrified of being sent to jail because he had heard accounts of prison rape and felt certain other inmates would rape him. He would rather die. He wanted to run away to Mexico, where he thought they couldn't extradite him.

Mom knew a crazy white boy wouldn't last five minutes in Mexico, so she brought him to my house in Alabama. "Here, Mary, see what you can do with him." He was like a frightened kitten. I took him to see an attorney and tried to convince him he wasn't in any danger. Seeing the attorney didn't make him feel any better. We called the Missouri State Trooper's office and proved to him there were no warrants out for his arrest. No amount of fact would persuade him.

PARANOID SCHIZOPHRENIC

My husband and I took Jim to see a psychiatrist. They diagnosed him *paranoid schizophrenic* and told us it was probably related to the methamphetamine use. The doctor told me it doesn't take very much methamphetamine to cause schizophrenia, and that it may not resolve. They put him on medication to treat his hallucinations and delusions.

The medication caused side effects, and it took several tries to get the right dose. He would go for days without sleep, and complained of itchy feet. We never knew whether we were dealing with a side effect of the medication or another hallucination. His speech rambled and he sounded incoherent at times. He would stare into space and forget what he was talking about.

He was obsessed with the conditions in the nation's prisons, how inmates were raped, abused, castrated and mutilated in the prisons. He claimed he had seen documentation of all of this on a "Nightline" news show a few months prior. My husband looked into it, we got a transcript of the show they had done on the prisons, and even a videotape of the episode in question. None of the things he 'remembered' were on that videotape, but seeing the show again did nothing to quell his delusions.

His short term memory was shot. He would forget what he was talking about in mid-sentence. He couldn't remember to feed the dog, turn off the lights, or shut off the gas on the grill. He would not take a bath and he smelled terrible. My husband tried to make him take a bath, but he would not use any soap. He would put his old, dirty clothes back on, even though he had clean things to wear.

After about six months on medications, Jim started getting a little better. He progressed to where he could hold a real conversation. We would ask him to do something and he could do it. We helped him get a job at a factory near our home. His first day on his new job, he met a dealer. He didn't even come home that night. He came running in at eight o'clock the next morning to get his badge. He had a hangover, he was dressed in yesterday's clothes, and he was late for work. He made it home about every third day, usually late at night, and he was running with a rough crowd. He brought his friends around and we got to know them. The next time I saw his best friend was three years later, at the county jail where he had just served twelve months.

> *After about six weeks of running*
> *with his new friends,*
> *he started hallucinating again.*

Jim found the liquor cabinet and drank all the Mexican tequila a friend had given us. When confronted, he told the truth. He admitted he had taken it, yet he continued to drink. He lost his driver's license because of DUI arrests, but he still had a state ID giving his age as twenty-two, and so his younger friends would take him anywhere he wanted to go, as long as he would buy beer for them. Our driveway was littered with beer cans every morning.

After about six weeks of running with his new friends, he started hallucinating again. This time it scared me. We had two children, ages five and two at the time, and I was expecting another child. Jim said he heard our little boy, the two-year-old, saying long complicated things that a baby can't say. My baby was telling him things about the future, telling him what he should do. I had had enough.

We went back to the psychiatrist. They wanted to admit him to an in-patient drug rehabilitation center. Jim refused. I paid his security deposit for an apartment and moved him into it. Over the next six months, he went through six jobs and had loud parties at his apartment. He got arrested twice for public intoxication, and acted surprised when I refused to bail him out of jail. He steadfastly declined rehabilitation, would not even go to AA meetings. He would not admit he had a problem.

He tried to work, but could not keep a job. He didn't pay the electric bill and they cut the power off. I reinstated it once, but when it happened again I let him sit in the dark for awhile. It was July in Alabama and it was hot. He cut his finger trying to splice a wire from the light fixture in the hall, so I turned the power back on again. I paid his rent a couple of times and bought him groceries. He let his hair grow real long, not because he wanted long hair, but because he couldn't get it together to get his hair cut. He couldn't take himself to get his teeth cleaned or his glasses fixed; we had to take him to the doctor when he got sick, like he was one of our children. He was twenty-two years old and he just didn't seem to understand how to take care of himself.

> *He was twenty-two years old and he just didn't seem to understand how to take care of himself.*

His apartment was full of beer cans and cigarette butts—not a clean dish in the house. I <u>didn't bring the kids around his place</u>. We went to get him for dinner on Sundays, but he would pick at his food and didn't talk much. When he did talk, he didn't make any sense. He was living in some other world. He would stare into space and flinch, and he couldn't hear what we were saying. He would play tapes of the music he had done on his guitar with his friends, and it sounded really bad. He would say, "Well, it sounded great when we were doing it."

Then one day, Jim called wanting a ride to the bus station. He wanted to go back home to our mother. "She needs me," he said. He told us that Mom was having lots of problems and he wanted to go back to Missouri to help her, so we took him to the bus station. The next day, we got a call from the city judge, a friend of ours, asking if we knew where Jim was. He had been due for a court appearance on his public intoxication charge and he didn't show up. My friend had to swear out a warrant for my brother's arrest.

SUICIDE ATTEMPT

Back in Missouri, Jim started hanging around with his old friends again. He kept late hours, couldn't hold a job, and he was hallucinating about the drug dealers. He thought they were following him everywhere and they were trying to kill him. He just *knew* they could read his mind, and they were going to find him and torture him and kill both him and his mother. He made a transparent attempt at suicide. He drank some toxic fluid and told Mom about it. She took him to the hospital, and had him committed under the 72-hour emergency commitment for a suicide attempt.

After the 72 hours were up, Jim had to sign papers to stay in the hospital. He refused to sign those papers. He thought the drug dealers were in the hospital, and they could read his mind. They were going to torture him, rape him, and kill him, and he couldn't protect himself in there. He checked out of the hospital. He didn't know what he was going to do. He knew he couldn't think right, but he was too scared to trust anyone.

> *He knew he couldn't think right, but he was too scared to trust anyone.*

Mom picked him up from the hospital and we met her at a lake house in Kentucky. We were having a summer get-together there with my brother Ed and his family. Jim was spacey and angry. He was delusional, and he had a headache that no amount of Advil would relieve. I couldn't take him back with me because of the warrants against him in Alabama. Our dad didn't have room for him in the travel-trailer he was living in. Ed had six children at the time, two of his own and four foster children. Jim went back home with our mother.

About three weeks later, he went with our mother to a cousin's wedding in Des Moines, Iowa, but he was 'out of it,' crying uncontrollably. He wanted her to leave him there in Iowa. He was afraid to go back to Missouri because he thought the whole state was full of drug dealers, and they were going to torture and kill him. Mom tried to take him home and back into the hospital, but he didn't want to go back to the hospital. He was afraid they would kill him there.

He found a gun at my uncle's house and blew his brains out on the 4th of July 2000. He was twenty-four years old.

After I buried my brother, I didn't even want to think about it for almost a year. I heard all the reports about methamphetamine busts, and I knew it was a national problem. I was seeing patients in my office who were addicted, and I saw the same symptoms in them I had seen in Jim. Then I started looking into it as a physician. I looked it up on Pubmed, an online medical research database, and read some scientific articles about the biochemistry of this drug. What I found out *appalled* me. It made the hair on the back of my neck stand up. Oh, my God, this stuff killed my brother. And they call it "Ice."

.2.

THE SCOPE OF THE PROBLEM

THEY CALL IT . . .
ICE, CRYSTAL, GLASS, GO-FAST, TINA, CRANK

Amphetamine was synthesized in 1887 and meth-amphetamine was developed in Japan in the 1920s as a stimulant and diet aid. It was quickly recognized to be dangerous and highly addictive. Its use as a recreational stimulant has waxed and waned in Japan for many years, with periodic epidemics of addiction. Some of the best research on the biochemical effects of methamphetamine comes from Japan, where it has been studied for sixty years.

Hitler was addicted to methamphetamine; his private physician gave it to him by intravenous injection for years during the war.[1] It was tested for use in combat, and was used by German troops during WWII. You will recognize many of the characteristics of Hitler as you read the biochemical and behavioral descriptions of addiction in this book; delusions of grandeur, paranoia, ruthless cruelty and mindless arrogance. These are all classic symptoms of methamphetamine intoxication.

It was widely used by the Japanese military during World War II. Remember the Kamikaze pilots? They were speed freaks. Everyone from the grunts to the High Command had access to methamphetamine in the Japanese military. The high from methamphetamine causes a feeling of confidence and power, you feel invincible and indestructible. It causes heightened alertness and endurance. You can go for days without sleep. The advantages to the fighting soldier are obvious.

After the war, the Japanese military released its stockpiles of methamphetamine to the general public, and the result was an epidemic of addiction in the 1950s that is still a problem now and has spread world wide. Methamphetamine has been a major drug of abuse in Southeast Asia for many years.

[1] Heston L, Heston R *The Medical Case Book of Adolph Hitler* Stein and Day 1980
Redlich F *Hitler: Diagnosis of a Destructive Prophet* Oxford University Press 1998

It is called *Ya Ba* and can be had for about sixty *"baht"* (currency in Thailand) or $1.43 on any street corner in Bangkok. It was, without a doubt, a factor in the Vietnam War.

Both military and civilian populations used methamphetamine throughout Southeast Asia in the years encompassing the Vietnam War. If you are fighting against forces who are on methamphetamine, you had better be on it yourself. More methamphetamine was used by American soldiers during the Vietnam War than was used by the whole world during WWII, with 25 to 50% of enlisted men using it. [2] There is no doubt that methamphetamine abuse contributed to the severity of the Post Traumatic Stress Disorder seen in Vietnam veterans after the war.

Soldiers were told over and over that drug use would not be tolerated by the Army, and yet these same soldiers were put into situations where amphetamines were necessary for survival. If the appropriate medications had been issued in suitable forms and doses, and with proper supervision, [as they are now] the men would not have had to purchase the locally available methamphetamine. As it was, they used the local supplies of cheap and abundant methamphetamine to fight, as well as the local supplies of cheap and abundant heroin to bring themselves back down after an engagement. In Southeast Asia during the war, it was sometimes easier to get heroin than it was to get alcohol.

Relatively few soldiers came home addicted to speed. They were rather revolted by the effects of methamphetamine, since it reminded them of combat situations they would much rather forget. The side effects of methamphetamine are eased by downers like alcohol and heroin, and huge numbers of servicemen came home from Vietnam addicted to heroin. The Drug Enforcement Agency was born in the aftermath of Vietnam and the epidemic of drug addiction that accompanied the war. Some veterans struggled for years against the addictions they had acquired in their effort to stay alive in Vietnam.

Post Traumatic Stress Disorder is a major risk factor for alcoholism and addiction to other drugs. Vietnam veterans came home and got drunk and stayed drunk, many of them for the rest of their lives. Some of these men came home addicted to heroin and methamphetamine, and joined the outlaw motorcycle gangs that perpetuated their addiction with the first illicit production of methamphetamine in *this* nation.

---

[2] Baker Col SL Drug abuse in the United States Army. Bulletin NY Accad Med 1971 47:541–9
Cook RF Hostetter RS Patterns of illicit drug use in the Army. AM J Psychiatry 1975 132:1013–17

As you are reading this book, consider the plight of American soldiers returning to this country after serving in Vietnam. They had to use methamphetamine in order to stay alive in a war against an enemy that freely used it. If you fell asleep at the wrong time, you could plan on getting killed. Methamphetamine was a major weapon in that war.

Think about how the war was fought. Snipers and ambushes, traitors and spies, booby trapped babies and land mines. The episodes like My Lai will make more sense when you understand the biochemistry of methamphetamine. After staying awake for a week or more, anything could happen.

Most soldiers knew better than to get 'high' on methamphetamine. An overdose was just as dangerous as none at all. If a soldier got delusional or paranoid, he might kill his whole unit. If he lost his temper or went into a panic, he might give away his position. They used just enough to stay alive.

Imagine what these men went through upon returning to this country. They were in withdrawal, a deep prolonged depression. They were having residual nightmares and hallucinations, not just the normal post war Post Traumatic Stress Disorder, but a superimposed methamphetamine withdrawal / Post Traumatic Stress Disorder.

When they finally got home, debriefed, deloused, fumigated and sanitized for American soil, the nation they served greeted them with jeers and insults, and spat in their faces. Is it any wonder that, forty years later, some of them are still wounded, in the heart, if not in the body?

WORLD WIDE SPREAD

Methamphetamine reached Hawaii from Japan and Southeast Asia in the 1960s, and became more popular in the 1970s, with an epidemic of addiction starting in the early 1980s that is still going strong today. It is now prepared differently, as the HCl salt, a crystalline form of the drug more potent and much more addictive than the powder form available in the Vietnam era— a form called **ice, glass,** or **crystal.** Ice reached the continental United States via California in the 1970s and has spread eastward across the continent and into Canada and Mexico. Methamphetamine is now a global problem. Of the truck drivers killed in accidents in Australia in the decade of the 90s, 23% tested positive for stimulants, including methamphetamine. Worldwide, over 35 million people use amphetamines, including methamphetamine, compared with 15 million users of cocaine, and 10 million users of heroin.

> *Over 35 million people use amphetamines,*
> *including methamphetamine, compared*
> *with 15 million users of cocaine, and 10*
> *million users of heroin.*

The most recent statistics for the United States from the National Survey on Drug Use for 2002 by the Department of Health and Human Services stated that 10% of the youth and young adult population [twelve to forty years old] had tried amphetamines as a recreational drug. That represents more than 10 million people in this nation alone. Locally, the problem can be even more pervasive. The Department of Human Resources survey of the students at the Arab City High School in Arab, Alabama, half a mile from my house, showed that 20% of the juniors and seniors had used crystal methamphetamine casually, and 10% were regular users. Of the job applicants at the local sewing plant in Guntersville, Alabama, 15% are positive for methamphetamine on their pre-employment drug screen. That represents an epidemic, and it is not confined to North Alabama.

For many years, methamphetamine was manufactured by motorcycle gangs on the west coast, and was made from 'phenyl 2 propanone.' When that precursor was outlawed in the late 1980s, a method of synthesis was developed using ephedrine or pseudoephedrine, an ingredient in most over the counter cold remedies, as the base chemical. Methamphetamine can now be produced by amateur chemists using household and industrial chemicals readily available in any hardware store.

As demand grew, megalabs proliferated in the California desert, and in Mexico where the manufacture of methamphetamine is tolerated by the local Mexican authorities. Its distribution in the United States followed the Interstate trucking routes, as long distance truckers brought their speed with them. A 2002 study found that 9.5% of commercial tractor-trailer drivers were positive for stimulants on urine drug testing at a road block.

Importation by drug cartels now accounts for most of the methamphetamine used in this country. Mexican cartels dominate the US market because the ingredients are not restricted there. Huge amounts of ephedrine and other precursors can be legally purchased in Mexico and other nations with little or no government oversight, and large plants produce nearly pure methamphetamine. It is imported using the same channels and smugglers that distribute cocaine, heroin, and marijuana.

DOMESTIC PRODUCTION

Interdiction, however, will never solve the problem of methamphetamine. Domestic production will always make up for any shortages in the import market. The Federal Government recently outlawed the sale of ephedrine as a dietary supplement in 2004, but even if we could eliminate the global supply of ephedrine and pseudoephedrine, we would not solve the methamphetamine problem. The cooks running clandestine meth labs can make their own ephedrine. It takes a while, it is a three day fermentation procedure with a low yield, but they can do it.

Regulation of the precursor chemicals does make a difference. In California the bulk powder ephedrine law of 1989 stopped a seven year rise in hospital admissions for methamphetamine related illnesses, and reduced them by 35%. The single ingredient ephedrine law reduced meth-related hospital admissions in Nevada, Arizona, and California by 40 to 60%. Oklahoma has recently passed a law requiring a signature and photo ID for the purchase of even a single package of ephedrine-based medications. These drugs are kept behind the counter at the pharmacy and are dispensed by a licensed pharmacist. Meth lab seizures have plummeted in Oklahoma since this law was enacted.

Methamphetamine is cheap. The average retail price is less than $25 for a hit, less than half the average cost of cocaine. It can be manufactured for less than $1 per dose, so the profit to the manufacturer is enormous. With that much money at stake, organized crime is sure to get involved. The same network of wholesalers and retailers distributing cocaine and heroin in this country is distributing methamphetamine. They can supply methamphetamine anywhere in this nation in response to increases in demand.

> *Wholesalers and retailers can supply methamphetamine anywhere in this nation in response to increases in demand.*

Most users can alternate between cocaine and methamphetamine based on availability and price. In the state of Washington, price increases led large numbers of methamphetamine addicts to switch temporarily to cocaine until supply situations improved and the price of methamphetamine came back down. It is sometimes dissolved in coffee, referred to as "Bikers Coffee," or combined with heroin, a process called "Speedballing." Methamphetamine is often marketed as "Ecstasy" at rave parties and concerts.

Methamphetamine use has classically been found in large cities on the west coast and Hawaii, where it has been a problem for twenty years.

Speed freaks are a common sight in homeless shelters and mental hospitals in many areas. San Francisco, Los Angeles, and San Diego, California; Seattle, Washington; Phoenix, Arizona; and Denver, Colorado are all major hot spots in the recent epidemic. It has spread eastward, and is now a *national* problem. Methamphetamine has recently become popular with the gay nightclub scene in New York City.

But "ice" is not limited to the big cities anymore. Methamphetamine is fast becoming a rural problem, with clandestine labs sprouting like clover in the countrysides. There are two reasons for this: First, the labs emit a strong odor that is difficult to hide in a metropolitan area. It is typically made in a chicken house on ten acres with no neighbors, thus one of its nicknames, 'high speed chicken feed.' Second, the level of law enforcement is usually lower in the rural areas of the nation, where three or four sheriff's deputies police up to 50,000 people. Labs are easily hidden and highly mobile. They can be dismantled and moved in one day. It can be made in a motel room or a college dormitory; some stages of the process can be done in a space as small as a shoebox. The trunk of a car is plenty of room for a lab.

METH LABS

In 1993, Colorado state officials busted twenty-five meth labs per year. In 2003 authorities busted 500 meth labs in one year, an 1800% increase over just ten years. The statistics are about the same for every state in the nation. There are meth labs in the middle of neighborhoods and next to elementary schools. They are run by intoxicated and armed men who are ready to shoot to kill. The "cooks" making this stuff are not concerned about where they dump the solvents and byproducts from the manufacture of methamphetamine.

The chemicals used to make methamphetamine are toxic, flammable and explosive, and a working lab is truly a dangerous place to be. The cook in charge of the lab is frequently high, paranoid, or in withdrawal, which makes the situation even more hazardous. Explosions and fires are common and deadly. Many of the solvents used in the manufacture of methamphetamine are themselves intoxicating, like sniffing glue. Long term addicts, who don't get high on crystal anymore, can still get high on the fumes from cooking it. That is an "inhalant high."

Many clandestine meth labs are housed in middle class neighborhoods where families live in close proximity. Children living in or near these homes are exposed to the toxic chemicals and fumes resulting in brain damage and other health problems. Two-year-olds play with canisters of nitroethane and breathe in the fumes of anhydrous ammonia. Babies crawl among puddles of phenylacetone, and then put their fingers in their mouths. Many states have made it a felony to have children living in a meth lab. Adding felony child abuse to the charges keeps the cooks in jail longer.

You are the eyes and ears of your local police department. You are looking for canisters of anhydrous ammonia and discarded cans of Red Devil Lye accumulating in the yard. Cooks go through thousands of packages of Sudafed or Actifed to get the ephedrine they need to make methamphetamine. They will dispose of the discarded packaging in their burn pile. You might notice large quantities of Coleman fuel, lithium batteries, and books of matches in the garbage, starter fluid, murantic acid for cleaning swimming pools, rock salt, toluene, or iodine. Be alert to unusual odors. The fumes may have the overwhelming odor of cat urine, or smell like the chemistry lab when you were in high school.

When you report a lab in your neighborhood, don't be surprised if it takes awhile for the authorities to crack down on it. They are a lot more interested in making arrests than shutting down the lab. It won't do anyone any good to just bust the lab and confiscate the chemicals if the cooks are still at large. Often, a set of cooks will operate labs in multiple locations, and the lab you see doesn't get busted at all, but the people responsible for it are arrested at another location. Police will often then watch the lab in your neighborhood to see if any more 'roaches' move in and resume production.

A meth lab is a serious toxic waste disposal problem. The cooking process yields five to six pounds of toxic waste per pound of product, which is usually dumped down the toilet or spilled on the ground. These chemicals are flammable and explosive chlorinated solvents and carcinogens, and they are in your local sewage treatment facility and ground water supply. Byproducts and waste include things like benzyl cyanide, sodium cyanoborohydride, benzaldehyde, and nitric acid. When a lab is dismantled, the waste has to be disposed of, and the chemicals are usually incinerated—an expensive process.

The cooking process yields five to six pounds of toxic waste per pound of product.

As mentioned, the base chemical used is ephedrine or pseudoephedrine found in cold tablets and diet pills. Common ingredients for the manufacture of methamphetamine include kerosene, lye, anhydrous ammonia, lithium from batteries, and toluene which are used in the "Nazi" method of meth manufacture. Drain cleaner [lye], red phosphorus from the heads of matches or from flares, and iodine are used in the "Red P" method. Recipes abound on the internet and circulate in jails. Click on "methamphetamine" on Amazon.com, and the first available selection is a cookbook produced by "Uncle Fester" out of Washington State with detailed instructions and tips for the home-brewing industry.

There are many different recipes for methamphetamine, and a good cook can make it out of whatever he can get his hands on. If one chemical is banned or traced by the government, they can adjust the recipe and find a substitute. Large quantities of these chemicals can be ordered from agricultural and industrial supply houses with no questions asked. Uncle Fester provides information on the legitimate uses of each chemical so the careful cook can say the right things when purchasing the ingredients for methamphetamine.

Most home-made labs turn out small volumes of poor quality crystal to be used by the cook and his friends. Home-made methamphetamine is usually only about 40% pure. Often, it is not really methamphetamine they are making, but one of the precursors or byproducts, some of which are more toxic than meth itself. The impurities are filtered out with a coffee filter, which does not do a very good job. Home-made meth might be yellow, red, green, or brown depending on the recipe and filtering equipment used, and on how much of a hurry the cook was in. Common impurities are lead, boron, and mercury, which are themselves poisonous.

"Ice" is 'crystalline methamphetamine hydrochloride,' and can be *smoked* or *injected* intravenously, whereas plain methamphetamine powder is *snorted* or taken *orally*. The ice form of the drug gives a more intense high, or "rush," than the powder form of the drug. It is many times more addictive than the methamphetamine powder available in the 1960s and 70s. Methamphetamine powder is frequently cut or diluted with other substances, but ice crystals are usually pure drug, which is much more potent. The high is longer-lasting than with either cocaine or methamphetamine powder.

ADDICTION

Methamphetamine is usually taken orally at first, in the form of a pill; home-made diet pills, or wake-up pills for driving long distances. It can be dissolved in a soft drink or coffee with little change in the taste, though it has a bitter taste when taken alone. The crystalline form, ice, can be snorted or smoked, or melted in a syringe and injected. Addicts commonly put some on a piece of aluminum foil or bent up soda can, and hold a cigarette lighter or small butane torch to the back of it. The drug is vaporized and inhaled through a soda straw or a rolled up piece of foil.

Some of the fumes will get in the user's eyes with this method, so most addicts eventually invest in a pipe. They can make a home-made pipe out of glass tubing for less than a dollar, or they can splurge and buy an ornate decorated pipe from a 'head shop.' Examples can be seen in the picture section beginning on page 257.

As the addict requires higher and higher doses to get intoxicated, the side effects become more annoying. The jitteriness and pounding heart are lessened if the ice is mixed with heroin. Of course, the easiest way to do that is to melt it down and inject both drugs intravenously in a single syringe. The casual user turns into a junkie almost overnight.

Methamphetamine addiction is not an occasional problem limited to the underclass and irrelevant to society at large. Addiction can happen to *any* person from *any* family in *any* community. Intelligent kids from good families get addicted to crystal; the police chief's son and the pastor's daughter. Typically, the dealer will give it to a kid for free for a few weeks. These kids are addicted within one month of using ice on a casual basis. Once addicted, they are back with Mama's pearls and Daddy's gun, trading them in for more dope.

Crystal methamphetamine has a 95-98% addiction rate. Of the people trying ice, 95% of them will become addicted to it within one year. By contrast, alcohol has a 10–15% addiction rate, nicotine has a 60–70% addiction rate, and cocaine has a 75–80% addiction rate. Methamphetamine is by far the most addictive substance known to man. *Almost nobody tries ice just once.*

> *Methamphetamine is by far the most*
> *addictive substance known to man.*
> *Crystal methamphetamine has a*
> *95-98% addiction rate.*

The high from using ice is a sense of energy and alertness, competence and intelligence, power and control. Loss of appetite, hyperactivity and endurance are common. You can go for days without getting tired or needing to sleep. It is a long lasting high, on the order of twelve hours or more. When used by inhalation, smoking or snorting, the high is more intense and has a more rapid onset. The euphoria is associated with delusions of power and invincibility, and with sexual arousal and desire. When injected, the rush is reported to feel like an orgasm lasting twenty-thirty minutes followed by lesser degrees of euphoria for many hours.

Common slang names for Methamphetamine

Ice	Jet Fuel	Sugar
Glass	Hillbilly Crank	Tina
Crystal	No Doze	Space Food
Crank	Methatrim	High Speed Chicken Feed
Go-Fast	Jenny Crank Program	Tweak
Chalk	Devil Dust	White Pony
Gak	Redneck Heroin	Zip
God	Satan Dust	Zoom

An updated list of more than 325 slang names for methamphetamine is listed on the Koch Crime Institute website www.KCI.org.

Long term consequences of methamphetamine abuse include memory loss, hallucinations, delusions, panic, and rage. The later stages of addiction are characterized by a form of dementia—mothers abandon their babies, teenagers shoot their parents, families are destroyed, and communities are crippled. Addicts are unable to hold a job or care for their families; they are consumed by their drug use and cannot do anything else.

A large proportion of the crime in this nation is drug related, with some areas reporting 95% addiction rates in their county jail inmates. The list of crimes associated with the use and sale of methamphetamine includes property crime to pay for the drug and violent crime associated with paranoia. Sexual crimes associated with the arousal aspect of the high are also prominent features of the community infested with crystal. Methamphetamine abuse is not a victimless crime. We all pay the price. Look fo. T

PROGNOSIS

Methamphetamine and cocaine have very similar modes of action, affect the same areas of the brain, and have similar side effects. The high is more intense and longer lasting with methamphetamine than with cocaine. Methamphetamine, however, is much more toxic to brain cells than cocaine. As devastating as the crack cocaine problem has been, ice promises to be much worse.

Crack cocaine is especially popular in inner-city black neighborhoods, whereas crystal methamphetamine is primarily used by blue collar white populations. The crack cocaine epidemic has resulted in 20% of young black men in America being incarcerated at least once in their lives. Methamphetamine promises to do the same for the white populations. In 1993, there were seventy-seven cases in predominantly white Marshall County, Alabama in which children had to be removed from a home because of drug abuse. In 2003 there were 465 such cases. There is nothing unique about Marshall County. We can look forward to 20% of our children abandoned, 20% of our work force in prison, 20% of our population brain damaged or dead.

> "Dependency cases are when kids have to go live with someone else because Mama and Daddy can't take care of them. 99% of the time, it's because Mama is on meth and Daddy is on meth. In most dependency cases, kids go to live with their grandparents or some other relative. Twice in the past six months, I've had to stop dependency hearings because everyone involved in the case—parents and grandparents—had tested positive for methamphetamine. The other lawyers and myself were the only ones in the courtroom clean and sober."
>
> District Judge Howard Hawk

Methamphetamine addicts sustain significant brain damage, as we will see. 'Methamphetamine psychosis' and 'methamphetamine dementia' are frequent admitting diagnoses for mental institutions in many areas. Addicts lose control over their drug intake, and very shortly thereafter, lose control over their lives. They lose their jobs, destroy their families, abandon their children, and eventually, lose their minds. My brother and his wife in Missouri have kept foster children for the past eight years. All of the children they keep are victims of drug abuse.

The long term prognosis for methamphetamine addiction is dismal. Most addicts never recover from their addiction. Many of them never even try. Only 6% of meth addicts who try to quit on their own are able to do so. Even with competent rehabilitation, only 50% - 60% are able to stay clean long term [more than one year] without relapse. Three-quarters of all meth addicts initiate drug use in their teens, and one-quarter start using under the age of fifteen. These children are starting life with a debilitating addiction that will destroy their minds in a very short time.

> *Three-quarters of all meth addicts initiate
> drug use in their teens, and one-quarter
> start using under the age of fifteen.*

Crystal meth: they call it— "ice"? This stuff isn't ice—this is fire! One dose will change a person's life; one spark will burn your whole house down. Ice *is* burning homes down, destroying families, polluting the environment, and corrupting our neighborhoods. It is destroying our workforce and flooding our prisons and mental hospitals with brain-damaged people. It is infiltrating our schools and killing children.

Stage IV ovarian cancer has a mortality rate of 90% at five years. The mortality rate for methamphetamine addiction is about the same. Within five years, 90% of addicts are either brain-damaged, dead, or in prison. Homicide, trauma, and suicide are the most common causes of death for methamphetamine addicts, but there are also many medical complications of methamphetamine abuse resulting in disability and death. If there were an infectious disease sweeping through our nation that caused this kind of death and destruction, the CDC would be camped out in every high school parking lot and the whole nation would be under quarantine.

> *Within five years, 90% of addicts are either
> brain-damaged, dead, or in prison.*

In this book, I will—

- Explain how methamphetamine works in the brain, its effects on other organs of the body, and on the unborn child of the pregnant user.
- Discuss some of the popular related drugs like ecstasy and cocaine.
- Discuss important risk factors for addiction, including Attention Deficit Hyperactivity Disorder and Post Traumatic Stress Disorder.
- Explain how to tell whether your child is addicted and what to do about it.
- Address the social and cultural factors that predispose to addiction and the spiritual poverty that precipitates them.
- Finally, I will offer hope.

I have been teaching this material to addicts in rehabilitation centers and county jails for the past three years. I also share it with groups of concerned parents and youth. A community that understands methamphetamine and the nature of addiction will be equipped to fight this scourge with intelligence and compassion. We don't have to stand by helplessly while our children march off the edge of a cliff and our society is brought to its knees by a drug.

SECTION 2:
THE SCIENCE

.3.

How the Brain is Supposed to Work - Anatomy

Why is methamphetamine so addictive? How does it cause these dramatic changes in personality? Why do addicts neglect and abuse their children? Why do these people use methamphetamine in the first place? Why can't they just stop? Don't they realize what this stuff is doing to them?

$$========$$

In order to really understand how methamphetamine causes so much damage to the minds and personalities of the people using it, we need to learn a little anatomy and physiology. Any drug causing such pervasive personality changes must affect multiple areas of the brain and multiple chemical systems. Please don't feel like you have to read this entire section and memorize all the body parts. The next several chapters will use the terminology introduced in this chapter, but I will remind you of what those brain parts do as we talk about them in future chapters. *If the whole thing looks too complicated for you feel free to skip ahead to Chapter 9.* You can come back to this stuff later, should you so desire.

The Neighborhood in Your Head

It gets a little complicated. There are people with PhD degrees in this stuff, and the literature is daunting. I have simplified it as much as possible while still getting the point across. A full set of references and citations is available in the fourth appendix. I can't begin to do justice to the investigators who have devoted their lives to increasing our understanding of methamphetamine and the neural pathways it effects. Their contributions are greatly appreciated. Can I hear a round of applause, please, for all the people represented in Appendix D?

Let's begin. The brain is organized into discrete areas with specialized functions, and the center of human consciousness cannot be localized to any one particular area, but rather transcends the brain. Each part is essential, no part is sufficient in itself, for the integrity of a personality. Some of these parts are familiar to you because you learned about them in the fifth grade. Others are obscure little nuclei in the middle of the brain most doctors don't know much about.

If this were a novel, we would introduce you to a collection of characters one at a time as they entered the story. If this were a science fiction novel, they would all have strange names and odd ways of doing things. In this 'story' we will meet a lot of _characters_ with long Latin names, and they all have '*personalities.*' They do things, they interact with each other, and *they all live in your head,* a _neighborhood_ if you will, and I've drawn maps of it. I'll use their proper Latin names, but if they are intimidating to you, feel free to give them nicknames. Amygdala, for instance, (pronounced A- mig- dah- lah) can be called Amy, with no loss to the accuracy of the discussion.

Along the way you will find boxed off areas called _Nerd Boxes._ This is where I put material I find fascinating—no one else may really care. The professionals and PhD types among you will want to read what's in the _Nerd Boxes._ Everyone else can safely skip them.

Cortical Areas Fig 1a

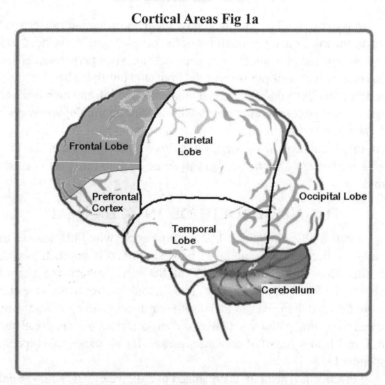

Frontal and Prefrontal Cortex: Rational thinking, judgment, and complex emotions.

FRONTAL LOBES

The **frontal lobes** are at the front of the brain, and they are important for complex thought and reasoning, awareness, logical thought, predicting the consequences of an action, anticipating the future—the stuff we call "thinking." When you see on the news that it's going to rain tomorrow, you think, "That means I can't go fishing." It didn't say in the newscast that you couldn't go fishing, you figured that out for yourself, and your frontal lobe is where you did it.

Underneath the frontal lobe is a subsection called the **prefrontal cortex.** It processes emotional information, like love, fear and anger. It processes these emotions into complex feelings like guilt, anxiety, and depression. In the old days, they treated mental illness with a prefrontal lobotomy; they just cut out the offending area of the brain. The result was a cardboard person, a kind of zombie, with no emotions at all.

The frontal and prefrontal areas work together to solve problems, like what to do when a huge truck appears in your rear-view mirror going twenty miles per hour faster than you are. Fear and logical thought work together to get you out of the way in time. A major function of the frontal lobe is what we call *judgment.* Complex decision making, weighing of alternatives, short term reward and long term consequences are evaluated in this part of the brain. You don't spend all your money on a new suit of clothes, you save some to buy groceries. That happened in your *frontal lobe.*

> *You figured that out for yourself, and your frontal lobe is where you did it.*

Anticipating the likely reactions of other people is also done in the frontal/prefrontal cortex, and has input from emotional centers. You knew your mother would get mad if you played loud music late at night, so you used your headphones. You could predict your mother's emotional response and make decisions based on that prediction. When the frontal lobe is not working properly, your judgment and reasoning are faulty. You misinterpret what people say, jump to erroneous conclusions and get angry about it. You stay out late at a party and miss work the next day, losing your job. You spend all your money on drugs and can't pay the rent or buy groceries. Those are frontal lobe functions, and they are essential for getting along in this world. People with poor frontal lobe function have a lot of problems communicating with other people and keeping a job.

TEMPORAL LOBES

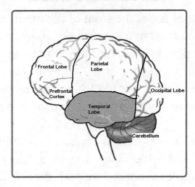

Fig 1-b Temporal Lobe: Language and long-term memory

The **Temporal lobes** are involved with language and long term memory. Memories are stored short term, for a few weeks, in the **hippocampus**, a little structure underneath the temporal lobe. If those memories are activated several times in those few weeks, they get transcribed onto the temporal lobe memory centers for permanent storage. You remember your dad in a different way than your next-door neighbor, and you know your neighbor better than the guy you met last week. All of those memories are stored in different areas of the brain.

Short term memory storage is extremely susceptible to disruptions caused by drug abuse. Alcohol, marijuana, inhalants, methamphetamine and cocaine all disrupt the function of hippocampus, causing loss of memory, loss of processing [learning], and prevent laying down permanent memories in the temporal lobe. Drug abuse makes it difficult to remember how to do your new job; you make a lot of mistakes and get fired.

Language ability is also housed in the temporal lobe. Your ability to articulate your thoughts, learn and remember verbal information, speak and write are all important functions of the temporal lobe. If you have a stroke and damage the temporal lobe, you have what is called 'aphasia.' These people can understand what is said to them, and know what they want to say, but they can't make the words come out.

Drug abuse causes a more profound defect. Addicts can't think of the word they want - that 'tip of the tongue' effect. They have an idea, and will recognize the word if you say it for them, but they cannot come up with it on their own. They talk too much, but don't really say anything, it's just disorganized chatter. They don't understand the verbal information they hear or read. You have to tell them everything at least twice. Addicts sometimes lose the ability to read. The letters are just jumbled up, and they have to read things many times in order to understand them.

PARIETAL LOBES

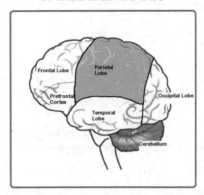

Fig 1-c Parietal Lobe: Motor control and sensory cortex

The **parietal lobes** are on the sides of the brain, and they control movement and sensation. The motor part controls your arms and legs. If you have a stroke and lose function in the parietal lobe, you will drag your leg around behind you. After using methamphetamine, the controls over your motor cortex don't work right, you may have a tremor or spasm in the muscle group involved. Your arm moves, you just don't have a lot of control over it. Your hand trembles and you spill your coffee.

Sensations are also localized in the parietal lobe. Lower parts of the brain know *something* hurts, the parietal lobe knows *where* it hurts. If somebody touches your hand, you know which hand they touched, how hard and how long, in your parietal lobe. Under the influence of methamphetamine the sensory cortex doesn't work right, your feet itch and you feel creepy crawly things on your skin, but there is really nothing there.

OCCIPITAL LOBE

The **occipital lobe** on the back of the brain is your visual cortex. This is your movie screen, the place where images are formed so you can *see* what your eyes are seeing. It has several layers of cells which distinguish things like motion, edges, contrast, color, and form. It compares one side with the other and tells you how far away something is. The image comes from your eyes, through the middle of the brain, and then gets played out on your movie screen out back.

If you've ever been in a car wreck, you've seen how this works. Everything happened so fast. You slammed on your brakes before you realized what was happening. Your midbrain saw the problem, and sent the message to slam on the brakes before the image made it all the way back to the visual cortex. Your brain saw it before you did. Cool, huh?

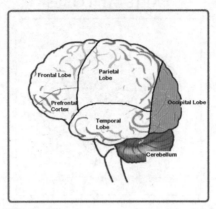

Fig 1-d Occipital Lobe: The 'movie screen'

You learned when you were six months old that if you see something on your movie screen, it's *real.* Crystal meth makes you see snakes on your movie screen, and you think they are real. You will get your gun and shoot those snakes, because they look that real. Nobody can convince you that what you see on your movie screen is not real. That is an hallucination.

Other parts of the brain can also experience hallucinations. On the parietal lobe, hallucinations are experienced as sensations that are not real. You feel bugs crawling on your skin, but there are no bugs. On the prefrontal cortex, they are emotional hallucinations. You feel anger, or even rage, when there is nothing to be upset about. You feel fear when there is nothing to be afraid of.

CEREBELLUM

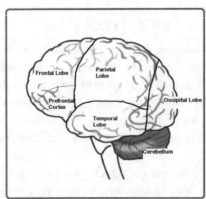

Fig 1-e Cerebellum, the balance and coordination center.

The **cerebellum** is at the back of the brain, and it is the part that coordinates movement and balance. It has fibers connecting to sensation, so you can feel the floor under your feet and sense the direction your car is turning. The cerebellum takes that information and uses it to fine tune your movements, so you don't fall over when your car turns the corner.

Cerebellum allows you to run up the steps real fast because it measures the first step, nine inches, and it knows all the other steps are also nine inches, so you can run up the steps without measuring each one. Cerebellum does the math for you. If you damage your cerebellum with too much alcohol, it does the math wrong, and you stumble on the steps.

Nerd Box

Between the two hemispheres of the cerebellum is a little structure called the cerebellar vermis. It looks like a worm, thus the name vermis. It is poorly understood, but seems to function like a 'miniature brainlet' with functions involving almost every other structure of the brain.

The vermis has connections with all of the personality centers, the pleasure center, the self control pathways, and emotional centers. It also has hormone receptors, and especially receptors for the stress hormones. That is why stress influences so many neurologic and hormonal functions.

The vermis is damaged by chronic over-production of stress hormones leading to Post Traumatic Stress Disorder. This structure is important for the regulation of emotions, and damage to it is a risk factor for drug addiction. We will talk a lot more about that in Chapter 8

If you enjoyed reading this, you will like the nerd boxes. They are not usually very complicated, but the information in them is not completely necessary to understand the rest of the material. There are just things I find fascinating, and maybe you do too.

Brainstem: The Light Switch

The **brainstem** is the connection between the brain and the spinal cord, and it functions as our light switch. It has a broad ranging network in it called the **reticular activating system** which radiates throughout the brain with two opposing chemicals, called **neurotransmitters**. One is the 'wake up' neurotransmitter, glutamine; the other is the 'go to sleep' neurotransmitter, GABA. Glutamine stimulates brain cells to fire at tonic levels and is experienced as waking alertness and responsiveness. GABA is the inhibitory neurotransmitter that makes every neuron in the brain less responsive, drowsy, and sleepy.

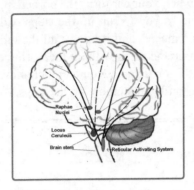

Fig 2 Brainstem; Connects brain with spinal cord

These two neurotransmitters are always in balance, and the predominance of one over the other determines whether you are asleep or awake. Some drugs over-stimulate the wake up chemical, glutamine, and you might stay awake for six or seven days, which is not uncommon on methamphetamine. Other drugs, like alcohol, over-stimulate GABA making you sleepy and relaxed. An overdose of alcohol will induce a coma, you quit breathing and die.

Just above the brainstem is a very small, very important area called the **locus ceruleus,** which also radiates throughout the brain using another chemical, called norepinephrine, as its neurotransmitter. It also mediates the sleep wake cycle, and contributes to vigilance and attentiveness. When it is over-active, in response to stress or pain, it causes anxiety, an ill defined feeling of fear or worry. It's not a response to any particular situation; rather it is an anxious tone that is there all the time. Locus ceruleus is over-active in the case of Post Traumatic Stress Disorder or Panic Disorder, causing insomnia and anxiety. Methamphetamine increases norepinephrine in this system and leaves you feeling wired.

Also in the brainstem, is a series of structures known as the **raphe nuclei** which project all over the brain using serotonin as their neurotransmitter. The best way to understand the effect of serotonin in this system is by analogy to the old mood lamps from the 60s. The soft light and a little pot made for a laid back mood. The level of serotonin in the brain will affect the basic mood or disposition of the brain. Methamphetamine and ecstasy initially increase serotonin in this system and make for a happy alert mood, but as serotonin cells are destroyed, they cause the long term depression associated with these drugs.

These three systems in the brainstem set the tone for the rest of the brain. When your mood lamp is working right, interruptions and annoying people, delays and bad news don't bother you. You are in a good mood, everything sounds good, you are alert and responsive, happy and energetic. When the mood lamp is disrupted by methamphetamine, you are irritable, jumpy and restless.

THE MIDBRAIN: PERSONALITY CENTERS

The **midbrain** structures are a collection of thirty-five or forty little nuclei and tracts, which all have long Latin names, and they control different parts of your personality and behavior. We will talk about several of them, but taken together, they contribute *continuity* to your personality. You are basically the same person you were yesterday, your temper, your disposition, your preferences and habits, because these brain parts have formed preferential ways of firing, connections that are used a lot, and your temper is hardwired into your midbrain. You can change these things, but in order to do it, you have to change the way your midbrain works, re-train it to better control your temper.

The **Nucleus Accumbens** is a small nucleus in the midbrain where pleasure is felt. Everything that feels good, feels good in the nucleus accumbens. This is where eating a good meal feels good, chocolate tastes good, a cold drink of water feels good, a warm bath feels good, your favorite music sounds good, and fresh baked cookies smell good. It is also the place where sexual arousal and stimulation feels good. Nucleus accumbens sends information up to the prefrontal cortex section of the frontal lobe, and the 'feel good' is experienced in all its richness there. The frontal lobe can then decide what to do about this thing that feels good, and a conscious decision is made.

Most midbrain structures use dopamine and serotonin as their predominant neurotransmitters. The dopamine reward system is linked to other parts of the brain, so activities like eating and sex are pleasant and rewarding. Dopamine and serotonin transmission are artificially increased by most drugs of abuse, even alcohol, and the result is a "high." Everything is funny, we all laugh and have a good time; the music sounds great, we relax and dance and enjoy ourselves after a few beers at somebody's cook out.

Drugs of abuse, almost without exception, stimulate dopamine release in the nucleus accumbens so the good feeling that is supposed to be elicited by sex or a good meal, is elicited by the drug. As the nucleus accumbens becomes addicted to the drug, the cells are changed, so they don't respond to sex or a good meal anymore. They need the direct stimulation of the drug in order to register any pleasure.

The **limbic system** occupies much of the midbrain and generates many of our emotions. It is a major contributor to our personalities. It also runs on dopamine and serotonin, and so drugs of abuse have a major impact on its function. The limbic system is made up of three different nuclei in the midbrain that work together to process emotions, hormones, and memories. Together, they mediate moods, motivation, energy level, and the emotional content of memory. This is the area where anti-depressants work; they reverse chemical imbalances in the limbic system and make you feel better.

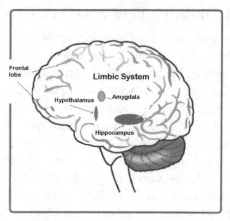

Fig 3 Limbic System: Emotional centers

The **Amygdala** mediates raw emotions like anger, fear, and love, and it increases your attention and arousal, wakes you up, when you see something threatening. Aggressive gestures and facial expressions, sudden movements and noises trigger a heightened alertness and a sensation of fear. The raw emotion of fear is communicated to the frontal lobe, so you can evaluate whether there is really anything to be afraid of or not. Amygdala works when you hear your child scream and go into high alert. You run to see what the problem is.

> *When these areas are damaged by methamphetamine, the mother abandons her child.*

You read the facial expressions of people, their body language and mood, in your amygdala; you sense what their feelings are 'in your gut.' Love and joy are also generated in the amygdala. Amygdala contributes the emotional content to nurturing impulses and maternal instinct, and damage to this area results in infant neglect. When it is damaged by methamphetamine, the mother abandons her child.

Another part of the limbic system is the **hypothalamus**, a kind of gland within the brain. The hypothalamus communicates with amygdala, and has hormone receptors allowing it to contribute to sexual feelings and responsiveness. It forms the neural basis for the feeling of erotic love which is associated with sensations of arousal. The arousal works its way through the nucleus accumbens [where it feels good] and from there to the frontal lobe [where decisions are made].

The limbic system also includes the **hippocampus**, the center for short term memory storage and processing. These areas are associated, so the memory of a certain person can elicit strong feelings about that person. The limbic system also communicates with the frontal lobe, allowing conscious experience of those feelings, and decisions based on those feelings. Simple feelings, like love, shame, and anger are generated by the limbic system and communicated to the frontal lobe, where they become complex feelings, like romantic love, guilt, and depression. The simple feeling is processed, in light of all the other things going on in the person's life, in the frontal lobe.

The limbic system produces situational anxiety, specific anxiety in response to a well defined problem, different from the anxious tone mediated by the brainstem [locus ceruleus anxiety]. A real threat is perceived, and real fear is elicited, which generalizes into anxiety when the threat does not immediately go away. For example, your kid is hooked on drugs and you are worried about him. You may not be the type of person who is always anxious and high strung [locus ceruleus anxiety], but this situation has you rattled.

LOWER MIDBRAIN–URGES, DRIVES, AND CRAVINGS

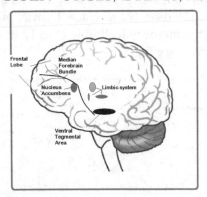

Fig 4 Lower Midbrain: Urges, drives, and cravings

Ventral tegmental area is a place deep in the midbrain where impulses, cravings, drives, and urges arise. It generates your sex drive, appetite, sleep cycle, grooming behavior, and maternal instinct, all strong primitive

desires and drives common to all animals and essential to life. When methamphetamine stimulates the ventral tegmental area, it gives rise to very powerful
cravings. Other drugs activating the ventral tegmental dopamine system are
alcohol, caffeine, marijuana, and nicotine. When you *need* a cigarette or a cup
of coffee, your ventral tegmental system is talking.

Ventral tegmental area communicates with nucleus accumbens, and
makes those drives, and the satisfaction of them, pleasurable. Sex is satisfying,
food tastes good, and rest is welcome. It also communicates with amygdala
and gives your drives emotional meaning, e.g. maternal instinct is experienced
as love. People express their love by providing things, like your favorite meal
or a cold glass of water. Your mother does that all the time, and you understand
she loves you.

When something feels good, the odds are good you are going to do
whatever made that happen again, if you get the chance. It is called a rein-
forcer. The 'feel good' component ensures that you will eat on a regular basis
and not starve to death, drink when you are thirsty, keep yourself clean, and
have sex to reproduce so we don't become extinct. It is a fairly primitive part
of the brain, a part shared with most other mammals, and so it is called the
'instinctual brain.' You don't have to think about it, you just do what comes
naturally.

Higher brain centers come in when there is a decision to be made:
what to eat and where to find it, what to drink, and who to have sex with. The
frontal lobe is the site of decision making, weighing of options, and prediction
of consequences. It takes into account emotional information from the prefrontal cortex part of the frontal lobe. This cortex allows you to exercise judgment,
and it communicates with lower brain centers by way of a network of fibers
collectively known as the **mesocorticolimbic tract** [Latin for connecting cortex and limbic structures]. See Fig 5.

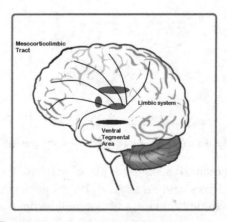

Fig 5 **Mesocorticolimbic tract: Conscious control over emotions**

The mesocorticolimbic tract enables you to control your temper, decide on a course of action, channel anger and subdue it. It allows you to evaluate fear and reason with yourself, test out the situation and see if there is really anything to be afraid of. You have conscious control over your emotions when mesocorticolimbic tract is working right. Malfunction in this area contributes to paranoia, which is one of the chief characteristics of schizophrenia. Hyper-vigilance and suspiciousness result when the amygdala [fear center] is hyperactive, and the frontal lobe has lost control over it.

Self Control

Median forebrain bundle is a two way street connecting nucleus accumbens [pleasure center] with frontal lobe [judgment], and is functionally part of the mesocorticolimbic tract. It forms part of the reward circuit. This circuit is actually a functional circle through the midbrain and frontal lobe. It is illustrated in fig 6.

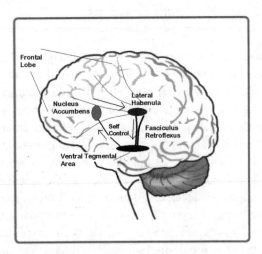

Fig 6 Midbrain areas responsible for self control

The mesocorticolimbic tract and median forebrain bundle collect information from all of the cortical areas and communicate it to the limbic areas, the nucleus accumbens [pleasure center], amygdala [raw emotions], hypothalamus [hormonal function], and hippocampus [short term memory]. They forward the most important parts to the **lateral habenula**, a sort of control center in the midbrain.

The habenula is listening to the stuff going on upstairs, in the frontal lobe, and acts to suppress the drives and urges coming from the ventral tegmental area. The connection between them is called **fasciculus retroflexus,** and it is a two way street. Ventral tegmental area says, "I feel really aroused. I want sex." Habenula says, "Not now, you're at work. Wait till you get home." It exercises inhibitory control over the cravings and urges coming out of the ventral tegmental area.

Lateral habenula/Fasciculus retroflexus is the connector allowing those higher brain centers, frontal and prefrontal cortex, to control cravings and direct impulses into constructive behavior. You can suppress your desire for a little more sleep, and get up to go to work in the morning. You get thirsty and drink water and not beer, you eat a sandwich and not candy, and you have sex with your spouse and not the neighbor's daughter. When fasciculus retroflexus is functioning properly, your conscious mind has control over urges, drives, and cravings. You can decide not to eat anything at all if you are on a diet.

> *When fasciculus does not function properly, you lose control over urges, drives, and cravings.*

When fasciculus does not function properly, you lose control over those urges, drives, and cravings. You don't control them anymore; *they control you.* You can't have one beer and enjoy it. You have to drink until you either run out or pass out. You can't control your sex drive anymore. You have to get sexual gratification right now, from the internet, when you should be preparing for the board meeting tomorrow. You are impulsive and aggressive, acting without much thought about the likely consequences of your actions.

Lateral habenula/Fasciculus retroflexus mediates maternal infant bonding, and damage to it leads to infant neglect. Lateral habenula takes the raw material of an urge to reproduce and nurture the young one, enhances it and channels it, and it is experienced as a strong desire to protect and feed your child, almost as strong as the desire to protect and feed your self. When lateral habenula is functioning properly, a mother will act to nurture her child, even at expense to herself. When it does not function properly, the mother neglects and abandons her child.

Fasciculus retroflexus is extremely sensitive to drugs of abuse. Alcohol can kill those cells over a course of months to years. Cocaine kills them over a course of weeks to months. Methamphetamine kills the cells in fasciculus retroflexus over a course of days to weeks. The tract in the brain that gives you control over urges, drives, impulses, and cravings is damaged. Some of the cells are destroyed. Now you don't care about going to work tomorrow, or paying the rent, or even feeding your children. All you can think about is getting your next hit of ice. Now the urges, drives, and cravings control you.

MIDBRAIN MOTOR MEMORY- THE STRIATUM

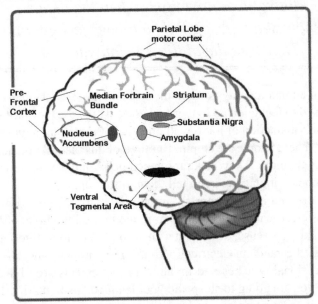

Fig 7 Striatum: The automatic pilot and reward center

The **striatum** is a collection of nuclei essential for reward-based learning. Striatum learns what feels good, and motivates you to look out for the opportunity to do it again. It remembers that a certain chewing motion is associated with something good to eat. The act of chewing was rewarding, and that's how you learned to feed yourself when you were six months old.

Motor habits are housed in the striatum: complex automatic behaviors like riding a bicycle or driving a car. You don't have to think about all the motor commands involved in driving; you are thinking more about where you are going and what you are going to do when you get there. Striatum manages the details of telling your hands are feet what to do to make that happen. Your striatum takes over when you are thinking about something else. It can drive you home and park your car, put slippers on your feet and fix you some hot chocolate, and *then* you remember you were supposed to go to the grocery store on the way home.

Some of the nuclei in the striatum are primarily involved with motivation and reward. They process emotional memories, the behavior that precipitated those memories, the desire to experience that again, and the cravings, preoccupation, and obsessions leading to addiction and relapse. Drug use becomes just as automatic as driving home. You just do it. You get in the car and drive yourself to the dealer's house without even thinking about it.

> *Motivational toxicity is when the things*
> *that used to feel good no longer feel good.*
> *They lose the ability to motivate you.*

Motivational toxicity is when the striatum has been damaged, and the things that used to feel good no longer feel good. They lose the ability to motivate you. The satisfaction of a job well done is not important anymore. "This job is boring. These people are stupid. I'm tired of this place." You don't enjoy your children anymore. They make too much noise and get in the way. They run into the house singing, and you tell them to shut up.

The striatum is also important for motor control. There is always a lot of extraneous electrical activity going on in the brain; little bolts of lightning that don't make any sense, so we filter them out. When the filtering system doesn't work, the random electrical activity gets through, and the result is a tremor, occasional twitches and involuntary movements. You have experienced this as you are going to sleep and your leg jerks involuntarily. The striatum modulates the extraneous electrical activity, so you can have purposeful movement. When striatum is hyperstimulated by methamphetamine, the result is hyperactivity and a sensation of being in 'fast forward.' Bodily motions seem faster than they really are, and the subjective feeling of coordination is enhanced. The sensations of fatigue are blunted and endurance is increased; you can dance all night. As cells are destroyed in this area, you get jitters and tremors, a type of Parkinson's disease.

THE SYNAPSE

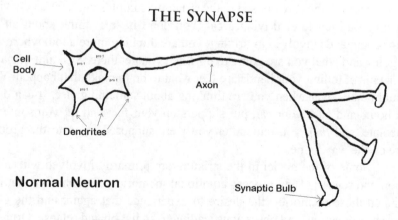

Normal Neuron

Fig 8 The Neuron: Basic anatomy of a nerve cell

How do signals get from one part of the brain to another? How does the frontal lobe make its wishes known to the rest of the brain? Brain cells have processes called **axons** that reach into other parts of the brain and touch on neurons there, to communicate with the cells in a distant part of the brain. Collections of these axons are called **tracts** in the brain or **nerves** in the peripheral parts. Some of these neurons are three or four feet long, so you can move your toes.

Brain cells don't actually touch directly; they are both electrically charged. If they touched, they would short out. They have to be separated by a layer of fluid called the **synapse**. They send their signals across that layer of fluid via the chemicals we met earlier, **neurotransmitters**, and by a process called **synaptic transmission**. Drugs of abuse work by artificially increasing the levels of these neurotransmitters, so the cells experience increased activity, even when there is nothing in the real world to stimulate them. The 'feel good' center [nucleus accumbens] feels *really good,* even though there was nothing going on that should feel good.

The sending cell, Cell A, generates an electrical impulse, called an **action potential**, and propagates that electrical signal by depolarizing the cell membrane, so that positively and negatively charged ions are displaced sequentially down the length of the axon. It is a chemical electrical charge, but it moves almost as fast as the power grid does to send current to your toaster. If you've ever hit your funny bone, you know how fast that is.

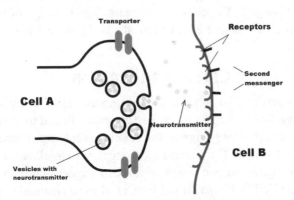

Fig 9 Detailed diagram of nerve transmission
Used by permission: United Nations International School

The sending cell, Cell A, makes an electrical impulse that reaches the end of the nerve, the **terminal**, and it releases a chemical, the neurotransmitter, into the gap between the cells. Vesicles loaded with neurotransmitter fuse with the cell wall and release their contents into the synapse. The chemical diffuses the short distance between cells and binds to its **receptor** on the Cell B side, and is recognized by the receptor for that chemical. Cell B says, "Hey, I know what sends that kind of chemical, this must be Cell A trying to tell me something."

Cell B sends a little bit of the neurotransmitter back to Cell A, and it says, "I heard you. You can stop now." Cell A then vacuums all its neurotransmitter back up into itself, and the signal ends. We recycle our neurotransmitters, using the same chemical over and over. Cell A has **transporter molecules** that are complex proteins on the surface of the cell. They vacuum up the excess neurotransmitter very rapidly, so the signal has a definite end. Signals start and stop abruptly, like a **click**. The reabsorbed neurotransmitter is recycled into another vesicle to be used again the next time an electrical signal comes along.

It took about a minute to explain all that; it takes only a *microsecond* for it to happen. Click. Click. Click, click, click—faster than that. If you put a transducer to it, it sounds like static on the radio. So how does Cell B know what Cell A is trying to say if it always uses the same chemical, and all it hears is a click? Cell B hears the interval and frequency of the clicks, and reads them like Morse code.

These cells have been talking like this for years, and they understand the Morse code. You can tell whether you are listening to Madonna or Beethoven, based on the interval and frequency of the clicks. When Cell B hears the right pattern and frequency of clicks, it fires its own electrical signal, and sends a message to the cells downstream. The *knowing* of the content of the message is a cumulative effect of all the cells that are firing on Cell B at any given time.

CELLULAR LEARNING

This transmission system seems unnecessarily complicated, but it allows for some fascinating features. Receptors are linked to chemicals inside the cell called **second messengers** that regulate gene expression and modify proteins inside the cell. The second messenger system allows for the amplification of the signal, so one receptor site can trigger hundreds of chemical reactions inside Cell B. It also allows for Cell B to be changed in some way by the reception of the signal. Cell B can respond by activating genes that code for receptors, and thus make more receptor sites, strengthening the connection between Cell A and Cell B. This process is called **sensitization**, meaning the next time the cell sees that stimulus, it will be more responsive to it.

Nerd Box

Repeated signals between two cells cause changes in the structure of the Cell B's in the midbrain that constitute cellular memory. The right combination of signals, at the right frequency, produce reactions in Cell B strengthening the synapse and making it more sensitive. **Calmodulin** is the chemical used, and it triggers changes in gene expression that change the structure of the cell permanently, storing a permanent memory. The ability of a cell to adapt to inputs by altering its gene expression is called **cellular learning.**

Cell B can be modified to make the machinery to produce a new synapse, a new axonal process, bigger dendritic spines, or a new connection with another cell. It can change the metabolism of the cell and change the protein mix within the cell. Changes like that modify the structure of the cell, and are thus 'remembered.'

Cellular learning Fig 10a

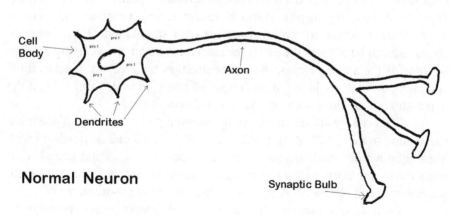

Cell Body

Dendrites

Axon

Normal Neuron

Synaptic Bulb

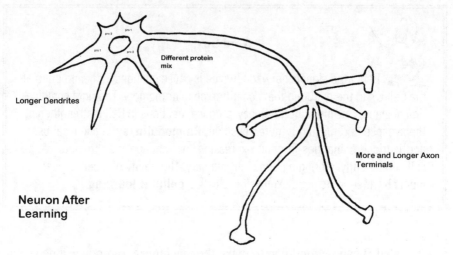

Fig. 10b Changes in the structure of a neuron with learning

This process is how connections which are used a lot become stronger, dominant, and habitual. Cells learn and adapt to the pattern of activity required of them. Frequently used connections become stronger and richer. Connections which are seldom used become relatively weaker. If you've ever left work intending to go to the post office and found yourself a few minutes later in your own driveway, you know what I'm talking about.

If a connection is *hyper-stimulated,* the cell **habituates** to it, or tunes it out. Cell B makes fewer receptors, decreases transmission, and becomes less responsive. It's like Cell B says, "Enough already, I heard you, you can stop now." First the cell **phosphorylates** its receptor, puts a molasses like covering over the receptor, to protect it against over-stimulation. With continued abuse, the cell inactivates the genes for receptors and quits making new receptor sites. If the abuse persists, the cell **sequesters** the receptor, pinches it off and internalizes it, so the offending chemical can't get to it. Eventually, if the hyper-stimulation does not stop, the receptor is destroyed.

This is a structural change in the neuron, and it takes more and more stimulation to get Cell B to respond to Cell A. When a cell is inundated with transmission from methamphetamine, this process is rapid and complete. It takes more and more crystal to get high because the receptors are protected, sequestered, and ultimately destroyed in response to hyper-stimulation.

Brain cells respond to patterns of usage. A frequently used neural pathway will stimulate additional fibers, or new lanes on the freeway, to accommodate the increased traffic. The synaptic strength of neural networks encodes memory, preferences, habits, and personality. A strong fasciculus retroflexus and mesocorticolimbic tract, with many projections and many receptor sites in the ventral tegmental area [impulses] and amygdala [emotions] makes for a person with good control over his temper. He gets angry, but he manages his response to anger and avoids saying harsh words.

Nerd Box

Neurotrophic factors in the brain also contribute to learning, memory, and habit formation. Adult neurons can secrete small amounts of the same complex chemicals that are seen in high concentrations in the developing brain of a fetus. These chemicals promote cell growth and differentiation, and repair of damaged tissue. Most people think brain cells do not divide and grow after birth. That is not true. The cells don't do it as much in the adult as they do in the developing fetus, but they do grow and heal after an injury.

Neurotrophic factors are large proteins secreted by damaged or overworked neurons that bind to receptors much like neurotransmitters do, [and in some cases function as neurotransmitters] but they use a different second messenger system, protein tyrosine kinase, which stimulates a neuron to make branches, and even to migrate to another location.

One cell can 'call' to another cell to join to it synaptically and establish communication. Only nerve cells with the appropriate receptors can 'hear' the signal and respond to it. Cells that do not respond to the signal atrophy. A cultured nerve cell can be led all over a petrie dish by dropping these chemicals in its path.

Examples of neurotrophic factors are Brain Derived Neurotrophic Factor [BDNF] Glial cell Derived Neurotrophic Factor [GDNF], Nerve Growth Factor [NGF], Ciliary Neurotrophic Factor [CNTF], Interleukins, Interferon, and Chemokines among many others.

A nucleus accumbens [pleasure center] bombarded with sexual stimulation becomes habituated to that level of stimulation, and gets no satisfaction from normal sexuality. He needs something kinky to get him going. Thought habits strongly influence the strength of connections in the brain and the patterns of neural activity. We have a lot of control over the structure of our brains.

NEUROTRANSMITTERS

Different parts of the brain use different chemicals for their neurotransmitter. There are about a dozen commonly used neurotransmitters, and some generalities about their roles in the brain. **Glutamine** is generally a stimulating neurotransmitter. It acts to make individual cells more likely to fire a signal and is associated with wakefulness, responsiveness and perceptiveness. **GABA** is generally a sedating neurotransmitter. It suppresses any given cell from firing and is associated with sleepiness, drowsiness, unresponsiveness and dulled perception. You feel the effect of GABA when you've been up too long and you can't focus on the book you're trying to read. Time for bed. [See you tomorrow.]

> *Thought habits strongly influence the strength of connections in the brain and the patterns of neural activity. We have a lot of control over the structure of our brains.*

Serotonin is used in cortical areas, like the visual cortex, the movie screen on the back of your brain. There are always extraneous electrical events going on, where one cell will fire just because it saw enough glutamine in its synaptic receptors to generate an action potential. It didn't really see anything in its retinal input from the eye, it just fired at random. None of the other cells in its vicinity saw anything. They know it's just one-of-those-things, so they put out a little serotonin to quiet down that hyper-excitable neuron over there on row four. When serotonin is blocked, using LSD for instance, those random signals get through to consciousness and you see bolts of lightning and flashes of color, or hear thunder claps and gun shots. Those are visual and auditory hallucinations and they seem very real.

Serotonin is also active in areas controlling mood and emotion, and distortions of serotonin transmission cause mood disturbances and emotional hallucinations. The mesocorticolimbic tracts [reality testing] use serotonin as a neurotransmitter, and its function is much like serotonin in the visual cortex. The mesocorticolimbic tracts distinguish the real from the unreal, and malfunction of serotonin transmission in these tracts causes hallucinations on the emotional cortex [prefrontal cortex]. You feel things that are not real. Under the influence of methamphetamine, you feel rage when there is nothing to be angry about, or fear when there is nothing to be afraid of. These emotional hallucinations lead to paranoia and violence.

> *Emotional hallucinations under the*
> *influence of meth lead to paranoia*
> *and violence.*

Under the influence of ecstasy [the hug drug], and methamphetamine you feel intense love and intimacy with other people. That is also an emotional hallucination, but you think it's real because it's on the emotional cortex where love is supposed to be. You feel intensely intimate with people you have never met before, but the feeling is so strong you suspend your intellect telling you this guy is a stranger. You feel like he's your long lost friend and you have always loved this person. You know him intimately and trust him completely.

There is a great deal of sexual arousal associated with those feelings. The hallucination of love is so real and convincing, it leads to a lot of unwise and unsafe sexual activity. I'll see the girls in my Gynecology office two weeks after the party with five different sexually transmitted diseases all at the same stage. They may have been in *love* with every man at the party, or they may have been gang raped. Ecstasy is popular with the gay night club scene for the same reason. It facilitates sex between people who have no real relationship.

Dopamine is the neurotransmitter used primarily in the midbrain. It mediates communication among the nuclei in the personality centers [midbrain], emotional centers [limbic system], and motivational centers [ventral tegmental area and striatum]. It is the primary neurotransmitter in the nucleus accumbens, the pleasure center of the brain. Any drug that increases dopamine release in this area is experienced as intensely pleasurable.

Mild elevations of dopamine, as in alcohol or marijuana intoxication, result in a giddy, giggly feeling. Everything is funny, and everyone is happy. Larger elevations in dopamine, as in a cocaine or methamphetamine high, result in euphoria, a feeling of power, confidence, intelligence, energy and control. Mega elevations in dopamine, as seen with inhaled free base or crack cocaine, or with smoked or injected crystal methamphetamine, cause an intense euphoria, or "a rush," characterized by intense feelings of sexual arousal, like an orgasm lasting twenty or thirty minutes, followed by a prolonged high.

Methamphetamine is neurotoxic to the cells in the pleasure center [nucleus accumbens], as well as many other brain centers. In the next two chapters, we will consider each of the major effects and toxicities of methamphetamine in the context of the normal function for that brain area, as well as adaptive mechanisms in the brain as it attempts to compensate for these effects, sometimes causing even more damage than the initial and direct drug effect.

> *Now, take your right hand and put it on your left shoulder. Pat vigorously. You now know almost as much neuroanatomy as the average physician does.*

FAIR WARNING

Fair warning, this will not be pleasant. Interesting perhaps, informative, but not pleasant. In the next few chapters, you will see why your child who is addicted to cocaine or crystal methamphetamine acts the way he does, and why he seems so distant, cold and distracted. You will see why he cares so little for his children, why he loses his temper and becomes violent, why he imagines and believes such ridiculous things, and why he seems so unable to stay away from this drug.

Some of the brain damage we will be discussing is permanent, especially in the case of methamphetamine, but much of it can be repaired, either by healing of the cells involved or compensation by other parts of the brain. The serious meth addict might never be what he could have been, he might never heal completely, but he can recover enough to be functional, much like the rehabilitated stroke or head injury victim. He can recover enough of his personality to have real relationships with the people he loves. He can recover enough self-control to be gainfully employed. He can recover enough to make tremendous contributions to the healing of other people in his community struggling with addiction. I've met many such people. I deeply admire the strength and courage they display.

The truly healed and recovered drug addict is a much stronger person than someone who has never faced much suffering. He is far more compassionate than someone who has never been held in the grip of powerful addiction. Take courage. There is hope.

WARNING:

If you are addicted to methamphetamine DO NOT proceed to chapter 4. It is much too depressing. Skip ahead to chapter 16. After you have healed a little you may come back to this material.

.4.

METHAMPHETAMINE - BIOCHEMICAL CHANGES

Methamphetamine is the chemical equivalent of a bolt of lightning striking a metal plate in the middle of the brain. Crystal meth and crack cocaine directly stimulate the release of enormous amounts of dopamine into the synapses of dopamine releasing cells in the midbrain, and especially in the nucleus accumbens, the pleasure center of the brain. An uncontrolled release of dopamine in the midbrain structures causes an incredible high, and has effects on many personality and motivation centers.

Methamphetamine sends shocks of electricity up to the cortex and down to the primitive areas of the brain involved in cravings, drives, and urges. Many of the mood, emotional, and personality centers we talked about in the last chapter use dopamine as their primary neurotransmitter. The huge release of dopamine in the limbic areas of the brain causes profound mood, emotional, and personality changes which are perceived as intensely pleasurable.

HOW METHAMPHETAMINE EFFECTS DOPAMINE TRANSMISSION

Dopamine transporter molecules are incredibly complex proteins on the surface of the neuron. They act as a vacuum cleaner in the synapse after a nerve fires. They bind dopamine molecules, change configuration, and draw the dopamine molecule up into the cell. And they do it really fast. They don't make mistakes; they draw up dopamine because that is what binds to their receptor. They transport it rapidly back into the cell, and reload the vesicles so the cell can fire again just microseconds after it has fired the first time.

> *Meth throws the vacuum cleaner*
> *into reverse.*

Methamphetamine binds to the dopamine transporter, the protein on the surface of Cell A that re-absorbs dopamine into the cell when an electrical impulse is completed. Meth causes the cell to release dopamine into the synapse by opening its dopamine channel chemically, instead of electrically. The transporter is supposed to re-absorb dopamine after a nerve fires, so we can recycle it, a process we call re-uptake. Methamphetamine throws the transporter into reverse, making it dump neurotransmitter into the synapse, instead of vacuuming it up.

Methamphetamine changes the configuration of the transporter protein, so that it picks up dopamine on the *inside* of the cell instead of the outside, and pumps it *out* of the cell instead of into it, and it still works incredibly fast. Within microseconds, the transporter can completely empty the cell of dopamine without a single nerve being fired. There was no real stimulus to feel good. Nothing felt good or smelled good or looked good. It's all artificial, and it is much more intense than any natural pleasure could possibly be.

> *It's like you took the lid off the fire hydrant*
> *and all the water comes gushing out.*

Synaptic levels of dopamine increase by 700% - 1200% after an intoxicating dose of ice. It's like you took the lid off the fire hydrant and all the water comes gushing out. The uncontrolled release of a neurotransmitter sends an uncontrolled message to the receptor on Cell B, flooding it with chemical stimulation. The rush is intense.

Methamphetamine also inhibits the enzyme, monoamine oxidase [MAO], which metabolizes dopamine, so the high lasts for many hours. A cocaine high lasts two or three hours at the very most, while a crystal high lasts twelve to fifteen hours. Every area that uses dopamine as a neurotransmitter, the whole midbrain, is hyper-stimulated for twelve to fifteen hours.

The Cell B's of nucleus accumbens [the pleasure center] are seeing far more pleasure signal than they have ever seen before, and the rush is described as "ten orgasms all at the same time." Methamphetamine also releases large amounts of dopamine in the emotional centers of the limbic system, and creates a feeling of well-being, confidence, and power. It stimulates motor centers in the striatum and causes hyperactivity, energy, and endurance. You can dance all night and never get tired. The effect is even more explosive with injected or smoked crystal than with the drug taken orally.

When the cell is completely depleted of dopamine, there is nothing left to release, you go into the crash, which at first is a mild depression lasting a day or two. Dopamine is replaced by the cell, and everything goes back to normal. Dopamine manufacture by the cell is metabolically expensive, it takes time and energy to synthesize it, and so dopamine cells are a little depleted for a few days after a high. Remember, we don't waste our neurotransmitters, we recycle them.

As the person continues getting high, and cells are damaged and killed by the drug, a process we'll describe in more detail in a minute, the recovery is slower and less complete. Dopamine levels don't quite get back to normal in between highs, and the crash gets longer and more intense. At the same time, the nucleus accumbens needs more and more dopamine stimulation in order to feel any pleasure. Normal amounts of dopamine, in response to a good meal for instance, aren't enough to cause pleasure, and the result is a generalized feeling of depression relieved only by another hit of ice.

Early Stages of Addiction
Sensitization and Habituation

Remember how cells become sensitized to repeated stimulation? They increase the number of receptor sites making the cell more responsive. They also learn by growing new and more abundant connections in frequently used tracts, adding lanes to accommodate more traffic. In the early stages of methamphetamine addiction, we see the same process. Dopamine receptors in nucleus accumbens become more sensitive to dopamine. Each hit of meth seems to feel even better than before. The crash is relatively mild, and the high is intense, long lasting, and easier to reach.

> *In the early stages of methamphetamine addiction, each hit of meth seems to feel even better than before. The crash is relatively mild, and the high is intense, long lasting, and easier to reach.*

The addict becomes more comfortable with his drug use, and feels like he is in control. He uses more often, not just in the context of a party or with his friends on weekends. He is already addicted; he feels a strong pull to use, a compulsion to do it whenever it is available, even though he is only using on weekends. He can't control his desire for the drug, because his fasciculus retroflexus is already damaged. Of course he thinks he can control it. He thinks he just *chose* to use it again.

As the crash becomes more and more noticeable, he starts using just a little every day, just enough to avoid the bad mood and anxiety that comes with the crash. He feels so bad without the drug, and feels so good with it, he starts regarding it as a *treatment* for his depression and bad mood, a depression and bad mood brought on by the drug itself. It takes more to get high now, but that's okay. He feels comfortable with his drug use now. He has a steady supplier, or he has learned how to make it himself. It becomes a natural part of his life.

Over time, and with escalating doses, the dopamine transporters are damaged by the over-stimulation and become non-functional. Dopamine transporters are supposed to vacuum up all the excess dopamine after a nerve fires, so as to reload the cell and allow it to fire again. Methamphetamine changes the configuration of the transporter molecule and makes it churn out large volumes of dopamine for prolonged periods of time. Cocaine blocks the transporter and prevents re-uptake of dopamine; it puts a sock in the vacuum cleaner so it can't suck anything up. Methamphetamine reverses the transporter and makes it put out dopamine; it makes the vacuum cleaner spew stuff out instead of sucking it up.

Cell A is spraying out dopamine like a pressure washer. It's like the cell is screaming at the top of its lungs for twelve to fifteen hours. What would happen if you screamed at the top of your lungs for fifteen hours? You'd get hoarse, wouldn't you? You would probably rupture your vocal cords. You wouldn't be able to talk tomorrow either. That's what happens to Cell A. It ruptures its vocal cords, damages its dopamine transporter, throws it into reverse, and now Cell A can't talk. A normal signal comes along and it tries to speak, put out dopamine, but the cell is dopamine depleted and cannot talk.

Cell B, on the other hand, has been listening to click, click, click all its life, and now Cell A is screaming in its ear for twelve to fifteen hours. Seven to ten times the normal amounts of dopamine in its receptor sounds like a siren. What would you do if somebody screamed like a siren in your ear for twelve to fifteen hours? First, you would tell them to shut up. You send your little feedback signal back to Cell A, "I heard you, you can stop now!" But it's not Cell A doing the screaming. It's "crystal" doing the screaming, and "crystal" won't shut up.

LATER STAGES OF ADDICTION
PHOSPHORYLATION AND SEQUESTRATION

Cell B has to defend itself against this chronic hyper-stimulation. It hears a siren in its ear, and the siren won't shut up. Cell B says, "Man I'm not going to listen to *this* anymore." It hangs up the phone. It disconnects and destroys its receptor by the processes of phosphorylation [the molasses covering over the receptor] and sequestration [pinches off the receptor and destroys it] and now Cell B can't hear. Cell A can't talk, and Cell B can't hear. The lines are down.

All the systems using dopamine as a neurotransmitter are broken down. Major malfunction. Does not compute. The limbic system [moods], nucleus accumbens [pleasure center], ventral tegmental areas [cravings], striatum [motivation center], prefrontal cortex [judgment and rational thought], and fasciculus retroflexus [self control] are all disconnected, and the personality is in shambles.

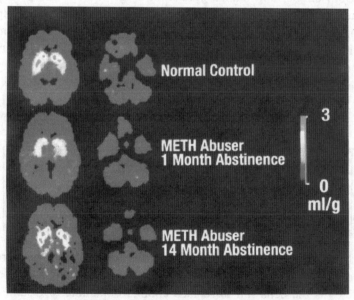

Fig. 11 Scans of the methamphetamine affected brain
Copyright 2001 Society of Neuroscience, Dr. Volkow, Full citation page 448

Figure 11 is a PET scan of a human brain on methamphetamine. Please look at the color plate on page 261, figure 1. The top picture is of a normal brain with red areas in the midbrain. The red stuff is dopamine transmission in the midbrain, an intact personality. His mesocorticolimbic tract works, and he can reason with himself and control his anger. His fasciculus retroflexus is functioning, so he can make himself get out of bed in the morning and go to work. His amygdala works properly, so he feels love for his children.

The middle picture is the brain of an addict who has been clean for one month. There is no red stuff, no dopamine transmission through his mid-brain. His personality has been disconnected. He has a vague feeling of being followed. He can't reason with himself and know that he is safe. He jumps to conclusions about the car behind him. He is convinced the man driving it is a narc and he takes off in a panic to lose the guy.

This addict has no control over his temper. He blows up over trivial things and everything annoys him. He has wild mood swings, happy and expansive one minute, angry and irritable the next, and a few hours later, depressed and tired. He can't get it together to go to work and do a good job. He fidgets and paces and can't pay attention to his work. He makes a lot of mistakes and gets fired. He is distracted by his drug, how to get more of it, where to hide it, and when he can use it again. He has completely lost control over his impulses and drives.

Both animal and human studies have shown the loss of dopamine transporters and receptors in multiple brain areas after even minimal exposures to methamphetamine. And the effect is not just temporary. Across multiple species, including humans, methamphetamine causes long lasting / permanent dopamine depletion with no incremental recovery over six day, or even six month periods, as would be seen if the effect were a temporary pharmacologic effect. It doesn't just wear off. Something structural and permanent is going on here.

> *In the later stages of addiction, he has a generalized feeling of profound depression relieved only by another hit of ice.*

Now, in the later stages of addiction, the crash has become more prominent and longer lasting. Dopamine depletion is more severe, and recovery is incomplete, as the cells fail to replace enough dopamine to resume normal function between highs. As the receptors are destroyed, you don't even get high anymore. After chasing the high for several days, no amount of drug will keep you up. You are shooting up every two hours, using $200 or $300 a day, just to stay out of the crash. It's not much fun anymore, and you don't really like doing it, but you *have* to because the crash is so miserable, and you know you can't live like that.

The crash feels like the worst flu you've ever had in your life. You sleep for the first two or three days, wake up on the floor wondering what day it is, and look out the window to see if it is day or night. You feel achy and depressed, tired, hungry and irritable. You get the 'wet dog shakes,' sweats and nausea. You are empty and craving. You have a low grade fever. Everything hurts. The anxiety is intolerable, your skin is crawling, muscles are tense night and day, and it lasts for seven to fourteen days. The only thing that relieves the misery of the crash is another hit of ice.

"I probably only have about a days worth left and I'm starting to stress out. I catch myself rationalizing and justifying why I shouldn't quit yet—you know . . . I have so much to do that I can't possibly crash now, it would be so much easier next week . . . on and on I could go with reasons. I know that it's time now, but I'm so afraid to come down. My internal dialogue is driving me insane, one voice telling me that it won't be that big of a deal and that I can do it no problem . . . my other voice is shrieking non-stop that it will be the worst crash ever and that I can't go back into my depression and why is this happening to me and just keep using Okay??? Please??? You won't be able to do it, and why do you want to quit anyway? I know that voice is my addiction—but why does it have to be so loud and persistent? My daughter is at daycare today and I feel like I don't have enough time before I have to pick her up, time to do what I couldn't tell you, I'm guessing it's time I need to fall apart."

And seven to fourteen days is just the beginning. The depression lasts for months, as the brain heals and the receptor sites reconnect. The anxiety and insomnia, depression and irritability are debilitating. You are crawling out of your skin with anxiety. You feel tired all the time. Month after month, the whole world is gray. Everybody gets on your nerves; you just want to be left alone. You can't concentrate, and it's hard to remember why you wanted to quit in the first place.

Gradually, over twelve to eighteen months of *complete abstinence,* receptor sites heal. See the third brain in that PET scan picture? The red transmission is back. The surviving Cell A's have built new dopamine transporters, and they can talk again. Cell B's have made new receptors, so they can hear, and transmission is re-established. Over twelve to eighteen months, the personality slowly heals, the depression lifts and the anxiety abates. Twelve to eighteen months. That's a long time to go around with a disconnected personality.

But, do you see what *else* is wrong with the third brain in that PET scan picture? Can you see those holes in the substance of the brain? Those are not just the normal fluid collections that are supposed to be there. Those are holes, non-functional areas, where vital brain tissue is supposed to be. PET scans measure function of the tissues. The active neurons have been replaced by inactive filler cells called Glial cells. They are a lot like scar tissue seen in other parts of the body. They are not neurons, and so they show up as a dark spot on a PET scan.

The holes do not continue to form after drug use has stopped. The addict in the third brain scan has been using ice for a lot longer than the person represented by the second scan. Those holes in the third scan indicate several years' worth of brain damage.

HOLES IN THE BRAIN

The first research paper I encountered in my effort to understand what happened to Jim was a paper by Dr. Ernst in the journal Neurology [2000]. Dr. Ernst showed that brain cell metabolites N-acetylaspartate and total creatinine were decreased, and the cellular breakdown products choline and myoinosital were increased in the brains of human methamphetamine abusers. Whole areas of brain were dying and releasing the chemicals that indicate cell death. It caused enough cell death to show up on an *x-ray*. The hair stood up on the back of my neck, and I couldn't breathe for a minute. I stayed nauseated for almost a week after reading that paper, and I honestly couldn't bear to read anymore of this literature for a while.

Jim was right. The drug *did* destroy his blood-brain barrier. It really did do some kind of structural damage to his brain. I was also right. Something inside him was dead, and there is no medicine to fix it.

Nerd Box

The blood-brain barrier is a complex layer of protein that separates the blood from the fluids bathing the brain cells, so that fluctuations in blood chemistry, toxins and most drugs do not penetrate to disrupt neural function. The chemical environment of the synapse has to be carefully protected. Psychoactive drugs can cross this barrier, but most medications do not.

Methamphetamine really does damage the blood-brain barrier. Blood-brain barrier degrading matrix metalloproteinases are increased in methamphetamine exposed brain cells [especially in the presence of HIV virus] and inflammatory cells gain access to the neuron to release a variety of potent neurotoxins.

Methamphetamine causes cell death in multiple areas of the brain, especially the limbic system, emotional, and motivational areas. The data to support this is overwhelming and includes biochemical evidence, microscopic evidence, radiographic evidence, electroencephalographic evidence, and behavioral evidence. You can measure it and see it and take pictures of it.

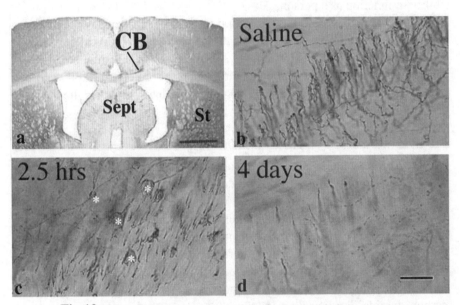

Fig 12 Brain cells exposed to a single intoxicating dose of methamphetamine
Micrograph courtesy of Dr Feng C Zhou c1996
Used with permission, Full citation page 449

In the picture marked saline, the cells are spread out like peanut butter so you can see them. Looks like about 100 cells there. Just 2.5 hours after a *single hit of ice*, those cells are swollen, disconnected, breaking up, they are dying right before your eyes. Four days later, how many do you have left? I count about six. We have turned 100 cells into six cells, and we did it in just one night. It takes alcohol six *years* to do that kind of damage; cocaine can do it in six *months*. Methamphetamine does it *overnight*.

There is permanent damage to serotonin pathways in the brain within 2.5 hours of injection, areas that include the median forebrain bundle [one of the major self control pathways], mesocorticolimbic tract [reality testing], and frontal lobe [where complex decisions are made]. Cell death in some areas is dramatic and immediate, with complete loss of these tracts at high doses. Serotonin pathways mediate impulse control, obsessive thoughts, reality testing, and mood. Damage to these tracts causes psychotic symptoms, paranoia, hallucinations, delusions and wild mood swings.

Methamphetamine also kills cells in the dopamine pathways, including nucleus accumbens [pleasure center], amygdala [anger and fear], hippocampus [short term memory], ventral tegmental area [cravings and urges], fasciculus retroflexus [self control], and lateral habenula [maternal behavior]. These areas are central to your personality, your attitude, relationships, and ability to function as a person.

Fasciculus retroflexus (self-control) is especially sensitive to methamphetamine damage because it is so small. It only has 200–300 cells. It doesn't take very much ice to destroy 80–90% of these cells. The amount of crystal that would only kill 20% of the cells in nucleus accumbens [10,000 cells] or 1% of the frontal lobe [10,000,000 cells] can completely wipe out the tiny little fasciculus retroflexus.

THE BATTERY ACID EFFECT

Teaching this to ninth grade students is a challenge, and I have learned to rely on a simplified but very vivid description to explain how toxic crystal is. I call it the **Battery Acid Effect**. Methamphetamine is made using a long list of toxic chemicals, including battery acid [lithium], kerosene, anhydrous ammonia, lye, all caustic corrosive chemicals. I show the kids a picture of a lab with jars of chemicals, hoses, and filters.

Look what this stuff is made out of. What do you suppose your body turns it back into? You can't break methamphetamine down into water and carbon dioxide like you do everything else. You break it down into caustic corrosive chemicals, the biological equivalent of battery acid, kerosene, anhydrous ammonia, and lye.

Methamphetamine is taken up by the pre-synaptic dopamine transporter into the cell where it is metabolized into dihydroxybenzoic acid, dihydroxyphenylacetic acid, methoxytyramine, and hydroxyindoleacetic acid, all of which are toxic to the cell. Of course, only small amounts of methamphetamine metabolites are formed. Much larger amounts of dopamine are released into the synapse, and the dopamine has to be broken down too.

The extremely high levels of dopamine released into the synapse are eventually broken down, and the metabolites are also caustic corrosive chemicals called **hydroxy free radicals**. They are every bit as caustic as battery acid. Hydroxy free radicals are of the same class of chemicals that a white blood cell uses to kill bacteria. White blood cells have the machinery to control and manage these chemicals. Brain cells do not. Crystal causes the cells to make seven to ten times the normal amounts of dopamine, and so seven to ten times the normal amounts of these metabolites are also made. The brain has systems that can buffer small amounts of these chemicals, but it cannot handle the huge amounts made after a meth high.

Nerd Box

Excess dopamine released into the synapse is metabolized first into 6-hydroxy dopamine, which is then further oxidized into nitric oxide, peroxynitrite and nitryl carbonate. Nitric oxide is a free radical with one electron available to bind to other chemicals. Peroxynitrite and nitryl carbonate are more potent two electron radicals that are capable of destroying DNA, cellular proteins, dopamine receptors, and lipid bilayers.

Free radicals break down the membranes around mitochondria and release chemical cascades of toxic enzymes and chemicals leading to cell death. It only takes a few hours for this to happen. A 50% increase in nitric oxide is found within hours after meth injection, and lasts for twelve hours in the striatum and hippocampus. Regional metabolic activity in brain tissue as measured by PET scans shows loss of glucose metabolism in the frontal lobe, parietal lobe, and midbrain that are long lasting, and in some cases, permanent.

Chronic unpredictable stress, which also increases dopamine release in the midbrain, has been shown to dramatically increase the toxic effects of methamphetamine in rats. Stressed rats had a doubling of the mortality rate, and more permanent damage to dopamine neurons in the survivors. Stressed animals had the same blood levels of methamphetamine as the other rats, but the damage to their neurons was much more severe.

Most human users are not kept in warm comfy cages with steady supplies of rat chow. Most of them live and use under extremely stressful conditions, with guns and narcs and dealers, which probably increases the brain damage they sustain. The rat studies most likely *under-estimate* the degree of damage caused by methamphetamine.

Nerd Box

There are mechanisms in the brain to heal damaged tissue, and the markers for these processes are all elevated in the methamphetamine affected brain. Fos r Ag 2 is a protein released by dead and dying brain cells, indicating both cell death and terminal degeneration. It is thought to be involved in the cell's attempts to repair and regenerate after cellular damage. Methamphetamine and ecstasy caused increases in Fos r Ag 2 beginning at day three after exposure, and lasting for two days after meth, and for twelve days after ecstasy.

Calmodulin dependent protein kinase and genes related to synaptogenesis, neuritogenesis, and mitogen activated protein kinase are increased in the nucleus accumbens, prefrontal cortex, striatum, and hippocampus, after even a single low dose of methamphetamine. Structural modification of neural networks, increased number of dendrites, lengthening of dendritic processes, neuritic sprouting and elongation are seen as the brain tries to recover from the acute effects of meth.

Calmodulin is depleted after a single dose of meth, and requires four weeks to recover to normal levels. Relapse after four or more weeks of abstinence results in even more pronounced decreases in calmodulin activity. The enzyme is dephosphorylated, leading to decreased enzyme activity with each additional dose, and chronic use leads to increased cellular toxicity after a prolonged withdrawal.

Sorry, I couldn't help it. It's the doctor in me.

"The first time I used it didn't affect me much, but after I'd been in jail for six months and got out, I used it again, and this time it made me crazy. I was hearing things and seeing things for months. I still have a lot of seizures and now I can't read anymore. Even simple things I can't understand. You can teach this class now, but I won't remember what you said tomorrow."

The brain makes a brave attempt to heal after methamphetamine exposure. When an addict stops using temporarily, neurotrophic chemicals are released to rebuild the neural networks that have been damaged. These processes are related to the hyper-sensitivity to methamphetamine seen after stopping it temporarily. Relapsing addicts sometimes die from taking the same amount of methamphetamine they had previously tolerated, because they are much more sensitive to the effects of the drug after a period of withdrawal.

THE ORIGIN OF CRAVINGS

I have been clean for eight days and the cravings are killing me. I wake up in the night and I can taste it again. I do okay during the day but I dream about it every night. I don't know how much longer I can hold out. Please pray for me.

Ventral Tegmental area Fig 13

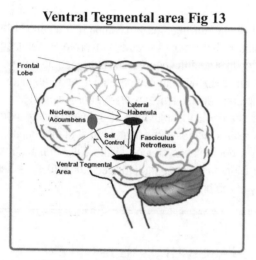

Brain areas associated with drug craving

  Cravings, drives and urges come from the ventral tegmental area which projects to the pleasure center [nucleus accumbens] with dopamine neurons. Ventral tegmental area has dopamine D2 autoreceptors that become insensitive to dopamine with overstimulation. Autoreceptors are supposed to signal to Cell A that Cell B has heard us; we can turn the signal off now. In the addicted brain, the off switch doesn't work as well, so the ventral tegmental area keeps sending its craving message.

  Intense cravings are elicited by a memory, a dream, the smell of marijuana or alcohol, the sound of party music or a friend's voice, or the sight of a piece of tin foil, spoon or syringe. Just like the smell of fresh baked chocolate chip cookies makes your mouth water, the sights and smells associated with drug use will make an addict crave crystal, and the craving signal does not just go away, because the off switch is broken.

  Ventral tegmental area craving cells also become hyperactive after exposure to methamphetamine, and send the craving signal more readily. Methamphetamine increases the number of glutamine [wake up] receptors on the cells in ventral tegmental area. They sometimes fire spontaneously even though there was no 'reminder' of the drug to trigger them to fire. They are jumpy and excitable because they have more than the normal number of gluta-mine [wake up] receptors on them.

Nerd Box

Ventral tegmental neurons are structurally changed by exposure to methamphetamine with decreases in structural proteins, reduced axonal trans-port, and reduction in size of the neurons in ventral tegmental area. Their ability to communicate and respond to inhibition from lateral habenula and fasciculus retroflexus is impaired, and so cravings are harder to suppress.

Repeated electrical stimulation of the ventral tegmental area over a period of fourteen days increases the neural effect of methamphetamine stimu-lation reflecting a neuroplastic change in the cells that results in dopamine supersensitivity. More lanes are added to accommodate increased traffic in the craving pathway of the brain.

FASCICULUS RETROFLEXUS

The second area we will consider is fasciculus retroflexus. Fascicu-lus is the descending self control tract in the midbrain that suppresses urges, drives, and cravings originating in the ventral tegmental area. It is a very small tract, only a few hundred cells, and 90% of them are destroyed by cocaine and methamphetamine, especially when these drugs are used in a binge type pattern, as they usually are. Fasciculus retroflexus is the tract connecting the lateral habenula with the ventral tegmental area. It has two major tracts, one of which is damaged by exposure to nicotine; the other is damaged by exposure to cocaine or methamphetamine. I call it your two lane highway to Nashville.

Nashville is the good life. In Nashville you can finish your education, start a business, pay the rent, and take care of your kids. You can show up for work in the morning and be motivated to do a good job. You get a big raise and a corner office; you can buy a nice house and eat steaks for diner. Nashville is where everybody wants to go. Fasciculus retroflexus is your two lane interstate highway to Nashville, your self-control pathway. When it is in good working order, you can subdue your craving for a little more sleep and you can get up and go to work.

Nicotine is toxic to the cells in the right lane of fasciculus retroflexus. In high enough doses, the cells die, but at normal doses, smoking one or two packs per day, they are not dead, they just don't work very well. It's like you have a speed bump every few feet in the right lane of your highway to Nashville. But that's okay, you just get in the left lane, and pretty soon you are doing 65 miles per hour headed to Nashville. You can start your business, show up for classes, and pay the rent. You *can't quit smoking*, but you can do everything else you want to do.

> *Then you start doing ice or crack cocaine, and you wipe out the left lane of your fasciculus retroflexus. Now you're not going to Nashville.*

Then you start doing ice or crack cocaine, and you wipe out the left lane of your fasciculus retroflexus. Now you're not going to Nashville. The control system over cravings and impulses is disabled. You don't care about going to work, you don't care about feeding the kids, and you don't care about paying the rent. All you can think about is getting your next hit, and you want it right now. You don't control the cravings; the cravings control you.

Fasciculus has projections to nucleus accumbens [pleasure center], limbic system [fear and anger], striatum [learning ability and motor control], ventral tegmental area [cravings and urges], and brainstem [alertness and waking]. All of these areas are also directly damaged by methamphetamine. Lesions to fasciculus cause regulatory dysfunction in all these areas, and as we will see, the personality changes and behavioral implications are profound.

.5.

PERSONALITY CHANGES ON METH

The personality of the methamphetamine addict changes dramatically. He's a completely different person under the influence of this drug. He is grouchy and irritable, moody and unpredictable. When he is high, he is energetic and happy, talkative and fun. He works fast and hard and for long hours every day. At the top, he is agitated and jumpy, aggressive and loud. In the crash, he is tired and depressed, even unresponsive. He doesn't enjoy a movie or a meal anymore. He tells his daughter, "Shut up and get out of here." He won't go fishing; he won't play ball with the kids. He loses interest in the things that used to be special to him. Nothing pleases him.

As the damage worsens, he gets paranoid and violent. He becomes abusive towards the people he loves the most, his family. He is irresponsible and can't focus on his job because of damage to the frontal lobe. He loses his memory, and his speech is garbled and halting, because of damage to the temporal lobe. He has damage to the parietal lobe resulting in loss of motor control, twitches and tremors. He has disrupted transmission in the occipital lobe, so he sees snakes where there are not really any snakes. He has lost impulse control and reality testing, and so he *shoots* the snakes that are not really there, and by the time he comes to his senses, all three of his children are dead.

Fig 14

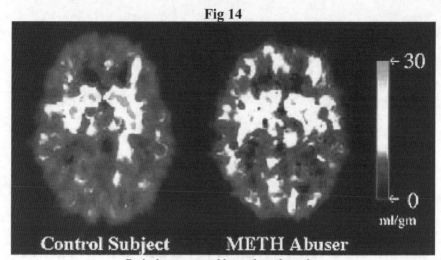

Control Subject   METH Abuser

Brain damage caused by methamphetamine
Image ©2001 Brookhaven National Laboratory, Dr. Nora Volkow
Full citation page 448

This PET scan shows the damage to the whole brain from methamphetamine. Again, look at the color plate on page 261, figure 2 in the picture section. This guy still has a little red transmission through this midbrain personality centers, though not very much. But do you see all those green areas? Large areas of the frontal, temporal, parietal, and occipital lobes are green because they have dramatic loss of cell function. The whole brain is affected.

NOTHING FEELS GOOD

Methamphetamine causes structural damage to nucleus accumbens [pleasure center] and frontal cortex [thinking part of the brain] with changes in length and density of dendritic processes. It's like they were singed in a fire. The terminals are broken off and the cell can't fire a message to rest of the brain anymore. Damage to the nucleus accumbens results in a loss of ability to feel pleasure and a resulting depression. Nothing feels good. Food doesn't taste good, playing your guitar doesn't sound good, and talking to your friend doesn't feel good. Cuddling your baby doesn't feel good, even sex doesn't feel good. Crystal is the only thing in your life that feels good.

Imagine a life where nothing tastes good, music sounds flat and unexciting, conversation is boring, people are annoying, sex isn't satisfying, and it goes on like that every day for twelve to eighteen months. And every day of those twelve to eighteen months you know that if you can get some more ice, it will all go away and you'll feel great again. Staying clean past about three months takes some real commitment.

The loss of ability to feel pleasure is called "anhedonia," and it contributes to relapse. You've been clean for three months, and nothing in this world feels good. Everything tastes like cardboard, everybody gets on your nerves, the music sounds flat, your kid won't shut up, and your job is boring. "Man, if I could just feel good again, just once, just for a minute. If I could just feel *good* again. This is so depressing." And so you get high again, because nothing else in this world feels good anymore.

Nerd Box

Methamphetamine causes structural and chemical damage to the cells in the pleasure center of the brain, nucleus accumbens. Over-stimulation of the cells causes genetic changes in the cells of nucleus accumbens and striatum. The cells produce large amounts of a transcription factor called Δ fos **B** which accumulates in the cells with long term exposure to methamphetamine.

Transcription factors determine which genes get expressed in a cell and which do not, which proteins are made and which are not, which receptors are produced and which are not. This chemical change is long lasting, on the order of months, and it changes the metabolism and firing rate of the cell, a chemical memory. Nucleus accumbens remembers what it felt like to be high and is not satisfied with anything less.

Certain cells in the nucleus accumbens are incredibly sensitive to methamphetamine, and are completely and permanently destroyed by even a single dose of crystal. Recovery of dopamine transmission is incomplete, even at eighteen months abstinence, in the striatum and nucleus accumbens.

Nucleus accumbens is one of the areas which gradually and partially heal over twelve to eighteen months. Many addicts do not get complete recovery of the sensation of pleasure, but some recovery is possible. During those twelve to eighteen months, the depression is oppressive. There is a generalized feeling of the blues, with loss of enthusiasm, energy, interest, and ambition. Accomplishments are no longer satisfying, and so there is no motivation to excel, no reward for the sacrifice of temporary comfort to reach a higher goal.

Pleasure [nucleus accumbens] and conscious control over drives [fasciculus retroflexus] come together in higher order functions like ambition, life goals, purpose and direction for your life. A formerly charged-up goal-oriented personality is replaced by an aimless existence and apathy, an 'I don't care' attitude. Life is made meaningful by the long term goals in life, the problems to solve and projects to complete, the impact you have on your family, in your job, your community, and future generations. When that is lost, or never developed in the first place, life loses its meaningfulness.

SEXUAL DYSFUNCTION

"I had never felt so sexual, nor had I wanted sex so badly. All the time it was IN MY HEAD. The idea of having normal sex with my husband was revolting to me. It was sick and dark sex that I wanted, anything deviant and wrong is what I wanted. I could sit in the f@#$%^ room for hours and hours while my husband slept, and act out these fantasies and I was never satisfied. I may as well say it outright, I would mas@#$%B@&e until I was exhausted and sickened by what I was doing, and not be able to stop doing it. Never satisfied, just this hunger and obsession. I would go into the bathroom at work and do that, I would do it driving, I'm so embarrassed, I'm just trying to convey how sick and twisted my mind went. I hope I haven't offended you or embarrassed you; truly that's not my intention. I've never shared these thoughts with anyone–it's something I've always felt great shame about. Have other women felt this way in the height of their addiction?"

When you first start using it, methamphetamine makes sex feel really powerful and good. It stimulates nucleus accumbens [the pleasure center], the hypothalamus [the hormonal center] and the ventral tegmental area [sex drive], with a whopping dose of their favorite chemical, dopamine. It causes intense sexual arousal with smoked or injected drug, and also causes alertness and endurance which enhance sexual performance.

Many people start using it primarily for the sexual effects. Married couples will use it to spice up an otherwise boring sex life. Some people [especially women] are so satisfied with the stimulation of crystal they don't want actual sex anymore. They can get all the pleasure of sex without bothering with the real thing. No need for a relationship, a condom, or birth control; they can just get high and forget about all the hassles of real sex.

Others [especially men] feel that stimulation and it makes them feel aroused all the time. Indiscriminant and promiscuous sex is part of the high. Formerly straight men will find themselves with an appetite for gay sex while on ice. They feel uninhibited, confident, and intensely aroused. They are around other people who are also intensely aroused, and so it is easy to hook up; guys, girls, it doesn't matter. Safe sex is not even on the menu. These men don't consider themselves gay, they have a wife and three kids at home, but they can swing both ways when the opportunity presents itself. The risk of HIV transmission is obvious.

Teenagers using methamphetamine are more than twice as likely as non-users to engage in promiscuous indiscriminant sex. The incidence of HIV and hepatitis is rising in these pediatric populations as 'street kids' with no permanent home stay more or less continuously intoxicated and sell themselves for another hit of ice. Sex is the common currency in the world of crystal.

A recent study looked at HIV negative heterosexual methamphetamine users, whose primary motivation to use meth was to get high, to have more energy, or to party. They weren't using it primarily for the sexual effects. These addicts reported an *average* of 9.2 sex partners over a two month time frame and sixty-eight unprotected sexual encounters during that time. They were using 7.9 grams per month, and using it an average of fourteen days per month.

---

*Methamphetamine stimulates an incredible appetite for more sexual stimulation, but after using it for a while, you can't have sex even when you're high. Of course, they don't tell you about **that** part at the party.*

Methamphetamine addiction is a prominent problem in the gay community, where it is primarily used to facilitate sex. Ice circulates at circuit parties and gay bars, and many homosexuals are addicted. The predominant drug at circuit parties is still ecstasy [75% of men at these events use ecstasy] but methamphetamine is also very popular with 40% of participants in a recent study using ice to enhance their sexual response. These parties are characterized as sexual marathons with abundant anonymous high-risk sexual activity over a span of several days. There are no relationships between these men, just raw sex.

Methamphetamine stimulates an incredible appetite for more sexual stimulation, but after you use it for awhile, you can't have sex unless you are high. After using it for a little while longer, you can't have sex even when you're high. Nothing happens. It doesn't work. You might wear your partner out trying, but it just won't come. Of course, they don't tell you about *that* part at the party.

EMOTIONAL CONTROL

"A forty-year-old man was arrested for the murder of his eleven year-old daughter. She was found in the backyard of their home. Her throat had been slashed and she had knife wounds all over her body. The girl's mother was at work at the time of the killing. The victim's nine year old sister escaped unharmed."

The crimes associated with methamphetamine are sometimes spectacular. Small people are capable of incredible violence when activated by a methamphetamine rage. Addicts are frequently armed and ready to pull the trigger at the slightest provocation. They seldom plan their crimes, acting on impulse in the heat of passion. They are unpredictable, moody, and aggressive.

Anger Fig 15

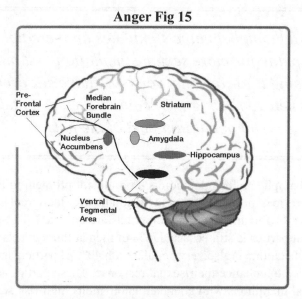

Emotional areas affected by methamphetamine

Damage to amygdala [limbic system] results in loss of emotional control. The fasciculus inputs to it are broken, so you don't have any control over your temper. The amygdala is also directly damaged by methamphetamine, so you have the inappropriate experience of some very intense raw emotions. The effect is very much like the emotional hallucinations caused by serotonin dysfunction, you feel anger when there is nothing to be mad about, or fear when there is nothing to be afraid of.

A study done in mice showed a dramatic increase in aggressive behavior after treatment with methamphetamine. A single dose did not increase fighting, but a series of multiple doses caused increased biting and shorter latency to the first attack in mice threatened with an intruder in their cage. The same thing happens in humans. The first dose does not usually increase aggressiveness. It is the cumulative brain damage caused by frequent use that causes the aggressiveness seen in human meth users.

Aberrant function in the limbic system, amygdala [emotions], frontal lobe [judgment], temporal lobes [language and memory], striatum [motor habits], and hippocampus [short term memory] have all been associated with violent anti-social behavior, anger and anxiety. Anger is first manifest as a short temper. The addict can't sit in the living room and talk to people without flying off the handle about something. He is irritable and grouchy, verbally abusive to his children, and seethes with anger for hours after some perceived offence that may not even be real. At the same time, his amygdala lights up like a Christmas tree under MRI imaging.

> *He had killed a man twice his size with his bare hands in a meth induced rage.*

Uncontrolled anger is experienced as rage. Jim had a cat, a little white cat he'd had since he was ten years old. He loved his little white kitty cat. One day he flew into a rage and beat his cat almost to death. He could see himself doing it; he knew he was killing his kitty, but he couldn't stop. What if that's your baby, not your cat? I met a man in jail that barely weighed 165 pounds, but he had killed a man twice his size with his bare hands in a meth induced rage. This rage is explosive and leads to senseless tragedy. People are horrified when they realize what they have done to their children.

ANXIETY

"Yesterday I was in Wal-Mart and I had a buggy full of groceries and all of the sudden I got scared and lost control. My heart was pounding, and I couldn't breathe. I had to get out of there. My kids were scared. They thought I was dying. Is this caused by meth?"

Anxiety is expressed as irritability, excessive talking, fidgeting, restlessness, and impatience. Hyperactivity and inability to focus attention is common. You can't sit still and watch a ballgame or enjoy a meal. You jump from one activity to another without finishing anything; your work becomes chaotic and nothing gets done. Sleep is impossible.

Uncontrolled anxiety is experienced as panic, and there are two types of panic attack associated with methamphetamine abuse. When Jim came to live with me he was in a catatonic panic attack. For almost a week, he stayed in his room, in bed, with a sheet over his head. He was crashing, he was paranoid, and he was panicked. He didn't even know what he was afraid of. He would not come out from under his sheet to eat or talk to anybody, all he could do was cry.

The other type of panic attack is the manic panic attack. It is associated with acute intoxication, and is characterized by hyperactivity and irrational fear. "Gotta Go Go Go." Get behind the wheel of a car, and you're going 200 miles per hour, running everybody off the road. Where are you going? You don't know. What are you afraid of? You don't know. "Just gotta get out of here. Right now."

The brain stem mood lamp [locus ceruleus] is also damaged, causing increased noradrenergic tone and a continuous level of anxiety. It generalizes into a manic depressive anxiety disorder, with recurring unprovoked intense anxiety attacks in a background of profound depression. The anxiety responds to medications, like Valium and Xanax, and so these drugs are very popular with the drug crowd. They reduce the side effects of using methamphetamine.

Over the course of receptor healing, the anxiety fades and temper is easier to control, but again, it takes twelve to eighteen months for receptors and transporters to heal. You recover your personality, your temper, and your emotional control a little at a time. Recovery is often incomplete. You may have a residual short temper and chronic low grade anxiety, perhaps for the rest of your life, but there is major improvement in the first year of abstinence.

BEHAVIOR PROBLEMS—SHAKES AND TREMORS

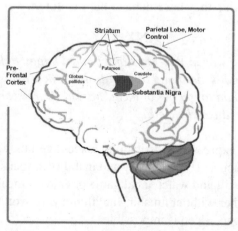

Fig 16 Brain parts associated with hyperactivity

"I still can't hold a cup of coffee without spilling it, and I've been clean for two years. The doctor told me it's Parkinson's disease. Will it ever go away?"

Hyperactivity is a characteristic of the methamphetamine high, and is associated with two distinct brain lesions. *First,* there is evidence of **parietal lobe dysfunction** which, on the sensory side, results in tactile hallucinations. Picking at imaginary bugs is so common they call it Ice Lice, or Meth Mites. I met a woman who had plucked out each and every one of her eyelashes trying to get the bugs out of her eyes.

On the motor side of parietal lobe, methamphetamine causes hyperactivity and jitteriness, twitches and tremors, involuntary movements and spasms, often called 'crack dancing' because of its association with crack cocaine. Tooth grinding, nail chewing, scratching, hair pulling, and head banging are common in acute intoxication with crystal. Seizure activity occurs as the levels become toxic, and some people use until they seize and can't work the syringe anymore. Severe reactions like this are usually associated with acute psychotic symptoms, hallucinations and delusions as well.

Second, there are multiple layers of subcortical damage in the **striatum** [motor memory], which cause a loss of fine motor control. Remember, there is always a lot of extraneous electrical activity going on in the brain, and that includes the motor cortex. Regulatory input from striatum allows you to filter out of the static so you can have purposeful movement. These are the very areas methamphetamine destroys.

The cells in **substantia nigra** [functionally a part of the striatum] have damaged membranes that stain for the same toxin we see in classic Parkinson's disease. You can see it under a microscope. And so you have tremors, not unlike those seen in Parkinson's disease. When a young person, under the age of forty, gets Parkinson's disease, he has been using ice until proven otherwise. The development of Parkinson's requires the destruction of 80–90% of the cells in substantia nigra. No other drug of abuse can kill those cells as quickly and as dramatically as methamphetamine.

Other centers in the striatum, **caudate, putamen, and globus pallidus**, also mediate motor control, and damage to them results in chorioathetoid movements, much like the movements characteristic of Huntington's chorea. Broad sweeping involuntary movements, jerks and grunts are typical. I had a pregnant patient in my office a few weeks ago, and she was having these sudden involuntary writhing movements, repeatedly sticking her tongue out. She was pretending nothing was wrong. When I asked her about it, she shrugged it off, just having a bad day. Any other patient would have been panicked that she was having these gross abnormal movements. Her blood pressure was also sky high. I checked her for crystal, and she tested positive.

> *"Doctor, I've been clean for eight months,*
> *and I'm still doing that 'arm behind the*
> *head' thing nearly every day. Is this ever*
> *going to go away?"*

I've met men in the jail still having these intense muscle spasms even months after their last high. The spasms typically draw their arm up behind their head like a vice. These are intense painful spasms, and these men can't get their arms back down. Sometimes the spasms last for hours. The guy said, "Doctor, I've been clean for eight months, and I'm still doing that 'arm behind the head' thing nearly every day. Is this ever going to go away?" It might not go away. I've met people who have been clean for eight *years* and still have spasms and tremors. In fact, most recovered addicts still have a twitch in the corner of their eye or a spasm in the back of their throat, perhaps permanently. You can often hear it in their voice. Spasms are frequently on a cranial nerve distribution, and they can be very subtle, like chattering teeth. Nobody else can see it, but the addict knows it's there.

ALERTNESS AND INSOMNIA

"Why me? I don't understand? I'm not an addict, why should I have to pay the price for having a boyfriend that is? Sunday night I left at midnight because he was still awake and would not let me sleep. I stayed with my sister. I went home yesterday after work and he was asleep after being up for however many days, I went in the room to go to sleep. I woke up in the middle of the night cold, trying to get some blanket from him. He wakes up and thinks that I am trying to go through his pockets, He told me to get off the bed. I told him no. Then he kicked me off. I went in the bathroom to get my stuff to go to my sister's again. In he comes irrate, yelling and cussing at me. I didn't want to make it worse, so I stayed quiet. Then he pushed me so hard I fell on the side of the bathtub and messed up my leg. I can barely walk today. Then he took my bag that had my stuff in it and hit me in the face with it and then took my full glass bottle of perfume and threw it at me, all because he thinks I was trying to get to his pockets while he was asleep. I sat in the bathroom and cried."

The hyperactivity associated with meth use leads to problems sleeping. Living with a meth addict is nearly impossible because they never sleep. They can stay awake for days at a time. They talk all night, and get angry when you won't talk with them. You go in on the couch to get some sleep, and they follow you around, picking and poking at you, turning on the stereo and making noise in the kitchen. It's two o'clock in the morning. They have no concept of being tired and needing sleep.

Nightmares and panic attacks also disrupt sleep, and the flashbacks of beatings and assaults are vivid. These are not like the pleasant flashbacks associated with LSD, pretty streamers of light and color flashing across your visual field. These are flashbacks, vivid memories, of the night you were raped. You can feel it again, your heart is racing, you can't breathe and you can't get away, just like the first time. You wake up in the night and you can feel a gun against your head. You can feel the punches. You try to run but you can't. Night after night.

Nerd Box

Habenular projections through fasciculus mediate the sleep cycle, and lesions to it disrupt normal sleep patterns, especially REM sleep. Methamphetamine changes the structure of the cells in locus ceruleus, one of the sleep cycle centers. Gene expression is altered and these cells become dysfunctional. The sleep cycle is disrupted at a genetic level and recovery is slow and sometimes incomplete.

Even when Jim had been clean for many months, he would go for days without sleep. No matter what time I got called out to deliver a baby, Jim was up; sometimes watching TV, sometimes just staring into space. We made him go to his room and turn the lights out, but he still stayed awake for days at a time. Continued exposure to crystal causes chronic anxiety and permanent damage to the sleep cycle. The resulting sleep deprivation contributes to the psychosis associated with methamphetamine.

HYGIENE AND APPETITE CONTROL

Addicts typically don't care much about their own hygiene. Grooming impulses come from the base of the midbrain [ventral tegmental area] and are reinforced by nucleus accumbens [it feels good to take a bath] and both of these areas are damaged by methamphetamine. Addicts also lose their sense of smell because of damage to the olfactory tubercle in the brain, and to the nasal mucosa from snorting meth. They honestly don't know how bad they smell.

When Jim lived with us, he had an aversion to bathing. He would wear the same clothes for days, and his body odor was frankly offensive. My husband tried to help him take a bath, and he could get Jim in the shower with a lot of direct supervision, but he wouldn't use any soap. He smelled just as bad after his bath as he did before, and he didn't even seem to notice.

> *He couldn't smell himself, and he couldn't smell his food either. Nothing tasted good because he couldn't smell it.*

He couldn't smell himself, and he couldn't smell his food either. Nothing tasted good because he couldn't smell it. A lot of different structures go into appetite regulation. The sense of smell is crucial to appetite; if you can't smell your food, you can't taste it either. You won't want to eat if every thing tastes like plastic. The loss of appetite is variable, with some addicts habituating to it and maintaining normal weight. Most, however, lose significant body mass and become malnourished.

This is serious malnutrition. A long term addict looks like a walking skeleton, gaunt and thin. I see the girl in my office, she's five months pregnant, all her teeth are falling out, her hair is falling out, she has sores all over where she's been picking at her bugs, and they won't heal. She's anemic. Her immune system is shot; she can't fight off infection so her sinus infection has turned into pneumonia. Go to check the baby? The baby is dead.

METHAMPHETAMINE PSYCHOSIS

"I was an average happy well adjusted guy until I got addicted to meth, and then one day I heard some movement in the bushes outside my window. I had some Ice cooking in my tractor shed and I was absolutely sure I saw movement in the bushes on both sides of the door to my shed. I heard somebody laughing and I thought they were laughing at me. I shot at the source of the noise. I killed my neighbor's daughter. She was out there playing Barbie's with my daughter. I thought I had control over my drug use, but I didn't. Please tell people what this drug does to your mind."

Psychotic symptoms including paranoia and hallucinations are very common as the addict progresses to chronic compulsive intake. He's using every day now, not just on weekends, and the changes in dopamine and serotonin transport are not reversed between doses anymore as cells are being killed. As dopamine function is destroyed in the frontal lobe and mesocortico-limbic tracts, psychiatric symptoms become more pronounced. The dopamine receptors and transporter molecules are lost and the psychosis becomes persistent, a phenomenon called **methamphetamine psychosis**.

Reductions in dopamine transmission are long lasting, on the order of twelve to eighteen months, and so the psychotic symptoms persist even after methamphetamine use stops. Reductions in blood flow to the frontal lobes are noted for years after the last dose of methamphetamine, suggesting a permanent loss of tissue with chronic high dose use.

Long term use of methamphetamine, particularly in people with pre-existing schizoid personality types, triggers a psychotic break in people who otherwise might have gone through life without any major psychiatric problems. Persons who started using methamphetamine as adolescents are more likely to become psychotic than those using for the first time as adults, and addicts using higher doses and more frequently are more likely to become more or less permanently psychotic.

The pattern of behavior in methamphetamine psychosis is indistinguishable from classic paranoid schizophrenia, and can last for years after withdrawal of the drug. Auditory hallucinations and command voices [kill yourself, kill yourself, kill yourself] are common. Jim told me all the things my two-year-old son had said to him, all the things the baby told him to do, and I got him out of my house that very day.

Visual hallucinations frequently involve threatening scenes and gestures, sexual content and phallic symbols are characteristic features. Smoke from a joint or bong takes the form of a gun or a knife growing larger and larger. Sticks on the ground become thousands of snakes striking at your ankles. The room is closing in on you, and there is no escape. The floor disappears and you fall and fall and fall.

> *You feel bugs crawling on your skin, spiders crawling in your hair. You can't wipe them off because they are on your sensory cortex, not on your skin.*

Tactile hallucinations are specific to crystal meth intoxication and can be useful to distinguish methamphetamine psychosis from classic schizophrenia. Hallucinations of bugs crawling on your skin are sometimes corroborated by the visual hallucinations of spiders or snakes. You can't get away from the spiders because they are on your visual cortex, not on the sheets of your bed.

The paranoid delusions are complex and confusing. Jim believed the prison establishment was corrupt, that gang rape was scheduled and encouraged by prison staff, videotaped for the entertainment of the guards, and young weak prisoners were helpless against it. Inmates were castrated and mutilated by the guards if they complained. Everyone knew about it and considered it just punishment for prisoners. If the truth of one of his assertions was challenged or disproved, he would manufacture another.

Ideas of reference are common, as the addict thinks news reports are referring to him. The siren he hears outside is a cop coming after him. Hypervigilance and a vague sense of paranoia solidify into paranoid delusions and threatening hallucinations. He sees cops in the bushes; he thinks his motel room is bugged. He sees a gun in the static on the TV, and it looks like it is aimed at him. The ceiling fan is raining acid on his head. The weather man is watching him through the TV, and he's pointing to his house on the map, broadcasting his location to the police.

Addicts frequently listen to emergency channels and police radio bands. They lace their homes and laboratories with booby traps, trip wires, and even land mines, explosive devices partially buried in the ground. They are heavily armed and poised to shoot in any direction. They are afraid of the police, and also afraid of each other. Rival gangs, customers who won't pay, thieves, and informants are all targets.

The hallucinations are differentiated from those associated with paranoid schizophrenia only by content. Methamphetamine hallucinations center on the drug experience, law enforcement, sexual content, and violence. When the delusions are threatening, they rapidly lead to violent and aggressive behavior, and thus the high rate of incarceration among meth addicts.

The violence is usually directed at someone they know, most often a family member or friend. Misunderstandings escalate to verbal abuse, which turns into a shoving match, a punch, a fight, and if a lethal weapon is available, a death. The underlying paranoia contributes to this process, and since both parties are frequently intoxicated, the altercation rapidly accelerates out of control. Drug related homicide is by far the most frequent cause of death in methamphetamine addicts.

Nerd Box

Methamphetamine damages the same structures that malfunction in classic paranoid schizophrenia, including the anterior cingulate gyrus, a part of the frontal lobe. The parts of the frontal and temporal lobes that are damaged with methamphetamine use are the same sections that are associated with violent anti-social behavior in the psychopathic personality, the person who commits mindless violent crimes with no sense of remorse.

Addicts are frequently violent. The delusions and the hallucinations contribute to their aggressiveness, but they are also angry, irritable, and impulsive. They fly into a rage and put their fist through a wall without even thinking about it. The violence is what most often lands them in jail. Those with severe damage to their frontal and temporal lobes cannot live anywhere except in a prison.

METHAMPHETAMINE DEMENTIA

"Now all I'm left with is a lousy short term memory and a case of screwy speech like a serious loss for words. It takes me many tries to grasp new thoughts. I'm doing better; I'm not depressed all the time anymore. I'm functioning as well as I can in life, but I am beginning to think that for the rest of my life I will not be who I was before my meth debauchery."

Damage to the temporal lobe affects both speech and memory, as both are centered in that part of the brain. Slow slurry speech, halting word pattern, and impaired memory are common complications from even short term use. He knows what he wants to say, but can't find the word for it. When you suggest the right word he knows it immediately, but he can't come up with it on his own. He tries to read, but the letters are all jumbled up, and he can't make sense out of them.

The mental disability associated with meth use is very much like a 'closed head injury' from a car wreck. After many years of high dose use, relapses, and concurrent use of other drugs, the brain damage is comparable to mental retardation. Recovery from brain damage like this requires some real work. The cells that know how to read, for instance, are dead. They are not coming back. The job of rehabilitation is to teach some other bunch of cells how to read.

In the case of frontal lobe damage, the likely consequences of any given act are not clearly thought out. You decide to climb up on top of the church next door and ring the bells. It looks easy from the porch of your house, just climb that wall, jump up on the roof, climb up the steeple and ring the bells! Come on, let's do it! That is called a delusion of grandeur, the Superman Syndrome. "I can go anywhere, I can punch that guy's lights out; I am the most powerful person in the world."

Confused thought processes, impaired learning ability, and poor judgment are long term consequences of methamphetamine abuse. Addicts, even recovered addicts, have difficulty keeping a job and learning new tasks. It takes them longer to catch on, and they make more mistakes, even years after their last use of methamphetamine. A single dose of methamphetamine is toxic enough to the hippocampus to impair short term and long term object memory. Memory loss is correlated with 30–40% loss of binding to dopamine and serotonin transport sites persisting for three weeks after a single injection. The rat couldn't find the cheese anymore. Just one dose can produce profound and persistent deficits in hippocampal [short term] memory.

Therapy for methamphetamine brain damage

You have to work the damaged area of the brain in order to talk the surrounding cells into picking up the lost functions. And so we recommend exercises like word search puzzles, comic books and picture books. "But doctor, all I can read is 'stop' signs." Well then, read 'stop' signs. And when you can read picture books, read picture books. And when you can read comic books, read comic books. Do the thing that is hard for you to do. Force those cells to learn how to do it. They are not going to learn how to read unless you force them to do it. You can't park yourself in front of a TV set and expect to get better.

Other types of verbal and memory deficiencies are addressed in much the same way. There are lots of children's games that build memory skills. Reading out loud helps with the speech problems. It is humiliating for a trained electrician to have to re-learn how to read like a second grader. But the alternative is even worse. This is the rest of your life we are talking about. Swallow your pride and do your letter books, get tutoring if you have to, and teach yourself how to read again. You are not stupid. You can do this.

Don't point out to me the obvious. The people who can't read are not reading this book. You are. And you can teach this kind of skill to your loved one struggling with the residual effects of methamphetamine. You don't need a PhD to offer hope and encouragement to a recovering addict.

Methamphetamine dementia can be severe and is associated with dramatic defects in the temporal lobes of addicts, with 11% less tissue in the cortex, and 8% less tissue in the hippocampus on SPECT and MRI studies. This is serious brain damage. It shows up on an x-ray, and it is reflected in clinical test of memory function. Short term memory loss, combined with damage to the frontal and temporal lobes, causes a profound learning disability impacting job performance.

This figure shows up much better in color on page 261, figure 3. It is a SPECT image of brain cell damage from methamphetamine in addicts who had been using ice for an average of ten years. The areas with the most severe damage are the hippocampus, association areas in the frontal lobe, language and memory areas in the temporal lobe, and the midbrain, especially the limbic area. This brain damage correlates with the holes in the brain seen in previous PET scan images.

Fig 17

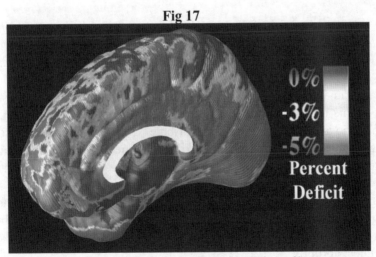

Large areas of severe brain damage in chronic users of ice.
© 2004 used courtesy of Paul Thompson et al UCLA School of Medicine, Full citation page 448

Treatment

There is some evidence that the Alzheimer's drug Aricept [donepezil] is helpful in treating methamphetamine dementia. It consists of one case study of a severely impaired individual, but further controlled studies are certainly indicated, since these people are usually quite young and otherwise healthy.

Verbal learning, memory tasks, nonverbal fluid reasoning, and executive functioning were all impaired in this individual, and significant improvement, especially in the area of memory, was noted after three months therapy with Aricept. Improvement was also noted in his academic performance and concentration.

Jim would repeatedly leave the water running, leave the back door open and forget to feed the dog. When I took him grocery shopping the day he moved into his apartment, he would get peanut butter but not bread, cereal but not milk; my seven-year-old daughter would have done a better job. I was trying to treat him like an adult. I didn't want to tell him what to do, but he just didn't get it.

"Stan doesn't understand why they keep turning the power off at his apartment. He got pulled over for expired tags on his car and he had to pay a fine. He doesn't understand why all these things keep happening to him."

Damage to the frontal lobe [and I am including all the many subdivisions of this lobe in one discussion] results in disordered thinking and judgment. Lesions in the frontal lobe contribute to the dementia, and also cause subtle changes in decision making skills. The methamphetamine brain does not function normally when making decisions, setting priorities, managing time, and remembering even simple things. Addicts can't focus on a job long enough to finish it. They get lost in the details and wander from place to place doing disconnected tasks. They fidget for hours, their mind is racing, but they don't get anything done. They talk in circles, can't finish a thought, and change the subject abruptly.

Nerd Box

This neural disruption can be seen on fMRI and PET scans and correlated with simultaneous performance on psychological tests measuring mental processes when making decisions. It is also correlated with disrupted neural integration seen in cortical areas under a microscope. In EEG studies, it shows up as increased theta band activity.

Chronic methamphetamine abuse disrupts frontal-striatal pathways involving both dopamine and serotonin transmission. Methamphetamine abusers have difficulty concentrating and focusing attention. They are highly distractible, much like patients with Attention Deficit Hyperactivity Disorder.

Meth addicts are more likely to choose a smaller immediate reward than a much larger delayed reward, a finding directly correlated with the brain areas activated on fMRI studies. These defects in complex thought slowly and incompletely fade over twelve to eighteen months in recovery. The longer these people are in recovery, the more the recovery of normal brain patterns, but healing is sometimes incomplete even many years after last use of methamphetamine. Similar behavior is noted in ADHD, and is associated with lesions to the prefrontal cortex and anterior cingulate gyrus, parts of the frontal lobe.

Addicts are guided by immediate rewards in an obsessive manner, and do not even activate the brain areas associated with predicting future consequences. They take longer to make a decision and consistently make poor choices, failing to take into account all the information given to them. This defect in reasoning results in defects in real life decision making. They can't deliver your pizza because they got the address wrong and didn't know who to call to get it right and decided to go to their friend's house instead and I guess I don't have that job anymore. Would you like some pizza? It has pepperoni on it. They live in a fog.

Methamphetamine users are much more dependent on the results of previous observations to solve problems. They do what worked yesterday, even if it is totally inappropriate to the situation today. You work at a body shop and yesterday the boss wanted everything painted white, so today you automatically paint everything white. But the order is for a red finish on the car you are painting. The customer is not likely to be happy with the result.

> *Mental ability is severely compromised*
> *and approaches the severity of*
> *mental retardation.*
> *It is an acquired learning disability.*

Adaptability to new demands is markedly lacking, and approaches the severity of mental retardation. You land a great job in a machine shop, and they are training you to operate the machine that stamps out parts for the manufacture of aircraft. It has to be done right. After a week of training, you are still making a lot of mistakes. Okay, we'll train you again next week. After two weeks, you're not doing it right. Half of the parts you make are not usable. After three weeks, we still have to stand over you and make sure you did it right. This isn't going to work. We can't keep you here. We don't *have* a job you can do. You've just lost a $20 per hour job because you couldn't get past the training sessions.

Jim went through six jobs in six months because he just didn't get it. He thought they were expecting too much, he didn't really want to work there anyway, they just didn't like him there, the supervisor had it out for him, she was against him from the very beginning, it was too hot, it was too cold, he couldn't get a ride . . . it was always somebody else's fault. He couldn't see how his own poor performance had anything to do with losing his jobs.

But Doctor, I've been using this stuff for 15 years and I'mmmm nottttt braaaain dammmaaaaggged!

CHILD ABUSE AND NEGLECT

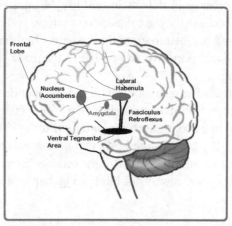

Fig 18 Brain areas important to caring for a child

"I was working late one night and I heard something as I was locking up. It was a child crying at the end of the Sunday School wing. He was about 18 months old, dressed in pajamas, and he had an old stuffed dog with him. They must have just left him there, he was scared, but he wasn't hysterical. The police came and got him."
    Pastor of a small church in Alabama

"I just want my children back. Will I ever be well enough to take good care of them again?"

Child neglect is so common and maternal bonding is so poor in methamphetamine moms that newborns are left at the hospital, two-year-olds left in the parking lot of a store, and six-year-olds left to care for babies. The children are not bathed or fed for days, they drink out of the toilet, and they wander in the streets hungry and crying. They are absent from school because nobody gets them up on time and takes them to school. They don't have clean clothes and their homework is not done. Mothers are oblivious to the needs of their children. The foster care system in some areas is crushed under the weight of parental neglect because of methamphetamine.

A great deal of complex thought, working memory, judgment, and emotional control go into raising a child. The basic drive to care for a child originates in midbrain structures that are damaged by methamphetamine. Lateral habenula and fasciculus retroflexus [self control], ventral tegmental area [cravings, drives, and urges], nucleus accumbens [pleasure center], and amygdala [emotions] all contribute to the maternal instinct. They mediate bonding with the newborn and nesting type behavior. When these structures are damaged in laboratory rats, the pups are abandoned. The same thing happens in humans.

> *When these structures are damaged in laboratory rats, the pups are abandoned. The same thing happens in humans.*

The feeling of love comes from amygdala. It is emotionally rewarding to love a helpless infant. Care, concern, compassion, the 'deep in the gut' feeling that hurts when the child is hurt, comes from amygdala. The moods and feelings of the child are understood in this midbrain area, different from the rational analysis going on in the cortical areas. He might be telling you everything is just fine, but you know in your heart it is not. You have read his body language, his facial expressions, and his mood using your amygdala.

The motivation to have a child comes from the ventral tegmental area. The drive to have children comes from the same place as the drive to have sex, and is almost as powerful. It is a desire to give your identity to another, to create a little person to love and nurture. We love our children before we know what they look like, before we know what kind of person they are going to be, before they are even conceived. We love them because they are ours.

Your ability to set aside your own needs to take care of a child comes from the lateral habenula/fasciculus retroflexus. It is capable of suppressing other drives and desires in the interests of the child's welfare. You can suppress your desire for sleep in order to get up and feed your infant. The child's cry empowers you to risk your own life and safety in the interests of your child.

Your attentiveness to your child's needs comes from the frontal lobe. You can anticipate the needs of your child and make conscious decisions and plans to meet those needs. You shop for groceries, save for college, buy clothes and diapers, talk to his teacher, make him a doctor's appointment, and read him stories out of your frontal lobe. You know he needs those things, and you make the necessary arrangements.

The enjoyment of the child's smile and play comes from nucleus accumbens. It feels good to hold your baby close and cuddle. Her soft skin and the smell of her hair, her chubby tummy, and her smile with the two missing teeth are all pleasant to experience. They feel good and warm and comfortable, and you want to do it again.

All these functions are impaired when these areas of the brain are damaged. The baby brings no pleasure to the methamphetamine mother. She doesn't enjoy the sound of her baby singing; it is just noise to her. She doesn't attend to his needs and buy milk and cereal; she can't get it together to buy any type of food. She can't set aside her own need for sleep to get the child up and ready for school. She can't feel his pain when he cries with an ear infection. She just doesn't care. She feels no compassion.

"It's been nine days now, and I still haven't heard a word from my daughter. My grandkids are miserable and worried and crying themselves to sleep every night. I am taking the nine-year-old to a therapist today. He blames himself because he was not real nice sometimes while she was here and had a lot of anger for stuff she did to him in the past. Now he thinks it's his fault she left, although that is ridiculous. He has horrible abandonment issues because she has left him so many times over the years. We are miserable in this house; and I doubt she even cares, or she would at least call her kids."

These functions recover slowly as the brain heals over twelve to eighteen months off ice. A methamphetamine addict can recover and be a good mother to her children, but she needs intense supervision for a least a year as her brain heals. Child Protective Services in Alabama require a mother to be drug free and employed for one full year to get her children back, and she can anticipate frequent visits from CPS workers for another year after that.

COMPULSIVE DRUG TAKING

"I had a great boyfriend, somebody I really loved, and I blew it. I started using again. I knew if he caught me it would be over, and I really loved this man. He was a wonderful man. But I couldn't quit using. Eventually he found out and he left and it was my own fault."

Repetitive compulsive drug taking can be understood just from the damage to the frontal lobe with poor decision making processes and loss of ability to weigh options and take all the data into account. But it goes deeper than that. Just informing an addict about the damage caused by drug use will not stop him from using.

Methamphetamine sensitized rats have a change in transmission patterns in the tracts between ventral tegmental area [cravings, drives, and urges] and frontal lobe [rational thought]. Normally, there is traffic in both directions, but after methamphetamine exposure, transmission is almost entirely from ventral tegmental area to frontal lobe, and almost none going the other way. Cravings, urges, and drives can talk to the cortex, but the cortex cannot talk to the cravings. No matter how much good information you give the frontal lobe, it cannot control the cravings and drives originating in the deepest parts of the brain.

> *No matter how much good information you give the frontal lobe, it cannot control the cravings and drives originating in the deepest parts of the brain.*

Obsessive thought patterns are established, in which an image or memory of getting high becomes impossible to ignore. The normal pathways we used to exert control over our thoughts are non-functional in the addict, and he cannot suppress those thoughts. He is constantly distracted by thoughts of getting high, remembering his last high, the people he gets high with, the status of his stash and how to get more, make more, or steal more. He can't turn those thoughts off.

Nerd Box

Drug craving is associated with the ventral tegmental area, nucleus accumbens, striatum, amygdala, hippocampus, and frontal lobe. The amygdala in particular is activated in craving situations. You can see it on a brain scan. Crave inducing imagery [descriptions of paraphernalia, for example] stimulates a huge increase in metabolic activity of amygdala, as well as other limbic structures. Interestingly, anger inducing imagery also activates many of those same areas. Angry, resentful thoughts that are nurtured and encouraged can also trigger cravings, and the thoughts themselves can be addictive.

Stress and drug associated stimuli activate circuits in the amygdala which are implicated in the memory of emotionally salient events. The amygdala in turn activates dopamine neurons of the ventral tegmental area, directly triggering cravings. Amygdala also triggers associations indirectly via the frontal lobe. Pleasurable memories are associated with the site of drug paraphernalia, stimulating obsessive desires and thoughts about drug use. These areas of the brain can remember the high. Anything that reminds them of crystal, a charred piece of tin foil for instance, will trigger cravings for ice.

Midbrain cells that have learned to seek out methamphetamine have 50% higher levels of a receptor system, called Sigma 1, in the frontal lobe and hippocampus, which was not seen in rats that are passively exposed to the drug. The triggers are wired into the brain at the cellular protein level, not just from exposure to the chemical, but from the act of seeking out the drug.

TRIGGERS

"After four weeks clean from meth, I still have these really bad times, like now! I woke up from a "using" dream. God I can feel the pipe in my hands & mouth, see the sh** melting, running down the pipe, then the smoke. Now I am awake & afraid to go back to sleep! Does it ever end?"

In order to recover, these obsessive and compulsive thought patterns have to be extinguished. If a tract is used a lot, it gets stronger, but a tract that is never used atrophies and gets weaker. How many of you remember the phone number at the house you lived in thirty years ago? There are a lot of rituals and associations connected with drug use, and the related brain pathways have to be extinguished in order to break the behavioral habits associated with those rituals.

The sight of a syringe, a piece of tin foil, the smell of pot, the sound of party music, all bring back vivid memories of drug use that will actually result in a 'high' by association, a kind of Pavlov's Dog response. Conditioned firing in the brain can reproduce the high, even in the absence of methamphetamine. You can taste it again, smell it again, even feel it again, by the strength of the association wired into the brain. It takes a long time for these associations to be extinguished, on the order of years.

> *You can taste it again, smell it again, even feel it again, by the strength of the association wired into the brain.*

The triggers of those memories and associations are endless. Drug paraphernalia like spoons, flasks, dollar bills, cigarette lighters, pipes, soda straws, and razor blades are obvious triggers. They are part of the ritual in preparing and using the drug. The music associated with the party scene is a powerful trigger for cravings. You pull up to the stop light, and the car next to you is throbbing with your favorite party music. It will make you crave.

Alcohol and marijuana are potent triggers. I met a man in jail who had been in for a year on methamphetamine charges. You can get it in jail, but he chose not to. He wanted to get off of it. The day he got out of jail, his friend picked him up and gave him a beer and a joint in the car on the way home from jail. The smell of pot triggered intense cravings and he wasn't expecting them, cravings for ice, not pot. He ended up back in jail that very same night with four new charges against him. He'd been clean for a *year*. The cravings had gone away. He thought it was over. He didn't think he'd ever have to worry about ice again. He was wrong.

> *He didn't think he'd ever have to worry about ice again. He was wrong.*

Pornography is another very common trigger. When they bust one of these places, they have to shove all the guns off to one side, and all the porno off to the other side, to get to the chemicals they're after. Porno is part of the experience. Violent and kinky sex is part of the high. I've met more than one man who is back in jail because of internet porno. They didn't know it could do that to them.

People and locations associated with the drug experience are potent triggers. The convenience store where you used to make your buys, the tractor shed where you used to cook it, the old neighborhood where all your drug buddies live, will bring back vivid memories and cravings. I know a woman whom I have delivered two children for, they are three and five years old, and those kids have never met their grandmother. They never will. That woman knows that if she ever goes back home, her mother will drag her back into addiction. Her mother uses, and the house is full of sights and smells that trigger cravings. This woman has been clean for five years, but she will never go home again.

Important relationships sometimes have to be broken to escape addiction. If your wife is still using, you might have to divorce her and move away. You may never be able to see your cousin or your best friend again. You are extremely fragile in your recovery for **two to three years** after getting off crystal. That's how long it takes for an old pathway to atrophy and the associations to dissipate. You are at risk for relapse for the *rest of your life.*

DRUG REHABILITATION

The cognitive-behavioral model for drug treatment, used in most rehabilitation programs, relies on an intact mesocorticolimbic apparatus, including fasciculus retroflexus, for its effectiveness. When those structures are damaged, no amount of arguing will influence the behavior of these people. They will agree with you completely that drugs are evil and dangerous, and yet use crystal again the next chance they get. It's irrational and you can't argue with it.

Control over craving requires working functional tracts between rational cortical areas and irrational limbic areas. The thinking part of the brain has to have authority over the craving part of the brain. Remember, methamphetamine is extremely toxic to the cells in fasciculus retroflexus, and other mesocorticolimbic tracts. Even a single dose of methamphetamine can destroy 80–90% of the cells in these tracts. Rehabilitation consists in strengthening these neural connections to restore communication between frontal lobe [command and control], and the ventral tegmental [cravings], and limbic [emotional] areas of the brain. We have to re-connect the wires. How do we do that?

If you have an accident with a chain saw and tear up the muscles in your leg, they put you in the hospital and treat you real nice for a few days, and then they put you in a rehabilitation center. What do they do in the rehabilitation center? They make you move that leg. Ouch! That's the last thing in the world you want to do. It *hurts* to move your leg. But that's what they make you do, all day - every day, move your leg, this way and that way, up and down. After a few weeks of working at it, the muscle fibers you have left hypertrophy. They get stronger, thicker, larger, and you can walk again. You might always have a limp, but you can walk.

> *He's doing bench presses with his self-control tract every time he gets up in the morning and does his chores.*

The addict has torn up the tracts in his brain that give him control over urges, drives, and cravings. How do we rehabilitate him? We put him in an inpatient rehabilitation center and make him use what's left of his self-control pathway, fasciculus retroflexus. How do we do that? By making him get up at 6:30 every day, make his bed and mop the floor. We give him chores to do. Ouch! That's the last thing in the world he wants to do. It *hurts* to use those self-control pathways.

We make him do it anyway [if we can keep him in the rehabilitation center]. He's doing bench presses with his self-control tract every time he gets up in the morning and does his chores. Over time, the twenty or thirty cells he has left in his self-control pathway get stronger. They grow richer stronger connections, new synapses, new dendritic processes, and new axons, and after some work, we can talk twenty or thirty cells into doing the job of a hundred cells. He regains control over urges, drives, and cravings. He might always have a limp, but he can walk.

FUTURE DEVELOPMENTS

Vaccines against methamphetamine are under development that induce specific antibodies that neutralize the drug before it can reach the brain. Vaccines against nicotine and cocaine are in clinical trials, and vaccines for heroin and methamphetamine are being investigated. Vaccines are specific to the intended drug and do not prevent abuse of other related drugs. Vaccines also do not curb the cravings that often precipitate relapse. In fact, they may increase drug intake by dampening the high, "It takes even more to get high now that I've had this stupid vaccine."

SSRI antidepressants have been found to be helpful in smoking cessation programs as they reduce the cravings for nicotine. There is some data for their use in methamphetamine addiction as well, and they are commonly used to blunt the severe depression seen in abstinent addicts. Mood stabilizers like lithium and Carbamazepine [Tegretol] are also helpful. Gabapentin [Neurontin] is helpful for the anxiety, muscle spasms and seizures. Some addicts need anti-psychotic medications like olanzapine [Zyprexia] or resperidone [Respirdol]. We try to avoid the major tranquilizers like Valium because they are themselves addictive.

Many drugs are under development for treatment of addiction, with catchy names like GBR12909 and BP 897. Their target is the biochemical basis for the cravings. The challenge is to find a treatment that is effective, is non-addictive, has few side effects, and is not itself toxic to any brain system. Names to watch for: lobeline, memantine, pemoline, acamprosate, ondansetron, isradipine, and tergutide.

.6.

Methamphetamine – Medical Complications

Methamphetamine affects other systems in the body as well as the brain. The heart, blood vessels, liver, kidney, and muscles are all affected by this drug. The immune system is weakened, nutrition is poor, and sexually transmitted disease is rampant. Every area of health is affected by methamphetamine. The mortality rate is high.

Methamphetamine causes dilated pupils, high fever, chest pain and profound increases in blood pressure and heart rate. A fever of 108 degrees is not uncommon, especially when the person is very active, for instance with vigorous dancing. When norepinephrine receptors in the heart and blood vessels are overstimulated, they cause blood vessels to constrict and go into spasms. Blood pressure can exceed 200/150 and heart rate can approach 250 beats per minute. Values like that are associated with heart attack and stroke, especially if there is preexisting heart disease or vascular malformation. A weak blood vessel in the brain [aneurism] can rupture, causing immediate death.

> *A weak blood vessel in the brain [aneurism] can rupture, causing immediate death.*

Headaches are very common and debilitating in methamphetamine addicts. Jim had a headache every day for two years. These are migraine headaches, due to vasospasm in the blood vessels in the brain, and they usually respond to migraine drugs. Serotonin deficiency causes the migraines, and drugs like sumatriptan succinate [Imitrex] that bind the serotonin receptor, alleviate the headache. Unfortunately, the headache comes right back when the medicine has worn off, because the serotonin cells have been killed by meth-amphetamine. These drugs are expensive. They are meant for the occasional migraine you get once a month or so. Ice addicts have migraines every day.

Seizures are also common, not just when using, but also in recovery. Some addicts use until they seize and can't hold the pipe anymore. Anyone will have a seizure if they are stressed enough. The addict, even in recovery, has a lower seizure threshold than normal. Every time he gets too hungry or too tired, he has a seizure.

MALNUTRITION

The malnutrition in methamphetamine addiction is profound, and underlies many of the medical problems we will discuss in this chapter. Some addicts habituate to it and maintain body weight and nutritional status, but most do not. A long term addict looks like a walking skeleton, with sunken eyes and grey skin, not exactly a fashion statement.

Addicts lose their appetite and their sense of smell. They run with a crowd that also uses, and nobody around them is interested in eating. The only thing they cook is methamphetamine, and the kitchen has been taken over for this purpose. All of their money is tied up in dope, and no one is interested in going to the grocery store. If there are children in the house, they also have nothing to eat.

After a year or two of chronic undernourishment, the body systems adjust; the small intestine atrophies and the stomach shrinks. Long term vitamin deficiencies lead to worsening of the neurologic symptoms and skin lesions. Bones are weakened, wounds don't heal, and teeth fall out. Addicts are severely anemic. They have poor immune function and abnormal blood clotting. Electrolyte abnormalities cause an irregular heart rhythm. Aggressive nutritional support is essential to successful recovery from drug addiction.

SKIN LESIONS

"I would break out immediately after doing meth, usually within a half hour of the drug hitting my system I would start getting "speed bumps" but what made them worse and infected was because I would pick at them and squeeze them–basically I would tweek on my face–it was so gross, too. I would spend hours picking at my face and I knew the whole time what kind of damage I was doing, but I JUST COULDN'T STOP MYSELF–it was because of the drug. Anyhow, after I picked my face to pieces, I would put rubbing alcohol on all the sores and use a blow dryer on my face . . . It would take a week or two for my face to clear up after I'd used and picked at it . . . . I have a really pretty face and I would just destroy it every time I used."

The medical complaint that most troubles addicts is the skin lesions caused by methamphetamine. They are called crank sores or speed bumps, and they commonly appear on the face, arms, and shoulders of the addict. They are not related to injection sites, and can be seen with only occasional use. They resolve when the drug is stopped, but sometimes leave scars.

Methamphetamine is detectable in the skin and hair follicles within 30 minutes of injection, with peak levels two hours after injection. The drug is then incorporated into the hair shaft, and can be detected by drug testing. It is worked into the core of the hair shaft and cannot be washed away. Some heavy users note a powder in their hair that looks like dandruff or nits. They can taste it in their sweat.

Methamphetamine is a crystal at room temperature. It crystallizes in the skin and forms a local tissue reaction, like a pimple. Often people burst the little pimples, and the crystalline contents come out. Jim had large keloids, thick raised scars around the speed bumps on his back, and the scars did not go away. Speed bumps itch, and the skin of a methamphetamine addict itches even when there are no sores. The itching is sometimes related to the hallucination of bugs that is so common on crystal. They pick at the bugs and dig deep sores into their skin.

> *Young people in their twenties can lose all their teeth within a few weeks.*

A similar process in the mouth and gums leads to the loss of otherwise healthy teeth. Even young people in their twenties can lose all their teeth within a few weeks. Some addicts grind their teeth down to the gums, and many have advanced tooth decay due to poor hygiene, decreased saliva and malnutrition, but even clean teeth will fall out if the root is destroyed and the enamel weakened by methamphetamine.

> *Needle tracks feel like a little pipe under the skin.*

When methamphetamine is injected, it leaves needle tracks. The injection sites get infected, and the blood vessels are burned by the drug. The vein just above the injection site gets hard and tender. Needle tracks are well hidden by the addict who doesn't want his mom to find out. Look between their fingers and between their toes, on their breasts and private parts, in the armpit and groin. They use a tiny needle, so you have to look closely. It is easier to *feel* needle tracks than it is to see them. The sclerosed vein does not compress like it should. It feels like a little pipe under the skin.

LUNG DISEASE

The entire respiratory tract is at risk with methamphetamine use, and the consequences are serious. The manufacture of methamphetamine involves skin and lung exposure to extremely caustic chemicals. Chemical burns to the airways cause a chronic cough, even in cooks who do not use the drug themselves. Snorting it causes a chronic runny nose, sinus infections, holes in the nasal septum, and rapid loss of the sense of smell. Smoking meth also causes sores in the mouth, and erosions of the corneas if a piece of tin foil is used instead of a pipe.

Cigarette smokers die of respiratory failure at sixty or sixty-five years of age. Methamphetamine smokers die at thirty-five or forty. This stuff isn't filtered and these are toxic fumes. The chemicals used to manufacture meth are carcinogens, and the fumes are toxic to airways and bronchioles. Methamphetamine is broken down in the lung into the same collection of caustic chemicals we met earlier, hydroxy free radicals, and they kill living cells wherever they find them. The cells in your airway that are supposed to kill bacteria cannot do it. Smoking methamphetamine is associated with lung problems, chronic bronchitis, recurrent pneumonia, emphysema, and scars on the lungs from pulmonary fibrosis. Of course, the pot you are smoking doesn't help matters. Pot is a lot more toxic to lung cells than tobacco is, and chronic exposure causes lung damage.

> *Death from respiratory failure is not pleasant. It is a slow suffocation, like trying to breathe through a pillow.*

The occasional cough becomes chronic, and the mucous becomes thick and foul looking. It often tastes like crystal when you cough it up. As the cough gets worse, you find you must limit your activity. You can't run and play ball with the guys because of your coughing spells. As the damage worsens and emphysema sets in, you can't even catch your breath. Even minimal activity leaves you winded. You start wheezing like an old man and have to sit down. Death from respiratory failure is not pleasant. It is a slow suffocation, like trying to breathe through a pillow.

The final event is usually a bad case of pneumonia; or the flu comes through the community, and you can't fight it off. The malnutrition associated with methamphetamine abuse causes immune deficiencies that predispose to these infections and make them more severe. Addicts are more susceptible to the sinus infections leading to pneumonia. It seems they always have a cold, a chronic cough and a low grade fever.

HEART FAILURE

"My biological father used methamphetamine for five years. He died of heart failure when he was thirty-eight years old. I was only twelve when he died. He missed my wedding. Now I see my cousin doing the same thing."

Heart failure is a common sequelae to methamphetamine abuse. There are three ways crystal causes heart failure. Acute methamphetamine overdose causes *ventricular tachycardia,* the same heart rhythm we see in heart attacks, and it kills in six minutes just like a regular heart attack does. Perfectly healthy people, with no history of heart disease, some of them just teenagers, die from heart attacks brought on by methamphetamine. First, they complain of chest pain, then they get nauseated and can't catch their breath, then they get dizzy and pass out, and then they die. And it only takes six minutes.

Methamphetamine causes the heart to race and blood pressure to soar. If you do that to your heart every day for a few months or years, your heart becomes what we call *strained.* The muscle walls get thick, and when the walls get too thick, oxygen can't get through to the deepest layers of muscle. The muscle gradually dies.

> *When you can't breathe anymore, even at rest, we put you on the list for a heart transplant.*

Methamphetamine is also a direct *toxin* to heart muscle cells. Animal studies have shown in detail the heart muscle degeneration and cell death caused by methamphetamine resulting in heart failure. Eighteen hours after injection, inflammatory cells and contraction bands are seen in heart muscle cells. By fifty-six days, cell death and spotty fibrosis are seen throughout most of the heart. The same chemicals that kill cells in the brain, peroxynitrates, kill muscle cells in the heart and cause heart failure.

The heart is a pump; it pumps blood all over your body. When the pump in your basement gets backed up, the water just sits there in the basement. When the pump in your chest gets stopped up, the water just sits there in your feet and legs. Blood doesn't get pumped back up to the rest of your body, including your muscles, and you have no endurance. You can't even walk up the steps.

Early signs of heart failure include breathlessness and palpitations, easy fatigability, and a feeling of being out of shape. Later you get swelling, especially of the feet and legs. When fluid accumulates in your lungs, we call that pulmonary edema, and you have a sensation like you're drowning. Symptoms are worse when you are lying flat, and you need several pillows in order to sleep.

We treat heart failure with medications to make the heart beat stronger, make the blood vessels stronger, and reduce the demand on the heart. We give you diuretics to help you get all the extra fluid off. When these medications don't work anymore, you have to restrict your activity, and when you can't breathe anymore, even at rest, we put you on the list for a heart transplant.

BLOOD VESSEL DISINTEGRATION

"An autopsy done on a 16 year old methamphetamine addict revealed massive hemorrhage into the lungs and body cavities. Cause of death, 1] hemorrhagic shock 2] methamphetamine toxicity"

Methamphetamine is pretty caustic stuff. Intravenous injection of it causes sclerosis of the veins involved. It also damages arteries all over the body. When blood vessels are damaged they leak, and you bleed into the tissue all around the leaking vessel. Damage to blood vessels is called vasculitis, and when it occurs in major arteries, the cells in the wall of the vessel die, and the artery disintegrates. This results in bleeding, hemorrhage into the surrounding tissue. If that happens in the brain, you get intracerebral hemorrhage and cerebral edema. A twenty year old kid having a stroke has been using cocaine or methamphetamine until proven otherwise.

Bleeding into the lungs makes you cough up blood. You can't catch your breath and you drown in your own blood. Bleeding into your kidney makes you urinate blood; it clogs up the function in the kidney and causes kidney failure. Bleeding into your stomach causes ulcerations, makes you vomit blood and causes profuse diarrhea.

Methamphetamine causes bleeding into the pancreas, resulting in pancreatitis. Under a microscope, they could see swelling and disintegration of the pancreas cells in 50% of exposed rats. Severe cases show cell death, fibrosis and cirrhosis like lesions. Human autopsy studies have confirmed severe acute hemorrhagic pancreatitis in meth users, and I have seen several cases. Pancreatitis causes intense unremitting pain in the area of the stomach and severe nausea and vomiting. The pain persists for weeks, and there is no effective treatment for it. You just have to wait for it to go away. [It does not cause diabetes or cancer.]

BLEEDING INTO MUSCLES

"Man I wanted to die, it hurt so bad. I couldn't walk, I couldn't even breathe. I was peeing pure blood. I felt it when they put the tube in my throat, but I don't remember anything after that. I guess I'm lucky to be alive."

Bleeding into a muscle causes rhabdomyolysis [disintegration of muscle cells], and the death of muscle cells releases toxic chemicals into the blood stream. These toxins cause fever, chills, headache, muscle spasms, and intense pain. They also cause nausea and vomiting, rapid heart rate, heart failure, kidney failure, and difficulty breathing. It comes on suddenly, usually in an experienced user. It does not depend on the dose, but is seen more frequently in IV users.

> *The addicts call it "trash fever,"*
> *[if it doesn't kill you, you will wish*
> *you were dead]*

The addicts call it "trash fever," [if it doesn't kill you, you will wish you were dead] and attribute it to bad dope or impurities in the syringe. It is not caused by bad dope, but is a toxic reaction to the drug itself. Of the people seen in emergency rooms nationwide with rhabdomyolysis over the past five years, 43% were methamphetamine abusers. Trash fever is rare, but it is frequently fatal.

One of the toxins released by dead muscle is called myoglobin, which is extremely toxic to kidney cells. Acute kidney failure and metabolic acidosis are common complications of trash fever. The toxins also interfere with blood clotting resulting in DIC, or Disseminated Intravascular Coagulation. Victims start bleeding through the nose, ears and throat, and bleeding into the kidney, lungs, and brain. You go into hemorrhagic shock and pulmonary edema. DIC has a mortality rate of at least 50%.

So they take you to the hospital and I'm supposed to save you. I'm the doctor, right? Well, honey, if you are in a bad enough metabolic acidosis, there's nothing I can do for you. I'm pouring medicine into you through two large bore IVs as fast as I can, and it's not doing any good. Your kidneys shut down, your liver shuts down, your brain shuts down, and your heart shuts down, and there's nothing I can do about it. You are going to die. It's the most sickening feeling in the world.

LIVER FAILURE

"I'm not doing so well today. My friend that has been very sick passed away Tuesday morning. They took him off life support . . . I'm hurting right now, and I can't stop crying. I knew this day was coming, I did, but never prepared myself for it . . . I know he is in a better place, and that he is not suffering anymore. He was my old using buddy and my dad's best friend. I keep telling myself remember the good old days. 95% of it was cooking dope together, but the other 5% was taking my son to the park and out to eat. He always promised me we would go to the Red Lobster, but we never made it."

Toxic chemicals are supposed to be filtered out of the blood by the liver, with the obvious hazard that the toxin it is filtering will damage the filter itself, the liver cells. They are amazing cells, and can regenerate almost overnight if you just leave them alone and let them heal for awhile. Methamphetamine injected into the liver results in cell damage that can be seen even just a few hours after an injection. [This is a chemical hepatitis which is different from the infectious kind of hepatitis we will discuss next.]

An animal study showed how it happens. There was disintegration of the cells closest to the blood vessels just 2.5 hours after injection with methamphetamine. At six hours, damage had spread to the midzones of the liver and large areas of cell death were noted. At eighteen hours, liver damage had progressed to diffuse spotty cell death throughout the liver. Symptoms of liver damage include chronic nausea and vomiting, diarrhea, jaundice [yellow eyes], itching all over, disorientation, and delirium. You vomit blood and your belly swells up like you are nine months pregnant [even if you are a guy].

There is no medication for liver failure, we just treat the symptoms and hope it gets better. If it does not get better, we put you on the list for a liver transplant. In later stages, the damaged liver releases so much toxic debris into the bloodstream that it causes kidney failure and death. Concurrent use of alcohol exacerbates the disease, and liver failure is a frequent cause of death in alcoholics.

AIDS AND HEPATITIS

AIDS and hepatitis are common in methamphetamine addicts, even if they just snort or smoke it. IV drug users face the additional risk of exposure to dirty needles. One third of the IV drug abusers in this nation are HIV positive, and one third of HIV infected people are IV drug abusers or their consorts, many of them unknowing consorts, the wife who didn't know her husband was using.

Methamphetamine addicts are much more likely to contract HIV than heroin abusers, especially if they inject, because of the promiscuity associated with methamphetamine addiction. The arousal aspect of the high leads to promiscuous and violent sex. Meth addicted men have sexual dysfunction that leads to longer and rougher sex, and results in abrasions and bleeding, increasing the risk of sexually transmitted disease, including HIV and hepatitis.

HIV infection by itself causes significant deterioration of mental capacity. AIDS dementia is well documented in the HIV positive population. The HIV virus produces toxins that attack the dopamine producing cells in the midbrain, and kills those cells by making hydroxy free radicals, just like meth does. Animals exposed to the HIV toxin, and then to a relatively low dose of methamphetamine, had five times more damage to the midbrain than with either toxin given alone.

> *HIV infected methamphetamine addicts sustain significantly more brain damage than those with either condition alone.*

HIV infected methamphetamine addicts sustain significantly more brain damage than those with either condition alone. They use more heavily than HIV negative addicts, partly to treat the depression related to having HIV. The dementia is more severe, psychosis is more pronounced, and Parkinson's symptoms are produced at earlier stages of addiction in HIV infected addicts. HIV positive methamphetamine addicts are more aggressive, more promiscuous, and more resistant to treatment than uninfected addicts.

Hepatitis exposure is nearly universal in IV drug users. Infectious hepatitis is a serious disease with few acute symptoms, but which seriously limits life expectancy as complications develop in later years. Acute symptoms are nausea and vomiting, low grade fevers, jaundice and fatigue. It feels like a flu, but it doesn't go away. Long term, the symptoms are just like the liver failure described above.

Sexually transmitted diseases are epidemic among crystal meth addicts because their sexual behavior is compulsive and indiscriminant. Syphilis is almost unheard of except in the drug abusing population, where it is making a comeback. Herpes, Gonorrhea, and Chlamydia are common whenever sex is used as a medium of exchange, and sex for dope is part of the drug culture. The girls don't consider themselves prostitutes because no money is exchanged, but that is exactly what they have become.

PREGNANCY, EFFECTS ON THE BABY

"I am 35 and having my first child next month. I use speed and have been on it for about 2 years. I was doing a few lines a day right before I got pregnant, and then I quit doing it the first 3 months of my pregnancy and then slowly started up again off and on doing maybe half a line a day. [a line for me is half an inch or so, not big at all] I am so afraid I will harm my son, and his father is also an addict. I love my son so much, and I know in my heart that it is wrong to be doing drugs while pregnant, and I cry and hate myself, yet I need that stupid little line to somehow get through, and I don't want to hurt myself or him anymore. I believe in God and know he watches over me and my son, and I pray nightly for my son to be OK . . . I'm scared, please help me."

I get calls occasionally from grandparents, adoptive, and foster parents inquiring about the effects of methamphetamine on the child exposed to the drug in utero. They have real concerns about the future of their child. How will he be affected by the mother's use of methamphetamine? Will the baby be brain damaged? Will he have learning disabilities?

Some birth defects, like heart defects, cleft lip and palate, limb reduction anomalies [a baby with no arms], anencephaly [a baby with no brain], and anophthamlia [a baby with no eyes] have been associated with methamphetamine, but reports are sporadic and no recognized syndrome has emerged.

Methamphetamine use during pregnancy is associated with prematurity and low birth weight in term infants; a four pound baby at full term is not unusual. There is a high risk of brain damage from oxygen deprivation during labor. An inadequate placenta causes in- utero asphyxia [oxygen deprivation], and placental abruption [where the placenta separates from the uterus and hemorrhages]. Together with the chaotic lifestyle, profound malnutrition, sexually transmitted diseases, and lack of prenatal care typical of meth addicts, it's a wonder some of these children even survive.

> *It's a wonder some of these children even survive.*

The children aren't the only ones that die. Mothers die in labor from hemorrhage, massive strokes, heart attacks, and blood clots. They have massive swings in blood pressure and heart rate during labor, and serious complications with anesthetics. They get overwhelming infections and spend weeks on strong antibiotics, having their wounds cleaned out three times a day. An addicted mother is twice as likely to die in childbirth as a healthy laboring woman.

Methamphetamine does cross the placenta, and animal studies have shown that fetal brain tissue levels are about 1/5 of maternal levels one hour post injection, with the heaviest concentration in the fetal midbrain, frontal lobe, and brainstem. Withdrawal symptoms are seen in about 40% of exposed newborns, including excessive crying and tremors lasting for weeks. They don't feed well, don't sleep well, and don't gain weight. We call that 'failure to thrive.' They have rapid heart rates, and some are in heart failure at birth, though they usually recover with no permanent heart damage.

The risk to the baby's brain is obvious. The early studies on this subject were grim and suggested permanent neurological impairment in the children exposed. An early ultrasound study showed detectable abnormalities in the brains of 35% of drug exposed neonates compared to 5.3% of unexposed babies. Lesions included interventricular hemorrhage, echodensities associated with cell death, and cavitary lesions especially in the midbrain, frontal lobes, and brainstem. The injuries were consistent with those seen in adult abusers.

> *As these children have matured, the effects seem to have lessened.*

As these children have matured, the effects seem to have lessened. A human brain continues to develop until the age of twenty-two. Much of the early damage appears to be compensated for by the growing brain. Methamphetamine exposed school aged children were studied by MRI and 1H MRS, and no visible structural abnormalities were seen. Metabolite concentrations of N-acetyl compounds, creatinine, choline compounds, myoinositol, and glutamate were all normal in the frontal lobe and striatum. Exposed children had minimal changes in these chemicals in the midbrain, and there were no behavioral differences between the two groups of children.

"I had four meth addicted babies. I used throughout my pregnancies, and I can tell you from experience that a meth addicted baby is not the bundle of joy everyone hopes for. Incessant crying for weeks on end, very small at birth (my smallest was 4 lbs 2 oz.), and I didn't even look pregnant; in fact I knew I was but lied to myself about it and everyone who cared. My third baby

died at two weeks old from a heart defect that I believe was related to my meth use. Babies two and four have severe learning and mental disabilities and have since been adopted by people who could properly take care of them. I have no idea about my first daughter. I left the hospital shortly after she was born, and never looked back, I was sixteen. Meth is evil in any dose."

Nerd Box

Animal studies are much more invasive, and can demonstrate cellular changes invisible to x-ray based studies. Adult rats exposed to daily doses of methamphetamine in utero did show neurotoxic effects with reduced norepinephrine uptake sites in frontal cortex, reduced dopamine sites in midbrain, and impaired serotonin uptake in hippocampus, hypothalamus, and striatum. Damage to cells in the nucleus accumbens and hippocampus is seen, with damaged dendrites and reduced numbers of spines per neuron. The parietal cortex was also affected, suggesting a neurologic cause for the learning disability so often seen after prenatal methamphetamine exposure.

There was evidence of reparative regrowth of axon terminals in surviving animals. These changes are associated with alterations in behavior and impaired maze learning ability. Prolonged neonatal exposure to meth altered several markers for dopamine in substantia nigra, caudate, putamen, and ventral tegmental areas that resolved by thirty days of life.

Molecular genetic studies show more ominous changes. In rat pups exposed to methamphetamine, a total of 913 genes in brain cells were damaged, and the effect was not reversed after the drug wore off. The genes that initiate brain development are not expressed properly, and depending on the timing of the insult, may have serious implications for behavioral and cognitive function.

The fetal sequelae of methamphetamine use by the mother appear to be limited to learning disability and hyperactivity, which can be severe. Language development is delayed and impaired, but intelligence appears to be normal. There does appear to be a lasting susceptibility to the addictive and toxic effects of meth in the adult survivor of prenatal drug exposure, especially in the male. Adult male rats were more susceptible to neurotoxicity if re-exposed to crystal as adults. The adult children of alcoholic parents are known to have a genetic predisposition to addiction, but children of methamphetamine addicts will have the additional burden of a biochemical susceptibility to addiction.

Children exposed to the chemicals used to make methamphetamine are being exposed to some incredibly toxic substances. The solvents and fumes associated with the manufacture of methamphetamine are volatile neuroactive chemicals, like the toluene found in glue and spray paint. Huffing these chemicals causes severe learning disability. So does breathing them day and night. Children get the residues of these solvents and reagents on their hands, and end up eating them along with their hot dogs. The extent of the brain damage they suffer is only beginning to be appreciated.

About 25% of the children removed from methamphetamine homes test positive for methamphetamine, their parents are giving it to them. The child is three years old, he's whining and crying, he's hungry and tired. If the parent gives him just a little meth, he'll quit crying and go play with his toys for a few days. Significant levels of meth have been found even in baby's bottles. These children are just as addicted as Mommy and Daddy, and their brain dysfunction is even worse. Some of them are five or six years old and can't even talk.

> *Seventy-five percent of pregnant drug addicts use two or more substances during their pregnancy.*

Prenatal exposure to methamphetamine is invariably associated with exposure to alcohol and nicotine, and smoking during pregnancy is linked to low birth weight and increased risk of ADHD in susceptible families. Fetal alcohol syndrome is also a concern, with consequent brain damage and other anomalies. Seventy-five percent of pregnant drug addicts use two or more substances during their pregnancy, making it difficult to distinguish among the influences of each drug upon the baby.

Pregnancy is often the only thing that can make an addicted young woman get off methamphetamine. The mother love instinct is strong, even in addicts, and some of these women will do for their child what they would not do for themselves. Of course, the withdrawal is even harder when combined with the normal discomforts of pregnancy. Morning sickness is bad enough without being in withdrawal at the same time. I have a lot of respect for these ladies I see suffering for the sake of their children.

PROGNOSIS

Every addict eventually quits using methamphetamine. Unfortunately, they have usually destroyed their lives by the time they quit. Some quit in jail, some quit when they hit bottom and make a decision to change, some quit in a mental institution or homeless shelter. Most quit in the morgue. The mortality rate for methamphetamine addiction is very high, with death due to homicide, suicide, overdose, or accidents related to intoxication. The life expectancy of a serious methamphetamine addict is markedly shortened, largely due to the drug related violence associated with methamphetamine, but also due to slowly progressive heart failure, liver and lung disease. Many addicts are also alcoholics, which also contributes to the early mortality.

Twenty years ago, you could make a mistake with drugs and you would probably get by with it. You might lose a few years, but you could eventually recover and have a normal life. Any recovered meth addict can tell you that's not the case anymore. If you make a mistake with crystal, you pay for it in brain cells. You pay for it in permanent neurologic symptoms, twitches and tremors. You pay in lost thinking ability, lost relationships, lost opportunities, and terminal disease.

You can't go back and be a mother to your children. They've grown up without you. You can't go back and get a professional degree. You can't go back and get your lost neurologic function, kidney function, or heart function. *Your life will never be the same after using ice.* The damage to fasciculus is permanent. The cells are dead and they are not coming back. Rehabilitation consists of training the remaining cells to perform the functions of the lost cells.

The brain damage caused by methamphetamine is devastating, but understanding it seems to help the people affected. I used to worry about how people would respond to the news about how serious this damage is. They are almost never surprised. They have wondered why they feel this way and do these things. Sometimes they are baffled by their responses to little irritations. Learning about the degree of damage caused by crystal clears up a lot of questions for them.

> *I used to worry about how people*
> *would respond to the news about how*
> *serious this damage is.*
> *They are almost never surprised.*

Some of this brain damage is permanent, and life may never be the same after using methamphetamine. About 30% of recovered users are seriously disabled by the brain damage caused by drug use. They are what we call 'burned out addicts.' They didn't really recover, they just quit using because they were too brain damaged to work the syringe anymore, or were incarcerated. Typically, they were from deprived backgrounds and had poor work skills in the first place. Now, they cannot function in any job, cannot take care of the simplest tasks, cannot even keep themselves clean. Most of these people are in mental institutions, homeless shelters, or in prison; they cannot live anywhere else. If Jim had survived, he would have fallen into this category.

About 40% recover with enough personality to be more or less functional. They have completed rehabilitation and remained sober for a year or two. They may have to take medications for their hallucinations and depression, perhaps for the rest of their life. They can work and take care of a family, make the rent payments and maintain a car, but they might never reach the full potential they had before using ice. Some of these people were capable of highly professional positions; they may have degrees in engineering, teaching, or other highly skilled work. They may never have their full capacity back, but they will be able to live independently.

The other 30% I have recognized as highly functional people. A trained eye can tell they have significant brain damage, but they are well compensated and fully rehabilitated. They are usually activists, highly motivated to helping other people get off drugs and educating youth against drug use. They are intelligent and motivated, insightful and compassionate.

But even the highest functioning recovered addict knows he is extremely fragile. Intelligent addicts know better than to expose themselves to situations that remind them of drug abuse. They are cautious about the company they keep, the medications they take, the neighborhoods they go into, and the jobs they take. Each relapse magnifies the brain damage and leaves more residual disability. These people know they may not survive another bout with methamphetamine.

SECTION THREE:
THE RISK FACTORS

.7.

RISK FACTORS FOR ADDICTION-
USE OF OTHER DRUGS

Why do most people become helpless addicts while others use a few times and walk away from it? Can biochemistry offer any explanations? If we understand the biochemistry of methamphetamine, can we use that information to predict addiction, or more importantly, to prevent it? There are several recognized risk factors that can be avoided or treated if we are aware of their potential for precipitating addiction.

Let me start off by defining the term "risk factor." There is a big difference between a risk factor and a determining factor. The only determining factor for meth addiction is trying it for the first time. You can't get addicted to it if you never try it. A risk factor is a condition that predisposes to the determining factor. ADHD is a risk factor. Alcohol use is a risk factor. Many people drink and have ADHD, but never try methamphetamine and so they don't get addicted.

Methamphetamine is not usually the first drug abused by the addict. There is a strong correlation with abuse of other substances preceding the addiction to crystal meth. The typical progression is to start with alcohol and nicotine, followed rapidly by second tier drugs such as inhalants and marijuana, and then hard drugs like cocaine, meth, and heroin. Multiple other substances stimulate the same brain areas and biochemical pathways that methamphetamine does, only to a smaller degree. The cast of characters in this chapter will be very familiar; we have met every one of them before.

There are a lot of Nerd Boxes in this chapter. You get extra credit if you read them.

NICOTINE

Cigarette smoking is a major risk factor for methamphetamine addiction. Twenty-five percent of the general population smokes cigarettes. Sixty percent of high school drop-outs smoke cigarettes. Eighty percent of alcoholics smoke cigarettes. Ninety-five percent of methamphetamine addicts smoke cigarettes. There are several good reasons for that observation.

> *Ninety-five percent of methamphetamine addicts smoke cigarettes.*

Nicotine damages one tract of the fasciculus retroflexus, the self-control tract in the midbrain, as we discussed in Chapter 4. Nicotine does not actually kill the cells like methamphetamine and cocaine do, at least not at the doses you get from smoking cigarettes. It just disables them. The right lane of your fasciculus retroflexus has a speed bump every few feet. Damage to this tract weakens your resistance to cravings coming from the ventral tegmental area and predisposes to addiction to other drugs.

There is also the psychological impact of sneaking around and doing something forbidden. Ten-year-old kids smoking behind the school building after class know they are doing something wrong. They get a rush out of getting by with behavior that could get them into trouble. Doing it and getting by with it is the most exciting part of smoking. Having once learned how to smoke tobacco, the skills are learned, the barrier has been breached and smoking other drugs becomes more acceptable.

If his parents then react with shocked dismay followed by rapid acceptance, the stage is set for accelerating rebellion. "Oh, Jimmy smokes. I wish he wouldn't, but he does." The passive acceptance of his smoking is taken as tacit permission to smoke anything and everything. If he can't shock his parents with a cigarette, maybe cocaine will work.

Nicotine is the single largest avoidable risk factor for methamphetamine addiction. We need to take it extremely seriously when our kids start smoking cigarettes. Jump all over that kid. Make him quit while he still can. He is damaging areas in his brain that predispose to all types of addiction, including methamphetamine and cocaine.

Nerd Box

There is a biochemical interaction between marijuana and nicotine. Co-administration of both causes changes in cellular metabolism and gene expression in the nucleus accumbens, amygdala, and hypothalamus increasing the sensitivity of these areas to marijuana. Nicotine makes pot work better and so contributes to the addictive potential of marijuana.

Nicotine also interacts with methamphetamine at the cellular level. Nicotine increases the levels of dopamine in the midbrain but it does it in a different way than methamphetamine does. Nicotine makes Cell A supersensitive to stimulation and causes it to release more dopamine in response to an *electrical* signal. Methamphetamine makes the cell release dopamine in response to a *chemical* signal. The use of nicotine makes the crystal even more potent.

Chronic daily use of nicotine causes increased hyperactivity in animals given methamphetamine. It increases dopamine stimulation to the striatum which mediates the hyperactivity caused by methamphetamine. It also increases the dopamine stimulation in the nucleus accumbens, the pleasure center. Nicotine primes the system to get a better high from crystal.

Nicotine induces basic fibroblastic growth factor and brain derived neurotrophic factor in rat striatum stimulating reparative growth in dopamine cells in the rat striatum. Smoking enhances the ability of the cell to heal and recover function after a dose of meth, allowing methamphetamine addicts to retain function in the face of insult. Addicts often realize they function better when they smoke, and so they increase their smoking as they use methamphetamine. Many of them are chain smokers.

ALCOHOL

"I've been drunk since I was twelve years old. I started shooting crystal when I was fifteen. I'm twenty-four now, and I'm pregnant. I've never been sober for as long as I can remember. I don't know what it's like to be sober. I don't know who I would be if I wasn't drunk."

Kids start getting into their parent's liquor cabinet after school at the age of ten or twelve. They have it at their parties, sometimes with the blessing of their parents, at thirteen or fourteen. These children are laying the foundation for a lifetime of addiction before they even enter high school. Alcohol abuse typically precedes drug abuse by several years.

The numbers are impressive. Half of all teenagers have drunk alcohol at least once before the end of eighth grade, and 80% by the end of high school. Twelve percent of eighth graders, 22% of tenth graders, and 28% of twelfth graders are frequent "binge drinkers" [five or more drinks at one sitting more than once a month]. Many of them are already alcoholics, but because they only drink on weekends they don't think they have a problem. The majority of these children will continue to have an alcohol problem into adulthood.

Drinking is considered socially acceptable in this age group; in fact they are mocked if they do *not* partake of the libations after a football game. Alcohol is so ready available, widely advertised, and condoned by parents; the teen who does not drink finds it difficult to find any validation in our society. Even some of his friend's parents sponsor drinking parties for their children under the guise that it is "safer for them to drink at home with us than out on the street somewhere. After all, at least he's not drinking and driving." The brain damage is the same whether the kid is at home or out on the street.

Alcohol affects all the neurotransmitter systems, including the dopamine and serotonin systems affected by methamphetamine. Drinking reduces inhibitions, encourages risk taking behavior, and exposes the teen to a rough crowd where other drugs are likely to be available. Alcohol is also addictive, causing damage to the fasciculus retroflexus and ventral tegmental areas that predisposes to addiction to other drugs. These children are ten and twelve years old, and they are using a drug which damages the self-control pathway in their brain and will impact the rest of their lives.

> *These children are ten and twelve years old, and they are using a drug which damages the self-control pathway in their brain and will impact the rest of their lives.*

Alcohol damages the cells in fasciculus retroflexus much like cocaine and methamphetamine do, it just takes a lot longer for it to happen, years rather than weeks. There is loss of control over behavior, "I don't feel like going to work [school]." There is loss of control over temper, you put your fist through the wall. There is loss of control over alcohol intake, you drink until you either run out or pass out.

The loss of cells in fasciculus predisposes to other addictions much like nicotine does, even if you are not an alcoholic, by weakening the self-control structures in the brain *even at the tender age of ten or twelve years old.* Remember, 25% of methamphetamine addicts start using crystal before age fifteen. They can't just try a little cocaine or crystal and walk away from it. They lose control over drug intake much faster when also exposed to alcohol.

Alcohol causes changes in the same set of neural markers for cell death and disintegration we saw with regards to methamphetamine, N-acetylaspartate, myoinositol, and creatine and choline metabolites. These chemical changes are seen in social drinkers that did not meet criteria for alcoholism, and the heaviest drinkers had the most severe cell damage. The brain cell death caused by alcohol is also correlated with poor performance on tests of memory and executive function. This subtle change in thinking ability impairs judgment and insight, so the most damaged of these people are the ones who think they are doing just fine.

Alcohol induces a pleasurable giddy feeling, a feeling of confidence and competence, much like methamphetamine does, by its action on dopamine and serotonin transmission in the nucleus accumbens. Alcohol causes hydroxy free radical formation and damages the hippocampus [short term memory] with loss of neurons and reduced numbers of dendritic branches and spines. White matter in all areas of the brain is diminished, and learning ability is impaired. A complete biochemical analysis of the effects of alcohol on the brain is beyond the scope of this book, but I will comment on the interactions between alcohol abuse and methamphetamine addiction.

ALCOHOL'S INTERACTION WITH METHAMPHETAMINE

Many methamphetamine addicts are also alcoholics. Alcohol is sedating. It stimulates the GABA [go-to-sleep] receptors and inhibits the glutamate [wake-up] receptors, so as to relax and sedate you. It takes the edge off the uncomfortable side effects of methamphetamine, the jitteriness, rapid heart rate, and headache. Of course, the hangover is significantly worse the next day, so you need a steady stream of drugs and alcohol to keep yourself going.

Animal studies of the interaction between alcohol and methamphetamine show that chronic use of alcohol increases sensitivity to methamphetamine dramatically. Dopamine and serotonin levels are 50% higher in animals that had been drinking for six weeks prior to their first experience with methamphetamine. Dopamine surges of 1200% with an intoxicating dose of methamphetamine have been reported in animals pre-treated with alcohol, compared with 700% in animals with no experience with alcohol. They are more sensitive to the high; they are also more sensitive to the neurotoxicity associated with methamphetamine.

Methamphetamine abusers who also drank heavily had about the same degree of mental impairment as meth addicted non-drinkers. Memory loss and poor judgment when faced with complex decisions was about the same. Alcohol dependent meth abusers are statistically *more* likely to develop psychotic symptoms, hallucinations, paranoia and delusions. They are also more likely to become violent when intoxicated.

> *Alcohol dependent meth abusers are statistically more likely to develop psychotic symptoms, hallucinations, paranoia and delusions.*

Alcohol and nicotine are the background environment behind methamphetamine addiction, both socially and biochemically. Their common use and social acceptability contributes to an acceptance of intoxication as a normal part of life, an expectation, a right, indeed a social obligation to get intoxicated and join the fun. They guy who just wants to enjoy the company of his friends and won't drink is seen as the party pooper, the stick in the mud who ruins everybody else's good time because he won't get smashed.

Many of our children are accomplished drinkers even before finishing high school. We frown on pregnant women drinking because they are exposing their babies to such a toxic chemical. And yet we allow our children to drink as teens, not realizing their brains are still developing. They are just as vulnerable to the toxic effects of alcohol in the ninth grade as their counterparts in utero are. A parent allowing a child to drink should be regarded as child abuse.

It is my humble opinion that beer and wine advertisers should face the same restrictions and controls cigarette companies do. Their product is just as hazardous to the minds and bodies of our youth as cigarettes are. The daily parade of commercials extolling the fun and freedom associated with alcohol use is a national disgrace.

MARIJUANA

Marijuana use is another common precursor to the abuse of hard drugs, and considering the prevalence of marijuana use, it represents a significant risk factor for addiction to methamphetamine. We are now seeing a generation of young people raised in homes where pot use was common and accepted behavior among the adults in their household. Marijuana use among adolescents has tripled over the past few years. Some of the people I have met in the jails started smoking pot in the fourth or fifth grade, even before they started smoking cigarettes. They got it from their parents.

> *Some of the people I have met in the jails started smoking pot in the fourth or fifth grade. They got it from their parents.*

The strength of the association between marijuana and hard drugs is hotly contested by pot aficionados, but is accepted by most addicts. Marijuana induces a dopamine based high in the same neural structures as methamphetamine does, but to a much smaller degree. Marijuana does not directly increase dopamine in nucleus accumbens. It increases dopamine by indirect routes involving neurotransmission in the ventral tegmental area. Marijuana is often used to 'come down' from a crystal or cocaine high. It replaces some of the dopamine deficit and eases the symptoms of the crash.

Nerd Box

Marijuana stimulates dopamine release in nucleus accumbens indirectly by reducing the inhibitory input from the ventral tegmental area, thus allowing natural levels of dopamine to be increased. There are receptors in the brain for THC, the active ingredient in marijuana; they are actually receptors for a neurotransmitter called anandamide. THC binds to anandamide receptors, called CB1 receptors, ten times more tightly than anandamide does, and blocks the inhibitory impulses [GABA transmission] from the ventral tegmental area, hippocampus, and amygdala, to the nucleus accumbens.

Under the influence of marijuana, the normal regulation of dopamine in the nucleus accumbens is disrupted, and dopamine release is unopposed. There is increased spontaneous firing of dopamine neurons and a feeling of giddy euphoria results. We're at a party and somebody tells a joke. Everyone laughs. Then we go on to talk about something else, but you are still laughing at the joke we told twenty minutes ago. Your suppressor system would have let you shut up and pay attention, but you've turned it off with pot, and so you're still giggling. You might giggle for two hours.

Nerd Box

The marijuana effect at the amygdala induces long term gene based changes, cellular learning, in the memory areas of amygdala and in nucleus accumbens, and a pleasurable emotional memory is established. Marijuana also influences firing rates and decreases responsiveness of the amygdala, so it is less sensitive to inputs from the frontal lobe. Judgment is impaired and an emotional memory is established that has reduced supervision by the frontal lobe.

Marijuana has long been recognized by methamphetamine addicts as a trigger to relapse, and it is more than just an associated memory of the drug experience like party music or a piece of tin foil. Marijuana stimulates the same neural network methamphetamine does and has been shown to trigger relapse to cocaine and methamphetamine seeking behavior in *rats* that had been withdrawn for many weeks. The rats had not been smoking any weed at *their* parties. This is biochemistry talking.

MEMORY LOSS AND COGNITIVE EFFECTS

Marijuana disrupts the activity of the hippocampus, causing memory loss and disorganization. It causes swelling in the synapse, and increases the distance the neurotransmitter has to traverse to get to its receptor on the Cell B side. Neurotransmitter release is also impaired. The signal is delayed and distorted. It's not the click-click-click it used to be, but rather a slosh-slosh-slosh effect. You're driving down the road, and somebody stops suddenly in front of you. You ram right into the guy, because you were slosh-sloshing instead of click-clicking, and you couldn't stop in time.

Intoxicating levels of THC in the blood are just as detrimental to driving skills and judgment as intoxicating levels of alcohol are, with impaired psychomotor function, judgment, and actual driving performance. A urine test demonstrates past use of marijuana and does not reveal this relationship, but blood levels of THC are strongly correlated with direct responsibility for car wrecks in a dose dependent manner similar to alcohol.

The impaired neurotransmission extends to the hippocampus as well, and short term memory is impaired. Information is encoded by the click, click,

click pattern of impulses, and you read it like morse code. Marijuana makes transmission sluggish and the clicks sound like sloshes. You can't read the interval and frequency between sloshes like you can clicks, so some of the information gets lost. You work at my fast food restaurant, and I tell you to close down the register, mop up the floor, and lock the door when you leave. So you close down the register, and you kind of remember something about the floor, "Oh yeah, I'm supposed to mop it up," and you completely forget to lock the door when you leave. "Hey, man, I forgot." Well hey, man, you don't work here anymore.

Nerd Box

Marijuana inhibits synaptic transmission between hippocampus cells in culture. Marijuana also inhibits formation of new synapses between hippocampal cells which interferes with memory function. Working memory is impaired and long term memories are not laid down. Learning is also impaired by direct toxic effects of THC on the cells in the hippocampus, with cell death, fragmentation, and shrinkage of neurons in the hippocampus after chronic exposure to the drug.

Marijuana also affects function in the frontal lobe, judgment and reasoning, and problem solving capability. It decreases GABA transmission and increases dopamine, serotonin, and glutamate transmission in the frontal lobe. Hyperstimulation of dopamine receptors in the frontal lobe impairs working memory, judgment, and decision making, much like the disruption associated with methamphetamine, but not as severe because the disruption is much less than seen with meth.

In human studies the EEG measurements of rational thought and memory retention are markedly impaired after smoking marijuana. Sustained attention, working memory, and episodic memory are impaired and EEG studies showed attenuated event related potentials.

Chronic marijuana use causes loss of motivation, memory impairment, learning disability, and poor judgment. Long term abuse produces behavioral and metabolic signs of frontal lobe dysfunction persisting even in abstinence. Dopamine metabolism is disrupted in the frontal lobe for at least fourteen days after withdrawal. Chronic heavy use causes a four point drop in IQ that is persistent even after you stop using, the equivalent of the brain damage caused by fetal alcohol syndrome. You probably won't notice if your IQ was 100 to start with, but if you were borderline in the first place, an IQ of 80, and you drop four points, you now have an IQ of 76 and you are clinically retarded. Even the addicts realize that. "Cooks" who smoke too much pot make lousy crystal.

Somebody who has been using pot for twenty years is obviously impaired. His speech is slow and ideas come haltingly. He can't finish a sentence. If you want to tell him something, you have to repeat it. If you want him to do something, you have to draw a picture. But of course, the marijuana lobby will assure you nobody is really brain damaged by pot.

> *No one gets out of the fifth grade*
> *and starts shooting crystal.*
> *They get you drunk first.*

In a Yale University study, exposure to THC changed the neurochemistry in the median prefrontal cortex, the part of the frontal lobe critical to higher thinking, judgment and decision making. Decision making processes in the frontal lobe are impaired by marijuana, and this contributes to the risk taking behavior involved with methamphetamine use. Pot removes the barrier of fear and hesitancy to try strong drugs. No one gets out of the fifth grade and starts shooting crystal. They get you drunk first, either with pot, alcohol, or inhalants. You think you can handle this stuff. That's what Jim thought.

ADDICTION

Marijuana is also addictive by itself. The same ventral tegmental cravings are established with pot as with any other addictive drug. Marijuana has direct effects on the ventral tegmental area, the place cravings and drives come from. THC increases firing by dopamine fibers by 3.5 times over normal levels, feeding 3.5 times more dopamine into nucleus accumbens. Inhaled toluene, the chemical in paint and glue which is intoxicating, has a similar effect on dopamine transmission in the ventral tegmental area. This is the same neural network that causes cravings for methamphetamine. The change induced in the ventral tegmental area by marijuana or inhalants predisposes to addiction to other drugs by altering the chemistry in this vital area of the brain.

Marijuana stimulates the nucleus accumbens with a dopamine release and causes habituation and sensitization much like methamphetamine does. Withdrawal from chronic marijuana use is associated with reduced dopamine transmission in the limbic system [emotional area] and nucleus accumbens [pleasure center] similar to withdrawal from other addictive drugs. Nothing sounds good, nothing feels good, and everything irritates you, until you get another booster shot of dopamine.

The swelling in the synapse also contributes to the withdrawal. This swelling occurs all over the brain, and the cell compensates for it by using more glutamine (wake-up chemical) each time it fires. "He can't hear me, I need to talk louder." It continues to put out chemical until its feedback receptor hears the news, "Cell B heard me, I can stop now." When the pot wears off and the swelling goes down, [around day four at the county jail] Cell A is making way too much glutamine. It is a feeling of harshness; the lights are too bright, the sounds are too loud, can't relax, can't sleep until you get another joint and swell that synapse back up where it feels more comfortable.

I know a woman who never lets her husband run out of pot. She makes sure they always have plenty. Whenever he runs out of pot, he gets angry and aggressive. He beats her and he beats their children. He's an okay guy as long as he's high, but she'd rather run out of milk for the kids than run out of pot for her husband.

There is eventually a functional tolerance and reduced sensitivity to THC in the synapses of nucleus accumbens after chronic marijuana exposure. After a while, pot doesn't give much of a high anymore. You need something stronger to get the same effect you used to get from pot. Your dealer, of course, knows all about dopamine metabolism, he studied it in Dealer School, and he knows cocaine or crystal will still give you a dopamine high now that pot doesn't work anymore.

DRUG OPPORTUNITY RISKS

Marijuana increases risk of addiction to other drugs because of the availability of other drugs. Pot does not exist in a vacuum. Any party featuring plenty of weed is also likely to have other appetizers readily available. The stage is set for taking risks and meeting the expectations of the other people at the party. Judgment is impaired by the pot or alcohol available, and an otherwise intelligent kid who knows better than to use hard drugs will find himself in a situation he isn't prepared for. They are passing the pipe and laughing, and everyone expects him to use it too. We will talk a great deal more about this in Chapter 13.

Pot is sometimes cut with other drugs, especially methamphetamine. You thought you were having a joint, just a little pot, Mom will never know. "Where'd you get this weed? Man, this stuff is great!" By the time you come down three days later, you are hooked on crystal, and you didn't even know you were trying it. Lacing pot with methamphetamine is nothing less than attempted murder, and believe me, it happens.

Marijuana use contributes to a level of immaturity in adults who used a lot as adolescents. You don't have to grow up and learn how to deal with people if you can escape the difficult situation by getting high. Have a problem at work, come home and get high. Have a fight with your mother, go out and get high. You end up with a thirty-three year old man who still acts like a ten-year-old. He has a disagreement with his wife and beats her up. That's something a ten-year-old would do.

Legalizing Pot

There is a very vocal lobby determined to legalize marijuana under the guise that its legalization would reduce the abuse of pot and contribute greatly to the common good by eliminating those pesky laws that harass the typical recreational user of marijuana. We are being asked to legitimize and endorse drug abuse simply because so many people use it that it cannot possibly be considered wrong. A common argument: it's no worse than alcohol.

Legalizing marijuana for medicinal use will give it the same status as any other medication, and however tightly controlled, it will inevitably be abused. Once approved for one indication, say intractable nausea associated with cancer chemotherapy, it can be legally prescribed 'off label' for any indication, from anxiety to hangnails, and doctors willing to game the system will get enormously wealthy.

Legalizing marijuana will not remove it from the party scene. It is still an intoxicant. Once legitimized, it will become many times more popular. Pot will be used more freely and abundantly, and no one will be able to tell their kid not to use it when it is so ready available and endorsed by the *government* as safe and effective for whatever ails you.

If it is released for recreational use, the results will be catastrophic. How can we tell our kids not to use pot when it is displayed right next to the cigarettes in every convenience store? How many people drank during prohibition? How many more people drank after prohibition was repealed? Need I say more?

For more information on this subject see appendix B.

Learning to manage strong emotions is what adolescence is all about. You learn to control your temper and channel your affection. You learn how to manage your impulses, anger impulses and sexual impulses, and exercise self-discipline. You learn to act in the face of fear; we call that courage. You learn to resist temptation and stand up for what you know is right; we call that character. You learn to negotiate and compromise with people, how to express your needs without throwing a temper tantrum. We call that maturity.

If you don't learn these things when you are thirteen, you have to learn them when you are thirty-three. You can do it before you get thrown in jail or after, but eventually you are going to learn these things. It's called growing up. One of the major problems we face in drug rehabilitation is teaching people how to grow up. You can't do it in twenty-eight days.

> *He gets mad at his wife and beats her up.*
> *He's acting like a ten-year-old.*

INHALANTS

The most common drugs of abuse in the eight to twelve year old age group are the inhalants, with up to 24% of adolescents trying them at least once. They are cheap, readily available, usually legal, and widely perceived to be harmless fun. Kids do them out of boredom, rebellion, or as an escape from loneliness. They can be highly addictive, but most kids only use them for a few months until they find something better to get high on, generally pot.

Examples of inhalants include spray paint, lighter fluid, hairspray, paint thinner, and glue. They are placed in a plastic bag, or used to saturate a rag and sniffed, or inhaled in larger concentrations [huffed]. They cause a high lasting fifteen–thirty minutes. The fumes from cooking methamphetamine are also volatile inhalants. Cooks and children exposed to these chemicals get intoxicated on them, and suffer brain damage from them.

Inhalants are truly addictive in that they cause tolerance and with-drawal. Tolerance means it takes more and more drug to produce the desired high. Withdrawal symptoms include chills, tremors, hallucinations, headache, delirium, nausea, vomiting, abdominal pain, and drug craving. I have heard of four-year-old children becoming addicted to the chemicals they found in the garage.

The high from inhalants is similar to drunkenness with dizziness, dis-orientation, confusion, slurred speech, and distorted perception. High doses cause hallucinations and delusions. Aggressiveness and anxiety are common. Withdrawal and apathy are long-term effects. These kids are always in trouble at school. They get in fights and spend a lot of time in the principal's office.

Inhaled toluene, one of the most common ingredients in these drugs, stimulates dopamine release in ventral tegmental area and nucleus accumbens much like methamphetamine and other drugs do. These drugs concentrate in the frontal and temporal lobes [complex thought and long term memory] and in the midbrain [personality centers], striatum [motivation centers], and cerebellum [balance and control]. The dopamine release is similar to that seen with alcohol, nicotine and marijuana, but not as strong as with cocaine, heroin, or methamphetamine.

The dangers of huffing any chemical are obvious. Asphyxia, or oxygen deprivation, contributes to the high. When it gets out of hand, it causes hypoxic brain damage. Oxygen deprivation can be mechanical–if you pass out with a plastic bag over your head, you have exactly six minutes to live. It can be chemical–high concentrations of fumes displace oxygen in the lungs. It can be physiologic–conversion of hemoglobin to meth-hemoglobin which does not carry oxygen to the tissue.

You were huffing all afternoon yesterday while your Mom was at work, but now you're at school and the coach tells you to run around the track. It's a quarter mile track, and you can't do it. You have enough oxygen carrying capacity to get to school and stand there, but your hemoglobin is mostly meth-hemoglobin which does not carry oxygen, and you are passing out trying to run around that track.

> *The most common cause of death with inhalants is called Sudden Sniffing Death Syndrome.*

The most common cause of death with inhalants is called "Sudden Sniffing Death Syndrome." It is caused by direct cardio toxicity, profound and immediate arrhythmias of the heart similar to that seen in a heart attack. If you go into ventricular fibrillation, you will last exactly six minutes.

NEUROTOXIC EFFECTS

Neurotoxic effects of these drugs are related to damage to the myelin sheath around nerve fibers. These drugs are industrial solvents, degreasing agents. They concentrate in neural tissue and they dissolve things. The myelin sheath is the insulation around the nerve axon. It is made out of lipid, or grease. Inhalants dissolve the myelin coverings of nerve cells and destroy the insulation around the nerve, disabling it. The effect is similar to the damage seen in multiple sclerosis. Numbness and tingling in the hands and feet, visual blind spots and tone deafness are seen in chronic users.

When these drugs accumulate in the cortex of the brain, they cause personality changes, learning disability, memory loss, and dementia. In the cerebellum, they cause loss of coordination, slurred speech, and tremors. These are permanent changes in the structure of the brain that show up on an MRI or CT scan. The syndrome is known as "toxic encehalopathy" and it causes significant disability.

A bright kid who did well in elementary school will develop a new onset learning disability and flunk out of high school, and have a poor work performance as an adult, because of the inhalants he used in junior high. People who used inhalants as teenagers are often irritable and aggressive. They get in fights at school, and get in trouble with the law as adults. Teachers can usually tell when a kid starts using because his temper and personality change.

ECSTASY

Ecstasy is a derivative of methamphetamine initially touted as a safe alternative to alcohol and other drugs. National prevalence studies have shown that ecstasy is the second most tried illicit drug after marijuana, with about 9% of twelfth graders having tried it at least once. It is a risk factor for methamphetamine addiction because it is commonly cut with methamphetamine, and sometimes the drug marketed as ecstasy is actually more or less pure methamphetamine.

Ecstasy's reputation for safety has been vigorously defended, even as study after study came out describing in detail the neurotoxicity of this drug. This field has been rife with controversy, with conflicting results, lab fiascos, and verbal wars, even within the scientific community. It is now conceded by all responsible parties that ecstasy is a neurotoxin, and long term use of it causes significant brain damage in humans.

Ecstasy's chemical name is 3,4 methylenedioxy-methamphetamine, MDMA, and that is certainly a mouthful. The *methylenedioxy* part is hallucinogenic, like LSD in nature; the methamphetamine part is identical to the methamphetamine we have been talking about. Just knowing that, you already know a great deal about ecstasy. You know its mode of action, dopamine and serotonin receptors. You know its metabolism, toxic hydroxy free radicals. You have a pretty good idea how it causes brain damage just by looking at its chemical name.

> *Of course, ecstasy does not come from the pharmacy, and you never know what you are really getting.*

Of course, ecstasy does not come from the pharmacy, and you never know what you are really getting. Even when an honest chemist thinks it's

pure, it likely has manufacturing impurities in it. It is often cut with methamphetamine, ketamine, or LSD, or thinned out with talc, caffeine, or ephedrine,
whatever was handy at the time. The dose varies between 10 and 150 mg of
real MDMA per pill. It is usually taken orally, but can be injected, sometimes
with disastrous results. Death or severe brain damage is a real possibility when
using this drug IV.

Laboratory rats take pure ecstasy, but humans don't. Human studies
are hampered by the fact that street-bought ecstasy is almost never pure, and
most users of ecstasy also take other drugs concurrently. We can study ecstasy
all day, but nobody really takes pure ecstasy. It is nearly always contaminated,
usually by methamphetamine. But most ecstasy pills do contain at least traces
of real MDMA. In this discussion I will refer to the drug available on the street
as ecstasy, and the chemical scientist have been studying as MDMA. They are
not necessarily the same thing.

Nerd Box

Other forms of ecstasy are also manufactured, and many of them
are even more toxic than MDMA itself. Methylenedioxyamphetamine [MDA]
"Adam" Methylenedioxy*ethyl*amphetamine [MDEA] "Eve" n methylbenzodion-
xazolylbutanamine [MBDB], and Para methoxymethamphetamine [PMMA], are
related chemicals that are actually byproducts of meth or ecstasy production.
They are intoxicating like ecstasy, but they are even more toxic and many deaths
have been reported.

When PMMA is substituted for MDMA, it takes longer to reach a high.
Thinking they must have a weak batch of ecstasy, the party people will then
take another one to get a high. Then, when it takes effect, they realize they have
ingested a toxic dose and they can't get it back out.

DOPAMINE AND SEROTONIN

The high from ecstasy has many features in common with methamphetamine. It causes a dopamine high, with a feeling of joy and wellbeing,
alertness and endurance; you can dance all night on one pill. It increases dopamine in the synapse much like pure meth does, by reversing the transporter,
[vacuum cleaner] and dopamine levels are increased by 700% in the synapse,
very similar to methamphetamine.

It also reverses the serotonin transporter [vacuum cleaner] and increases serotonin levels by 700%, a much larger increase than methamphetamine produces, and this causes the enhanced feeling of self confidence, well being, and good mood. It also causes a detached feeling, increased sensory perception, and at high doses, hallucinations. The glow stick looks great, the music sounds fabulous; you can feel it in your bones.

They call ecstasy the "hug drug" because the feeling of intimacy and desire for closeness is so powerful. It is a hallucination of love on the prefrontal cortex, where love is appreciated consciously. The combination of dopamine stimulation at nucleus accumbens, and serotonin stimulation in cortical areas, causes sexual arousal at low doses and with oral use, whereas methamphetamine causes arousal only at higher doses.

> *Sexual arousal is more prominent with ecstasy than with pure methamphetamine, and the sexual content at a rave is correspondingly higher.*

Sexual arousal is more prominent with ecstasy than with pure methamphetamine, and the sexual content at a rave is correspondingly higher. It is very popular with the gay night club scene for this reason. People will have open intercourse in the corner of a crowded room, mostly ignored by the other people at the party. These people, of course, have never met before and don't even know each other's names. The risk of sexually transmitted disease is obvious.

The hangover from ecstasy is a profound drowsiness, fatigue, muscle aches, and depression lasting one or two days, the "Tuesday Blues." Anxiety, irritability, and sometimes paranoia are also seen. With continued use, the hangover becomes more prominent and the high less intense, a function of cell destruction. There is some recovery of serotonin stores within 24 hours of use, but then cerebral serotonin concentrations decline due to the neurotoxic effects of MDMA on serotonin fibers in the cortex.

In most settings, MDMA is not considered addictive. It is used only on weekends and at parties, and the unwanted side effects increase with repeated use. However, there are chronic users who continue to take ecstasy despite serious unwanted side effects and hangovers, suggesting at least some addictive potential. The side effects are related to release of norepinephrine and include rapid heart rate and palpitations, anxiety and panic attacks, sweating, watery eyes, and tremor. In high doses, it can cause delirium and fever, respiratory depression, coma and death.

Nerd Box

The ventral tegmental area is also affected by MDMA suggesting a risk for true addiction with cravings and compulsive use. Sensitization is seen with MDMA which cross reacts with the stimulants, cocaine and methamphetamine. MDMA increased the speed with which rats became addicted to cocaine and methamphetamine. The rapid spread of methamphetamine addiction through the nightclub set is testimony to the power of this effect.

Ecstasy causes many of the same physical effects as methamphetamine does, including fever, liver and kidney damage, and disintegration of muscles and blood vessels. Most users do not consume the drug daily and hourly like methamphetamine addicts do, and so physical effects are limited to the acute effects of a single dose. But even that is frequently lethal. A single high dose, particularly in combination with alcohol and other drugs, leads to death in a small, but significant, number of users. Fever is common and body temperature can get as high as 108 degrees. You will survive a fever of 108 if you are well rested and hydrated, but if you've been dancing all night and drinking nothing but booze, you will die from a fever of 108.

Nerd Box

Since many ecstasy users are of childbearing age, it is important to know the effects on the fetus. MDMA exposure in utero studied in rats showed significant alterations in dopamine and serotonin systems in the frontal lobes, nucleus accumbens, hippocampus, and striatum. Offspring had lasting behavioral changes with hyperactivity, impulsivity, and learning disabilities, similar to the changes seen with methamphetamine.

DOPAMINE TOXICITY

There is good evidence for dopamine neurotoxicity associated with ecstasy, along the same lines as we saw with methamphetamine. Remember, there is a huge release of dopamine with acute intoxication [700%] almost as much as with pure methamphetamine. MDMA binds the dopamine transporter, but not as tightly. MDMA releases its grip on the transporter after about four hours, whereas methamphetamine does not. The dopamine activation in the nucleus accumbens contributes to the addictive potential of MDMA.

The huge influx of dopamine triggered by MDMA causes cell death in the same way dopamine released by methamphetamine does. It produces hydroxy free radicals that nitrate and oxidize the cell's proteins, break down cell membranes and inactivate genes within the cell. Since dopamine fibers and serotonin fibers are closely associated, the toxic metabolites damage cells in multiple areas of the brain.

Repeated exposure to MDMA causes disruption in the nucleus accumbens, both serotonin and dopamine fibers are affected. The frontal lobe can not send its signal to the nucleus accumbens like it should, and so it has no input into "What are we going to do about this thing that feels good?" Rational decisions are not made; we just do what comes naturally, in the corner of the room with somebody we have never even met before.

MDMA is especially toxic to the serotonin fibers from the dorsal raphe nucleus [mood lamp] leading to whole brain depletion of serotonin lasting at least four months after a single intoxicating dose. Once those cells have been destroyed with multiple doses, they no longer produce serotonin. This serotonin depletion contributes to the anxiety and depression seen in long term users, and it is very difficult to treat.

The mainstay of antidepressant treatments are the SSRI's, selective serotonin reuptake inhibitors like Prozac. These medications have been demonstrated to be effective in the post-ecstasy depression if the damage is not too severe. But if the serotonin system has been destroyed, there is nothing for the Prozac to work on. Large doses of good medications do not relieve the long term depression from chronic ecstasy use.

TOXIC METABOLITES

Ecstasy is made using the same manufacturing methods and precursors as methamphetamine. Its metabolites are just as caustic as those of pure methamphetamine. In fact, pure MDMA injected into a brain causes no effect at all. It is metabolized in the liver to glutathione-alpha-methyl-dopamine and when *that* is injected directly into a rat's brain it causes hyperactivity, teeth chattering, tremor, head weaving, splayed posture, clonus, and 'wet dog shakes' in the rat, and without any hip-hop music!

The other metabolites of MDMA are oxygen and nitrogen free radicals, the same collection of hoodlums we met in Chapter 4. Ecstasy's metabolites include dihydroxymethamphetamine, trihydroxymethamphetamine, N acetylcysteiene, alpha methyldopa, and 2,3 dihydroxybenzoic acid. These chemicals cause lipid peroxidation and disruption of cell membranes in the frontal lobes [complex thought], the striatum [motor control], and in the hippocampus [short term memory]. When cell membranes are disrupted, the cell disintegrates. The cells killed are serotonin producing cells leading to long term serotonin depletion.

A study was done a few years ago, where monkeys were given two pills per day of pure MDMA, standard doses, for four days . . . one long rave party. Two weeks after the party, they cut five of the monkey's brains open, and saw serotonin fibers that were damaged. If you touch the cell with an electrode, nothing comes out the other end. *Seven years later,* they cut the other five monkey's brains open, to see if there had been any recovery. The answer? Well, not really. There was some regeneration of axons, but they didn't do what they were supposed to do. A total of forty brain areas were studied, and all showed dramatic loss of serotonin fibers. Recovery at seven years averaged 60%, with some areas regaining only 24% of normal function.

Fig 19

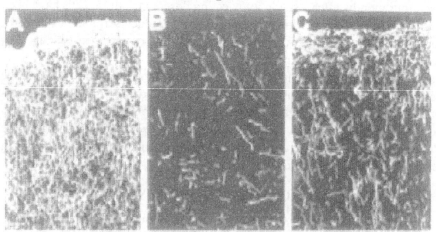

Brain cells exposed to ecstasy
© 1999 Society for Neuroscience, Dr. Hatzidimitriou, full reference page 455

A is normal monkey frontal lobe tissue, B is two weeks after the party, C is seven years after one long rave party in the monkey house.

Nerd Box

PET and SPECT scan studies of humans have shown similar loss of serotonin transporters diffusely in humans. The serotonin depletion has been measured in many ways and involves the frontal lobe, hippocampus, amygdala, and striatum. The cells have whorls of protein debris in them called inclusion bodies. The axons degenerate and the terminals dissolve, leaving severely reduced serotonin function in the brain.

Remember Δ fos B, the transcription factor in the nucleus accumbens that methamphetamine knocks out? Ecstasy knocks out c-fos, a transcription factor in the amygdala that changes gene transcription in the emotional center of the midbrain. Direct effects on social interaction measures in mice have been documented after MDMA administration.

Other neurotransmitter systems are also disturbed by MDMA. Gene expression analysis shows that four different proteins are decreased in the brain cells exposed to MDMA, and all four of them are important for GABA transmission, that go-to-sleep chemical in the brainstem that radiates all over the brain to relax and sedate you.

The loss of serotonin terminals is permanent, though the cell body survives and regenerates serotonin axon terminals over a period of years. The re-grown fibers are not normal; they don't distribute to the right areas of the brain, and some function is permanently lost. Serotonin depletion is associated with anxiety and depression as the raphe nucleus [mood lamp] is disabled. The circadian rhythm, sleep wake cycle, is disturbed so nights and days are all mixed up.

"I just can't think straight anymore."

Abstinent ecstasy users have reduced cerebrospinal fluid 5-HIAA, a metabolite of serotonin and reduced density of serotonin transporters. Long term depletion of serotonin receptors has been demonstrated in human ecstasy users. These biochemical changes are associated with higher cognitive deficits, disorganized thinking, and memory loss. "I just can't think straight anymore." Various psychiatric disorders are seen, including anxiety, depression, psychotic symptoms, altered appetite, and loss of sexual interest. These functional deficits persist long after drug use has ceased, and are consistent with serotonin nerve fiber loss in many brain areas.

Nerd Box

MRI and SPECT studies of human ecstasy users have demonstrated loss of neurons in grey matter in the neocortex, brainstem and cerebellum, and have confirmed the loss of serotonin transporters in the cortex of ecstasy users. With chronic use, serotonin stores are depleted by 50% to 80% as seen in an autopsy study of a long term ecstasy user. Adolescent ecstasy users studied with fMRI showed deficits in working memory and attention, which were correlated with impaired function in the hippocampus.

Human ecstasy users have been shown to sustain serious damage to the globus pallidus, a part of the midbrain. These people were frankly psychotic, one of them after taking just one half of one pill on one occasion. The damage was documented on MRI scans and correlated with subsequent autopsy studies. Of course, it is impossible to know exactly what these people took, even their chemist doesn't know for sure.

Of course, the brain damage from ecstasy is added on to the damage associated with whatever drug it is cut with or used with. Since it is often cut with methamphetamine, the personality changes are often profound. The combination of MDMA and meth causes more dopamine depletion and brain damage than with either drug given alone. A common variation on the theme is to use ecstasy alternating with LSD, a process called "candy-flipping." The residual thought disorder after candy-flipping is significant with hallucinations and delusions being the most prominent features.

CONTROVERSY

But what about all the papers saying ecstasy does not cause brain damage? A careful review of those papers invariably reveals deficiencies in the data or analysis. A recent paper by De Win et al [Psychopharmacology 2004] is a good example. It showed no increase in depression scores in ecstasy users, and no correlation with SPECT measurements of serotonin dysfunction seen in ecstasy users. The control group, however, was a group of other drug users. There was no real control group of healthy non-drug users with which to compare depression scores or serotonin transporter density data. If you are trying to prove that ecstasy does not cause any more brain damage than other drugs of abuse, this is the right control group. But if you want to say that ecstasy does not cause *any* brain damage, you have to use a sober control group. And yet, even this study showed a trend for increasing life time doses of ecstasy causing increased depression.

Multiple other drugs also cause serotonin dysfunction and depression including methamphetamine, cocaine, and alcohol. Surely there are residents of Amsterdam who do not use any drugs to call upon to serve as a control group. Another paper in the same issue of Psychopharmacology, [McCardle et al] using appropriate control groups demonstrated a dramatic loss of memory, learning, and attention, as well as significantly higher scores for depression in ecstasy users.

Other studies suffer from short follow-up, irrelevant endpoints, small numbers of subjects, poor control for use of other drugs, and variable amounts of lifetime ecstasy use, some as little as one pill on one occasion. The best studies available offer conclusive evidence that ecstasy is a potent neurotoxin in the doses and conditions under which it is used by humans.

Legalizing Ecstasy

Ecstasy got its start as a psychiatric drug useful in counseling to help people open up and communicate difficult subjects. In small doses, once or twice in a lifetime, it was considered safe and effective. [This was before very much research had been conducted on it.] It was not outlawed until it began its career as a party drug, with the death and destruction following its recreational use.

Some scientists, seeking to legitimize their favorite drug, are investigating its use as a treatment for Post Traumatic Stress Disorder. These people are on the government payroll, and their goal is to legitimize the use of ecstasy in much the same way as the marijuana lobby seeks to legitimize the use of pot.

There is no doubt in my mind that ecstasy will prove to have an effect on PTSD. It is a powerful psychoactive drug, and with proper statistical manipulation, its proponents will be able to prove it 'works.' We will then give already profoundly depressed people a drug known to cause depression. Somebody needs to think out the legal ramifications of this form of treatment.

There is also no doubt in my mind that its medical use will not be confined to bona fide PTSD. It will move out of the world of illegal drugs and into the medicine cabinet. If the ecstasy activists can't open the front door, they will pry the back door open, with a crowbar if necessary.

LIQUID ECSTASY, GHB

I have to include a word or two about GHB, even though it is only peripherally related to methamphetamine. Both drugs are part of the same culture of raves and circuit parties, and while the mechanism of action of GHB is radically different from ecstasy, its intoxication is very similar. GHB stands for gamma hydroxy butyrate. It is made out of gamma hydroxy butyrolactone, a degreasing agent found in industrial floor cleaners, combined with KOH, a drain cleaner. Sounds appetizing, doesn't it.

At low doses, GHB is relaxing and sedating like alcohol. You are happy and contented, you feel the music deeply, and the glow stick looks great, much like the ecstasy experience. Higher levels of intoxication result in loss of motor control. You flop around like a fish out of water; you are intermittently unconscious, incoherent, and have no recall of events taking place while you were intoxicated. GHB is extremely toxic at high doses, especially when mixed with alcohol, as it usually is. GHB stimulates the GABA receptors in the brain stem, much like alcohol does. The GABA receptors are the ones that put you to sleep, make you go into a coma, quit breathing and die.

> *She was sore in all the right places; she knew she had been raped. Her friends were nowhere to be found.*

The dosing in GHB is extremely tight; tiny increases in dose cause profound increases in intoxication. It comes as a liquid, and since it doesn't come from the pharmacy, you have no idea what you are getting. The stuff you bought last week was watered down and it took an ounce to get high, two ounces to get plastered, and three ounces would have killed you. This week, you got some straight stuff from an honest guy, and a teaspoon is enough to get high. An ounce will kill you. But you didn't know that, so you put an ounce of it in your girlfriend's drink. Now she's dead. You can't get the stuff back out.

A few years ago, I saw a girl in my office who went to a party with her friends and woke up the next day in a strange house on a strange couch. She had no idea where she was, and she had no clothes on. She was sore in all the right places; she knew she had been raped, and she could not find her clothes anywhere. Her friends were nowhere to be found.

GHB is addictive in the same way alcohol is, and the withdrawal is very similar to alcohol withdrawal, featuring anxiety, agitation, tremors and delirium tremens. Addicts stay more or less continually plastered on this stuff, reaching consciousness only long enough to secure a steady supply of GHB and a safe place to crash.

COCAINE

Cocaine is used in settings similar to crystal meth use, and it is often available from the same sources as meth. The high is very similar, though not as harsh as the methamphetamine high. It also does not last as long as a methamphetamine high. That, in combination with the lower cost associated with crystal, has resulted in crystal methamphetamine largely replacing cocaine as the stimulant drug of choice in many areas.

It is snorted, smoked, and injected like methamphetamine, and the paraphernalia are much the same. Powder cocaine is much less potent than the free base 'crack' cocaine that has devastated many inner city areas. Crack cocaine has been processed with many of the same chemicals used to manufacture crystal. Cocaine stimulates dopamine release in the same areas of the brain methamphetamine does. It blocks the dopamine transporter, like you got a sock caught in your vacuum cleaner, and causes a surge of dopamine in the synapse. The high does not last as long as a crystal high, two to three hours, but the crash does not last as long either.

> *Free base crack cocaine can cause brain damage just as severe and just as rapidly as methamphetamine.*

Powder cocaine damages the same areas of the brain methamphetamine does, it just takes longer, on the order of months instead of weeks. Free base crack cocaine can cause brain damage just as severe and just as rapidly as methamphetamine. Rats given a single dose of crack cocaine develop a strong addiction after just one exposure, and the memory persists for up to a year.

Cocaine users have shown significant loss of tissue in the frontal lobes, with corresponding deficits in higher order thinking, much like methamphetamine addicts. Compromised decision making contributes to the violence, the erratic thinking, and to the risk of relapse. Cocaine addicts' performance on decision making tests showed the same aberrant activation of frontal lobe areas as was seen in methamphetamine abusers, and it also persisted for years after last use of the drug, suggesting a permanent change in the way the brain works. Connections from the frontal lobe to the rest of the brain are broken, emotions are uncontrolled, thought patterns are disrupted, and psychotic delusions and paranoia are seen with crack cocaine, much like the ones we have discussed with regards to crystal.

Cocaine kills the cells in fasciculus retroflexus just like methamphetamine does, causing addiction, cravings, and compulsive use. It damages the pleasure center, nucleus accumbens, just like crystal does, and often that damage is permanent. Nothing sounds good, nothing feels good, nothing looks good, and there is no pleasure in life. The addiction to cocaine, especially crack cocaine, is every bit as severe and life changing as methamphetamine addiction.

HEROIN

Heroin used with methamphetamine, "speedballing," becomes more common as the methamphetamine addict requires higher doses to get intoxicated. The side effects of high doses of methamphetamine are reduced by heroin, and the heroin rush enhances the high. Large numbers of people are addicted to both methamphetamine and heroin, which complicates treatment by orders of magnitude.

Heroin is a derivative of opium poppies, a natural painkiller contained in a flower. In its highly purified form it is highly addictive and extremely potent, causing many deaths by overdose. John Belushi died speedballing heroin and cocaine, and his death drew national attention to the problem. The combination of heroin and methamphetamine is considerably more addictive than methamphetamine used alone. The breakpoint for rats addicted to speedballs was much higher than for any dose of methamphetamine tested. They would press that lever till they *died* to get another speedball, where they gave up after awhile if all they got was ice.

We have opioid receptors in our bodies, and we produce natural opioids, called endogenous endorphins. They are released whenever we suffer acute pain. There is a natural release of endorphins, for example, in the later stages of childbirth, giving a natural little rush that makes a mother forget the pain of giving birth as she is holding her newborn baby.

Heroin and its congeners, Oxy-Contin, Dilaudid, Darvocet, etc, are all metabolized to morphine in your body. They stimulate the morphine receptors and cause total body numbness and relaxation. Methamphetamine does not stimulate opioid receptors [though cocaine does to a small degree], but high doses of heroin can stimulate dopamine receptors. IV injection of concentrated heroin causes a rush, much like a crystal rush, by stimulating dopamine receptors in, you guessed it, the nucleus accumbens. The effect is not as powerful as that seen with methamphetamine, only a 170% increase in dopamine levels in nucleus accumbens, but the effect is additive and the chemical mechanism is similar.

Nerd Box

The G protein is a second messenger system in brain cells that interacts with dopamine receptors and triggers a cascade of chemical events inside the cell in response to dopamine. GTP is liberated, ion channels are opened, proteins are phosphorylated, genes are activated, the signal radiates all over the cell. When the neurotransmitter is released from the receptor, the GTP is bound once again to the G protein, and the cascade ends.

An autopsy study of human heroin and methamphetamine abusers showed a 50% decrease in G protein in the nucleus accumbens in both heroin and methamphetamine abusers. The resulting decreased responsiveness of the cell could account for addiction and tolerance at the level of the nucleus accumbens in the midbrain.

Interestingly, cholera toxin, pertussis toxin, diphtheria toxin, and wasp venom also interact with this system and cause neurologic symptoms.

I think the Nerd Boxes are cool.

Tolerance to heroin is rapid, even the second dose doesn't feel as good as the first dose did. The brain acts immediately to protect itself from the overstimulation of opioid receptors. The receptors for heroin undergo the same phosphorylation, sequestration, degradation pattern seen with dopamine receptors exposed to methamphetamine. It takes more and more heroin to get a rush, and eventually you require a toxic dose just to get high. The result is death by overdose. It's not that the guy made a mistake and took too much. The amount he needed to get high was enough to make him quit breathing, and he died.

Chronic exposure to narcotics, even mild narcotics like Lortab or Vicodin, causes hyper-sensitivity of the nerves all over the body. They become ten times more sensitive to pain than normal. They took some rats and got some of them hooked on heroin. Then, they dissected out the little spinal cords of these rats, exposed the neurons to caustic chemicals, and measured the sensitivity of these neurons to painful stimuli. The narcotic addicted rats were ten times more sensitive to painful stimuli than non-addicted rats. That's not somebody complaining about their backache. That is real pain transmission in the dorsal horn of the spinal cord of a rat. It really hurts.

Withdrawal from heroin is the most painful withdrawal of any drug. Combined with the withdrawal from methamphetamine, it is almost unbearable. In withdrawal from heroin, everything hurts. Your hair hurts, your eyeballs hurt, your teeth hurt, even the food moving through your gut hurts. You get intense bone and muscle pain as all your muscles go into spasm. You have intense anxiety and irritability. You get sweaty and nauseated. Your nose runs and you vomit. You get dehydrated from the diarrhea and you can die in withdrawal. This is not to be taken lightly. Heroin withdrawal needs to be carefully supervised. Combine all that with the misery of methamphetamine withdrawal, and you are faced with a true horror.

> *Withdrawal from heroin is the most painful withdrawal of any drug.*

The Garden of Eden had opium poppies to chew for your toothache and coca leaves to chew for a stimulant. Alcohol in low concentrations is a natural sedative found in over-ripe fruit; it is a natural preservative for grape juice. Psychedelic mushrooms are an ancient anesthetic. Most drugs of abuse *started out* as medicinal herbs to ease our painful lives on this planet. They don't become dangerous or addictive until we smoke them, refine them, and exploit their medicinal properties to get high.

Then God said, "I give you every seed bearing plant on the face of the whole earth and every tree that has fruit for seed in it. They shall be yours for food." (Gen 1:29)

.8.

RISK FACTORS FOR ADDICTION-
MEDICAL CONDITIONS

There are some common medical and emotional illnesses that predispose to addictions, especially addiction to methamphetamine. Amphetamines have a long history of medical uses. For many years they were the only antidepressants we had. In 1885 you could buy cocaine toothache drops in a box featuring pictures of innocent children. It could even cure dandruff and irritations of the scalp. Cocaine wine was used for neuralgia and despondency, a pleasant tonic and invigorator, and a bottle of it could be had upon the receipt of one dollar from Theodore Metcalf and Co. Until 1903, Coca Cola™ contained 60 mg of cocaine in each 8 oz. bottle.

Cocaine is still used as a local anesthetic, and it is the drug of choice for use in the nasal mucosa for severe nose bleeds. In its natural state, it is no more dangerous than caffeine. The leaves are chewed by indigenous peoples in South America with about the same effect we get from a cup of coffee. Unfortunately, it is not left in its natural state. In an unnatural state, it is a potent neurotoxin.

Amphetamines are also used medicinally, most commonly for the treatment of Attention Deficit Hyperactivity Disorder, ADHD. Ritalin and Adderal are both amphetamines. Methamphetamine was first marketed in the United States as Benzedrine, an effective decongestant and a treatment for asthma. Under the brand name Methedrine, it was a stimulant used widely by truckers and athletes. It has also been used in the treatment of obesity and narcolepsy, and as a stimulant in war time. Of course, we have many other drugs for these indications that are much safer and more effective than methamphetamine, but the illness itself, especially if untreated, predisposes to addiction to the 'medicine' that treats it.

(Author's Note): This is by far the hardest chapter in this book. It gets very technical. If you enjoy this stuff, march on. It's worth the effort. If you

don't ever want to see the word dopamine again as long as you live, skip to Chapter 9. It's okay. Really. I'll catch up with you later.)

ADHD ATTENTION DEFICIT HYPERACTIVITY DISORDER

Our twenty-three year old son is facing 105 years in prison and over $100,000 in fines for use and distribution of meth. We were forced into giving him Ritalin in his youth and we are angry. It was implied to us by the arresting detective that there is a connection between Ritalin and meth addiction. Is there a basis to this and do you have any statistics?

Attention Deficit Hyperactivity Disorder, ADHD affects 6–12% of school age children and 4–6% of adults. Sixty percent of cases persist into adulthood, but even the remaining 40% still have some residual symptoms; not enough to make the criteria for diagnosis of ADHD, but enough to affect their lives. True ADHD, not unreasonable expectations or chronic discipline problems, but true biochemical ADHD, is characterized by inability to concentrate and focus attention, and impulsivity. It leads to poor social relationships, failures at school and at work, demoralization and poor self-esteem.

Around 30% of addicts seeking treatment have Attention Deficit Hyperactivity Disorder, and addicts with concurrent ADHD have much higher risk of severe addiction. ADHD addicts have high rates of violent crime and incarceration, family disintegration and abandonment. Learning disabilities and poor job performance, motor vehicle accidents and trauma are all more common in the ADHD addict. Appropriate treatment for ADHD *reduces* the risk of addiction by 50% and improves the success of drug rehabilitation dramatically.

Appropriate treatment for ADHD reduces the risk of addiction by 50% and improves the success of drug rehabilitation dramatically.

The physiologic and anatomic characteristics if ADHD are very similar to those seen in methamphetamine use and toxicity, and some chemical properties of untreated ADHD clearly put patients at risk for addiction to methamphetamine. The National Institutes of Health consensus conference found that the *appropriate* use of Ritalin or Adderal, both of which are amphetamine derivatives, does not increase the risk of methamphetamine addiction. Untreated ADHD most certainly does.

Military Use of Amphetamines

Similarly, the appropriate use of amphetamines by military personnel during combat duty for defined periods of time and at regulated doses does not predispose to addiction or brain damage for military personnel. Chronic daily use at escalating doses, however, as was commonly seen during the Vietnam War, most certainly can result in both addiction and brain damage.

The dosing recommendations in the Naval Strike and Air Warfare Center's Performance Maintenance Manual for Continuous Flight Operations define the appropriate use of amphetamines in war time. When those recommendations are followed, *including the recommendations for catch up sleep*, the drugs are safe and effective in saving lives.

Brown Capt D, Belland Cdr KM Performance Maintenance During Continuous Flight Operations, a guide for flight surgeons. Naval Strike and Air Warfare Center 1 Jan 2000

The ADHD adult has trouble focusing attention, finishing a job, and prioritizing simultaneous demands. It's like somebody is always tapping his shoulder and distracting him from what he's trying to do. His mind is scattered, he feels incompetent, he can't even control his own behavior. He has trouble controlling impulses and making decisions. He can't set a goal and expect to reach it, seldom gets the satisfaction of a job well done, and his professional life is a shambles. Now somebody offers him a drug, methamphetamine, that makes him feel powerful, confident, intelligent, and in control. It helps him focus his attention. He feels energized. He will gravitate to methamphetamine. It solves all his problems. He doesn't know how he ever got by without it.

When the crystal wears off, all the ADHD symptoms come flooding back in, along with the withdrawal and toxic effects of the methamphetamine, and he is miserable until he gets another hit. As the methamphetamine induced brain damage sets in with symptoms of anxiety, scattered thought processes, and loss of mental focus, he uses even more. He thinks his problem must be getting worse and he needs more crystal to be able to cope. Addiction is much more rapid and severe in the ADHD adult than in the normal healthy person trying methamphetamine. He's using it therapeutically, and it 'works.'

ADHD AND DOPAMINE RECEPTORS

True biochemical ADHD is primarily a genetic problem. Eighty percent of cases are familial. Several genes that code for defective dopamine receptors have been associated with ADHD, including the D4 receptor and the D2 receptor, among others. Variants of the dopamine D2 receptor gene have been associated with impulsive, addictive and compulsive behavior, a "reward deficiency syndrome." This genetic defect is associated with alcoholism, drug addiction, obesity, smoking and gambling, as well as ADHD.

ADHD and Television

A recent study has shown an association between excessive television watching, especially in the pre-school years and the development of ADHD. Passively watching as a series of fast moving images flashes before your eyes is thought to be damaging to the developing brain. I don't think it is a causal relationship. TV does not cause a dopamine receptor deficiency. But if you already have a dopamine receptor deficiency, the constant stimulation from the TV is likely to cause further disorganization of thought patterns.

It's hard to fix dinner with two preschoolers wrapped round your ankles, and thirty minutes of a Barney video every afternoon won't hurt a child, but if you have a family history of ADHD, and you let your preschool child watch hours of TV every day just to have that electronic babysitter, you are asking for a problem. ADHD has been with us for centuries, but has clinically gotten much worse in the years since television.

The ADHD child will gravitate to the TV because it helps him hold still. The ADHD parent is grateful for the TV because it calms the child for awhile. The visual hyperstimulation of the television makes him feel better, just like the chemical hyperstimulation of amphetamine makes him feel better. There are much better treatments for ADHD than the television set.

ADHD is also related to prenatal exposure to alcohol, tobacco, and other drugs of abuse, as was discussed in Chapter 6. Prenatal exposure to tobacco increases the risk of ADHD by 200 to 300%, especially in susceptible families. Prenatal exposure to alcohol, or Fetal Alcohol Syndrome, is associated with decreased dopamine transmission in the ventral tegmental area causing hyperactivity and inattention indistinguishable from ADHD. Fetal Alcohol Syndrome is also treated with Ritalin, which normalizes the dopamine transmission in the ventral tegmental area.

The dopamine receptor is defective in ADHD, whether by genetic causes, toxic chemicals or a combination of both. It does not respond to normal levels of dopamine. The defective dopamine receptor has a poor linkage with its second messenger system, affecting the gene transcription response to dopamine. Dopamine binds to the receptor, but does not trigger the internal cellular changes dopamine is supposed to cause. Remember, that's how brain cells learn. ADHD brain cells don't learn as well. The defective dopamine receptor is, however, responsive to epinephrine and norepinephrine, a detail that becomes important when we talk about treatments.

The stimulants Ritalin, Adderal and Concerta, at the low doses used for ADHD, increase norepinephrine levels in brain tissue, and the norepinephrine drives the second messenger system dopamine was supposed to drive, thus relieving the symptoms of ADHD. These drugs do not trigger a dopamine release in the nucleus accumbens *at the doses used for ADHD,* so they do not cause a high and do not cause the type of cell death methamphetamine does. But all of these drugs are amphetamine derivatives and can be diverted for the manufacture of methamphetamine, or simply used in high enough doses to get a dopamine release in the nucleus accumbens, and thus a high. Long acting formulations of Ritalin are very resistant to diversion. They cannot be snorted, and the residue is too gummy to make good crystal.

Nerd Box

The dopamine transporter has also been implicated in ADHD, the vacuum cleaner that mops up dopamine after an impulse. MRI and PET scan studies of children with ADHD have been done showing subtle abnormalities in dopamine transporter densities in the striatum. The only animal model for ADHD we have is a strain of mice that have deficiencies in the dopamine transporter and slow clearance of dopamine from the synapse. They also show hyperactivity and impaired learning ability that responds to treatment with stimulants like amphetamine.

PET studies in humans show that Ritalin blocks some of the dopamine transporters [vacuum cleaners], causing a mild increase in extracellular dopamine, and amplifies dopamine signals in the striatum [not nucleus accumbens, which is not as sensitive]. The defective dopamine receptors can't respond to normal levels of dopamine, but are stimulated by these increased levels of dopamine, and they start responding. The increased dopamine transmission in the striatum enhances task specific signaling and decreases 'noise' resulting in improved attention and decreased distractibility.

Nicotine has been noted to have a therapeutic effect on ADHD. It is a cholinergic drug that enhances dopamine transmission in the midbrain and relieves many of the symptoms of ADHD. Many adults smoke primarily to relieve the restlessness and poor mental focus caused by their untreated ADHD.

Marijuana also increases dopamine transmission and relieves the symptoms of ADHD, and some irresponsible physicians are recommending it for treatment of adult ADHD. Dopamine receptor deficiencies in ADHD are also 'corrected' by the use of cocaine and methamphetamine, and many patients are self-medicating their dopamine deficient states with illegal drugs. We have much safer and more effective medications for ADHD than street drugs that cause irreversible brain damage.

Nerd Box

There are also structural changes in the brain associated with ADHD. ADHD adults were studied under fMRI as they did a complex task, and instead of activating the normal brain pathways for complex work, they activated an ancillary pathway that got the job done, but took longer. MRI studies have shown smaller caudate volumes, a structure important for motor memory and control.

The MRI's of ADHD patients also show smaller volume of the cerebellar vermis, which regulates dopamine transmission in the nucleus accumbens and also has projections to the ventral tegmental area. Inadequate tissue in the cerebellar vermis is associated with heightened risk of addiction. We will discuss the vermis more when we talk about PTSD.

This study also showed decreased blood flow in the frontal lobe and midbrain suggesting that ADHD is mediated by poor functioning of frontal lobe and subsequent connection to limbic system. Impulse control is mediated by the frontal lobe's control over limbic areas. These connections are weaker in ADHD adults.

ADHD TREATMENT

ADHD adults have to work a lot harder than the rest of us just to cope with normal life, job demands, and scheduling. They have to concentrate to pay attention at work. They are more impulsive and have to use a lot of mental energy to control those impulses. Add in the fact that their children also have ADHD, and you have the recipe for a real problem.

Most ADHD adults are not receiving any treatment for their problem. They have fewer symptoms than they did when they were young, and they manage to control themselves well enough, but they are extremely susceptible to addiction to stimulants. An ADHD adult who stumbles upon methamphetamine will feel so much better when using the drug, and so much worse when he stops, he will become addicted much faster than a normal person.

Treatment of ADHD with long acting low abuse potential stimulants improves success rate of substance abuse treatment dramatically. The problem has always been the obvious risk of diversion or abuse of the treatment stimulant. A new drug, Atomoxetine [Strattera], has been developed that is a non-stimulant, selective norepinephrine re-uptake inhibitor, and has been shown to be effective in a high percentage of ADHD children and adults.

Remember, the dopamine receptor is also sensitive to norepinephrine, allowing a pharmacologic back door to treatment. Some serotonin based drugs are also effective in some patients, including the anti-anxiety drugs and anti-depressants like buproprion [Wellbutrin], venlafaxine [Effexor], fluoxdetine [Prozac], and buspirone [BuSpar]. Most of these drugs also have effects on the norepinephrine receptor. These drugs are not as effective as the stimulants for most people, but when they work, they are very safe.

Of course, the combination of ADHD and methamphetamine addiction is going to result in some very significant brain dysfunction. Methamphetamine addicts with concurrent ADHD have severe problems with memory, learning, abstract thinking, attention, focus, and verbal fluency. The thought disorders associated with ADHD are characterized by impulsiveness and poor decision making that contribute to the severity of the addiction. Educational therapy and psychotherapy are helpful for developing skills to cope with the challenges of ADHD, but pharmacologic therapy is still essential in most cases to long term success and prevention of relapse.

POST TRAUMATIC STRESS DISORDER

At least 75% of female drug users, and more than 50% of male drug users, are survivors of childhood physical, emotional, or sexual abuse which contributes to their drug use and severely compromises their recovery. Many are children of alcoholic homes, a subject we will cover in detail in a later chapter. Some were sexually victimized by aunts or uncles, grandparents, baby-sitters, or other unrelated adults.

There is a large and growing literature about the neural effects of trauma and abuse, especially childhood trauma and abuse, upon the developing brain. It is almost as frightening as the literature about methamphetamine itself. Post Traumatic Stress Disorder [PTSD] is characterized by chronic insomnia, obsessive thoughts and compulsive behavior, nightmares, flashbacks, anxiety and depression. The anatomic correlates are lesions in the frontal lobes [complex thought] and limbic [emotional] areas of the brain.

> *At least 75% of female drug users,*
> *and more than 50% of male drug users,*
> *are survivors of childhood physical,*
> *emotional, or sexual abuse*

Post Traumatic Stress Disorder is well described in veterans of the Vietnam War, and is strongly associated with high rates of alcoholism and other drug addictions. Veterans with PTSD had high rates of severe mental impairment and suicide in the years following the war. Eighty percent of PTSD veterans studied were addicted to one or more substances, and the mortality rate from suicide in this population was 17% over six years.

Stressors causing PTSD include child abuse, rape and incest, war time trauma, witnessing a violent death, car accidents, and catastrophic events like the events of 9/11. The more directly threatening the event, the more likely it will result in permanent problems for the person exposed to severe stress. Chronic severe stress upon a child has similar effects, for instance growing up in an alcoholic home, even if there was no overt abuse, commonly predicts major depression and other psychological problems. Children of alcoholics report more life stress, more personal dysfunction, and have less effective stress management techniques as adults. The changes in the brain and personality of the trauma victim predispose to addiction to alcohol and other drugs of abuse.

Severe early stress and abuse initiates the release of stress hormones in the body, much like the adrenaline rush you feel when someone almost hits you in traffic. That hormone rush includes adrenaline, and also several other neurohormones that are also neurotransmitters. Stress induced hormones include cortisone, epinephrine, vasopressin, and oxytocin, all of which act as neurotransmitters in the central nervous system.

Chronic over-production of these neurohormones, especially in the developing nervous system, causes over-stimulation of the brain areas involved in the appreciation and response to stress. Remember what happens when a brain area or function is over-stimulated? The brain cells adjust to accommodate the level of activity required of them by producing structural changes in the neurons involved. Cellular learning occurs in response to chronic stress. Young children are especially vulnerable to these effects because their brains are still forming.

> *Real brain damage occurs at a cellular*
> *level whenever a child is abused.*

Lesser degrees of abuse and trauma result in lesser degrees of PTSD symptoms, but the same neural pathways and structures are damaged and dysfunctional. Mild to moderate cases that would not show up on a structural study like an MRI nonetheless have chemical and cellular basis. Real brain damage occurs at a cellular level whenever a child is abused.

STRESS EFFECTS ON THE BRAIN

High levels of stress neurohormones cause inhibition of neurogenesis, synaptic remodeling, and selective myelination of certain tracts in the brain that are potent enough to change the structure of the brain. Those changes can be measured by PET scans and MRI scans showing dramatic differences in the size and structure of the amygdala [emotions], hippocampus [short term memory], frontal lobe [rational thought], and cerebellar vermis in survivors of severe chronic stress.

The **cerebellar vermis** is particularly sensitive to stress hormones, having the largest concentration of stress hormone [cortisone] receptors in the central nervous system. Over-stimulation by excess stress is ultimately toxic to these cells and kills them. The loss of cell volume is apparent on PET and MRI studies. Atrophy of the vermis of the cerebellum is especially marked in the case of childhood sexual abuse and wartime trauma, two situations in which it has been measured in detail in fMRI studies.

The vermis regulates dopamine transmission in the nucleus accumbens, and when it is not well developed, there is less control over the nucleus accumbens. Vermis also has projections to the ventral tegmental area [cravings and drives], the caudate nucleus [reward based learning], and the hypothalamus [hormonal control over the whole body]. Damage to the vermis radiates effects throughout the pleasure reward circuit making the brain more vulnerable to addiction.

The hippocampus is the structure that processes short term memory, encodes it for permanent storage in the temporal lobe, and communicates it to emotional and motivational centers in the midbrain. It functions largely below the level of consciousness, and thus sub-consciously. It is also seriously damaged by severely threatening events, enough to show up on a MRI study of PTSD patients. Hippocampal damage is documented in both combat veterans and survivors of childhood sexual abuse, and is seen in PTSD patients with no history of substance abuse. It is not caused by the alcohol or drug abuse, but rather is associated with trauma.

> *The memory is literally burned*
> *into her brain.*

Prolonged and severe stress damages the dendritic spines on the cells of hippocampus, much like singeing the hair on your arm when you get too close to the fire. Excessive stress also reduces the expression of brain derived neurotrophic factor, especially in the hippocampus and amygdala [memory and emotion], so they cannot repair themselves. These structures process emotional memory, so that the memory of a certain person can elicit strong emotions related to that person. Stressful stimuli trigger unexpected recall of traumatic memories due to dysfunction in the amygdala and hippocampus, the areas that initially processed those memories. A mother experiences vivid flashbacks of her own childhood sexual abuse when she sees her two-year-old daughter climb out of the bathtub. The memory is literally burned into her brain.

Nerd Box

Structural changes in the amygdala, hippocampus, nucleus accumbens, anterior cingulate gyrus and hypothalamus have all been documented in human survivors of child sexual abuse. Damage to these areas is associated with impulsivity, aggressiveness, depression, anxiety, panic attacks, flashbacks, and insomnia. The sleep cycle is disrupted and the mood lamp is non functional. The severity of symptoms was correlated to the degree of anatomic abnormality.

Childhood abuse has been associated with fMRI and EEG changes indicating deficient cortical maturation and differentiation in the frontal and temporal cortex areas. These areas are critical to judgment, reasoning, and decision making. Executive functions in the cortex are weakened, and emotional limbic areas are less controlled and regulated.

Fig 20

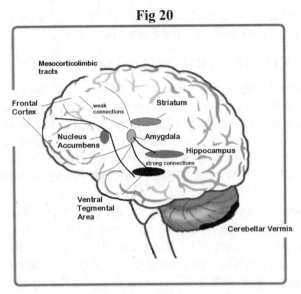

Areas of the brain affected by child abuse and other major trauma

The structural changes in the brain resulting from childhood trauma weaken the connections between the higher cortical areas and the emotional limbic areas, so emotions are harder to control. The imbalance between cortical [reasoning] and limbic [feeling] brain function leads to uncontrolled thought processes [obsessions], and disruptive memories [flashbacks].

Obsessive thoughts and feelings of worthlessness, ugliness, rejection, and humiliation require a conscious effort to 'stop thinking like that.' As soon as the reasoning cortex lets up its command to 'stop thinking like that' [around two o'clock in the morning] the limbic circuits revert to their old pattern of obsessive thoughts and compulsive behaviors.

These neural alterations increase the risk of PTSD, depression, ADHD, borderline and dissociative personality disorders, and substance abuse. There is an interaction between ADHD and PTSD. ADHD kids are more likely to be abused because of difficulties controlling their behavior. The brain abnormalities associated with child abuse worsen the functional problems associated with ADHD; the impulsivity and difficulty concentrating get dramatically worse.

My brother and his wife keep foster children, and every few months, they will get a ten or twelve-year-old child, usually a boy, who is completely out of control. He can't focus his attention, he is loud and aggressive, he is three or four years behind in school, and if you look closely, he has a crooked arm and cigarette burn marks all over his body. They can't keep him because he is so cruel to their other children. He ends up in a group home for juvenile delinquents, and spends his adult life in jail. These kids are good examples of what ADHD and PTSD look like in the same person.

CORRELATION WITH DRUG ABUSE

We have always known that adult survivors of child abuse and war combat veterans have a much higher that normal incidence of drug and alcohol abuse, beyond what may be attributable to being the children of alcoholics, for instance. The permanent and significant loss of neurons in the vermis, amygdala, and prefrontal cortex produces a life long state of susceptibility to stress, and resulting vulnerability to addiction to any substance that offers to relieve that stress.

A genetic defect in the dopamine receptor is associated with Post Traumatic Stress Disorder, suggesting that abnormal dopamine transmission predisposes to the development of PTSD in much the same way that the genetic defect in the dopamine receptor predisposes to ADHD. Some families have multiple members with severe PTSD resulting from trauma that would not bother people from a less vulnerable family. They are just more sensitive to stressful events than other people. Any drug that enhances dopamine transmission is going to be perceived as an effective treatment for the symptoms of the underlying chemical imbalance.

The use of cocaine or methamphetamine is initially very effective in relieving the mental torment and physiological dysfunction caused by abuse or traumatic memories. The endless negative thoughts and feelings of disgust disappear on ice. The feeling of power, confidence, intelligence, competence and endurance is exhilarating. The chronic under-stimulation of nucleus accumbens is corrected, and he feels good for the first time in his life.

> *These patients are treating themselves with cocaine or methamphetamine, and it 'works' for the short term, but in the end, worsens the very symptoms they are trying to avoid.*

PET scans of cocaine abusing Post Traumatic Stress Disorder patients show different patterns of blood flow in the amygdala, prefrontal cortex, and hippocampus than stimulant abusers who did not have a history of PTSD. The drug temporarily relieved the neurologic effects of the PTSD. These patients are treating themselves with cocaine or methamphetamine, and it 'works' for the short term, but in the end, worsens the very symptoms they are trying to avoid.

Treatment of PTSD consists of psychological counseling with ventilation and validation of the feelings involved. Most cases also require treatment with anti-depressants which reverse some of the biochemical changes associated with PTSD. The selective serotonin re-uptake inhibitor class of anti-depressants, like Prozac, cause a delayed increase in neurotrophic factors that promote regrowth of the damaged neurons in the hippocampus and other areas. That's why they take two or three weeks to take effect. Pharmacologic treatment with serotonin re-uptake inhibitors is needed for at least one year, and is sometimes life long. The structural changes in the brain should be considered permanent.

It is important to recognize the drug addict who is also a PTSD patient. The PTSD has to be addressed in order to adequately treat the addiction. Relapse is inevitable if the underlying problem is not addressed effectively. This issue is addressed more completely in Chapters 11 and 15.

DEPRESSION

Lesser degrees of psychic distress can also precipitate addiction. The biochemistry of depression is not well understood because there are no animal models for it. We can't interview our rats and ask them how they are feeling before we dissect their brains. The roles of various neurotransmitters can only be deduced from human responses to various medications we have studied in rats.

The role of stress and stress related hormones have been confirmed as a cause of depression. Lower degrees of chronic stress that would not precipitate a full blown PTSD can nonetheless cause significant depression. Studies of the hippocampus and amygdala [memory and emotion] anatomy in depressed patients show many of the same abnormalities seen in PTSD, but to a smaller degree.

The current mainstay for treatment of depression is the selective serotonin re-uptake inhibitors as mentioned above. Many lives are saved by these drugs, as suicides are prevented and quality of life improves with the effective treatment of depression. They increase the amount of serotonin in the synapse thus improving mood, sleep, and concentration. The mood lamp is turned up a shade and the depression lifts. It is a natural feeling, so natural that patients will often conclude, "Hey I'm better now, I don't need this stuff anymore." They feel normal again.

Of course, no anti-depressant will give you quite the lift methamphetamine does. Untreated depression preceding the onset of drug abuse is temporarily relieved by methamphetamine. Patients with manic-depressive disorder are especially prone to methamphetamine abuse, because they have already learned to prefer the manic stages of the illness. They are euphoric in the mania, while the depression is equally profound. Methamphetamine gives them 'control' over their illness; they can induce a manic state using crystal, and maintain it with continued use.

The similarities between methamphetamine intoxication and manic-depressive disorder [bipolar disorder] are so striking that methamphetamine treated rats are used as an animal model for the study of manic-depressive disorder. Meth treated rats develop a manic condition that responds to lithium and carbamazepine [Tegretol] just like humans with manic-depressive disorder.

Later stages of addiction are marked by profound depression that responds poorly to medications since the biochemical pathways affected by anti-depressants have been disrupted. Serotonin pathways are among the first to be destroyed by methamphetamine, and recovery, as we have seen, is slow and incomplete. High doses of SSRI anti-depressants are required to relieve the symptoms, especially during the first year off methamphetamine.

Relapse into addiction is very common in patients with undiagnosed and untreated depression. Addicts often assume their depression is normal and there is nothing anybody can do about it, and so they don't even seek help. They just cave in after a year or two, and treat themselves with the only anti-depressant they know, methamphetamine.

SITUATIONAL DEPRESSION

Otherwise healthy people can find themselves severely depressed as a result of social factors in their lives. The woman whose husband left her for another woman, for instance, feels rejected, humiliated, and angry. Unresolved grief at the loss of a family member, guilt at the acquisition of a sexually transmitted disease or in the aftermath of an abortion, anger at the loss of health or bodily function, the hopelessness of an AIDS diagnosis, the failure of an important relationship, can all cause the kind of unremitting grief and depression that leads to substance abuse. Situational depression does not respond to medications as well as endogenous depression does. The external situation has to either change or be accepted, and that takes time.

Situational depression can generalize to a chronic depression when there is no resolution to the problem. Worry, anxiety, and obsessive thought patterns take on a life of their own. Inability to forgive oneself, for instance after an affair or an abortion, leads to feelings of disgust and self hatred. The pain of rejection by a spouse becomes a self image of inadequacy. "He doesn't love me because I am unlovable. I am worthless. Nobody loves me." Anger becomes chronic, and generalizes to other situations. The anger at being rejected by your husband becomes irritability at work, a short temper with the kids, and hyper-sensitivity to criticism. Friendships are strained, family members are alienated and you become isolated.

You may be able to distract yourself during the day, but at night it is impossible to sleep. Chronic insomnia makes a bad situation even worse. Sleep deprivation causes mood swings, crying spells, worsening irritability, headaches, and increased anxiety. Obsessive thought patterns are almost impossible to stop, or even to recognize as the obsessions they are. You can't just quit thinking about it. It possesses you, torments you, night and day.

Depression of this nature predisposes to drug and alcohol addiction. You can turn those thoughts off by getting drunk or high. You get tired of feeling so bad all the time. Methamphetamine makes you feel a lot better, and the stimulant gets you through the day when you are bone tired. Methamphetamine is a lousy anti-depressant in the long run, but the first intoxication with it feels great. You feel powerful, confident, happy and energetic. Remember, the crash at first is mild and short lived. The serious depression is not seen until the late stages of addiction. The stuff your friend gave you 'works' a lot better than anything the doctor's office has.

> *You think you can control it. You think of it as a medicine, and some people use at low doses like this for years.*

You think you can control it. You think of it as a medicine, and some people use at low doses like this for years. They never get 'high' on it; they just use it to help with their depression or ADHD symptoms. Eventually the brain damage catches up with them. They get irritable, paranoid and irresponsible. They lose control over their drug use, and shortly after that, lose control over their lives.

Intelligent people get hooked on methamphetamine. They innocently take the pill their friend gives them for their hangover or for their depression, or they stumble upon a treatment for their ADHD symptoms, and they feel so much better they think, "This can't possibly be bad for me. This stuff works!" It 'works' so well, they get sucked in to a trap, and by the time they realize it, they are seriously addicted to crystal meth.

.9.

CULTURAL RISK FACTORS -
THE ALCOHOLIC HOME

Of the addicts I work with, a county jail population, 50% are basically healthy people who made a bad decision and ran with the wrong crowd, or went to the wrong party and stayed too long. They may be college-educated professionals, smart people who thought they were too smart to get hooked on a drug like methamphetamine. They came from good families, went to good schools, and lived in nice neighborhoods. Sunday School teachers get hooked on crystal. High School principals get hooked on crystal. Professional athletes get hooked on crystal. I've met former *policemen and substance abuse counselors* addicted to crystal.

Some incredibly intelligent teenagers get hooked on crystal, too. Straight "A" students from good homes who went to good schools and ought to know better, get hooked on ice—the teacher's daughter and the fireman's son. Good honest people who loved and disciplined their kids, taught solid values and lived honorable lives can still lose their children to crystal. There is no vaccine against methamphetamine.

The other 50% of addicts are the kids we call "bad kids." They are angry, tough, insolent, and rebellious. They are in trouble with their parents, with the principal, and with the law; they despise any authority figure in their lives. They drop out of school and roam the streets. These are the kids who act bad, talk bad, dress bad, the kind of kids we don't want our kids running around with.

Who are these kids? Can we understand them? Is there anything we can do to help them?

Let's take a closer look at one of them. When he was five years old, he came home from kindergarten and woke his mother up. He said, "Mommy, I'm hungry, can I have something to eat?" Mommy slapped him up the side of the head and said, "Get out of here, you noisy brat! You woke me up." She was drunk. He went to the pantry and all he found was stale crackers and beer. No food in the house. He was five years old and he was hungry. He was crying. Nobody cared.

Alcohol is the family idol.

Alcohol is the family idol. The whole family is organized around the alcoholic. Mom has to have her booze and nothing else matters. She explodes if anybody interferes with her gin and tonic and she rules with her rage. She has to be taken care of or everybody else will suffer the consequences. The child's legitimate needs are not important. The rest of the family covers for her. They lie for her, do for her, comfort her, and bend to her wishes. She is the center of attention in the family. All the money goes for liquor. Nobody's needs are met but hers. Everything is sacrificed on the altar of Mom's problem. The child defends her and looks out for her. That's his mother, and he loves her. But nobody is meeting his needs.

She verbally or physically abuses the child, not just by neglect, but also by overt words that are degrading to the child. "Shut up and get out of here. I'm tired, leave me alone." She loses her temper and tells him he's 'stupid, he'll 'never amount to anything.' She beats him when he makes too much noise and ignores him when he cries. Formative years have gone by, and the child has internalized all the messages he got from his alcoholic home. "I am not important. I am stupid. I am unlovable. I am not wanted. My feelings don't matter. Nobody cares."

As he gets older, he realizes this is not normal. He grows angry and rebellious. Authority figures are especially despised. Parents are irresponsible and selfish, punitive and uncaring. Teachers, principals, and coaches are all seen through the same lens. He overreacts to constructive criticism from his teacher and explodes in school. He withdraws from his coach and won't participate in school activities that could have given him some validation and acceptance if he had been open to the authority involved. His ten-year-old friends don't understand his hostility. They withdraw from him, and that just confirms what he already knew—he is unacceptable, unloved, and unwanted. His attitude is "Nobody likes me and I don't care." It hurts too bad to care. Rejection hurts, even if it's self imposed.

ANGRY AND REBELLIOUS

Fast forward a few years—now he's fifteen years old. He's angry and aggressive. His home life is chaos. He looks to his peers for emotional support and guidance. What kind of guidance is he going to get from his seventeen-year-old drug pusher friend? "Here, kid, take some of this. It will make you feel better." And you know what? It 'works.' It makes him feel better. It relieves his depression, his feeling of inadequacy and powerlessness.

> *"Here, kid, take some of this. It will make you feel better." And you know what? It 'works.'*

Methamphetamine makes him feel confident and powerful, intelligent and energetic. When he gets high with his friends, he feels accepted and valued, part of the group. He finds his need for love and acceptance met, a need his parents should be meeting, but they are too caught up in their own psychopathology to meet anybody's needs but their own. When he gets high, he can forget about all the trouble back home. He has a new 'home' of sorts, a place where he feels comfortable, where he belongs.

Of course, the new home has rules, too. First is, Don't Snitch. Don't tell anybody on the outside what we're doing. Don't let your parents find out. If they do, the party's over. Second, we demand Absolute Loyalty. You can't decide you want to quit and go somewhere else to get your love and acceptance. That would be a betrayal. If anyone leaves voluntarily, that is an admission that this 'family' is not good and perfect, meeting every need and desire of its members.

In order for a teenager to resist pressure to use drugs, he has to be willing to make his friends mad. He has to stand up to them and say, "Hey, I'm outta here" when they get out the dope. This kid is not emotionally strong enough to risk losing the approval of his friends. He can't deliberately refuse their offer of acceptance, even if they require his obedience to mind numbing cruelty, participation in crime, the violation of every value he has.

What we have just described is a gang, a mind-controlling group. These people are not just friends. They tell him how to think, what to value, and how to act. They have codes of honor, discipline, expectations, and rewards for 'good' behavior. Sounds like the kid finally found a parent.

Fast forward another ten years. Now the kid is twenty-five years old, he's addicted to methamphetamine. He is self-centered and abusive, demanding and manipulative, paranoid and violent. His five-year-old daughter comes home from kindergarten and says, "Daddy, I'm hungry, can I have something to eat?" Same song, second verse. *"The sins of the fathers are visited upon the children to the third and the fourth generations."* That's not a curse. That's a description of how it really is. That verse is in the context of the Ten Commandments, the first of which has to do with idolatry. When we worship other gods, we affect our children for many generations.

> *His five-year-old daughter comes home*
> *from kindergarten and says, "Daddy, I'm*
> *hungry, can I have something to eat?"*

ADDICTION AS IDOLATRY

Addiction is a form of idolatry, the worship of something other than God. It is the worship of pleasure, feel good at any cost. It is a life controlling desire for an object offering satisfaction and pleasure. Methamphetamine promises to meet the needs of its worshipper, make him feel competent and powerful, intelligent and energetic. He does whatever it takes to appease his dealer and obtain more ice. Methamphetamine has become his god.

His need for acceptance and belonging is met by methamphetamine. His need for affirmation and approval is met by crystal. His sexual response is enhanced by crystal. His relationships have been destroyed, but he finds gratification in ice. As his brain pathways adjust, the drug takes center stage. He feels so bad without it; he needs it just to get through the day. He craves it, desires it, longs for it, can't think about anything else. As his brain pathways are destroyed, he is possessed by it, controlled by it, and obsessed by it. In the end, it reduces him to a slave. He feels he can't survive without it.

Addiction focuses a person's life on the pursuit of pleasure, feeling good, and being happy. If methamphetamine accomplishes that, he will worship the drug, long for it, adore it, desire it, and spend time, energy and resources to get it. He will buy more meth, steal more meth, con more meth, or make more meth. He will sacrifice his money, his career, his family, and even his personality to feel good. Anything that feels good can and will become an idol. It will elicit desire and longing, restructure priorities, and form new habits of gratification which intensify the desire and longing. It is the desire, the compulsion, the preoccupation with pleasure from any source that makes it an idol.

The thing we long for and desire, the thing we are preoccupied with, the thing we adore, meditate on and plan for; the thing we want more and more and more of, the thing we devote time, energy, and resources to; the thing we obey, that is what we have chosen to be our god. The thing we value the highest, the unspoken priority of our life choices is the thing we worship.

Methamphetamine is one vicious god.

Methamphetamine is an all consuming god. It not only takes all the emotional and financial resources of its worshipper, it also takes his very identity. It takes his temper and makes him violent and abusive. It takes his caring and makes him careless. It takes his ability to love and nurture his children and makes him indifferent to their needs. It takes his self-control and makes him a slave to his urges, drives, and cravings. It rewires his brain and turns him into an animal instead of a person.

He "passes his children through the fire" to his idol, an ancient form of human sacrifice. He gives time and attention, emotional and financial resources to the object of his desire instead of to his children. God would never demand that of us. He strictly forbade child sacrifice. Idols don't care. They absorb all the energy we are willing to devote to them.

Of course, methamphetamine is an empty god. Methamphetamine does not really make anyone happy, it just gives an illusion of happiness, a hallucination of pleasure, while it steadily destroys your life and robs you of any real joy you might have had. While you are high, your business fails, your wife and kids leave, your home is repossessed, and your life is destroyed. You were worshipping a drug, a feeling the drug gave you, and it was a mirage.

Humans are hard-wired to desire, to long for, things that give pleasure. It is worked into our brains to appreciate and anticipate pleasure. God gave us nucleus accumbens, the pleasure center. He knows what it's for, and He wants us to feel pleasure. He does not want us to worship it, desire it above all else. When we worship pleasure we destroy it. That kind of worship is reserved for Him. Addiction is the natural result of the Godlessness and spiritual emptiness of our culture. We can't find satisfaction in God because we don't really believe in God.

WE DON'T BELIEVE IN GOD

A large proportion of the people in this nation do not really believe in God. They learned in school that this God thing is a fairytale; the universe created itself and this world is an accident of nature caused by blind physical laws having nothing to do with God. They sometimes profess a belief in God, on certain holidays, when national tragedy strikes, or when their lives are threatened. But when if comes right down to the brass tacks, they don't really believe in God. *They live as if He does not exist.*

Even some people who grace the church with their presence every Sunday don't really believe in God. They put in an appearance, get their name in the attendance record, just in case God is real, but no matter what they *say* they believe, their actions Monday through Saturday make it obvious they don't really believe in God. There are people calling themselves Bishops and Pastors in the Church who don't believe in God, His sovereignty and His moral law. They believe in a caricature of God that bears no resemblance to the God of the Bible.

People who really believe in God don't despise their children for a bottle of whiskey. People who believe in a righteous, all powerful God don't have affairs and betray and humiliate their spouse. People who really believe in a Holy God don't lie to spare themselves the embarrassment of the truth or make an extra buck. People who believe in a loving God don't harbor hatred and hostility, vengeance and violence.

> *We don't deliberately choose to do what we know is wrong, rather we don't believe anything is really wrong.*

Our nation is not so much *immoral* as it is *amoral*. We don't deliberately choose to do what we know is wrong, rather we don't believe anything is really wrong. Anything can be right or wrong. It's all relative. Right and wrong are according to what our friends say and do, or what we see people doing on TV. Right and wrong are defined moment by moment according to our own whims, lusts, and desires.

As a society, we have evicted God from our schools and our government, both of which were founded on Christian principles. The intellectuals led the crusade against God with the 'discovery' that nature could explain itself, no outside force is needed or desired to explain the existence of the universe, life, or mankind. Science has tried to deny God, reduce our concept of God to a myth and a story people tell each other to make each other feel better.

There is a widespread attitude of mocking the faithful, as if they were superstitious or ignorant or both. God is the mental construct of the needy personality, a cozy security blanket for immature people. He is irrelevant to us big people in the real world. He can be safely ignored. He certainly has no claim upon our lives or behavior, no basis for authority, no validity as God.

People look at the story of creation in the Bible and compare it to creation myths of other cultures in which the gods copulate and give birth to a universe, and they put Genesis in the same category. It is a nice story that has nothing to do with reality, and we can safely ignore this ancient book. The Bible is irrelevant to our lives in this space age world of lasers and telescopes.

In our enlightened world, we now know the universe is billions of years old, and this quaint little story about the six days of creation couldn't possibly be true.

> *Since the creation story is obvious fable, we can dispense with the rest of the book as well.*

Since the creation story is obvious fable, we can dispense with the rest of the book as well. Biblical morality has been relegated to the Victorian era, and our ethics have been reduced to a utilitarian yardstick that allows almost any behavior as long as it benefits somebody or feels natural. There is no absolute right and wrong. There is no authority, no moral law, no responsibility to a real and powerful God. The natural result of this moral vacuum is anarchy, broken families and abandoned children, addicted and promiscuous teenagers. *The Lord of the Flies* has come true.

IS GOD REAL?

We have been teaching evolution in the schools for so long many people don't really believe that God created the world. They might believe there is a fluffy Cosmic Security Blanket Up There Somewhere, but they don't believe God is real and powerful here and now. Some people want to believe, but are unable to reconcile what they know about the world with the teachings of the church. Some pretend to believe, and go through the motions on Sunday morning, but their lack of faith is revealed in their actions Monday through Saturday. Many more have such a weak faith that their lives are marked by profound apathy. They won't stand up for what they believe in the face of opposition, or when their income or professional reputation is at stake.

If God really created this universe, then He has authority over every aspect of this universe. If God really created this world, His sovereignty is absolute. Even if He were the most hateful, arrogant, spiteful God you can imagine, He is still God, and His authority is unquestionable. We, as creatures, are responsible to this Being who created us. We don't want to hear that. We want to be our own authority. If we can get rid of God in the physical realm, then we don't have to deal with Him in the realm of morality.

And so, modern science tries to take creation away from God. Evolution tries to explain the complexity of life without God. Molecular biology tries to explain the origins of life without God. Cosmology tries to explain the origin of the universe without God. They can't do it. They go to tremendous lengths and mental gymnastics to think their way around God. They would rather believe in ridiculously unlikely events, with odds of 1: 1x10 to the 44000th power, i.e. impossible, than admit to the existence of a Creator, a Creator they would then owe perfect obedience and submission to.

> *If we can get rid of God in the physical realm, then we don't have to deal with Him in the realm of morality.*

Science looked at the "Big Bang" and understood that such an explosive event had to have a cause. They looked at the condition of the universe before the explosion of light occurred, and saw a mass with all of the matter in this entire universe compressed into something the size of the period at the end of this sentence. Realizing how incredibly unstable such a thing would be, they sought an explanation for how it came to be. All the equations break down when they try to go back in time. Time itself disappears. Matter disintegrates. Energy dissipates. Science scratches its head and wonders where it all went? How can we explain this? The rest of us are on our knees before the Living God.

> *Science scratches its head and wonders where it all went? How can we explain this? The rest of us are on our knees before the Living God.*

Science can't imagine where primordial matter could possibly come from, so it makes up imaginary time and imaginary space to go with it. We can imagine other universes with different physical laws to make up for deficiencies in the known laws of physics. Proposals that would be laughed out of the college in any other discipline are tolerated in theoretical physics because the stakes are so high. If God is real, then we are in trouble. Let's not look too hard, we might find Him.

Graduated from Church
A Personal Note

I was raised in the church, and when I graduated from high school, I graduated from church, as many young people do. I knew about God, but I had no real relationship with God, and I couldn't believe that He could possibly want a relationship with me. God was "up there somewhere" and was totally unapproachable by the likes of me.

I didn't come to God in any real way in the church. I came to Him for the first time in a biochemistry class in college. Having studied chemistry and physics, I had an understanding of chemical bonds and the energy contained in them, and in biochemistry I witnessed the miracle of chemical bonds and energy bringing forth life. I saw the hand of God in *this* world touching real things and giving them life.

I saw Him in the development of plant and animal life in my ecology class, in comparative anatomy, in embryology, in physiology, and in genetics. I saw His powerful hand in the fossil record which I saw faithfully reproduced in human embryology. I was struck by His tenderness in the way He handled the life He had created out of inanimate dust, chemical bonds and orbital energies. I witnessed the vast intelligence of God, His precision and carefulness. His awesome power intrigued me and I wanted to draw nearer, but I had a problem with the Bible. All of natural history seemed to conflict with the story of creation in the Bible. I began to pray, but I wasn't sure "Who" I was praying to.

The sheer impossibility of a spontaneous Godless creation had always been obvious to me, but the Genesis story alienated me. It seemed like a hocus-pocus magic show, and as much as I wanted to, I couldn't believe it. I wanted to draw close to the God of the Bible, He seemed like a really good God, but this book read like a fairytale. I couldn't believe it just because I *wanted* to believe it. We all want our favorite fantasies to come true. I was looking for the TRUTH. Maybe the Buddhists are onto something. Maybe the Hindus have it figured out. I was searching.

Then I read Steven Hawking's *A Brief History of Time* and I saw Genesis with new eyes. The heavens—the spiritual world; the earth—the physical world; formless and void; darkness over the surface of the deep; let there be light; it was all there. The tremendous odds against such a singularity occurring spontaneously spoke life into my faith, and brought the Bible into the world of reality. *To deny Him is idiocy.* It takes far more faith to deny God than it does to accept Him.

"Let There Be Light," the command that resulted in the most massive explosion in history, the after shocks of which are still measurable in the cosmic background radiation field. The formation of a planet, water separated from denser elements at the core of the planet. This is the Guy who *did gravity!* The God of the Bible really did this. The poetic accuracy of Genesis astounded me. The eternal and infinite Creator of the universe really did reveal Himself to us, mere creatures, in a Sacred Writing which perfectly reflected the physical realities I was so familiar with.

I dove into the Bible with the same enthusiasm, wonder, and dedication I had applied to biology, science, and medicine. I couldn't get enough of it. His Holiness was constantly before me. I saw His beauty in everything He created, and in everything He said. I saw His vast and infinite intelligence, His vast and infinite beauty and rightness and truth. I still can't take my eyes off of Him, He is so beautiful.

Please don't be offended at the term *poetic accuracy.* Poetic accuracy is *more* than literal accuracy, not less. Poetic accuracy captures the cosmic meaning of the words, not just their literal translation. It captures the power and majesty of the words and images used. We don't appreciate poetry in our culture to our great detriment. Ancient people were not so uninformed. *"He spoke all these things to the crowd in parables; He did not say anything to them without using a parable"* [Matt 13:34]. That's not something new He came up with at the last minute. He had been speaking in parables and metaphors from the very beginning, living breathing parables; whole lives were lived as parables, with meanings far deeper than any of them realized as they were living them.

People got in trouble with Jesus when they took Him too literally. Three times in the Gospel of John people misunderstood what He was saying. Nicodemus [John 3] should have known better, he was trained in poetry. The lady at the well in John 4 caught on right away; she knew her poetry. But the crowd in John 6 never did understand what Jesus was talking about, so they left Him, "Many of his own disciples went back and walked with him no more." Even His twelve best buddies didn't understand Him, but they loved Him enough to stay with Him. When we misunderstand God's poetry, we leave Him in a spiritual way. We leave His mercy and become judgmental; we leave His love and become condemning.

> *The tremendous odds against such a*
> *singularity occurring spontaneously spoke*
> *life into my faith, and brought the Bible*
> *into the world of reality.*

"Let there be light." The command that resulted in the most monumental explosion in history, the creation of a universe, was the work of a Holy God, an awesome and powerful Being. He has inspired the Scriptures, a sacred writing that accurately describes the creation of this universe. And He has made a way for me, *even me,* to know Him, the One who said, "Let there be light." What an amazing God!

IN THE BEGINNING

Our national assumption that God is a fairytale and Biblical morality is a joke is based upon the teaching of a science and natural history curriculum that deliberately skews the facts in favor of an atheist interpretation of the origins of the universe and of life. Our kids learn in school that the universe just appeared, the natural result of the laws of physics, and that humans arose accidentally, independent of any Creator or Cause. The science teacher who dares to present Intelligent Design as a valid interpretation of the facts is shown the door. These same kids are then faced with a choice of whether they should obey an authority which restricts their right to pleasure, sex and parties. What is the basis for this infringement on their right to do whatever they want? Is it wrong to have indiscriminant sex and use drugs? Says who?

"In the beginning God created the heavens and the earth" [Gen 1:1 NIV]. Time was created by God. It is a thought of God spoken by Christ. This is a hard concept to visualize. From out of timeless eternity, God made a beginning. In the beginning, God created the heavens, the spiritual world of angels and spirits, things we cannot see. And He created the earth, the physical world, atoms and molecules, things we can see and touch and handle. And the physical world was formless and void, and darkness was over the surface of the deep.

Science by and large admits that the physical world had an origin in time; they just describe it in slightly different terms. All of the matter of this entire universe just appeared one day, about 14 billion years ago, in the form of something very small, even subatomic in size. It was of infinite temperature [energy], infinite density, even light could not escape its gravitational field. Formless and void and darkness was over the surface of the deep.

And then God said, *"LET THERE BE LIGHT"* and a massive explosion occurred as the mass expanded, space was created, and light escaped from the gravitational field with its release of the energy God had stored in that matter. Light was separated from darkness, and God saw that it was good. The beginning and the end of the first day.

Light was separated from darkness, and that was defined by God as the first day, a day having nothing to do with 24 hour rotational days, those didn't exist until day four, but a day defined by the separation of light from darkness, energy separated from matter, something only God can do. Time was created by God. Energy was created by God. Matter was created by God. All the laws of physics have their origin in God.

> *All the laws of physics*
> *have their origin in God.*

There are hints of the spiritual world in this physical world. Physicists have described the movements of subatomic particles that can only be explained by the existence of multiple dimensions of reality which we do not participate in or experience directly, but they are no less real. We cannot measure them, but they are undeniably real. The spirit world was created by God, but He is not confined to it. He transcends all that He has created, even the spiritual world.

> *The spiritual world and the moral laws,*
> *and the physical world and the laws of*
> *physics were spoken into existence on the*
> *same day, by the same God, and they carry*
> *the same power.*

God also separated the light from darkness in the spiritual world. Good was distinguished from evil, truth opposed to lies, right separated from wrong. The process is described in Isaiah 14:12–15 dramatized as the fall of Lucifer from heaven. These truths are understood by every person in every culture on this planet in the form of taboos and moral laws of decency. Every human society recognizes the value of truth, justice, fidelity, and respect for others.

Biblical morality is burned into our conscience, and however these universal laws may be distorted by human cultural mores, every one of us recognizes their power. Biblical morality was spoken into existence by God on the very first day of creation.

> *How you have fallen from heaven O morning star, son of the dawn! You have been cast down to earth you who once laid low the nations! You said in your heart "I will ascend to heaven; I will raise my throne above the stars of God; I will sit enthroned on the mount of assembly, on the utmost heights of the sacred mountain. I will ascend above the tops of the clouds; I will make myself like the most high." But you are brought down into the grave, to the depths of the pit.*
>
> Isaiah 14:12–15 NIV

The force of gravity, electromagnetic force, the weak and strong nuclear forces, they all have their origin in Him. All of the matter of this universe is held together by Him in the strong nuclear force, and it was created on the first day. The physical world and the physical laws were spoken into existence by God on day one. Truth and morality, right and wrong also have their origin in Him, The spiritual world and the moral laws, and the physical world and the laws of physics were spoken into existence on the same day, by the same God, and they carry the same power.

> *For by Him all things were created: things in heaven and on earth, visible and invisible, whether thrones or powers or rulers or authorities; all things were created by Him and for Him. He is before all things, and in Him all things hold together.*
>
> Col 1:17 NIV

THE APPEARANCE OF LIFE

The six days of creation, properly understood, establish the authority of God to rule our behavior, our sexuality, and our lives. They establish the authority of the Bible as a book of fact. Without the authority of truth, the Bible is a long list of do's and don'ts, a collection of lovely poems, and it can safely be ignored since there is no real power behind its claims. If the Bible accurately describes the creation of life, then its credibility is unimpeachable. So let's take a look.

The second epoch was qualitatively different from the one before. It was a new day. This day was defined by the separation of water from the atmosphere and from the earth. This planet was formed from of the dust of an exploded star. In the heat of that primordial star hydrogen and helium underwent nuclear reactions forming the higher elements. Dense elements were separated from lighter elements by gravity, a force created by God.

The hand of God is obvious in the formation of the planets. No two are exactly alike, even the moon has trace elements not present on the earth. The debris coalesced into a more mature star and a series of planets, one of which could support water on its surface in all three phases, solid, liquid, and vapor. The water was separated from the land, the denser elements at the core of the planet, and from the atmosphere, the gasses lighter than water, and it was the end of the second epoch.

The third epoch was the maturing of the planet and the creation of life. "Let the earth bring forth life." The first life forms to appear on this planet were subterranean bacteria, the fossils of which are 3.6 billion years old. These bacteria were found in deposits of rock beneath the surface of the planet. The earth brought forth life, just like God said.

> *The spontaneous accidental appearance of something as complex as life could not have formed in such a brief span of time.*

This planet was formed 4.5 billion years ago. Molecular biologists were stunned when those early bacteria fossils were found. It meant that life had appeared on this planet less than 1 billion years after it was formed. How could that be? It took at least 500 million years for the crust to cool enough to be solid. The spontaneous accidental appearance of something as complex as life could not have formed in such a brief span of time.

Again, science did mental backflips trying to explain life without God. Proteins are made using nucleic acids, and nucleic acids are formed using proteins, and both had to be protected by a cell wall to allow them to exist long enough to replicate. Scientists proposed catalysts of various natures, none of which stood up under the evidence. Proteins and nucleic acids are so fragile chemically, they would immediately denature if exposed to the harsh conditions on earth at that time.

So large numbers of otherwise intelligent people believed that life occurred on this planet spontaneously despite overwhelming evidence to the contrary. When the obvious impossibility of this was exposed, it became a sound scientific hypothesis that perhaps life formed on some other planet and got here on asteroids, tunneled down many hundreds of yards, and became established deep in the ground in a uniform fashion all over the planet. What an amazing asteroid!

The short answer is that for life to have formed spontaneously, survived to replicate, and be organized enough to metabolize [the scientific definition of life] *purely by random chemical processes* on inert materials would have required at least 100,000,000,000,000,000,000,000,000,000,000,000,000 . . . add a billion more zeros . . . years. It statistically could not have happened in the 14 billion years since the big bang, before which there was neither organized matter nor time.

Scientists have recently announced that they are on the verge of creating life in a laboratory, a living cell made out of inanimate chemicals. It's easy, just shake up some oil and water and put in amino acids, enzymes, and DNA, and voila, life! Wait a minute. Where do you plan to get the amino acids, or for that matter, the oil and water? Let's really push the envelope and assume you can make your own nitrogen, oxygen, and carbon, no small feat I might add. Can you make your own enzymes? Can you make your own DNA? Maybe if you look long enough at the picture on the box, you might be able to assemble the pieces, but don't give yourself credit for painting the masterpiece this jigsaw puzzle is a picture of. That's not creation, that's plagiarism.

> *I am continually amazed at the great humility of God.*

I am continually amazed at the great humility of God. DNA, enzymes and proteins didn't 'just happen.' They are the product of an intelligent power. Natural and physical forces can not and did not create this incredibly complex thing called a living cell. His fingerprints are all over His creation, but He does not sign the picture. He does not force us to acknowledge Him. He stays behind the scenes and makes it all look so 'natural' that many do not believe in Him at all. Who owns the copyright for the vast array you see in front of you? Who owns the patent, the intellectual property rights, to the quark, the atom, the molecule, the protein, the DNA, the brain cell, and the organism?

I know the naturalists are sneering at me, saying the laws of nature do not need a "God" to explain anything. Okay guys, I have an assignment for you. Explain to me the nature of the strong nuclear force, the force holding positive and neutral charges together in the nucleus of an atom so tightly that to break that force results in a nuclear explosion. Explain to me the origin of life out of inanimate chemicals, the sudden appearance of living cells complete with metabolism, replication, and complex interacting chemical systems. Explain to me the accidental appearance of an intelligent genetic code found even in the most primitive mitochondria. While you are busy with that, I will be worshipping God.

And so the earth brought forth life. Metabolism required a source of energy, there was nothing to 'eat' yet, so life relied on the radiant energy from the sun, which is the definition of a plant, vegetation. This marked the end of another epoch, the appearance of life.

THE MEASUREMENT OF TIME

Day four is where everybody gets confused. This is the first time the sun and moon and stars are seen, and they are to be to be markers of days, seasons, and years. Plant life gives off oxygen as a metabolic by-product. Oxygen forms ozone, and both are essential to our atmosphere. The thick haze of the pre-oxygenated air would have precluded the sun, moon, and stars from being visible from the earth until the epoch after the formation of metabolically active life.

The sun is also a product of the explosion of the primordial star, and it went through several stages in the process of becoming the well organized star it is today. The hand of God, cloaked in gravity, was forming the sun as we know it at the same time He was forming the planets. It matured on day four. Unless we claim God speaks nonsense, we have to acknowledge that the sun existed *in some form* on day three, because vegetation was created on day three and vegetation requires radiant energy from the sun for metabolism. That is the definition of vegetation.

> *Solar days of 24 hours did not exist until day four of creation.*

"Let the greater and the lesser lights be a sign to mark the seasons, days and years." The wording in Genesis strongly implies, indeed clearly states, that days measured by the rotation of the earth in relation to the sun are not what God had in mind when He used the term 'day' in the chronology of creation. Solar days of 24 hours did not exist until day four of creation. In many places in the Bible, a day can mean an epoch, an era, a long expanse of time that is qualitatively different from some other long expanse of time. In this day . . . In that day . . .

Now the Six Day camp is sneering at me, insisting that a day can only mean 24 hour spans of time as defined by the rotation of the earth with respect to the sun, and no other possible interpretation of that word is allowable. God defined His days long before there *was* an earth to rotate around the sun. We're arguing semantics about a language neither one of us speaks, and using it as a stick with which we beat people over the heads. God uses symbols and metaphors throughout the Scripture beginning on page one. He uses them to explain extremely complicated and abstract truths, and He chooses His symbols very carefully. A measurement of time is used as a symbol for a Measurement of Time.

Did God really create this universe? You bet He did. He created physics and mathematics. He created chemistry and biology. He created natural history, the dinosaurs, and the geological strata. He created the fossil record, the genetic code, the dust of the earth from which He formed human beings. There is nothing that was made that He did not create.

EVOLUTION

What about the evolution thing? Did we just happen by accident, as some scientists would have us believe? Are we just fancy animals with no higher meaning, no spiritual significance? The fifth day, the next major epoch, is the development of animal life, again an era qualitatively different from the epoch preceding it. Animal life arose in the seas; let the water teem with living creatures. Birds were next, based on a reptile skeleton, and the Age of the Reptiles is well documented in the fossil record.

Many people of faith are frightened by the word 'fossil.' It implies evolution, which is a dirty word in Christian circles. Darwinian evolution is indeed Godless. It states that life evolved from simple to complex simply by a principle called survival of the fittest. The same thought process that insists the universe formed itself and life happened accidentally, also attributes the development of higher animals, intelligence and reason to random forces of nature on a brutal planet that kills off its weak and its young.

> *The fossil record, examined in an*
> *open minded way,*
> *shows clearly the hand of God.*

The fossil record, examined in an open minded way, shows clearly the hand of God molding and shaping the life He has created, with brain cases and jaw bones, vocal apparatuses and appendages, senses and mental abilities. It is awesome to witness in the fossil record the tenderness with which He formed the bodies of His creatures. Gently molding with each new species a stronger frame, a keener eye, a bigger brain. God formed creatures that moved along the ground, and reproduced *each according to its own kind.*

If natural selection were the only force shaping life, there would be no such thing as genetically discrete species. Life would meander around aimlessly, clusters of organisms distantly related, a mishmash of life forms with features convenient and specific to the habitat, and genetically identifiable species would not exist. Races of humans would have become so different they would not be able to interbreed. Isn't 36,000 years long enough for that to have happened if it were going to happen? Dogs can still interbreed after even more intense and longer natural selection pressures to speciation. Isolated variants such as the wolf can be generated by natural selection, but natural selection cannot account for the formation of entirely new genetically discrete species. It has never been observed, not even in the microbial world where it should be easy to identify. Natural selection readily accounts for variety within species [micro-evolution], but does not account for the development of new species [macro-evolution]. The genetic information to produce a new *kind* of animal cannot be generated by natural selection. Evolution is a tenet of faith. It is not science.

The fossil record is informative as to the origin of new species. Darwinian evolution requires a new species to be a mutant of an old species, and if that were true, the fossil record should record huge numbers of intermediate forms between species. This has never been observed. New species arise abruptly in time with no intermediary forms. The fossil record of the Cambrian explosion of species is the best evidence we have for the creative power of God.

All animals have the same basic metabolism with respect to energy, and the same basic framework with respect to genetics. Our blood, hearts, kidneys, intestines, and nerves are all remarkably similar. We can study rat brains and understand how our own brains work. He formed us from the dust of the earth, the living, metabolizing, replicating dust of the earth. The earth brought forth life, and we were formed from the dust of the earth.

We don't know exactly how God made each new form and species. He may have used genetic material from older species to do it, since the genetic material is so similar. After all, He does own the patent for DNA. The new car is built on the old model's chassis. *But the old car did not turn itself into a new car.* Each one was individually designed by an incredibly intelligent Being with a great sense of humor and a knack for the original. No mindless force, not this Guy; He's a real Character.

THE SIXTH DAY

The appearance of human beings marks the sixth and final epoch. Male and female He created us. An impersonal cosmic force cannot create a person. Only a Person can create a person. God is a Person with character, emotions, and will, and He made us to be persons with character, emotions, and will. He blessed us and gave us dominion over the animals. He breathed into us an eternal spirit. We are not just animals; we have an eternal spirit given to us by God. When He gave us dominion over the animals, He gave us dominion over the animal natures within us. We have dominion over our animal drives and desires, appetites and impulses. Failure to exercise that dominion is the source of many of our sins. The lament of Romans 7 is about our struggle to subdue the animal [flesh] within us.

> *He blessed us and gave us dominion*
> *over the animals.*

Our reptilian nature, [the limbic system of the brain] acts like a lizard. It lashes out and snaps at any one interfering with its will. Anger, rage, resentment and bitterness come from our reptilian nature housed in the amygdala. Our urges, drives, cravings and impulses are part of the 'instinctual brain' which lies anatomically in the ventral tegmental area in the depths of the midbrain.

Our mammalian nature [also in the midbrain] acts like a mother bear, willing to fight to the death for its cub, or a tiger killing to defend its territory. Our ability and urge to nurture and protect our children, groom and clean ourselves, and control our environment is anatomically housed in the habenula, parts of the amygdala, and striatum, in the midbrain. We are also given a fasciculus retroflexus, mesocorticolimbic structures, and median forebrain bundle, so we can control and subdue the animal impulses within us.

Our sex drive is a powerful reminder that we have an animal living inside us. We routinely use our fasciculus retroflexus to control our sex drive and channel it in socially acceptable ways. Those of us who are single and sexually continent learn to sublimate that energy and make tremendous contributions to the arts and sciences.

God gave us these structures, dominion over the animal natures within us, as our heritage as human beings, created in His image. We are not just animals. We have eternal spirits within us, and we are equipped with the necessary neurons to house such a spirit. In our unfallen state, we had effortless natural control over the animal within, our temper, our sex drive, and our appetites. In our unfallen state, we could take one grain of a poppy flower and use it to treat the pain of an impacted wisdom tooth. We did not eat the whole plant, smoke it, or inject it. We could use the herbs and flowers God gave us for their legitimate purpose and not worship them. We tended His Garden and we worshipped Him.

> *We are like God, created in His image,
> when we are fully and truly human.*

When tracts in the brain, like fasciculus are used a lot, they hypertrophy and become stronger, grow richer connections, and willpower becomes habitual and effortless. We are faithful, righteous, patient, kind, and compassionate, we are like God, created in His image, when we are fully and truly human. When we fail to subdue the animal within, fail to be truly human, our brain pathways adjust to the pattern of activity required of them, and lust becomes a way of life. We live in our limbic systems, and our desires and impulses control us. Greed controls our daily activities. We love and adore ourselves, do what pleases us; we make ourselves to be our own god. That's what the fall was all about. You shall be as gods, deciding for yourselves what is good and what is evil.

We are much more than just the product of our neurons. We are spiritual beings, and we are responsible for the condition of our neurons. We damage the brain cells He entrusted to us when we abuse drugs. We destroy the priceless treasure He has made, this bit of star dust that has the capacity to appreciate the eternal God, an animal with the ability to enjoy its animal functions without being a slave to them. We were created to be human and holy. And He said it was very good.

WORSHIP

Humans were created by God to worship Him, to love and be loved by Him. By our nature we desire, love and adore, organize our lives around something larger than ourselves. It is hardwired into our brains. If we can't worship God, we'll find something else to worship. Every person on this planet worships something. The thing you long for, the thing you meditate on, the thing you sacrifice your time, energy, and resources for, the thing you *obey* is the thing you have chosen to be your god.

If your whole life revolves around getting high, all you can think about is how to get more ice, make more ice, steal more ice, con more ice—you are worshipping ice. The addict devotes his whole life to the interests of his god. He sacrifices his money, his career, his time, and his energy to get more methamphetamine. He sacrifices his family, his children, all of his important relationships. All of them are far less important than his next high. He gives everything he has and everything he is, even his personality, on the altar of methamphetamine. That is high worship. That kind of desire and dedication belong to the God who spoke this universe into existence. What would this world look like if we worshipped God the way most addicts worship ice? It would be a different world, would it not?

PHYSICAL AND MORAL LAWS

The physical laws and the moral laws have their origin in the same Person, and carry the same validity and power. If we violate the laws of gravity we fall flat on our face, and if we violate the laws of morality we destroy our lives, the lives of the people around us, and especially our children's lives. When we worship other gods, serve and obey them, we twist ourselves and everyone around us.

Society bears the scars of this influence in broken families, drug abuse, and loss of discipline in the schools and homes; the result of anarchy. If there is no God, there is no absolute, no authority. I can make up my own rules, be my own god, pursue pleasure and if it feels good do it. There is no reason to suppress my impulses for the sake of morality. Hedonism is the official religion of our day.

> *We have taken the Book that accurately describes the origin of this universe, and relegated it to the fairytale department because we don't like what it says about our urges and desires.*

Biblical morality is especially despised. It makes demands upon us in the name of God, and we all know in our hearts that those demands are right and proper. We also know that we do not *want* to suppress our animal lusts and desires. We would much rather believe there is no God, and so we have the right to indulge any desire we feel coming from within us. After all, those desires are natural and authentic to us. We have taken the Book that accurately describes the origin of this universe, and relegated it to the fairytale department because we don't like what it says about our urges and desires. We go to incredible lengths to get rid of God, sacrificing even our intellectual integrity, because we prefer to be our own gods.

We violate the laws of morality with no more compunction than violating the laws of the Girl Scout's manual. We don't feel like we are violating any real Person, only a set of inconvenient rules which interfere with our will. If we considered the laws of morality to reflect the will of a Holy God, we would not flaunt them so readily. If we respected and revered that Holy God, appreciated Him for the Person He is, we would absolutely love those laws. They are the blueprint for having an intimate relationship with Him.

The laws of God reflect His character; truth, justice, fidelity, courage, humility, compassion, generosity, wisdom, and respect for life. When you take an honest look at the glory and majesty of God, the timeless eternal Being who is the source of all other being, His vast intelligence, His awesome power, the only intelligent response to that is worship. When you understand yourself as His creature, the personality He has made, you will understand why you are not satisfied and fulfilled apart from Him.

Hear O Israel: the Lord our God, the Lord is One. Love the Lord your God with all your heart and with all your soul and with all your strength. These commandments that I give to you today are to be upon your hearts. (Deut 6:4 NIV)

.10.

CULTURAL RISK FACTORS - FAMILY IDOLS

SPIRITUAL LIFE

Drugs and alcohol are not the only idols that destroy our families and lead to drug abuse in our youth. When the focus of our attention is on something other than God, we distort our priorities and fail to meet the needs of our children. Remember, God created children and he knows how much of our time, attention and emotional energy they need. When we invest that time, attention and energy in the objects of our desire instead of our children, we deprive our children of the love and discipline they need. When we desire status, money and sexual pleasure more than truth, justice and faithfulness—that is, more than God—we deprive our children of the nurture and security they need. We drive them into the arms of drug dealers because we fail to provide them with a real home. Again, the key to understanding this concept comes from Genesis.

The second chapter of Genesis reads completely different from the first. It's like He's talking about another planet. In this story, before anything other living thing was made, God created man and breathed life into him, and then set him in a garden He had already planted. It's like the picture was in black in white and it all came into full color when humans were introduced. The garden *had been planted,* but everything came to life when a spiritual being was there to appreciate it. "The Lord *had formed* out of the dust of the earth all the beasts of the field and all the birds of the air." Before, it had been physically alive, but had no spiritual meaning. Now it was truly alive.

"God formed the man from the dust of the earth and breathed into his nostrils the breath of life, and man became a living being" [Gen 2:7 NIV]. When God breathed a spirit into His creature, it was *His Spirit* that He imparted. Man was created to be filled with the Holy Spirit of God, to be both holy and

human, in constant communion with God, expressing His character in this physical world, and enjoying the fruit of His Spirit: love, joy, peace, patience, kindness, goodness, faithfulness, gentleness and *self-control* [Gal 5:22].

> *Man was created to be filled with the Holy Spirit of God, to be both holy and human.*

It was spiritual life, the Breath of God, the indwelling of the Holy Spirit, which was introduced into the world when man was created. This is the kind of life Genesis 2 is about, and this is the kind of life that ended when we exalted our own wills above the will of God and died spiritually to our relationship with God. "In the day that you eat of it, *you will surely die.*" But Adam lived for many years and had children after he disobeyed. He was still physically alive, but physical life and death, the extinction of whole species had existed for centuries before the fall. We're not talking about mere physical death. Adam was *spiritually* dead the day he rebelled.

No longer would we have unbroken fellowship with our Creator. No longer would His Holy Spirit live within us. No longer would His law be written on our heart, and our will be aligned with His. No longer would we have effortless control over our impulses and desires. The subjugation of our animal nature would not come naturally and spontaneously to us, we would have to struggle to be honest, concentrate on being faithful, and consciously evict selfish thoughts. We would turn the soil and fight the weeds from now on.

THE FIRST MARRIAGE

When no suitable spiritual being could be found to be a companion for Adam, God put him to sleep and took from his body the material to make woman. He had already created them male and female. He now took spiritual life from the man and used it to make spiritual life in the woman. There's a lesson here. Men are supposed to be providing spiritual life to the women in their lives, praying for them and helping them find spiritual nourishment. Marriage was inaugurated by God between man and woman to make the two one. When we divorce or decide to just 'shack up,' we break the flow of spiritual life that is supposed to flow from man to woman. Animals copulate. Humans marry. It is a spiritual event with eternal meaning.

The casual attitude we have toward marriage in this nation is extremely destructive. Even a 'good marriage' usually contains virtually no spiritual intimacy. If we can get along without insulting one another, we consider that a healthy marriage. God had something far more powerful in mind for us. When

we worship and pray together privately and honestly, real heartfelt and spontaneous prayer, we see into one another's hearts and we form bonds of cement, a
love which sees deeply, loves deeply, and would die for the other person. And
we do die, every day. We die to our desire for kinky sex. We die to our desire
for a big beautiful house. We die to our expectations of perfection in each
other. We die to those things because our love is so great.

> *Animals copulate. Humans marry. It is a*
> *spiritual event with eternal meaning.*

We have raised a generation of people who don't know how to form
deep relationships like that. They were raised in daycare centers and were
unable to bond with their daily caregiver. Their role models, their parents,
changed relationships like they were changing cars, trading them in on a new
model every few years. The magazines they read have headlines like "Jennifer Dumps Her Lover" and "Trista and Ryan Say Goodbye". Temporary
and casual relationships are glorified in the media, serial sex partners are the
norm on television. Our kids can't form meaningful committed relationships
because they have never seen or experienced a real committed relationship.
They wouldn't recognize one if they saw it.

"I'll love you forever." is translated, "I'll love you until something
better comes along, or at least until the end of the week." Or, "I'll love you
until I get bored and decide to do something else." Or, "I'll love you as long as
you are fun to have around, but don't go getting depressed or angry or tired or
boring." Or, "I'll love you as long as the sex holds out, but when you hit meno-
pause, I'm out of here." There is no such thing as, "I'll love you forever."

The broken family and loss of security precipitates a lot of drug addiction and alcoholism, in the children and in the adults involved. The parents are
ashamed, hurt and angry; the children are abandoned by one or both parents.
The child thinks, "Daddy didn't leave Mommy. Daddy left me. I have been
rejected; I have to go to daycare now. I wasn't good enough. That's why Daddy
left." If the child can't find acceptance and belonging at home, perhaps his
drug buddies can give him a place to feel welcome and valued.

BAAL WORSHIP

Since we won't worship God, we'll have to find something else to
worship. Baal was everybody's favorite idol in Old Testament times, and its
popularity has not waned over the centuries. Baal was the fertility god of the
ancient Canaanites, and was worshipped with ritual sex using temple prosti-

tutes, images and symbols of breasts and sex organs, not unlike the contents of contemporary porno magazines.

Baal worship is alive and well in 21st century America. You can't turn on a TV or open a magazine without seeing a shrine to Baal, scantily clad women hawking beer, erotic scenes on television movies, and sexual innuendo on prime time sit-coms. Adulterous sex is so much a part of our culture that the school age child still living with both parents is the exception rather than the rule. The disintegration of the family is the direct result of this nation's preoccupation with sexual pleasure. If your whole focus in life is the pleasure of sexual stimulation, in fantasy or in fact, if you long for the chance to get on the internet and see some really kinky stuff, things your wife would never consider doing, you are worshipping Baal.

We enjoy the titillation of sex scenes in commercials, sit-coms, and soap operas. Indiscriminant and casual sex is the dominant theme of prime time TV, movies, and popular music. Women's magazines have "Ten Secrets for Great Sex" and "How to Drive Your Man Wild in Bed." The covers of fashion magazines feature lots of cleavage and alluring poses. The soft porn that passes for normal media drives a national preoccupation with sex.

> *The soft porn that passes for normal media drives a national preoccupation with sex.*

Then there's the hard porn industry, which obviously enjoys a thriving business. Internet porno saves men the embarrassment of checking out at the register with pornographic literature. Pornography produces an appetite for more stimulation much like methamphetamine does. The biochemistry of sexual addiction is much the same as with crystal. A frequently used neural pathway hypertrophies and becomes 'habitual.' It takes more and more stimulation to get the same arousal. Normal sex with his wife is boring after an evening spent with 'Jennifer' on the internet. His wife is a perfectly good woman, anybody else would be glad to have her, but he's not satisfied with her.

Soap operas and romance novels are verbal pornography, and have the same effect on women as the visual pornography the men prefer. The woman immersed in soap opera porn is less than impressed with her boring old husband who always does the same old things and never jets her off to Acapulco like they do on TV. He's a perfectly good man, anybody else would be glad to have him, but she's not satisfied with him. She becomes just as disappointed with normal life as her husband is while he's getting his fix on the internet.

Adultery happens in the mind a long time before it happens in the flesh. When you feed your mind a steady diet of pornography, you encourage fantasy which turns into spoken words, and shortly after that, into actions and relationships which destroy an otherwise happy marriage. Your beautiful and loving wife isn't good enough anymore. She doesn't get you off like the other woman does. It had nothing to do with the character of either of the women. It all happened in your mind.

From the Gynecologist in Me
[and having been married for 20 years]

Every day I see women in my office complaining of a loss of sex drive that is threatening their marriage. Some of them are profoundly depressed or have serious gynecologic problems and need treatment, but most of them are badly overworked soccer moms trying to do too much in a day, and they run out of gas long before bedtime.

Your sex drive is the canary in the coal mine. When it dies, you can be sure there are toxic fumes around. You are burning the candle at both ends, stressing yourself far too much, and the next symptom will likely be some kind of nervous breakdown, overwhelming illness, or cardiovascular event. It's not just about sex. It's about life. What you are doing is sacrificing your sexuality to get something else. Sometimes you have to set priorities. When you have too many things on your list, you end up crossing off the stuff at the end of the list. Is that really what you want to cross off your list?

There is a prevailing assumption that we are unable to have sex unless we *feel like it*. The idea of being a servant lover to our husband has never even crossed our minds. We do his laundry when we don't feel like it; we cook his meals when we don't feel like it. We do those things because we love him and we know he needs them. It is not impossible to give ourselves sexually to our husbands, even when we don't feel like it. The feeling comes later. Grandma learned that 100 years ago, but our generation seems to think there is something wrong with giving ourselves to our husbands. There should be something in it for us. Well, there is. It's a relationship.

It is okay to let your husband initiate activity, and it is his responsibility to help you get in the mood. Let him seduce you. A well placed kiss while you are drying the dishes helps a lot. He can give the kids their baths and clean up the kitchen while you take a long soak in the tub, and stuff like that makes a huge difference. But if you make him wait until *you* are in the mood, he will be waiting for a long time. He will never demand it. If he did, it wouldn't be love. He wants you to give it to him. Then it's love.

FAMILY DISINTEGRATION

In a world from which God has been evicted, and pleasure is the commanding principle, adultery and fornication are so accepted as to be considered normal. The concept of 'moral and immoral' sex has been reduced to 'safe and unsafe' sex. Our youth are mocked and derided if they maintain virginity until marriage. Marriage is a temporary expedient to convenient sex, and is dispensed with when the sexual experience is less that expected, or less than what is seen in the movies. When the marriage crumbles under the pressure of unrealistic sexual demands or infidelity, the family collapses. Children are deprived of a safe place to grow up. There is no understanding of unconditional acceptance so essential to healthy psychological development and secure self image. Mom and Dad don't love each other anymore.

> *Adultery does not even have to be consummated to cause family dysfunction.*

Adultery does not even have to be consummated to cause family dysfunction. If one parent has a crush on someone else, even if it is just in their fantasies, all of the sudden their spouse loses appeal. Nothing he or she does is good enough. Little faults previously overlooked for the sake of love are now glaringly obvious, and since no one is absolutely perfect, the marriage is doomed. Arguments and fights are daily occurrences, and confidence in the love of the other spouse dissolves in a sea of harsh words. There is no sharing of common interests, no emotional intimacy, not even common courtesy. Things are said in the home that would never be said in public; hateful, spiteful, condemning words, jumping to conclusions, maligning the spouse's intentions, unreasonable expectations and deliberate hurtful remarks.

This type of emotional abuse, even when directed at the spouse, is deeply harmful to the child. The child identifies with and often tries to protect and defend the offended parent. Insults directed toward the parent are felt by the child. When a child's mother is demoralized, the child is also demoralized. Physical abuse of a mother is especially harmful to a child. Now the threat is to the immediate survival of the mother, and the child feels terror and horror as his mother is brutalized. He feels helpless to defend her and he often feels responsible for her plight, "If I had been a better child, this might not be happening."

> *A child's emotional needs for attention,*
> *affirmation, acceptance, and safety cannot*
> *be met in an abusive home.*

A child's emotional needs for attention, affirmation, acceptance, and safety cannot be met in an abusive home. An abused mother cannot affirm her child if she is constantly insulted and humiliated by her husband. The constant conflict and uproar wears on the child, makes him feel tired and depressed, helpless and powerless. He can't concentrate and he can't relax. It is often a relief when the marriage finally ends.

Young children are extremely egocentric. They think everything happening around them is directly related to them personally. If Dad leaves Mom, the child feels, "Dad left me." The child feels abandoned. The world is not safe. Abandonment is terror. Horror. Death. Abandonment means rejection, and rejection by a parent is devastating to the personality of the child. The child internalizes the message, "I am not good enough. My Daddy doesn't really love me." The child doesn't know it was really his mother who had the affair and ended the marriage. All he knows is, "Daddy's gone, he doesn't love me."

Dad marries his girlfriend, and the first thing the new couple wants to do is legitimize their relationship by having a child. They want that tubal ligation reversed post haste, sometimes even before the nuptials have been completed. Dad has a new wife and a new child, and there is no room for the old child who looks like the old wife. The rejection is now complete.

> *"Here kid, try some of this. It will make*
> *you feel better. You don't have to be lonely.*
> *Hang around with us."*

Daddy disappears and Momma disappears too. She has to go to work. No one is there when he gets home from school. There is no one to talk to; no one to care about his little problems. He tries to talk to Mom when she gets home from work, but she is unloading groceries and fixing dinner and paying the bills and there is no time for him. Where is this kid going to go for emotional support and guidance? To his seventeen-year-old drug pusher friend's house. "Here kid, try some of this. It will make you feel better. You don't have to be lonely. Hang around with us."

And it 'works.' Ice makes him feel better. He has to sneak around in order to do it, but that's easy now. Nobody is looking for him after school, so he has a lot of privacy. Nobody notices a subtle change in his attitude, a drop in his grades, or his new set of friends. His friends are all latch key kids too, so they have their choice of homes to hang out at. The one with the least supervision, fewest nosy siblings, and best supply of beer will be their new home.

Divorce multiplies a discipline problem by a hundred times. A single mother cannot enforce the rules like a couple can. She has no back up when her teenager rebels [not *if* he rebels, but *when* he rebels]. Her teenager learns right away what he can and can not get by with. Children raised in single parent homes are more than twice as likely to abuse drugs or alcohol as kids raised in intact homes, even abusive intact homes. A single parent cannot supervise a child and also work full time, keep the groceries bought, the car tuned up, the bills paid, the lawn mowed, the kitchen cleaned, the laundry done, and the meals fixed. It can't be done. The child ends up fending for himself. Nobody at home disciplines him, and he doesn't know how to discipline himself yet, so he runs wild. His overwhelmed mother just throws up her hands.

A Dad who shows up every other weekend is worse than no Dad at all. Weekend Dads are not interested in disciplining their children. They want to spend 'quality time' being the kid's friend, and a lecture about doing homework would mess up a nice weekend. The rules are different at Dad's house, and the teenager is going to prefer his lax rules to the regimented rules at Mom's house. She has to keep order even when she's not there, so the rules are pretty strict at Mom's house.

Age appropriate discipline is essential, and must be consistent between households. It's not easy, but you will have to communicate with your ex-spouse. Kids are slippery and they know there are hard feelings between you and your "ex." They play one against the other and accuse one parent of abuse if he or she is stricter than the other.

MOLECH

Another favorite family idol is money, professional success, the stock portfolio, the boat, the lake house, more stuff. We are up to our eyeballs in debt trying to buy all these things. Whenever the focus of our time, attention and energy is on money, prestige, or professional success, we are worshipping Molech. In Old Testament times, Molech was the god of conquest and the spoils of war. When properly appeased, Molech would provide its worshipper with gold and silver, land and crops, financial success. Molech was worshipped by passing the first born child through the fire in a sacred ritual of human sacrifice. That's how much value ancient people placed upon riches and prosperity.

The mere possession of money does not make it an idol. It is the constant preoccupation with money, the unspoken goal of obtaining as much of it as possible that makes it an idol. The *desire* for money is idolatrous, not necessarily the possession of money. Poor families can worship money just like wealthy families can. If all you can think about is making the big killing, the fast deal or winning the lottery, you are worshipping money.

If your mind is always centered on your investments, your income, your next big deal, if you are distracted by the stock market and don't even notice your kids talking to you, you are passing your children through the fire to Molech. If you are working lots of overtime, making long business trips, bringing work home, and haven't even seen your kids in a week or more, you are passing your children through the fire to Molech. Where is your son going to go for encouragement and conversation? To his seventeen-year-old drug pusher friend's house. That's where.

> *If you haven't even seen your kids in a week or more, you are "passing your children through the fire to Molech."*

It reaches the level of high worship when we sacrifice other things to the pursuit of money. When we sacrifice our integrity and engage in shady business deals, charge exorbitant prices for our goods, or outright steal or embezzle funds; that is high worship. When we sacrifice dinner with the family, time in the backyard, conversation with our spouse or children for the sake of the big business deal or the overtime hours *above what is necessary to feed and house our family* that is high worship.

When you put your child in daycare so you can feed and shelter the family in a home with hot and cold running water, even the smallest child realizes this is right and necessary. He knows that by going to daycare at six o'clock in the morning every day he is making a contribution to the family. He is two years old and he is going to 'wook.' When you send your children to the babysitter at six weeks of age so you can have power, prestige, possessions, and wealth, that is high worship. Your child knows those things are more valuable to you than he is. The only one who knows whether your use of daycare is appropriate or not is you, and you know it in your conscience.

Sure, it's a sacrifice to give up professional advancement and pension benefits to be a full time parent. My husband, an engineer, has done it since the oldest was a baby. You get accused of 'wasting your education' on your children. A college educated stay at home parent is not wasting his education. He is using his education for its highest purpose, training his children, teaching them how to think, what's really important, and what their value is in this world. A child measures her value by the time and attention you give to her, talking to her, listening to her, being with her, preferring her company to that of the TV set, the newspaper, the stock market, and the computer. She wants to know she is more important to you than any of those things.

> *Why do I call money, "Molech"? Because that is what we, as a society, pass our children through the fire to.*

Why do I call money, "Molech"? Because that is what we, as a society, pass our children through the fire to. It is considered a respectable thing to worship money. People think there must be something wrong with you if you don't. You must not be very ambitious. You're not dedicated to the company. You're not a team player if you don't do the overtime, the travel, the weekend work and the twelve hour days. The needs of our children have to be more important than the needs of our careers. Our kids know how important they are to us. They know what really matters to us. They know it by the way we spend our time.

Employers make these demands on workers because they feel they will not be competitive in the marketplace if they can't get sixty hours of work per week out of each employee. After all, the law firm across the street can get that kind of productivity out of its work force, and we have to be able to compete. We are very short sighted when we value short term profit so highly we abandon our children in order to get it. Who do we think is going to fund our social security checks when all of our children are in jail for drug abuse? The children of our workers are very important to us, and we have to make some sacrifices to make sure our employees are able to raise them right.

As a society, we have decided our children are less important than our incomes, our productivity, our egos, and our sexual gratification. Are we really surprised when they forsake our 'morality' and get drunk at thirteen, get involved in drugs at fourteen, get pregnant at fifteen, and drop out of school at sixteen? What exactly did we expect?

Abortion

Of course the ultimate in passing your children through the fire is abortion. The relevant idol is usually money, [we can't afford a baby right now] but may include such deities as comfort and convenience, or personal and family reputation. Wedding pictures and even dress size are more important than the life of a child in our society. At the end of the day, however it is Baal who is most honored by abortion. Illicit sex is stripped of the usual natural consequences, and therefore enjoyed with impunity by teens and adults of all ages.

The girls know their mothers will not force them to carry the pregnancy; after all she never forced them to clean up their room, obey a curfew, or do anything else they didn't want to do. The idea of forcing a girl to face the consequences of her behavior never crosses anybody's mind, and the fact that another child is being destroyed doesn't matter.

I have yet to meet a woman who has had an abortion and feels absolutely no shame over it. Every woman knows in her heart that this is wrong. The mantra that we are saving these girls a heart-ache by encouraging them to abort is the lie of the century. Their heart-ache is magnified by orders of magnitude. They not only have the shame of an illicit sexual encounter, and the grief of losing a child, but in addition, the horror of knowing that they were responsible for the death of their child.

Sometimes the father of the child is most responsible for the abortion. The threats and coercion by abusive men who refuse to take responsibility for their children force many women to end otherwise wanted pregnancies. These women are tortured by the loss of their child; some of them are still grieving thirty years later. Two people die at every abortion. I bring these women to the cross of Jesus Christ every time I find one. No one else has the power to heal their guilt and shame.

POWER

A related idol is the lust for power, which may or may not involve money. The consuming desire to control other people, by direct order or simply by manipulation, is also a form of idolatry. It is expressed in the work place with unspoken expectations, power plays and passive aggressive behavior. You will get your way and exert your influence whether overtly by demand, or if you lack the authority to do that, you do it covertly by delaying, avoiding, sabotaging the thing you are supposed to do.

The civic club wants to plant flowers in the highway median and you think it's a waste of time and money. No one else agrees with you and they vote to do it, but you are the treasurer. You exert your power and control by forgetting to pay for the flowers, avoiding the issue until it is too late to plant flowers. That was a power play.

When you do that in your family, the results are very destructive. The wife would like to go to Disneyland with the kids for a family vacation and you don't want to go. Rather than express yourself directly, you proceed to sabotage the trip. You come up with an unexpected illness or an emergency at work. If that doesn't work, you mess up the reservations and can't get a room.

> *You couldn't enjoy it because it wasn't your idea.*

When you finally get there, you make everyone else miserable by your sullen attitude. You're too tired to do any of the activities and spend the whole trip in the motel room. You're not happy with the food, not happy with the long lines, the attractions aren't that much fun; this was a waste of time. You made it a waste of time because you weren't in control and you couldn't humble yourself enough to give control to someone else. You couldn't enjoy it because it wasn't your idea.

In everyday life, that kind of arrogance and control is expressed by working long hours to avoid the hassles of child care in the evening. Your husband didn't do the flower beds right, so you withdraw into a corner and won't interact with him, the silent treatment. You don't like all those silly Christmas decorations, so you are not going to help your wife put them up. You are too busy with important things.

You change the rules so nobody knows what to expect, make unreasonable demands, and get angry when your unspoken expectations are not met. You have no respect for the wishes and needs of the people around you. You have a desire for control over other people, and when that desire is not met, you get angry. Power and control are your idols and you have passed your children through the fire to worship them.

ASHERAH POLES

In Old Testament times people accumulated collections of symbols and artifacts, and assembled them into tall structures called Asherah poles. Wealthy people had tall impressive Asherah poles with ornate symbols and bright colors, poorer people had plain ones. They were ancient status symbols. Not much has changed, has it?

We wear our Asherah poles on our bodies in our culture, a preoccupation with our physical appearance, clothing and makeup, body size and shape. You dress provocatively, not only to seduce, but to attract attention, to feel desirable and attractive, to appear wealthy and intelligent. Not satisfied with enough clothing to meet your needs, you want more and better, smarter and nicer clothes. You can overcome your anxiety about being less educated or less qualified than the other guy if you look better than the other guy.

This idol takes on a life of its own, wanting more and more, better and better. Never content with the pretty things you have, you desire more clothes, more shoes, more coats, and more makeup. The fashion magazine feed that desire with glowing examples of all the things you do not have, better hairdo, nicer clothes, bigger boots; and all the things you will never have, larger breasts, a thinner waistline, and longer legs.

Men worship vanity in the field of influence; more people working under you, more books you have written, more power over events in the workplace, in the city, in the state, in the world, or in your professional field. Any opinion contradicting your authority has to be attacked and dismembered immediately, and with as much pain and bloodshed as possible. You can't just correct people when they are wrong; you have to also attack them, demoralize them, and publicly humiliate them. If someone makes a mistake, you feel compelled to make sure as many people as possible know about it.

Vanity can also be expressed in your house, bigger, better, more impressive, on the most prominent corner so everyone can see it. You fill it with more flowers, more vases, more knickknacks, redecorating, new wallpaper, new furniture, adding on rooms, taking out walls, a three car garage and three cars to put in it, original art work, antiques and sculptures, gardens, pools and gazebos, more, more, more. Never satisfied with what you have, you desire more, bigger, better, and faster, the tallest Asherah pole on the block.

> *Lonely unhappy people with very large Asherah poles.*

You teach your children to desire more and more stuff, more toys, more clothes, and more money. They cannot be satisfied with the things they have, they have learned from the cradle to desire more. When you teach your children to want more, more, more, they are never content with what they have *or with what they are.* They desire more education, more power, and more influence. They cannot be satisfied with a normal job and its humble demands, time sheets, and difficult personalities; they have to be the big guy, the MBA, the boss. They cannot be satisfied with their relationships either. They are looking for the best looking, richest, most educated man or woman from the best family, best neighborhood, best Ivy League College. Never content to be small and insignificant, they have to be bigger, smarter, better, and faster than their peers, and they are destined to be lonely unhappy people with very large Asherah poles.

Vanity extends to the children themselves in the form of excess parental pride. *Our* son gets straight "A"s, has lots of friends, plays three instruments, and went to state in basketball. *Our* daughter got a full scholarship to Harvard, won a beauty pageant, and played in the symphony. These are Trophy Kids and there are millions of them.

Trophy Kids get hooked on drugs too. Trophy parents are destroyed when their kid gets hooked on drugs and thrown in jail, *not for his sake, but for theirs!* "What will they say at the country club? We have to keep this quiet!" They deny he has a problem. They bail their addicted son out of jail and protect him from the consequences of his drug use. They tell all their friends he is studying in Europe when he's really in the most expensive rehabilitation center they could find. They don't want anybody to know, so they don't get him any follow up care for fear of what it would look like. They blame it on his little sister; people will talk bad about his little sister. It would destroy her reputation.

INTELLECTUAL PRIDE

Sometimes our Asherah pole is in our heads. As a nation, we collectively worship our intellectual prowess and intelligence. We have read the best books, gone to the finest schools, and subscribe to the most provocative theories, magazines, and ideas. We pride ourselves on adopting the ideas of the most intelligent and forward thinking people of our time. The most outlandish ideas are heralded as *avant guard.* We are skeptics of everything handed down to us from our culture, our religion, and our heritage. Even the oldest truths are only valuable if re-packaged into something new and exciting, something our old fashioned ancestors would never have considered. But of course, we are so much more sophisticated than those fuddy duddy old people.

Only new ideas, new religions, and new moralities have any value. We forsake the morality that has been proven correct over many centuries, and replace it with the sexual revolution and open marriage. Our fathers told us to avoid debt, but the standard now is to owe twice our annual income just in mortgage debt, and much more besides in short term debt. Those old ideas about morality are just too restrictive, to confining for our liberated consciousness. Those old people were trying to confine us and spoil our fun. We are free from that kind of moral bondage now.

> *We are free from that kind of moral*
> *bondage now.*

We discard valuable things just because they are old. We bring in new math and whole language reading, not because there was anything wrong with the old math or phonics, but because those ideas are so old fashioned. The newest and latest in child rearing is valued above the time honored methods of discipline that have worked for thousands of years. We know better than our parents did, now that we have been enlightened by our technology, our new philosophy, and our new morality. We pass our children through the fire to our intellect when we allow the newest theories to displace the discipline we know is right and proper.

And so our children have absolutely no respect for us, because now *we* are the old people, whose ideas are obviously old fashioned and irrelevant to the realities of contemporary life. Our children run around behind our backs, reject our authority, mock our morality, despise our advice, and ignore their obligations to us. They are doing what we so diligently taught them to do. They feel no obligation to obey us; our commands are not based on anything more permanent than our vacillating opinions. Who says marriage is between a man and a woman? Marriage can be anything we want it to be.

TELEVISION

The whole family is gathered around the glowing shrine in the living room. It holds their complete and exclusive attention. No one speaks while it is speaking. If someone wants to talk it is considered an interruption. "Don't bother me, I'm watching my show." There isn't even any conversation at the family dinner table because there is a shrine in the dining room, too. Everyone eats in silence while the evening news is on. When are we going to nurture and guide our kids if the TV has everyone's attention at the dinner table?

Even if the content of television programming were perfectly wholesome and healthy [which it is not] it would still be a major problem for healthy family functioning. When does the family talk together? When do the parents listen to the problems the children are having? When does the husband sympathize with his wife, when does the wife admire her husband's accomplishments, if there is no conversation in the home?

Family intimacy is made up of lots of little things all added up. It is smiling and laughing together, doing homework together, and watching the children play. It is getting down on the floor and playing Momma Cat and Baby Kitten with them, my personal after work favorite [all I have to do is lay on the floor and meow from time to time]. It is making up new games, word games and story games. It is reading to them and letting them read to you, playing chess on a cold day and football on a nice day. There is no time for TV when you are painting pictures and making cookies and reading the stories they write.

None of that is going to happen if every one's attention is directed at the glowing shrine in the corner of the living room. Kids need emotional support in the form of conversation, attention and listening, and they need it every day. If they don't get it from you, they will get it from somebody else. Who do you *want* listening to and supporting your child? His seventeen-year-old drug pusher friend? If the only person in the world listening to him is a drug dealer, that is who he is going to talk to.

CONTENT OF TELEVISION

The content of television is also destructive to the family. Illicit and irresponsible sex and sexual innuendo are common, even on family sit-coms. Fidelity in marriage is mocked. Children are insolent and disrespectful of their parents and everybody thinks it's funny. Fathers are portrayed as incompetent fools. Parental figures are deceived and something good comes of the deception. It's okay to lie to your parents as long as you cover up for it. Is this really what we want our children to see?

The violence and viciousness that passes for drama and intrigue are damaging to our children. They are developing a conscience, building the neural connections which give them a sense of right and wrong. They are learning from the television set that honesty and compassion are stupid and even dangerous qualities to have, while ruthless, conniving, vengeful actions are rewarded with success and admiration.

> *Is this really what we want our children to see?*

Shocker, chiller, violent death scenes are especially damaging to the developing conscience. Like any good narcotic, it takes more and more to get a thrill, more shock, more cruelty, more blood and more gore. We see senseless violence receiving the approval of society, not its condemnation. The violence extends to the videogames our children spend hours on whenever they are not watching TV. They get to participate in the killing and violence. They live vicariously through their characters, adopting the conscience offered to them on the videogame. Why then, do we act so surprised when a pair of teenagers shoots and kills classmates and teachers?

The music our kids listen to celebrates mindless violence and irresponsible sexuality, and sets it to a seductive beat. Music is a powerful medium. Our minds hold on to rhythm and rhyme tenaciously. Our kids walk around all day singing about sex and violence in their heads. Is it any wonder they act out what they are thinking about? Music is a prominent part of the drug experience. We teach our kids to enjoy that thumping beat and the aggressive lyrics when we allow them to saturate their minds with their favorite CDs.

APPROVAL

Why do we tolerate the garbage on TV, the raunchy music and violent videogames? Because the kids like it. If we restrict their TV watching, they might get upset. If we take the TV or computer out of his room, he's been robbed, deprived of his rights, and abused. Editing your teenager's CD collection will make a scene; cause a confrontation, a conflict. We don't like conflict.

We are all greatly distressed at criticism, we want to be liked and approved of. That is natural. It becomes idolatrous when we sacrifice our integrity by doing and saying the thing that will be approved of, instead of the thing we know is right and true. We risk other people's condemnation when we take a stand that is unpopular or less than flattering.

In the same way, we are afraid of 'offending' our children. We want to be liked and approved of by our children, and so we're afraid to discipline them because then 'they won't like us.' It is not our job to be our kids' friend. They have lots of friends who don't really care whether they turn out to be people of integrity or not. We have to show them the consequences of lying and cheating. If we don't, they will not be people of integrity when they grow up. As the people in Littleton, Colorado found out, you can and will be held responsible for the actions of your children, if not by the law, then by God.

Our source of approval has to be something much larger than the opinions of others, including our children. We have to say the unpopular and do the unwanted. As parents, we have the unenviable job of breaking the bad news to our kids, **"you are not the center of the universe."** Nobody likes to hear that. My four-year-old spent one full year in all of the various stages of a temper tantrum because she didn't want to hear all this stuff about, "I am not the center of the universe." Fourteen-year-olds have temper tantrums too, even worse than the babies.

> *Fourteen-year-olds have temper tantrums*
> *too, even worse than the babies.*

Disciplining a child is hard work. It requires our full attention and a lot of emotional energy. We have to be willing to listen to the whole story, voice our opinion, provide rewards for good behavior, and consequences for bad behavior. We have to pay attention to what our child is doing, both the good and the bad. If we never notice and reward their good behavior, they learn it really doesn't matter if they are generous or kind, honest or courageous, because nobody really values those things anyway. They won't work to develop strong character because the payoff is so small. We develop our kids' conscience by rewarding good behavior just as much as by punishing bad behavior. If we never notice and punish their bad behavior, they learn they can get by with being selfish, aggressive, thoughtless, abusive, and demanding. They won't learn to police the impulses arising within themselves if we never voice our disapproval.

CASE HISTORY

I took care of a teenager about ten years ago who really broke my heart. She came in pregnant at fifteen years of age, having a miscarriage, and her mother was sickeningly supportive of her. Never a word of rebuke, never a statement of disapproval, not even a threat of closer supervision. It was okay by her for this fifteen-year-old girl to be sexually active. She couldn't see anything immoral or selfish about it.

Naturally, six months later, the girl was back, pregnant again. The mother was 'shocked' that she would do such a thing again, but accepting of her child no matter what she did. The girl had the baby, and her mother took care of both of them, letting the daughter have a normal teenage life with her friends, while she took care of the baby.

Five years later, the girl grew up and married, but the five-year-old boy was 'too much' for her and her new husband. They didn't want him, and the husband was abusive toward him. She had another baby, a little girl, and made herself a nice little family without her inconvenient son whom she couldn't control and got no pleasure from. The mother came crying to me, complaining of depression and overwork. She was fifty years old, raising a five-year-old, and she had no time for herself or her numerous health problems. Her marriage was in shambles. Her self-centered daughter didn't care that she had to work so hard.

Can you see the selfishness in this woman? Unwilling to have a confrontation with her daughter because it would be uncomfortable to her, she let a fifteen-year-old girl destroy her own life, the life of her son, and her mother's life. Families unwilling to confront their drug abusing kids are doing the same thing. Yes, it's uncomfortable to face the situation. It's a lot easier to ignore it and hope it will go away. It won't.

DISCIPLINE

Age appropriate discipline may mean exile to his room for a ten year old, taking the computer away at age twelve, taking the door to his bedroom off the hinges at age fourteen, or taking the car away at age sixteen. If your kid is getting into trouble with his car, don't be afraid to take it away from him. You say, "But it's his car. He paid for it." No it's not. As long as he lives in your house and eats your groceries, it is not his car. It's *your* car and you can take it away from him.

If you are not willing to effectively discipline your son, don't worry, your local law enforcement agency will be glad to do it for you. The kind of behavior you may be willing to tolerate will not be tolerated by the rest of society. Your addicted child will lie to you; he will get abusive and violent with you. He'll steal from you for a long time before he'll steal from anybody else because he thinks you'll ignore it. Don't tolerate it.

> *Which would you rather sign, an arrest warrant or a death certificate?*

Don't be afraid to have your teenager arrested if he is getting in serious trouble with drugs. This is his brain we're talking about, and drastic measures are sometimes called for. An adult arrest will be on his record for the rest of his life. A juvenile arrest will not. When you have him arrested, he will see that you take this extremely seriously. But even an adult arrest he has to report to every employer for the rest of his life is not too great a price to pay to get your adult child to see the light and recognize what he is doing to his life. Every day he uses is another layer of irreversible damage to your son's brain. Which would you rather sign, an arrest warrant or a death certificate?

When you suspect your child is using drugs, you have to take action. You have to inspect his room and his car and be willing to admit that yes, this funny looking pill, this burnt piece of tin foil, this joint butt is probably the real thing. You have to confront his denial and resistance, and force him to take a drug test. You have to get him counseling and rehabilitation, and forcibly separate him from his friends.

> *He will accuse you of invading his privacy,*
> *as if that were some kind of crime.*

He's going to argue and complain and accuse you of invading his privacy, as if that were some kind of crime. He will refuse to cooperate, make threats and get violent. He will threaten suicide and run away. You have to do it anyway. If you don't, you will soon have a brain damaged kid who is either dead or in jail. The consequences of meth abuse are real.

If we shrink from disciplining our teenagers because we will lose their approval, that is a very destructive family idol. Your kids learn they can manipulate you with their approval. They learn that 'keeping the peace' is more important than speaking the truth. They learn to worship the approval of other people, too. They go along with what their friends are doing because they want to be liked by them. They can't stand up for what they believe and tell the pushers to get lost because they are afraid of a confrontation. They can't leave the party when things start getting out of hand because they might make a scene. They have learned all about worshipping the approval of other people.

We need to recognize where our approval and acceptance really come from. They come from God, and God alone. If you are doing the will of God, however unpopular that may be, you will know His approval, and you will not need anyone else's approval. You will also indirectly teach your child to value God's love, and to not be afraid of the scorn of other people. That is important when he has to stand up to peer pressure and be willing to make his friend mad. We model by our behavior the kind of independent thinking that enables a kid to walk away from drug abuse.

WE HAVE A CHOICE

I have worshipped each and every one of these idols, [and many more besides] at one time or another in my life, some of them for years. In every case, it has led to tragedy and heartbreak. Once faced with the majesty of God and the rightness of His worship, they fell out of my hands. The worship of God makes for good medicine, good parenting, and good relationships. I still occasionally realize I have an idol in my hands, most recently the worship of time, efficiency, wanting to 'save some time.' I was sacrificing gentleness patience and precision on the altar of efficiency. The moment I realized what I was doing, I renounced it.

We can choose to worship God, or we can choose to worship something else. We exercise our choice every day with every decision we make. We either desire God and everything He is, love, purity, mercy, truth, righteousness, or we desire something else and put it ahead of Him. We can't say we love God when we consistently put monetary profit ahead of honesty, or our own sexual pleasure ahead of faithfulness, in our daily lives. We cannot serve both God and idols. The choice we make determines every other decision in life.

I know a man who despised God because of the agonizing cancer death of his wife. He was doing the books for his business one day, and he was being honest in his books. In his mind he thought, "Why are you doing that?" and he answered, "Because I love honesty." He continued doing his books and he heard it again, "Why are you doing that?" and again he answered "Because I love righteousness and truth." Then, realizing he was praying, he demanded, "Who are you?" and the Lord answered, "I am Righteousness, Whom you love." This man was worshiping God with the work of his hands, the highest form of worship, and didn't even know it.

> *We cannot serve both God and idols.*

So, are we going to do what's right, or do what feels good? Speak the truth, or say what sounds good? Do what's honorable, or do what's convenient, cheap, easy, and painless? Are we going to engage conflict and face the uncomfortable situation, or let the injustice slide? We make that decision a thousand times a day every day.

God typically punishes idolatry by allowing us to live with the natural consequences of our sin. When the nation of Israel worshipped idols for a few hundred years and would not listen to Him, God let them be conquered by the Babylonians and led off to live with the idols for seventy years. "You want idols? I give you idols!" [my paraphrase of the book of Jeremiah] Excavations of Jerusalem show early layers of debris littered with idols up until the conquest by Babylon, [marked by a layer of ash and blood] and in all layers after that, there are no idols. The nation learned its lesson.

The captivity is a central story in the Old Testament, and it plays out in each of our lives. He lets us live with the consequences of our rebellion until we learn to appreciate His goodness and mercy. He restores us, like He restored them, when we admit our need, accept His forgiveness, and renounce our idols. Then, we embark on the hard work of rebuilding the temple of our lives, centering our lives on Him, loving the One who spoke us into existence and redeemed us, and living in obedience to Him. If we thought for even five minutes about who God really is, and if we loved Him even the tiniest fraction of the way we should love Him, our worship would flow from within, and no earthly pleasure would even come close. That's what we were created to do.

THE END

Someday we are going to see the END. There was a beginning, and there will be an end. Some day we will witness the end of this created order. The strong nuclear force will let go, and every atom in this universe will fly apart with explosive force to be reorganized into a new heaven [spiritual world] and a new earth [physical world]. "The heavens will disappear with a roar, the elements will be destroyed by fire and the earth [physical world] and everything in it will be laid bare." 2 Peter 3:10 NIV

When we see the Reality that lies behind this veil we call reality, the time for choices will be over. We can't choose to love and obey God when it is impossible to deny Him anymore. We will find that the choices we have made are eternal choices and we are eternal beings. He gave us fair warning of the judgment to come in the time of Noah and Jeremiah thousands of years ago. Even natural history, with its record of extinctions and ice ages, testifies that there will be a day of reckoning. We can't pretend we don't know any better. We will either sing with joy or burn with regret for eternity. Eternity is not just a really long time that eventually ends. Eternity does not end. We have a choice now.

You are worthy, our Lord and God, to receive glory and honor and power, for you created all things, and by your will they were created and have their being. (Rev. 4:11 NIV)

.11.

POST TRAUMATIC STRESS DISORDER-
CHILD ABUSE

Post traumatic stress disorder is a common precursor to substance abuse, especially child sexual abuse. Three quarters of female addicts and more than half of male addicts are survivors of rape or molestation, child abuse or abandonment, or other major trauma experienced before the age of eighteen. Most men are extremely reluctant to admit to a history of abuse, especially sexual abuse, and so this figure may be an under-statement of the truth. Incest survivors are twelve times more likely to become addicted to drugs or alcohol than the general population.

Classic PTSD is usually the result of overwhelming life threatening trauma, and the criteria for diagnosis are well defined. The neurologic and anatomic sequelae of severe PTSD are dramatic enough to see on a PET scan. Lesser degrees of trauma cause cellular damage in the same way, but to a smaller degree. Tracts not outright destroyed are none the less affected chemically by the trauma of abuse, witnessing traumatic and threatening events, or natural disaster. The brain learns to fear each time it is threatened.

> *Even bad love is better than no love at all.*

The pain of this type of abuse is felt throughout the child's personality. Constant turmoil, conflict, fear and anger predispose to methamphetamine addiction because the drug makes him feel better. Anything that relieves his pain will be welcomed and embraced by that child, even if it is illegal, dangerous, and immoral. Drugs and alcohol make him feel better, and premature sex makes her feel loved and cherished. Abused kids gravitate to these things, because they temporarily relieve their pain. Even bad love is better than no love at all.

Every experience of abuse or violence, every threat, insult and angry outburst, every act of torment and teasing is remembered, not only consciously, but also in the deeper areas of the midbrain, and thus subconsciously. These cellular memories change the way we process information. The nonverbal assumptions a person has are based on the things he learned in the rough and tumble of growing up. He approaches life the way he learned to as a child.

ALL IN THE FAMILY

Sibling squabbles are normal as kids grow up. They misunderstand each other because they are at different stages of growth. The eight-year-old tells a joke he thinks is funny, and the eleven-year-old thinks it's stupid, while the four-year-old gets upset because she misunderstood the pun and took him literally. That happened this evening at our house.

"Mommy, what's the nuffel on cumbus?"

"What?"

"The nuffle on cumbus. What is it?"

"Huh?"

That is the eight-year-old interpretation of "The NFL on CBS." The eleven-year-old thought it was stupid. The four-year-old wanted to know what a nuffle is.

Kids get possessive of their rooms and their toys, they won't play together, they object if one gets a special favor, they compete for their parent's attention, and they resent each other's accomplishments. Sounds rather like a typical office full of adults, doesn't it. Obvious unfairness in the treatment of siblings really is painful. They all want to be special to you in some way, recognized for some talent or characteristic, and they can get competitive.

Sometimes sibling rivalry can become abusive. Constant teasing and torment by a sibling is deeply painful, especially if the abuser is older, bigger, smarter, or somehow 'better' than the other child. If you compare the two children, you encourage that type of verbal abuse. The kids don't have to intentionally attack one another for this to happen. If the parent obviously prefers one child over the other, the child is going to blame the other child before he will blame his parent.

Physical abuse between siblings is also common. The larger older child is jealous of the attention the younger one gets, and takes his frustration out on the smaller child. He will beat the other child, invade his room and destroy things of great value to the other child, or play 'practical jokes' to humiliate the other child. If no one intervenes, a pattern is established, and real harm is done to the smaller child. He's just as helpless against his brother as he would be against an abusive parent.

If this kid finds a drug that makes him feel powerful, confident, and intelligent he will be strongly motivated to use it again. Crystal makes him feel like he is in control of his emotions and relationships; he's not a helpless little boy anymore. With this stuff he can feel like a real man.

THE SCHOOL YARD

Emotional abuse can occur outside the home as well. A child who is raised in a loving healthy home is still exposed to bullies on the playground and at school. High schools are famous for cliques and crowds that run together and mock and exclude outsiders. Even little kids in kindergarten and elementary school say and do hurtful things to each other.

My daughter came home from kindergarten one day in tears because the other girls had made fun of the pink flowers on her shirt. She refused to wear anything pink or with flowers on it to school, even though she had liked her pink sweaters before. I asked her, "If the kids in school thought it was stupid to like cats, would you stop liking cats?" She loved cats, they were and are her passion. She caught on that she didn't have to let anybody else tell her what to like or do. She has shown independence in many ways since then. But to this day [she's eleven years old now] she will not wear pink sweaters or anything with flowers on it.

Kids tease and torment each other for no reason at all. They gang up on classmates who look funny or dress different. They magnify and mock slight accents, learning disabilities and school failures. They point out ears that stick out and embarrassing birth marks. Sometimes a whole group of kids will gang up on one individual, and torment that child to tears for many years. They typically mock him for something he has no control over, like his name, his weight, his skin color, or the type of house he lives in. They call him "trailer trash" or "nigger." That's an insult, no matter what color your skin is.

> *Nobody wants to be the reject, the outcast,*
> *the one with no friends.*

Some kids are impervious to such abuse; others are deeply affected by it. If your child internalizes the message sent to him by the school bully, he will feel pain and humiliation, rejection and alienation, which is almost as painful as parental rejection. If he allows himself to be victimized because he's been taught that fighting back is bad, the bullies will pile on, knowing he will not defend himself. A small problem turns into a large problem. Nobody wants to be the reject, the outcast, the one with no friends.

If somebody in the grocery store bumped your cart, called you names, and made fun of the things you are buying, the manager would escort that person out. If they got violent with you, they would be arrested. And yet our kids put up with similar abuse and everybody says, "Oh that's just 'kids doing what kids do.'" Yes, it is "kids doing what kids do," and somebody has to step in and discipline them effectively. We teach our children right from wrong by what we tolerate, not by what we say.

School yard abuse gets physical, and for fear of lawsuits, school officials don't feel they have the right or authority to stop fights and bullying in the schools anymore. In some situations, you are going to get sued no matter what you do. If you break up the fight, you get sued for manhandling a kid. If you let the fight continue, you get sued for the fractured arm, the cracked rib, or the broken neck. Let's get sued for doing the right thing; it's a lot more defensible in court. That's why we have liability insurance.

A tormented child will inevitably get angry and lash out. If he can't lash out in a controlled manner, he'll lash out in an uncontrolled manner. He may lash out at the kids in school, but they may not be the ones who are tormenting him. He may lash out at some other little kid who looks safe and non-threatening, and turn into a bully himself. He may lash out at his little sister at home, or take it out on the neighbor's dog. He turns into the kind of person who is mad at the whole world and everybody in it. Sometimes he takes it out on himself, expressed as a major depression with significant risk for suicide.

We can't stand by and let our child be tormented by his peers. The child doesn't know how to defend himself. If he sees us standing by as if nothing is wrong, he gets the message, "I am not important. My pain doesn't matter. People can abuse me and it's okay." He feels helpless, humiliated, and rejected. If somebody offers this kid acceptance and belonging, he will sign right up, even if the acceptance and belonging come from a gang of drug addicts. If his new friend offers him a drug that makes him feel powerful and confident, he will take it, even if he believes drugs are wrong. *This* drug must not be wrong; it makes everything feel better.

> *If somebody offers this kid acceptance and belonging, he will sign right up.*

Even if we can't stop the abuse, when we step up to the plate and defend our child, we send him the message, "Yes, you do matter, you are important, and nobody has the right to abuse you." So don't be afraid to speak to the principal, the coach, or the teacher about the situation. Don't assume they already know about it, they probably don't. Don't be afraid to talk to the bully's parents. They might meet you with a pit bull dog and a gun, or they might be horrified to hear their child is acting like that, and put their foot down on him. Remember, the bully's parents also want their child to grow up to be a good person and not a career criminal.

THE HOME FRONT

Physical and emotional abuse by a parent is far more harmful to a child than anything that happens to him on the playground. His parents tell him who he is at the deepest levels of his personality. Emotional abuse of a child is verbal and relational. It attacks the child's worth as a human being. Hurtful and destructive comments made by a parent are taken as truth by the child. "You are stupid; you will never amount to anything." is taken literally and internalized. A comment like that holds as much power as, "You are a boy and boys play rough." It is a statement of truth about him, and he will live up to it.

If you continually remind a child how much pain he causes you, how much trouble he is, how he ruined your life just by being born, that is debilitating emotional abuse. He can't help the fact that he is, and if you resent him just for being there, he knows what his value to you is. If you tell your kid everything was fine in your marriage until he came along, he understands that he is not wanted, not important, his feelings don't matter and nobody cares.

> *If you have no respect for your child, he will have no respect for himself.*

Some parents habitually treat their children as objects instead of persons. It is an almost unconscious attitude that the child is not really a person, but rather a possession. The kids are in the way, noisy and annoying. "Tell them to shut up." It is easy to treat your child like an object to be dealt with; [one of the kids is crying about something] instead of a person to be consoled, [Cindy got her feelings hurt, let's talk to her]. You ignore your child when he talks to you; you are more interested in your newspaper or your TV show than your child. You wouldn't do that to a person, but your child is not a person. He's just an object, and a noisy inconvenient one at that.

If you tell your child to "shut up" more than once a day, you are telling him he is an object to you, not a person. If you don't even call him by his name, he's 'the mouth,' she's 'the ugly one,' your child is *less* than an object. Even the toaster has a name. The child learns that he doesn't matter and nobody cares. If you have no respect for your child, he will have no respect for himself.

The same message is communicated non-verbally by a lack of interest in the things the child does and says. You can tell your son he's good and talented, but if you don't look at what he did, use the potholder he made, and display the picture he drew, the message comes through loud and clear, what he did was really stupid. You can tell your daughter she is beautiful, but if you don't talk to her, spend time with her, and enjoy her company; she understands that she really isn't valuable or lovable after all.

If your child is valuable to you, you will make the effort to appropriately discipline him. Good discipline is an expression of respect for a child. It means you care enough about him to correct his behavior. Good discipline does not condemn the child, just his behavior. It is just physical enough to get his attention, but does not seek to inflict punishment. Disrespectful discipline is an attack on the child himself, not just his behavior. It reflects an attitude of irritation and resentment, and the child feels rejected, not just corrected.

The ADHD child is especially vulnerable to this type of abuse, frequently disguised as concern for his disability. He knows he is different, and he gets the idea he's really pretty stupid and can't do what the other kids do. If he isn't getting appropriate treatment, he really is a discipline problem and has to learn how to control himself. His academic and social failures make him hyper-sensitive to criticism.

The non-verbal message he gets is much more believable than the verbal message he hears. If he thinks he's incompetent, he will have no confidence in his abilities, and will never really try to do anything. His lack of confidence and lack of respect for himself is depressing and painful. It hurts to think you are worthless and stupid. When somebody offers this kid a drug that makes him feel confident and intelligent, you can be sure he will like it. It 'works'! It makes him feel a lot better. This stuff is great!

CONTROL PARENTS

A more subtle type of emotional abuse is a possessiveness and dependence on a child that is inappropriate. Mothers do it differently that fathers, but both can have similar unreasonable expectations of a child that hinder his development. Typically, the mother looks to her child for emotional support she is not getting in her marriage. She wants her child to listen to her problems, sympathize with her, care about her pain, in essence, to be her husband. Taken to an extreme, she is clingy, possessive, needy, and dependent on her child. She makes him feel guilty for pursuing his own interests, gets uncomfortable when her daughter gets a boyfriend, falls apart when her son gets married, and often interferes significantly in the child's marriage. She is the dreaded 'mother-in-law.'

The son who feels responsible for his mother is tied to her by strings of guilt. He cannot fulfill her needs; they are way too much for him. He cannot be her confidant, absorbing all her complaints about the inadequacies of his father. He cannot be her constant companion, faithful to her need for attention and validation. She is looking to him for things her husband should be providing, but is not. Her constant manipulation of him is cloaked in the guise of concern for his welfare, causing conflict and guilt when he attends to his own developing relationships. He feels guilty for leaving his poor mother all alone when she is only concerned about him.

> *He feels guilty for leaving his poor mother all alone when she is only concerned about him.*

This kid feels suffocated and controlled. He is kept a child, and not allowed to experience his manhood. He is afraid to leave her; afraid he will offend her and make her angry, or hurt her feelings and make her cry. He feels childish, powerless, and incompetent to be a real man. Now he finds a drug, methamphetamine, that instantly makes him feel competent, powerful, independent, and manly, he will be strongly attracted to it. Ice meets a real need in his life.

The controlling father projects his own deficiencies, desires, and inadequacies onto his son, and tries to live through his son. Often, he is looking for the affirmation and approval he is not getting from his wife. He wants his son to be the jock he never was. He wants his son to be the financial success, academic success, or romantic success he never was. He is not free to be the musician he wants to be, the author, the artist, the plumber, or the preacher. When he pursues these things anyway, he loses the admiration of his father, who doesn't really appreciate him for what he is. He might be really talented and have a lot going for him, but he feels rejected and empty inside.

When subjected to this type of expectation abuse, he longs to be himself, but has no freedom to be himself, and eventually rebels at the expectations put upon him. He rejects the law school his father chooses, he rejects education in general, and he rejects everything his father tries to ram down his throat, including his religion, his values, and his legitimate discipline. His efforts to be his own man lead him into places he would never have chosen had he been allowed to choose for himself. Instead, he reacts against everything being forced upon him, whether he might have actually wanted it or not. The seeds are planted for a major rebellion that is likely to include drug use just because he knows his dad would not approve.

> *He reacts against everything being forced upon him, whether he might have actually wanted it or not.*

Some fathers are so determined to make a man out of their son that they provoke him, tease him, and torment the child, even at the tender age of seven or eight. They want to make the boy angry enough to fight. "Come on! Be a man!" If the child cries, he is humiliated. If he fights back, he is overpowered. Eventually, the child gets big enough to defend himself, and the game stops, but not before the boy is turned into a hostile angry young man. This child hates his father, and for good reason. He is guaranteed to reject any and every value his father teaches him. He will then prove his manhood with his gang membership, his criminal record, his tattoos, and his drug use.

ABANDONMENT

Abandonment of a child by one or both parents is very common in this country. It's called divorce, or perhaps the parents never married in the first place, and the child knows he has been rejected, usually by his father. Of course, everybody tells him daddy left mommy, but to a child, it comes across as, "Daddy left me." He's not there when I get up in the morning and he's not there when I go to bed at night. He's not there when I'm sick, he's not there for my birthday. He doesn't come to my baseball games. I send him letters and he doesn't write back. He just doesn't care. And he should care. He's my daddy and he should care.

The child thinks there must be something wrong with him that his daddy doesn't care. He must be unacceptable in some way for his own father to reject him. He thinks he is fundamentally flawed, unlovable, unworthy, distasteful, and defective. If he also has ADHD, he's sure the problem is him. He's too noisy; he is always in the way. Nobody likes him. It never occurs to him that the problem is his daddy, not him.

I deliver babies for a living, and at least twice a week I deliver a baby for an unmarried young woman who has only a casual relationship with the father of her child, with no intention of forming what we might call a family. Often, she has no idea whom the father of the child is, has no contact with him, has been abused by him, or the young man is in jail and faces many years behind bars. These children will never have a daddy. Even if the mother eventually marries, the step-father is not his own daddy. It makes a difference. I belong to my daddy, and my daddy belongs to me. If this relationship is broken, or never established, there is a deep pain in that child's life.

I've been watching this progression for almost fifteen years now, and remember, I'm the one who treats the sexually transmitted diseases. This woman will have a series of brief sexual relationships with a parade of men coming in and out of her life, and her child's life. She doesn't consider herself promiscuous. She tells me, "I wouldn't want you to think badly of me." She's only having sex with her boyfriend and he is a good man, and she's been with him for over a year and she doesn't sleep around. Of course they never marry, and eventually the relationship ends, to be replaced by another boyfriend who's really a nice man, and she insists that she *never* sleeps around.

It's not just the 'lower class' women living like this. Middle-aged educated professional women don't think there is anything wrong with having sex with your boyfriend. Often they have been married once and have realized how meaningless marriage is when the husband they trusted left them. They're not about to trust another man with their heart. That would hurt too much. So they just have sex with their boyfriends and take whatever intimacy they can get. What kind of example is she setting for her teenage child? He has seen the revolving door since infancy and thinks that this is the normal way to conduct your sex life.

At the same time, this child has had a series of five or six 'fathers' who are not really emotionally invested in him. They don't really love him like a father should. They are here today and gone tomorrow. They are not interested in him as a person, only as a way to get in favor with his mother. When the relationship with his mother sours, he is rejected once again. It happens once a year or so. He has never had a real daddy.

Where is this kid going to go for emotional support and guidance? Who is he going to look to for a sense of belonging and acceptance? Who does he look to for affirmation and approval? Who can he look up to as a role model, an example of a successful life? Why, his seventeen-year-old drug pusher friend is someone he can look up to. His friend always listens to his problems. His friend has been there all his life. He knows his friend really cares about him.

And besides, the crystal he gets from his friend makes everything feel great. He feels confident and intelligent, energetic and powerful. He can fill the void in his life with a chemical and never have to be rejected again.

THE *RAGE*-AHOLIC

Some fathers are so consumed with their own anger and arrogance, they can't offer their son anything approaching acceptance and approval. He is right and everybody else is wrong. His wife can't do anything right, his children can't do anything right, his employees can't do anything right, his boss can't do anything right. He stays in a bad mood and barely contains his rage. He lashes out over little inconveniences, minor delays, and trivial problems with verbal diatribes that are vicious and insulting. He controls his family with his temper and his outbursts. He is worshipping power. This idol is just as ugly when worshipped by a mother as it is when worshipped by a father. For the sake of clarity, I have phrased this discussion in the masculine.

The parent who rules with his rage demoralizes his family. They live in constant fear. They tip toe around, dreading the inevitable explosion. Much like the alcoholic home, life revolves around the raging adult. He controls everything and everybody with his temper. The family dreads his coming home. They tell little lies and hide what they were doing, not out of guilt, but out of fear. "If Dad catches us watching TV, he'll blow up." Many times, his rage is completely unpredictable. Coke and popcorn in front of the TV was okay last week, but today we get verbally abused for it. The kids are afraid to bring their friends home for fear of what Dad might do. The rules are always changing, and you never know where you stand. Nobody is safe when he's around.

> *"If only we were perfect, Dad would like us."*

Everything that happens is somebody's fault. If the door knob falls off [the one that has been loose for two weeks] it's because you were to rough with it. "You kids are always running around here like a bunch of wild Indians and it's a wonder the house hasn't fallen down by now." Little things get blown all out of proportion, and big things leave the whole family shaking in fear for weeks.

Even if there is no actual physical abuse, the family is living in constant terror. The fact that there is no physical abuse makes it even harder to deal with. If he beat them, they could understand that Dad is the one with the problem. But since he doesn't, they think maybe *they* are the problem. "If we would just do right, he wouldn't get so mad. It's our fault he's always so upset." They think *they* are unacceptable, instead of realizing that his behavior is unacceptable. They think, "If only we were perfect, Dad would like us."

It Gets Physical

Physical abuse usually starts around the age of two, when the child begins to assert some independence. Alcoholic parents can usually tolerate a helpless baby, but when their two-year-old runs into the street or plays in the toilet, they are incensed. Child abuse beginning at this age is going to have profound effects on the neuroanatomy of a child. Tracts and connections are laid down in his brain that will be with him for the rest of his life. Tracts that should have formed at age two are not developed, and there is now no possibility for those connections to form. The window of opportunity has closed.

Child abuse predisposes to methamphetamine addiction, not just because of the psychological component, but also because of the biochemical changes in the midbrain structures we discussed in chapter 8. PTSD causes dopamine deficiencies in the midbrain, and there are serotonin tracts which do not develop properly. There are major biochemical differences between the abused child's brain, and that of the normal child who gets bumped around on the playground.

ADHD kids are often abused in an effort to control their behavior without medications. The ADHD child has poor impulse control. He is distracted and he honestly doesn't hear what his parents tell him to do. He has to be trained to pay attention, and that requires careful patient discipline, consistent rules and consistent consequences. It takes a lot of emotional energy to raise an ADHD kid without losing your temper. If the parent has untreated ADHD himself, his poor impulse control often results in significant child abuse.

Any type of physical abuse, whether real or threatened, is hurtful to the child and predisposes to addiction. Even vicarious abuse, witnessing the abuse of another child, especially a sibling, is deeply threatening to the child. Graphic television news reports of child abuse send a stab of fear into a child. It doesn't have to actually happen to him in order to have an effect on a child.

The physical pain is only a small part of the pain a child feels when he is abused. A well deserved swat on the behind hurts just as bad, but is understandable to the child. He knows it is right and just that he is hurt. It's almost a relief to get the well deserved swat. Now his infraction is paid for, and he can be part of the family again. Abuse is undeserved and unjust, and the pain is much more than physical. The unfairness is evident to even the youngest child. He has an innate God-given sense of what is right and what is wrong, of what is fair and what is unfair. He knows when he has been violated.

> ## *Why did she hurt me? Am I really bad even when I think I'm good?*

"Why did she hurt me? Am I really bad even when I think I'm good? Am I really such a bad and evil person that I deserve to be hurt?" If he gets spanked for natural functions, like soiling his clothes when he's trying to learn to use the bathroom, he learns that *he* is bad, not just the thing that he did. Sometimes days go by with no spankings. The child hopes things will be better now. But then, Momma gets mad and flies into a rage and, for no apparent reason, beats and bruises the child again.

"I'm not safe here. I can't trust anyone. I can't predict her response to me. She gets mad if I do something, she gets mad if I don't do something, no matter what I do, she gets mad." An authority figure can't be predicted and can't be pleased, but holds tremendous power over the child. The child is powerless and helpless. His parents hold the power of life and death over him. If they reject him, he is abandoned, and abandonment means terror, death, disintegration. Better to be beaten than abandoned.

His feelings are conflicted. Someone he loves is hurting him. He cares deeply about pleasing them. His love for them is mocked. He is made a fool for loving them, he should have known better than to love and trust his parents. The father or mother, whom he loves and wants to please, turns on him and becomes savage and brutal. The parent, whom he needs, condemns him and humiliates him. It doesn't really matter if she beats him with her fists or beats him with her mouth. He learns to fear the thing he loves, and hate the thing he needs.

INJUSTICE

As he gets older and realizes the injustice of it all, he gets angry. If he can remember the beatings, the humiliation of being helpless and controlled, he will hate the people he wants to love. He resents not having a safe place to live. If he cannot remember the specific abuse, he will have a generalized rage. He will be mad at the whole world and everybody in it, a short fuse, an angry disposition, and he won't even know why. He generalizes his feelings about his parents to anyone who reminds him of his parents; teachers and coaches, employers and supervisors, police and judges, any and all authority figures are potential abusers.

If his rights and feelings are not important, then neither are anybody else's. He will be cruel to animals, classmates, and smaller children. He will have fantasies of hurting people, enjoy videogames that feature mindless violence, be drawn to movies and television shows that display and glorify the feelings he has inside. Violent television that gives a thrill to a healthy kid, meets a *need* in this kid, a need for justice and revenge. He thinks he will find fairness and peace in violence.

He resents being dominated and controlled by the big bully at home. He looks for things he can control. He resists even appropriate discipline because he won't be controlled. He can't play on the baseball team because the coach tells him what to do. He can't get along with his teachers because they insist on telling him what to do. If he thinks his girlfriend it trying to control him, he leaves her. He will not be controlled by anybody or anything.

Being around his family makes him feel bad, scared, powerless, and angry. Pleasing his parents is not important to him; he takes pleasure in displeasing them, doing the very thing that would hurt them the most. He hangs around with tough kids because he knows his mom would not approve. She gets pregnant by a black man because she knows her dad hates blacks. The kid acts out, and then watches his parent's reaction to see if they care. He hopes against hope they will care enough to notice and rebuke him, but he rebels against any discipline they do offer.

If the family is religious, they sometimes use God as a means of controlling their children. They threaten the child with the wrath of God. They convince him that God is always watching, always angry, and impossible to please. He is ready to strike them with lightning for any mistake they make. The child is constantly reminded of how unworthy and unacceptable he is. Scripture is used as a club to verbally beat him with. Of course, in such a family, prayer to God is the last place that child is going to go for comfort. He doesn't expect any mercy from God. He's been taught from the cradle that God is the back-up authority to his 'big bully' dad.

> *God is The Big Guy with the Stick.*
> *He can't be pleased, so we might*
> *as well give up.*

This kid also rebels against God. He sees God through the lens of his father. God is The Big Guy with the Stick, a punitive hostile figure who doesn't really care about him. God is just another authority figure who can't be pleased, so we might as well give up. He hates his father and he hates God, the ultimate authority figure. This hatred may be consciously realized as a violent, militant atheism, or it may be deeply felt and expressed toward everything and everybody except God. He finds lots of help with this in a society which has decided that God is a fairytale. If he thinks about God at all, it's to defy Him, to prove he doesn't really need Him.

Sometimes, the adult survivor of child abuse will grow up and do well, until he sees something, hears something, or feels something that reminds him of the pain, the injustice, and the humiliation from the past and he explodes. He becomes a little kid again. He feels helpless and controlled again. He beats his wife, abuses his child, hates the neighbors, and shoots his boss. He is consumed with rage and loses control over himself. His desire to control something is expressed at home, where he possesses his wife like an object. He won't let her talk on the phone, visit her mother, or even go to the doctor. He is insanely jealous of her friends, her job, her family, and even her children [his children].

And he uses drugs to numb the pain. All the bad feelings of helplessness and fear, rejection and abandonment go away when he gets high. The drug 'works.' It makes him feel better. Instead of weak and helpless, he feels powerful and confident. Instead of stupid and worthless, he feels intelligent and competent. He fits in with his drug friends; they all feel the same way he does. He has a new family where he is understood, respected, and liked.

CHILD SEXUAL ABUSE

All these feelings are magnified in the case of sexual abuse. A large percentage of female drug addicts, and no small number of male addicts, are survivors of incest and other sexual abuse. The damage from incestuous abuse extends deep into the personality, even to the level of brain anatomy, as we saw in Chapter 8. The effects vary according to the age of onset of abuse, the duration of abuse, and the identity of the perpetrator. Structural changes are seen in the brains of incest survivors. This is serious stuff. Even a single episode of parental incest is devastating to the personality of a child. For the sake of clarity, I have described a male abuser and a female victim, since that represents the majority of cases. Boys are victimized almost as often as girls are, and incest is no less devastating when committed by a woman upon a child of either sex.

Incest is the dirty word that no one talks about. Victims are reluctant to come forward, even with clear physical evidence to substantiate their case, because of the emotional pain involved. The likely reaction of the rest of the family is frequently more than they are willing to deal with. The possible violent denial by their attacker, rejection by the rest of the family, the exposure of their own shame, makes it nearly impossible for an incest survivor to come out and talk about their experience.

> *Even a single episode of parental incest is*
> *devastating to the personality of a child.*

Children often feel dirty, shamed, like they were at fault for the incestuous relationship. Frequently, they are told by their attacker just how filthy and shameful they are. They believe it because of the credibility of their attacker. They are unable to believe daddy is dirty; it is much easier to believe *they* are dirty. Older victims are even more ashamed, because of the illusion of cooperation on their part. They feel that they in some way *wanted* to do these shameful things, and so they feel just as disgusted with themselves as they do with their attacker. They remember the contribution they made to the relationship, and take most, if not all, of the guilt over it upon themselves.

Incest is, by its broadest definition, inappropriate sexual contact, whether physical, verbal, or visual, imposed by a person of more power upon a person of less power. It can occur between persons of roughly the same age, and still be incest if one person had power or authority over the other. The perpetrator is not always a relative. It may be a trusted neighbor or babysitter. It may be a teacher or professor, boss or supervisor, pastor or priest, physician or counselor. Someone you trusted, someone you had a *right* to trust, violated you. That is incest.

Incest in the Bible

The story of David and Bathsheba in the Bible [2 Sam. 11] is commonly presented as an example of adultery. It clearly was not. Bathsheba was not a willing participant of equal power in that relationship. It was a rape, and not just an ordinary rape, but a rape by a king upon one of his subjects. Bathsheba was taken by force by a man who should have been her protector, her king. David was a *Jewish* king; he was responsible for her spiritual guidance and nurture.

Can you imagine what Bathsheba went through that day? She was home alone, her husband was off at war, and she was taking a bath in her bathroom. Everybody took a bath on the roof in those days; it was the second story of your home. The water was warmed by the sun. A wall around the roof protected your privacy, and if any one did happen to see you up there, they looked away out of respect.

But David was the king, and his palace had three stories, so his roof looked down upon hers, and, when he should have been at war with his troops, he was leering at Bathsheba, not looking away out of respect. She wasn't seducing anybody; she was just taking her bath, no doubt thinking about her husband whom she loved. The next thing she knew, two guards from the palace [with sick looks on their faces] were rushing her off in her bathrobe, with her hair still wet, telling her to come to the palace. I'm sure she immediately thought, "Oh my God, my husband has been killed in the war."

When she got there, frightened and all out of breath, they took her to the king's chambers, pushed her in the door and closed it behind her. Then she saw the king, and horror of horrors, he was taking her clothes off. He was taking his clothes off, and he was obviously aroused. What choice did she have in the matter? She was obviously just an object to him, not a person. He was the king. She was at his mercy.

Of course, it wasn't David's reputation that was shot, it was hers. To this day, this episode is called an adultery, as if she had seduced this man. This was *not* a consensual relationship. She had not been flirting with the king. He didn't even know her name. He had to ask his servant who she was. She was not a stripper or a prostitute. She was minding her own business, taking a bath in her own home where she should have been safe.

Can you imagine the next time he came to her and wanted to make love? Do you think she was happy to see him? The man who raped her and killed her husband? The consequences are obvious in the subsequent relationship between David and his sons, marked by disrespect and sexual dysfunction that resonated through the rest of the family. Solomon was Bathsheba's son. The rank idolatry of Solomon's later life likely had to do with the lack of respect his brothers had for David, the King who represented God. Solomon loved God, but had no respect for Him, and freely worshipped other gods.

ANGER AND SHAME

Anger is the universal response to the betrayal of trust that is incest. "You have made me dirty and disgusting. It wasn't my fault." This anger is a sign of significant healing. It acknowledges that the abuse was undeserved, and puts the shame where it belongs, upon the attacker, rather than on the victim.

The shock and disbelief of the rest of the family is a huge deterrent to coming out in the open about the abuse. The whole family structure is built upon secrecy. The perpetrator may have sworn the child to secrecy with overt threats, or he may have just made clear the likely consequences of telling. If she tells, the policeman will hurt Daddy. She loves her daddy, and she doesn't want the policeman to hurt him. The child will die first before she will tell.

He makes her feel like she deserved it, she got too close, she touched him first, she was dirty, seductive, a slut. She is convinced he would never do such a thing to a good girl, so she must be a bad girl. She is not worthy of respect, not worthy of protection, unlovable and unloved. The threat of rejection and abandonment is real, and extorts cooperation from the child. "If I don't let him do it, he'll get mad. If I cry or scream, he'll hurt me. Just stare at the ground and wait for it to be over." Helpless, overpowered, humiliated, exposed, all she can do is tolerate it. It isn't safe to go to sleep. It isn't safe to take a bath. It isn't safe to be at home.

The two-year-old game of 'run away and giggle' is fun when it is a celebration of love. It is not fun when there is a very real possibility of abandonment. Abandonment is a powerful threat to a child. Trust has been destroyed. "If he leaves me, I'll be all alone."

Abandonment means terror, death, disintegration, the end of the world. She clings even more tightly to her abuser because of this threat, adding to her confusion about whose idea the sexual activity really is.

> *Just stare at the ground and wait*
> *for it to be over.*

The child feels responsible for the abuser's sexuality, especially if he has revealed deficiencies in his legitimate sexual relationship, his marriage, or if he has no legitimate sexual relationship. "If I don't satisfy his needs, no one will." She senses his need for her, and responds to it with love, but is unable to satisfy him. Some children of incest are still the reluctant sex partners of their abuser even into adulthood.

Incest, especially chronic ongoing incest, also involves an element of pleasure, which is extremely confusing to a small child, and shameful to the older child or adult. It feels good to be loved; it is sexually stimulating to be touched. The child likes it and hates it at the same time. She knows its coming and makes no effort to avoid it, yet feels guilty and shameful because she didn't resist. Even the smallest child knows this is wrong, this is bad. The secrecy and denial confirms it. The shame and guilt are palpable even to a two-year-old. The young child is pre-verbal, she can't express her feelings; she just knows coldness, exposure, bad/good touch, wetness, penetration. It hurts, but she's afraid to cry. She knows that nobody cares.

WHEN SHE TELLS

Eventually, most children make at least a veiled attempt to tell somebody. She is afraid to come right out and say anything direct, but she drops hints, hoping her mother will ask the right question. When she does open up, and the person she talks to rejects her, avoids her, treats her like a slut, she thinks, "Am I really that disgusting? Am I really that revolting?" She feels exposed and humiliated all over again. If they don't believe her, she thinks maybe she really is crazy. She knows it really happened; maybe she deserved to be treated like that. There must be something wrong with her.

The step-father situation is more complex. Her mother doesn't want to know what is happening to her, and goes out of her way to avoid seeing it. If the child tells her mother, she will destroy the new marriage, and she and her mother will be all alone again. Her mother will be angry and may not believe her. She will be accused of lying and breaking up the family with her lies. The mother chooses her new husband over her daughter. When her mother refuses to defend her against her abuser, she feels completely worthless, like her pain and humiliation are unimportant and she must have deserved it. Her pain is increased by orders of magnitude. The child is threatened with the loss of both father and mother if she objects or resists. She is clearly just an object to both of them.

The abuse frequently escalates after she tells. The abuser may get more violent in retribution for telling. "Nobody is going to believe you. I'm the principal, the pastor, the cop. You do what I say." If she is sixteen years old, she runs away from home. If she is eight, she runs away emotionally. She clams up and won't talk to anybody, she just endures. She is depressed and anxious. She is distracted and can't concentrate on her school work. She can't sleep at night, so she's tired and irritable. She withdraws from her family and looks for a new family. She gets enmeshed with her friends, often older friends who can act as her parents.

SHE BELIEVES A LIE

The attacker had no respect for her, and so she has no respect for herself. Her body is not sacred, her will has no power, her needs and feelings are not important, she is an object and not a person. She learns to hate and fear intimacy. She learns that if it feels good, it must be bad. She feels worthless; her only value is for the sexual pleasure of her abuser. She internalizes all of that. She believes a lie.

Control issues are even stronger in incest than in other forms of physical abuse. She couldn't even control her own body. Somebody else took her clothes off. Somebody else made her do things, nasty things, painful things, disgusting things. She may try to re-establish control by under-eating [anorexia] or over-eating, trying to make herself less attractive to her attacker. She may refuse to have bowel movements and become profoundly constipated. Chronic pelvic pain and bowel dysfunction are common in adult survivors of incest.

Girls reject their femininity, deny or distort their sexuality, leading to lesbianism or frigidity. They may find their sexuality revolting, and become physically sick at the thought of having sex with a man. Attempts to have sex anyway result in intense involuntary vaginal muscle spasms precluding penetration. Other girls may internalize the filthy feeling and become promiscuous. Unable to value her sexuality, she debases it with a series of casual relationships, or in the case of prostitution, no relationship at all. She thinks everyone knows what a slut she is. They expect it of her.

Abused men also reject or distort their sexuality, either becoming effeminate and feeling intense attraction to other men, or seeking to control a woman as an object. They frequent prostitutes and enjoy pornography, and do so compulsively, but are unable to relate to real women. They have always felt this way, because the damage was done at such an early age, they cannot recall ever having normal feelings toward their own sexuality. They were unable to identify with and bond appropriately to their same sex parent, or successfully relate with and feel accepted by their opposite sex parent.

> *They were unable to identify with and bond appropriately to their same sex parent, or successfully relate with and feel accepted by their opposite sex parent.*

Boys suffer the additional threat to their masculinity, experienced as the loss of autonomy, loss of control, and the humiliation of being used by another man, or even deeper humiliation of being manipulated by a more powerful woman. They may identify themselves as weak and powerless, or they may seek to reestablish their masculinity by dominating and controlling other people or things, cruelty to animals, or gang violence. The boy wonders what it must have felt like to sodomize somebody, so he tries it on his younger brother. So now a twelve-year-old boy is sodomizing a six-year-old boy.

When baby monkeys have been neglected or abused, they self-stimulate [masturbate] and do so compulsively. The same thing happens with children, especially boys, and it turns in to a life long problem. I met a young man in jail who had been in and out of institutions most of his life. His mother was an alcoholic; he had been basically abandoned at the age of eight, and had spent his childhood in juvenile detention centers. "You don't want to know what they did to me there." He was eighteen years old, addicted to methamphetamine, and tormented by his compulsive masturbation.

In the case of ritual, family, or group abuse, the conflict is even deeper. Her mother knows about it and accepts it as the price she must pay to have a husband. Other parties join in and make a public spectacle of her humiliation. The child knows this is wrong, but everybody else says it's okay. She doubts her own sanity, her own understanding of what is really happening, her own knowledge of right and wrong, good and bad. Denial and suppression are almost universal in these cases. The fractured personality and self-doubt are obvious in the adult survivor of such abuse.

HEALING

Healing requires that the victim place the badness and the shame where they belong, upon the attacker, and accept herself [or himself] as a good and innocent child. Anger is the natural result of that, and when expressed, is a sign of significant growth and healing. Unexpressed anger may be turned inward as depression or anxiety, or acted out in aggressive or promiscuous behavior.

The child's "daddy need" is still strong, and the need for acceptance and love from a daddy will drive a young woman into sexual relationships that would never appeal to a healthier woman. She may seek to be dominated and controlled, so she seeks out aggressive and abusive men. She may reject heterosexual relationships altogether, finding comfort and love in a lesbian relationship. She is seductive and promiscuous, longing for someone to love her and care for her, but also feeling unlovable.

She forms powerful attachments to things or people promising unconditional love and acceptance, and is then crushed and disappointed when they cannot deliver. She makes demands of her relationships that cannot be met, and the relationships fail, proving to her once again that she is ugly and unlovable. Her deep neediness for time and attention drives people away from her.

Living in such a state of worthlessness and depression, it is any wonder incest victims are so prone to addiction to a drug like methamphetamine. Crystal makes you feel powerful, competent, intelligent, and confident. Such a person is extremely vulnerable to addiction, whether drug addiction, sexual addiction, fantasy addiction, or work addiction. She feels incomplete and longs for completeness. She feels out of control and longs for control. She may become a prostitute because it gives her control over a man sexually.

WOMAN AT THE WELL

When Jesus met the woman at the well, [John 4] He recognized in her the incest survivor who had had five husbands and the man she was with now was not her husband. She was the social outcast, dressed poorly, drawing water in the heat of the day when she wouldn't have to deal with the snide remarks of the other women. He didn't have to be God to know all about her.

John 4:6–34 NEB

It was about noon, and Jesus, tired after his journey, sat down by the well. The disciples had gone away to the town to buy food. Meanwhile, a Samaritan woman came to draw water. Jesus said to her, "Give me a drink." The Samaritan woman said, "What, You a Jew, ask a drink of me, a Samaritan woman?" [Jews and Samaritans had no dealings and did not use vessels in common.] Jesus answered her, "If only you knew what God gives, and who it is that is asking you for a drink, you would have asked Him and He would have given you living water."

This was the polite way of speaking, referring to yourself in the third person. He was speaking to her about spiritual things in a very polite way, and offering her something of value. 'Living water' was a clear reference to the presence of God.

"Sir," the woman said, "You have no bucket, and this well is deep. How can you give me living water?" Are you greater than Jacob, our ancestor, who gave us the well, and drank from it himself, he and his sons and his cattle too?" . . .

But He was God, and He cared enough about her to talk to her. And notice, there was a conversation. He listened to her as well. He treated her with respect, spoke of spiritual things with her, and responded to her comments. She'd never been treated like that before in her life. All of the sudden she was not dirty, she was not shameful, she was not an object. She was a person, with whom a man wanted to converse.

She pushed Him away verbally at first, aware of her inferiority. When He persisted, she resisted with literal arguments. Surely you don't really care about me! Let's talk about Jacob and his well. He continued to give her His time and attention, and finally she couldn't resist any more. He broke down her defenses, and she received real love.

He spoke to her of worshipping God in spirit and in truth. He offered her the abundant and unconditional love of God, His acceptance, His approval. "I, who speak to you, am He." He spoke to her! She's not filthy after all, He spoke to her! She dropped her water pot and ran! A life transformed by the love and acceptance of God.

She took him literally at first, wary of discussing deeply spiritual things with a Jewish stranger. The well itself was sacred to her people.

Jesus said, "Everyone who drinks this water will be thirsty again, but whoever drinks the water that I shall give him will never thirst any more. The water that I shall give him will be an inner spring always welling up for eternal life."

He made it perfectly clear that He was talking about spiritual things with her.

"Sir," said the woman, "Give me this water, and then I shall not be thirsty, or have to come all this way to draw."

Jesus replied, "Go home, call your husband and come back." She answered, "I have no husband." "You are right in saying I have no husband, for though you have had five husbands, the man with whom you are now living is not your husband. You told me the truth in that."

"Sir," she replied, "I can see that you are a prophet."

Her response indicates that Jesus did not know her from previous encounters, but knew about her from supernatural means. . . .

It happens every day, and Jesus is still just as pleased as He was when He told the guys with the turkey sandwiches, "I have food to eat that you know nothing about" [John 4:32]. Jesus treats you like a real person. God wants to be with you and enjoy your company. Your Father listens to you and answers you. He notices you. He cares about you. In a prayer relationship with Him, He joins you every day, takes interest in what you are doing, and cares about your feelings and needs. You've got a real Daddy, more powerful and loving than any human father could ever be.

LEARNING TO TRUST

Abuse survivors have a real problem learning to trust God. God is The Big Guy with the Stick. Your father, an authority figure, a representative of God, is not to be trusted. He will act one way in public, and be a completely different person in private. He will mock your trust, manipulate your need for him, and betray your love. The only cure for mistrust and suspicion like that is time.

Years of constant tender love, frequent, daily, even hourly reminders of your worth and value to Him, loving provision of your needs, attention, affirmation, approval, acceptance, and even affection—All of these can be experienced at the hand of God in prayer and in listening prayerful Bible study.

> "But the time approaches, indeed it is already here, when those who are real worshippers will worship the Father in spirit and in truth. Such are the worshippers whom the Father wants. God is spirit, and those who worship him must worship in spirit and in truth."
>
> The woman answered, "I know the Messiah [that is the Christ] is coming. When he comes he will tell us everything." Jesus answered her, "I who speak to you, am he."
>
> At that moment, his disciples returned and were astonished to find him talking with a woman, but none of them said, "What do you want?" or "Why are you talking with her?"
>
> *They knew better than to ask a question like that.*
>
> The woman put down her water-jar and went away to the town, where she said to the people, "Come and see a man who has told me everything I ever did. Could this be the Messiah?" They came out of the town and made their way towards him.
>
> Meanwhile, the disciples were urging him. "Rabbi, have something to eat." But he said, "I have food to eat of which you know nothing." At this, the disciples said to one another, "Can someone have brought him food?" But Jesus said, "It is meat and drink for me to do the will of him who sent me."

Take your "daddy need" to Him in prayer, and He will fill you with the most incredible love. You'll sense His delight in you. "I have food to eat that you know nothing about."

It's hard to believe it at first, but He never gets tired of telling you how much He loves you. Every time you realize it, on a deeper and deeper level, it's always a surprise; it's always this "Eureka" event. You'd think you would eventually catch on and not be so surprised every time it hits home that this God really loves you. You have believed a lot of lies, and each one has to be disarmed. It takes a long time for the fear to dissipate and the brain circuits to be rewired. God is very patient.

Eventually, over a period of years, it does sink in, and a kind of joy steals over you, a calm expectation of love and caring, a quiet trust in His goodness, a feeling of confidence in Him. You make a mistake and He still loves you. You forget about Him for awhile, but He doesn't lock you out. You start to understand what unconditional love really is, not by reading about it or hearing about it, but by experiencing it.

Experience His love in prayer, constant daily prayer. Know that He is with you all day every day. "In Him we live and move and have our being." [Acts 17:28] He's always there and He's always interested in what you are going through. You don't have to explain anything, He's seeing it right along with you, and you can inwardly discuss it with Him as you go along. When did you start praying? You don't know. You are always praying. He is always with you.

> ## *In Him we live and move*
> ## *and have our being.*

His love is a warm, comfortable presence you don't have to go out looking for because He's already there. He won't tell you to shut up; He won't get bored and tune you out. You can trust this Guy. He loves you. You can't earn it, you can't deserve it, and you can't talk Him out of it. It has nothing to do with who you are; you can't possibly be 'good enough.' It has everything to do with who He is. He loves you. He can't help it. That's just the kind of Guy He is.

Don't do like I did for a few years. I let Him love me on Monday, Wednesday, and Friday, but allowed myself to feel stupid and ugly on Tuesday, Thursday, and Saturday. It took twice as long to get to confidence and joy as it should have. Let Him love you every day. If you can't feel it, go to the Bible and get some there. Don't let a single day go by without knowing your Daddy loves you.

Don't let anybody take it away from you, either. If somebody hates you, that's their problem, not yours. When someone you love rejects you, pray for help coping with it. Don't let these people tell you who you are. Your Creator is the only One who has the right to do that. *"Sir, give me this water, and then I shall not be thirsty, or have to come all this way to draw."* He gives you fountains of love and acceptance within you, so you don't have to seek out the love of other people, or be devastated by their rejection.

The true knowledge of His unconditional love strengthens your personality. Relationships can fail, and you don't disintegrate. People can reject you and you survive. You don't die inside, because your Daddy still loves you. You can stand up for what you believe and take your punches from those who disagree with you, because your Daddy really loves you. *"I have come that they may have life, and have it to the full."* (John 10:10 NIV)

A MALE GOD

Some feminists want to emasculate God with gender neutral terminology. God has many 'feminine' qualities and should be understood as both male and female. We were created in His image. Male and female He created us, and so both male and female share in His image. God accepts His femininity gracefully in Isaiah 66:10–13. He doesn't have a problem with it. Women need to accept their Godlikeness and quit being so defensive about the gender pronoun thing. God put God's hat on God's head. Come on, now. Women are He as much as men are He. When the H is capitalized, it stands for both male and female.

Some women say they have been wounded so badly by the men in their lives that they cannot approach a male God. Exactly. That's what the Father thing is all about. All of us have been wounded by men in our lives at least once. Jesus came to heal that wound, not deny it, avoid it, or pretend it doesn't exist. He reconciles us to *"My God and your God, My Father and your Father."*

A Father to the fatherless, a defender of widows, is God in His holy dwelling. (Psalm 68:5 NIV)

Isaiah 66:10–13 NIV

Rejoice with Jerusalem and be glad for her, all you who love her; rejoice greatly with her, all you who mourn over her. For you will nurse at her comforting breasts; you will drink deeply and delight in her overflowing abundance. For this is what the Lord says: "I will extend peace to her like a river, and the wealth of nations like a flooding stream; you will nurse and be carried on her arm and dandles on her knees. As a mother comforts her child, so I will comfort you; and you will be comforted over Jerusalem.

.12.

POST TRAUMATIC STRESS DISORDER-
ACTS OF GOD

GOD GETS A LOT OF BAD PRESS

Many addicts [and many people who are not addicts] harbor a tremendous anger at God. Sometimes it is conscious, a militant atheism and contempt for believers. Other times, it is expressed as a hatred for society, an antisocial psychopathic disposition that holds all righteousness, honesty, honor, authority, and law in disdain.

The first representative of God we meet is our parents, and for better or worse, we think deep inside that God is just like our parents. When you are two years old, your dad is God. He is big, you are little. What he says goes, he is the authority. You believe what he tells you about yourself. You are not two years old anymore, but you carry your notions about God with you into adulthood.

On a larger scale, people think God is just like the church. They see the crusades and the witch burnings and conclude that God is judgmental and cruel and so they reject Him. Jimmy Swaggart and Jim Bakker claim to represent God, they even claim to speak for Him, and yet they have worshiped money, sex and power. The only Person who has ever truly come in the name of God is Jesus Christ, and we see no such judgmentalism and cruelty in Him.

It is inevitable that we are going to misunderstand God. All of us were fathered by human beings, and all of us think God is like human beings. We cannot conceive of an eternal and infinite God, because we are not eternal or infinite. We cannot comprehend his wisdom, because we are always learning. We cannot understand His unchanging-ness, because we are always changing. God is essentially unknowable to us because He is of a different order. He is "I am that I am." [Exodus 3:14] He is the essential Being from which all other things exist. We cannot comprehend Him. If we could, He wouldn't be God.

Our misunderstandings lead to animosity and denial. We see Him through the lens of our human relationships, especially our relationship with our parents, and we misunderstand His dealings with us. When tragedy strikes, we accuse him of not caring or of deliberately hurting us. We transfer the fear and resentment we feel towards our parents to God, the ultimate authority figure.

The deep pain of unresolved grief drives many into addiction. They cannot accept the death of a child, the unfairness of inherited disease, or the agony of a slow painful death. It seems cruel and unfair; it collides with our God given sense of justice. Suffering should be deserved. A thirty-two year old woman should not die from cancer. A mother and child should not die in an ice storm. All babies should be perfect. When a little girl is paralyzed for life by injuries to her spine in a tornado, we feel a sense of outrage. God should have prevented that.

Unresolved grief carries with it anger and helplessness, which lead to depression. When the grief is intense, it distracts us from normal daily activities. There is a constant preoccupation with the unfairness of it all. Unable to find relief from this pain in any other way, people look to drugs, whether alcohol, prescription drugs, or illegal drugs, to make them feel better. It hurts to think about these things. If we get high or drunk, we don't have to think about it for a little while.

It's A Real World And God Is A Real God

Post Traumatic Stress Disorder is oftentimes the result of a natural disaster, not an assault by another person. Car wrecks, tornados, even thunder and lightening can cause the recurrent nightmares, flashbacks, and obsessions characteristic of PTSD. The wiring of the brain can be permanently changed by a traumatic event, even an act of God.

One of the most common arguments against the existence of God is this. A loving God would not permit . . . and then they name all the evils in the world as evidence against a Creator. What about house fires that kill innocent people, an industrial accident that takes the life of the father of four children; what about babies with spinal bifida, or three young sisters killed in a car wreck? Those things are good evidence against a big Teddy Bear in the Sky, but they are not evidence against a Creator.

Some people cannot love a God who would allow such senseless and unnecessary suffering. They cannot see a reason for it in this world, and so they cannot accept it. It makes no sense if seen only in the context of this world. It can only make sense when seen in the context of the eternal and infinite world, which God can see, but we cannot. If we refuse to accept the reality of an eternal world, we can never make sense out of tragedy. It remains unresolved.

> *If we refuse to accept the reality of an*
> *eternal world, we can never make sense*
> *out of tragedy. It remains unresolved.*

God reveals Himself in the tragedy of life as much as He does in the flowers and sunshine. He shapes us and molds us by hardship and pain, and forms character within us. How could we develop perseverance if there were no hardships to endure? How could we learn mercy and forgiveness if no one ever offended us? How could He form compassion and empathy in us if there was no pain or loss in our lives?

You say, "If there were no pain in life, there would be no *need* for compassion. It is a cruel God who values compassion so much He makes innocent children suffer with birth defects if that is the only good that comes of it." I know a woman who had always been a very self-centered person. All she could think about was her problems, her aches and pains, her needs, and her rights. Any minor discomfort or inconvenience brought her to my office expecting instant and permanent relief. One day, she came in with a lump in her breast, and it was cancer. I thought, "Lord, why did you let that happen to her? Couldn't you have found somebody who would have handled it better?"

Six months later, in the throes of chemotherapy and wearing a wig, she came back a completely different person. She is filled with compassion for the people she has met at the oncologist's clinic. She is far more concerned with them than she is with herself. She no longer notices her own aches and pains, which are much more numerous and serious than anything she has ever experienced before. She has been transformed by her suffering into a joyful and generous servant of God, and she is truly a beautiful person because of it.

We can only understand a very limited type of love, a love that wants to spare the loved one all pain and suffering. It is a far greater love that is willing to subject His children to pain and suffering in order to develop in them character that can only come from pain and suffering. God is eternal, and He has given us an eternal spirit. He knows we will need compassion for the rest of eternity, and he feels it is so valuable that innocent suffering is not too great a price to pay for it. We cannot comprehend eternity, and so we cannot comprehend the need for the character He is developing in us. That is not His problem. That is our problem.

UNEXPLAINED SUFFERING

The central message in the book of Job, a story of unexplained suffering, is our inability to comprehend God. At the end of the story, God tells Job,

"Hey, I'm God and you're not. Get used to it." No explanation, no justification, not even a list of virtues gained from the experience. Just an understanding that God has a will and a purpose we cannot comprehend, and we have to accept the fact that He is God, and we are not.

He spoke this universe into existence in precisely the way He wanted it. There are no mistakes, no errors in judgment, no reckless gambles. This world is not a cosmic science project gone bad. It is a real world where real things happen and real choices are made. He has made a world where good things can happen, babies can be born. It is also a world where bad things can happen, babies can die. It is a real world and real things happen in it. He is not a Teddy Bear and this is not a toy world.

> *God is not a Teddy Bear,*
> *and this is not a toy world.*

If metal is hard on Monday so you can drive your car, metal is still hard on Tuesday when you get hit by a car. If the microbes in your gut can break your food down for you, microbes in the cut in your hand can turn to gangrene. If cell division can make new tissue to repair the damage of an injury, cell division can make a cancer and kill you. Reality does not bend to our wishes, like a fantasy world where nobody ever gets hurt. Gravity is not suspended when it is inconvenient to us and our purposes. I always get a charge out of 'cartoon physics,' in which gravity is suspended and smashed animals get back up with no harm done. I think some of us expect the world to really work that way. It doesn't. This is a real world and real things happen in it. We suffer real pain and we enjoy real pleasure.

Our actions have real consequences in this real world. If we neglect a great duty, that role goes unfilled. If we cause pain to another person, that person suffers real pain. The bullet does not magically turn into a nerf ball. If we shoot somebody, whether with a gun or with our mouth, they are shot, and we can't take the bullet or the harsh word back. This is not a play, and we are not actors. This world is real.

This world is, however, a fabulous boarding school. We are learning things here we could not learn anywhere else, and the lessons we learn here, we will never forget. The character we develop here will be our eternal character. In this world we are becoming, and our life experiences shape the eternal being we will be stuck with forever. In eternity we will *be,* as God *is,* unchanging. [1 John 3:2] God is far more interested in our eternal destiny and character than He is in our temporary comfort on this planet.

---

1 John 3:2 NIV

Dear friends, now we are children of God, and what we will be has not been made known. But we know that when He appears, we shall be like Him, for we shall see Him as He is.

BIOLOGICAL DETERMINISM

Some people look at the functions of the brain cells, and see themselves as the product of their neurons, attributing every thought and motivation to the mindless workings of their brain, molecular interactions that are predetermined by genetics, the cellular environment, nutrition, ingested toxins, cellular aging, fatigue, hormones, and blood sugar level, and feel that they really have no identity other than the product of their brain cells.

They assume that consciousness has no spiritual meaning, because their thought processes depend upon the actions of atoms and molecules gyrating around in response to electrical charges and orbital energies. Evolution has taught them to believe their ability to think, feel, will, and act is merely the product of cellular mechanisms, and they have no real free will, but can only do what their orbital energies do. This line of thinking, of course, absolves them of any responsibility for their thoughts and actions, since they are only doing what their brain chemistry is making them do. They are the children of alcoholics, with ADHD and damaged neurons, and their only alternative is to get drunk and stay drunk.

If I were just the product of my neurons, I would be a hateful spiteful person, controlled by the resentments left over from years ago, incapable of meaningful relationships. Obviously, I am more than the product of my neurons. So are you. You can be beaten and betrayed and humiliated, and still be a loving person. No one can destroy your spirit. You still have a choice.

No one can destroy your spirit.

We are essentially spirits, and the brain is an organ that you use, much like you use your heart and muscles. You are responsible for the condition of your brain, just like you are responsible for the condition of your heart and muscles. If you exercise and eat right, you have a healthy heart and strong muscles. Similarly, if you think right and nourish yourself on healthy ideas, you have a healthy brain.

If you damage your brain with methamphetamine, that limits what you can do with it, just like if you damage your leg you may not be able to walk. But you are still you. Methamphetamine might damage your ability to care for your children, it might damage your ability to control your impulses, but even methamphetamine cannot destroy you. Your thoughts, your beliefs, your desires, and your will belong to you. You use your brain to express those things, but they exist apart from your brain. They exist in your spirit. You *are* a spirit, and you *have* a brain. I could cut out half of your brain, and you will still be you - disabled no doubt, but still you.

Your brain states do influence your conscious thoughts. The Alzheimer's patient does not think like a normal person. But so also your conscious thoughts influence your brain states. Your thought habits change the wiring of your brain. Your conscious decisions affect your neuroanatomy. Science cannot account for your consciousness and free will simply on the basis of neural activity. It's impossible. Your consciousness and free will account for your neural activity. Your brain is your servant, not your master.

> *Your brain is your servant,*
> *not your master.*

Even the more deranged schizophrenic, the most brain damaged child, still has an identity and a will. He uses his brain, however handicapped it may be, and expresses himself, however unintelligible it may be to you and me. If you have ADHD or Bipolar, you have a choice about how you will react to that. Both of these problems are treatable with appropriate medications, and both require adaptations on your part to compensate for the tendencies arising in your brain. It takes more focus to control the impulses and distractions you feel, and a good therapist can teach you many good techniques. You can take charge of your brain and its biochemistry; you don't have to let your biochemistry take charge of you.

Your neurons do not control you, your genes do not control you; you have a free will, a real identity. You are a person, not an object or a machine, and not just an animal. You live in a world that permits you freedom to act, to choose, to initiate, to desire, and to see the consequences of those choices in real life. You can choose to take a hammer and pound a nail into a piece of wood, and that piece of wood is permanently altered by that act. You can make a remark and pound it into the head of your child, and that child's personality is permanently affected by that remark.

GOD DOES NOT CONTROL US

A world that did not allow bad things to happen would be a world of automatons, robots that can respond, but cannot initiate. In this world we have choices, real meaningful choices. We have a human will, a self that desires and chooses and acts. We have freedom that is meaningful; it is not an illusion. We have a choice in our response to the people around us, a real meaningful choice. We are not hypnotized by our friends; we are not blinded by our society. People offer us the opportunity to reject God and choose pleasure, power, money, and drugs over Him. We are not controlled by those people. We have the power to walk away from those influences and think for ourselves.

We are not controlled by God or fate or the stars. He made sure of it when He created a real world where bad things can happen. It is also a world where real choices are made, and we are really responsible for our choices. But, you say, if God is sovereign, does He not really control us? If He is really God, then nothing happens that He does not control. If we have choices, real meaningful choices, then our will is really sovereign. How can He give us a free will and still be God? God is *so* sovereign He can *even* do that. He can choose to give us a will which can oppose His will, and He can still be the final authority and the ultimate judge. He can still be God.

> *If God had wanted robots,*
> *He would have made robots*

His goal is that we should be His people, and He should be our God. He wants a real relationship with real persons. If He had wanted robots, He would have made robots. He wanted real people, with whom He could have a real relationship, people who would freely choose to have a relationship with Him. In the final analysis, God wants us to love Him. That's what worship really is. He made us in order to have a love relationship with us, to love us and be loved by us.

Why does God tolerate evil in this world? So we could have a real choice. He had a choice whether to make us or not; He gives us a choice whether to love Him or not. If we were not free to hate him, our love would have no meaning. Love cannot be forced. If it is, it's not love. It becomes slavish servitude. We cannot accept Him unless we are free to reject Him. We cannot love Him unless we are free to hate Him. We cannot love him deeply unless we are free to despise Him.

We are all free to choose Whom or what we will worship. Many of us worship God with all of our hearts, minds, and actions. We honor Him with every word we say and with every thing we do. Some of us worship drugs or alcohol, some worship sex or money, some worship their own egos. We choose our god with every decision we make.

> *Each and every one of us is free to reject Him. He wouldn't have it any other way.*

Each and every one of us is free to reject Him. He wouldn't have it any other way. He does not force anyone to obey Him. He does not compel anyone to believe in Him, and so He didn't sign the picture. We can see Him in creation if we choose to. He reveals Himself in a Sacred Writing which has been preserved for thousands of years. We can believe it if we choose to. He gives each one of us enough evidence that we *can* believe if we really want to, but He will not force anyone to acknowledge Him.

WE DO NOT CONTROL GOD

God doesn't control us. We can't control or manipulate God either. People misunderstand prayer because they misunderstand God. We get frustrated with prayer because we don't see any results. If we don't really believe in the spiritual world, we will quickly get disillusioned about prayer. We don't see the answer in this world, and we conclude there was no answer. Often, we overlook the answer to our prayer because it isn't what we expected or even wanted. I prayed for God to make me more patient, and all I get is these slow poke people pulling out in front of me.

Prayer is not an internet order form with instant e-mail response, because God is not a vending machine, and He refuses to be treated like one. Prayer is all about a relationship with God. It is about experiencing His presence, hearing His voice, responding to His requests, and growing to be more like Him. It is best done with an open Bible in front of you, so you can hear Him better. It cannot be rushed, programmed, scripted or delegated to somebody else.

> *God is eternal and infinite, and there is plenty of room in Him for you.*

Prayer is communicating with the eternal infinite Being who spoke us into existence. It has always astounded me that this Being even allows us to address Him, never mind ask Him for things. And yet that's exactly what He invites us to do, even *commands* us to do. He actually listens to all the whiney little stuff we bring to Him. His Mind is so vast and so large, He can hold each one of our little minds inside His Mind, each one of our little broken hearts inside His Heart, each one of our confused spirits inside His Spirit. He doesn't tune us out, or tell us to shut up, or get busy with somebody else. He is eternal and He is infinite, and there is plenty of room in Him for you.

RAZOR BLADES

We make our requests, but we always remember, we are asking our Father for something, and sometimes the answer is, "No." If your child were asking for a razor blade, and he wanted it really bad, would you give it to him? Probably not. "But it's shiny and pretty, and it's not very big, it will fit in my pocket." Sorry, kid, no razor blade. "But the teenage boy down the street gets one! Why can't I have one?" You've asked for a razor blade, and He will not give it to you.

The razor blade may be a certain person you want to be your spouse, someone He knows is wrong for you. It may be success in a certain career which would lead you into abject cruelty and injustice, spiritual blindness, or the neglect of your family. It may be a friendship which would be destructive to your other relationships. It may be a child of your own who would distract you from doing something He wants you to do ten years from now. You may get your razor blade, by your own skill and cunning, but if you're asking Him, the answer is "No."

Sometimes that is hard to take. We are asking for something, like the life of a child, and we feel betrayed when our child dies. Our hopes are dashed. We feel mocked, feel like a fool to have trusted this God who is supposed to care. "I must have been an idiot to trust God. He's either a phony or He doesn't exist." We are praying for something which is very important to us, and we can't imagine why He would refuse our request. Many years ago, I prayed for the life of my baby. My baby died. He didn't give me the life of my child. What did He give me instead? He gave me love and compassion for hurting people. Is that worth the life of a child? God thought so. Who am I to argue with Him?

We have to trust that He knows what He is doing, and be willing to take "No" for an answer. He will not substitute our temporal happiness for the kind of eternal character He wants for us. Whenever He says "No," it's because He has something far better to give us than the small thing, the little toy we are asking for. All we can see is the toy. We can't see the eternal value of the priceless treasure He is giving to us.

When we pray for our addicted children, sometimes we don't like the answer. The kid gets thrown in jail, perhaps for life. He loses his job and his wife leaves him. Things get worse instead of better. "What are you doing, God? I asked you to bless my child!" It's hard for us to understand how life in prison could be a blessing. God measures it against eternity in hell. Can life in prison be a priceless treasure? Sure.

> *God will not destroy your free will to get you to love Him.*

We are asking Him to remove our child's free will, to force him to quit using and get better, and that is the one thing God will never do. He has decided to make beings with a free will. He will not then destroy that free will in order to get somebody to love Him. He will manipulate events in order to get your son's attention; He will make sure your child has the opportunity to choose to do what's right, even if that means life in prison, but He will not force him to do what's right.

So why pray if God is going to do what He wants, when He wants, anyway? We pray because that is the way He set things up. He wants us to communicate with Him. He really does respond to our requests, and things are different when we pray. He created us to be persons, and He respects and responds to us as persons. Prayer works primarily in the spiritual world. Your prayers for your addicted child are answered deep in the heart of that child. Your child has a choice in how he will respond to the movements of God in his spirit. It breaks your heart when your child says "No" to God. It breaks God's heart, too. [Ezekiel 18:32]

GOD HAS A GOAL

People, in the back of their minds, think God is a lot like them. They think He agrees with them on most issues, hates the same people they hate, feels pain over the same things that cause them pain, wants the same things they want, and thinks the same way they think. [Wouldn't it be a horrible world if that were true?] He will not be like us. He wants us to be like *Him*. God has the big picture foremost in His mind. No amount of finite temporary suffering is too much to pay for the glory of being the people He wants us to be, in the world of eternal timelessness that He lives in and that we are destined for.

There is a lot of pain and tragedy in this world. Some of it is our own doing, and some is clearly an act of God. But God does not just dump us here and say, "See ya later, good luck, guys". He is with us in this world. *"In Him we live and move and have our being."* This universe exists within Him, and nothing happens in it that He does not know about. This harsh and unyielding world is real, but He is also real, and we are not left to fend for ourselves. We experience His presence with us in prayer, not just *talking* prayer, but *being* prayer. Staying in His presence through the heartbreak and agony draws us closer to Him. We draw strength from Him and enter His peace; the peace that doesn't make any sense [passes all understanding].

None of the pain and tragedy in this life has any meaning apart from Him. It is all just a mockery of our human capacity to suffer, mindless purposeless anguish. Apart from God, life is meaningless and futile and there is no reason to continue to live [my paraphrase of the book of Ecclesiastes]. Yet in Him, the eternal Being who created our universe, even the most abject suffering takes on meaning and purpose. Nothing is wasted. Every tear, every heart break, has an effect on the eternal infinite world we are destined for. Every grief shapes us for the world we were really made to live in.

He calls us to a real relationship with a *real* God, not the figment of our imaginations. We cannot create God in our own image. He will not play along with our delusions about Him. He insists upon being Himself, even at the expense of being badly misunderstood. One long look at His revelation of Himself, in the Bible and in our lives, will dispel all our delusions about a cuddly "Teddy Bear in the Sky" God, and we find a God who is truly sovereign, and truly worthy of worship.

Oh Lord you have searched me and you know me. You know when I sit and when I rise, you perceive my thoughts from afar. You discern my going out and my lying down; you are familiar with all my ways. Before a word is on my tongue you know it completely O Lord. You hem me in behind and before; you have laid your hand upon me. Such knowledge is too wonderful for me, too lofty for me to attain. (Psalm 139:1–6 NIV)

.13.

SOCIAL RISK FACTORS - PEER PRESSURE

"Dr. Holley;
Hi my name is Rachel and I have been a victim of methamphetamine. I am only 15 years old and got addicted from the first hit. It started out as I just wanted to try new things and I promised myself as well as my friends I would never do it again. I couldn't help myself and every time I was around it I did it. Then all I ever thought about was the drug and did anything to get to it. I lost my best friend because she was scared and didn't know how she could help me, as well as my boyfriend. I didn't care about my friends or my family and I used my friends to get to the people with the meth. I would never have got help if I didn't get caught by my mother and stepfather. They knew something was wrong from the time I walked threw the door. I wasn't myself and I was like a whole different person. My heart was racing and couldn't be still. When I got to the ER of course I failed my drug test. I was sent to rehab and stayed for . . . I realized that how bad what I was doing was. Now I have permanent damage from it. I have lost all of my short term memory, and it's very hard to concentrate, I wish that I could go back but I cant. I only did it for a short time, but the pain I caused for my family and affects will last forever. [all spelling errors original to the document]"

IT CAN HAPPEN TO ANYBODY

Nobody gets up one morning and says, "Gee I think I'll become a junky and lose my mind on methamphetamine." Addiction can happen to anybody. No person is resistant, no family is immune. Even healthy well adjusted people can make a mistake with methamphetamine and become addicted. More than half of all drug addicts are from abusive tragic situations like we discussed earlier. The others come from good homes where they were loved and nurtured, intact homes in which both parents were involved and caring. Drug addiction can happen to anybody.

> *They teased him about being a virgin,*
> *and passed him the pipe.*

A smart kid thought he was too smart to get hooked on drugs. He wanted to be cool with his friends, fit in with the party crowd, the 'in people.' They were using it in front of him, daring him to try it, too. They teased him about being a virgin, and passed him the pipe. The girl who gave it to him was really good-looking and she was standing real close. He was only fifteen years old. It never occurred to him that what he was doing would destroy his life.

The kids in high school think methamphetamine is just for fun. They see it as safer than cocaine, cheaper than cocaine, and better than cocaine. They've heard about 'crack babies' and the horrors of cocaine addiction, and they think crystal is safer. They don't consider it a real drug. The high is a feeling of power and control, confidence and intelligence, energy and endurance. They can't see anything wrong with that, and they get angry when their drug use is challenged or questioned.

It's not just youth falling into the peer pressure trap. Educated adults who should know better will also do things that they know are stupid because they want to fit in with the after work crowd. It's hard to go home alone when everybody else is partying. If you want to play basketball with these guys, you need to do what they are doing. If you don't, you are eyed with suspicion. "This guy might be a real narc. We can't let him into our inner circle unless he uses like we do."

> *Basically healthy people made a mistake.*

A third grade teacher started with a little diet pill, just for a few weeks, to lose a few pounds. Her friend lost fifty pounds on this stuff, it 'works' great. After taking it a few times, she realized it made her feel great, energetic, lively, and life was fun again. She hadn't felt that good in years. She felt a craving for the feel good it gave her, and started using it more. Within six months, she was injecting it daily. She was missing a lot of work and losing control over her life. She felt so bad the days she didn't take it, she couldn't function without it. "Doctor, is there anything you can do to help me?"

A truck driver needs to go another hundred miles to get home tonight. A factory worker wants to work a double shift. A nurse is working a swing shift. A student is cramming for finals, or trying to work and go to school at the same time. Basically healthy people with no significant psychopathology made a mistake. It looked so innocent, just a little pick-me-up, and it turned into a rattlesnake.

Occasionally, an adult is faced with a new social situation. A middle aged couple goes out with some new friends and feels pressure to fit in, go along with the crowd. Finding themselves in the middle of a rave party, they think, "Why not?" In a new setting they feel anonymous. No one has any expectations of them, they can try something new. After all, life was getting kind of boring.

Or, you find yourself in the midst of a crisis. Your husband leaves you, your mother dies, or your child is seriously injured in a car wreck. Your stress level just went through the ceiling, and you need some help to cope. A well-meaning friend offers you something sure to help. "Here, try this. It will make you feel better."

A whole new world is opened up; a world of chemical well-being. With one little pill you can feel highly intelligent, powerful, confident, and energetic. It is intoxicating to think you can have that kind of control over your moods. If you're feeling down, you can do something about it. Keep that Prozac, I've found something that really 'works!'

"I recently tried meth and I was shocked by the addictive powers of only one dose. I want to avoid it, but at the same time I remember that wonderful feeling. I find it strange that I've only done it like 2 or 3 times and I'm thinking about it that much."

Just once, on a special occasion, you suspend your values. You feel pressured to try it, just once, and you give in. Just once. With this drug, just once is enough to destroy a life. Even a single dose does subtle damage to the brain in key areas of the reward pathway, the mood centers, and in the pleasure center in the brain. More than 90% of people who try methamphetamine get another dose within one month of the first, 75% of them within one week of the first dose. You maintain control over your drug use for about two weeks. By the third hit, you feel a strong compulsion to use it again. You don't control it anymore. Of course you think you have control over it. You think you could walk away from it, you have just consciously *chosen* to use it again.

Okay, prove it. Quit using and prove to me, and prove to yourself, that you can just walk away from it. It's harder than it sounds. Even after just one or two doses, you will feel a definite pull to use it again. "Aw come on. It won't hurt. It'll feel so much better." Is hard to walk away from that, especially when the drug 'works' so well. Once you are addicted, the downward spiral gets steep and fast. The crash feels so bad; the high feels so much better. The bad mood doesn't go away with anything else, only crystal methamphetamine 'works.' You don't control it. It controls you.

Do you see what has happened? The free-will that God went out of His way to give you has been taken away. You no longer have control over urges and cravings and impulses. You have a *desire* for another hit, and you have no control over that desire. The cravings control you. The parts of your brain that give you control over cravings, median forebrain bundle and fasciculus retroflexus, have been damaged with just one or two hits of this stuff. But the effect of the drug is a feeling of power and control. It is a hallucination of power and control, because you already have no power and no control.

> *This is the last time. I promise.*

Every time you use is "the last time. I promise." You deny that you have a problem. You only use it on weekends, only with your friends, only when you have to work a double. You still work and support your family. "Hey, I give you enough money to pay the bills. I want to have fun with this little bit of money. I have a right to it. It's my money. I work for it. Just leave me alone, *all right?"*

Crystal makes you feel so good and energetic you feel you don't need anything or anyone else; nothing is more important or rewarding than ice. You sneak around and manipulate events to get more of it. You make excuses why you have to use it again, a double shift, a hard day at work, a fight with your wife. Pretty soon, anything is reason enough to get more, a difficult assignment at work, a night spent with a sick child, even just a bad cold. It alienates you from your family and co-workers and you really don't care. You are preoccupied with ice, how to get more, buy more, make more, and there is no time for normal relationships in your new and improved life with crystal.

THE ADDICT IS BLIND TO THE PROBLEM

Addicts are oblivious to the problems methamphetamine is causing. They think everything is just fine and they don't understand what all the fuss is about. They get defensive and hostile when their drug use is questioned or challenged. "Hey, I can do what I want, Okay?" They want to protect this fantastic feeling of power and self-esteem, and they resent anyone who threatens their source of pleasure, their new identity.

They don't see how crystal is causing them to be irritable with their children and abusive towards their spouse. They don't realize they haven't fed their baby in two days, spent the grocery money on ice, or missed their daughter's high school graduation. They curse at their children, blow up at their wives, and pull their toddler's arm out of its socket because the little one can't walk fast enough.

They don't catch on until their wife leaves or Child Protective Services comes to get the kids. They realize they might have a problem when they lose their job or their business goes broke. They are forced to face it when they get arrested and thrown in jail. In the meantime, they have broken their children's hearts. Daddy loves his drug a lot more that he loves us.

Think you are too smart to get hooked on a drug like crystal? Addiction happens to doctors and lawyers, teachers and preachers, policemen and high school football coaches. Intelligent and educated business people and professionals get addicted to methamphetamine. It is seductive and deceptive. It is a lot smarter than you are.

PEER PRESSURE

If adults have that much trouble with this drug, imagine what an immature teenager goes through. Even if a teen has been taught from the cradle, drug use is wrong, drugs are dangerous, they cause brain damage, even if he knows all that, the allure of ice is powerful. Teenagers can't think past today, even tomorrow doesn't matter. The long term brain damage caused by crystal seems insignificant compared to being cool with his friends right now.

They use it in front of him and pass him the pipe. The music is playing loud and everybody is laughing. He's had a few beers and he's feeling relaxed. A good looking girl is there. He wants to impress her and be cool like the other guys. These are all his best friends, or people he would like to be friends with, the popular guys who have lots of money and girlfriends and drive nice cars. Sometimes it happens when he is the social outcast with no friends, and he realizes he has lots of friends when he uses ice. When his best friends use, it's real hard to say, "Sorry, guys, I don't do that." The kid who resists and declines to use is mocked and derided. They call him names, the narc, the nerd. They pressure him to try it, "See, we all use it, and you don't see us growing a third eyeball."

Your son goes to his friend's house after school, and his friend pulls some crystal out of his drawer and offers some to your son. Your son says, "No thanks." Can you see what an awkward position your son is in? The friend says, "What's the matter? You scared? 'Fraid your mommy will find out?" Most kids will cave at this point and try the drug, but let's say your son has been educated and warned, so he says, "No, doing ice is stupid." Now the situation has changed. By refusing the drug, your son has told his friend that he is wrong. He doesn't want to be told he is wrong and he gets angry. The tone changes.

"What are you, some kind of snitch? You a narc? You gonna turn me in?" The words get hostile and the friendship is clearly threatened. If this friendship is meaningful to your child, he will cave in and say, "No, I'm still your friend, I'll try a little." Multiply by two, four, six friends at a party and the pressure is increased exponentially. Now it's a public humiliation to refuse the drug.

Nobody wants to be the only guy at the party who won't play along. Even if your son went to his friend's house determined to stay off drugs, he will try it once to avoid being teased and poked at. He'll do it to get everybody off his back, to fit in and be accepted. Once he has used it, he finds the party is great and he has all kinds of friends when he gets high. He has a new girlfriend and is experimenting with illicit sex under the influence of ice. All that bad stuff his mother told him about methamphetamine seems far away and long ago. This stuff is great!

If the only friends your child has are drug-users, your child is going to use drugs. Kids don't live in a vacuum. They are strongly influenced by their friends. You don't get out of the fifth grade and start shooting crystal, first thing. They get you drunk first. Remember, cigarette smoking, drinking, and marijuana use are significant risk factors for drug use. You let your guard down. You are with people you know and trust. They are using it too, and you want to fit in.

You the adult, you the teenager, *you* are responsible for your choice of friends. Your friends do not choose you. You choose your friends. You are responsible for what goes on at your parties. You are responsible for your choice of which parties you go to and how long you stay. You are not a helpless victim of your social situation. You can fit into any group of people if you really try. You make a friend by being a friend, and you can choose the people you will be a friend to.

> *You the adult, you the teenager, you are responsible for your choice of friends.*

Parents can help their kids in this regard. You can encourage them to participate in sports programs, after school special interest clubs, social service organizations, scouting, and church youth groups. Invite families over for dinner and let the kids mingle and have fun together. Take an active role in your child's social life, especially if he is shy and withdrawn by nature.

Peer pressure to use drugs and party is strong and powerful. So is peer pressure to stand tall and stay off drugs. A church youth group, math club, chess club, or sports team will exert a powerful influence on a teenager to stay clean. He won't want to disappoint his friends who are counting on him to be sober and play half back in the Friday night football game. Our teens need a social support system that validates and reinforces their decision not to use drugs. They need friends who expect them to be sober, smart, and sane. They need peers who value accomplishment and excellence in school, in work, in sports, and in life.

COUNTERING PEER PRESSURE

"I was raised in a Christian home, church and all, every summer we went to church camp etc. But most of all I remember the morals and values I was raised with. And even when I was using I remember thinking . . . Man this is not cool . . . but I was so addicted. But always those morals and values were right there in my mind."

The spiritual health of a teenager is extremely important to resisting pressures to use drugs. The strength of this association was described eloquently by the National Center on Addiction and Substance Abuse at Columbia University in 2001. Teens who never attend worship services are four times more likely to abuse drugs as those who attend services weekly. Adults who never attend worship services are eight times more likely to abuse drugs.

There are many factors going into that figure, income, education, marital status of the parents for example, but the most important variable was the spiritual condition of the teen's *father*. The father's attendance at church was the single most predictive factor for prevention of drug abuse among teenagers in this study. *The most important thing you can do to reduce the risk of drug abuse in your family is to take your kids to church.*

> *The most important thing you can do to reduce the risk of drug abuse in your family is to take your kids to church.*

The kid who understands God, and understands himself as the priceless child of God, is empowered against the kind of peer pressure we have been talking about. He doesn't need anyone or anything in order to feel confidence and joy, it wells up within him. He doesn't need the acceptance of a gang when he has the acceptance of the Living God. He can choose for himself what he is going to do, and he doesn't really care what anybody else thinks. He will seek out friends who agree with him, instead of agreeing with whatever his friends say and do.

I tell a story when I speak to groups of teens. It's from Mark 6:45. Jesus was a happy, friendly guy. He had lots of friends. One day a bunch of His friends were in a boat going across the lake. These guys were fishermen, big strong men who knew how to run a boat. But they weren't getting anywhere because they were rowing against a stiff wind.

It was getting dark and they still weren't there. It was getting late and they still weren't there. It was three o'clock in the morning, the fourth watch of the night, and they were getting scared. They were up against a wind that was a lot stronger than they were. Jesus came passing by, "as if to pass them by." He didn't ram Himself down their throats, He just passed by. They called out to Him, and He got in their boat; then the wind died down and they got to the other side.

> *He doesn't need the acceptance of a gang*
> *when he has the acceptance*
> *of the living God.*

Jesus knows all about peer pressure, and He knows it is a vicious wind. Even strong experienced adults have trouble rowing against that wind. A teenager all by himself doesn't stand a chance. Even if he has a healthy personality, even if he's not depressed, even if he's secure and happy in his family, peer pressure is intense. Nobody likes to be left out. They call him the nerd, the twerp, the narc. They badger him and tease him, stuff it in his pocket and use it in front of him. It's a hurricane-force wind.

Parents can help a teenager develop a strong relationship with Jesus. You can teach your child all about Jesus, but you have to show him how to *know* Jesus by knowing Him yourself. A youth minister can teach your child all about Jesus, but your child has to experience Him for himself. There is no substitute for a real relationship with Him. When a child really *knows Jesus,* not just all about Him, when he really believes that God is real and powerful and involved in his life, he will have more than enough courage to stand up to the dealers and friends who encourage him to use. When Jesus is a constant daily presence in his life, not just a character out of book, he will find it easy to avoid the situations that lead to drug abuse. That kind of party will not even appeal to him.

When you know Jesus, you get to know all His other friends, the folks who hang out at His place. Church youth groups are vital to success against the peer pressure to use drugs. Teenagers need a sense of acceptance and belonging, and they will join a gang if they can't get it any other way. He needs friends who will support him in his decision to not use drugs, people who know how to have fun without getting smashed.

A well-run church youth program will make sure no individual teen is ostracized by the group, keep cliques from forming, and counsel individuals who are having problems. A good youth minister will recognize the new kid and help him fit in, make friends, and make a contribution. If your son feels like he has something to offer the group, he will be much more comfortable in it.

Don't think you can drop your teenager off at church and they will fix everything for you. That church will have absolutely no credibility with your son if you don't go too. If you don't believe this stuff at least enough to participate in the church yourself, he will resent your efforts to manipulate him by putting him in this church thing.

It can't be just Mom's idea either. If church is really important, adult and manly, Dad will want to go, too. If he doesn't, the kid knows that church is just a toy, a gimmick to force him into a mold. Remember, he is breaking all the drug culture rules by going to this church thing. He's going to take some abuse about it from his old friends. They will call him the "church-boy," the "narc," the "twerp." He'll take that kind of abuse for something he really believes in, but he will not take it just to make you happy.

HYPOCRITES

If you have decided church is just a bunch of hypocrites and there is no real substance to their beliefs, check your facts first. You've been disappointed and disillusioned by a pastor, a priest, a church leader who wasn't what he should have been. You're right. You had an *illusion* about what a Christian leader should be like, and you have been *disillusioned.* That leader represents God, but he is not, and never will be God.

Pastors say things that hurt your feelings. Deacons jump to conclusions and make accusations that are not true. Preachers defer to the people who make the big donations. Priests have molested children, pastors have had affairs, and youth group leaders have been addicted to drugs and alcohol. It happens. These people are not robots, they are men and women with hurts, feelings, and hormones, just like the rest of us.

> *You hold spiritual leaders to a
> higher standard in their ethics and
> behavior. So does God.*

You hold spiritual leaders to a higher standard in their ethics and behavior. So does God. It is a fearsome thing to fall into the hands of the Living God. Offending pastors are held to the fire by Almighty God. They are brought to their knees, face to face with their sin, and in humility and repentance they are restored by Him, but not always to their previous position of power and service. God is choosey about whom He allows to serve Him.

The church represents your best hope for coping with your at-risk teenager. Don't try to go it alone. Get some people around you to pray with you and for you. Your child needs people around him who support his values, and so do you. Talk with other parents who are going through the same adolescent nightmare you are, compare notes and ideas. When your daughter makes a friend at church, get to know her friend's parents and have a cookout together. It's good for your daughter, and it's good for you, too.

NO RIGHT TO PRIVACY

"I used to hide my stash in a hollowed out spot under the thing that goes on the top of my bedpost. It would hold a gram, and I could make that last four or five days. Every day after school I would "go do my homework" and everybody thought I was some kind of angel."

As parents, we need to watch our children very closely for early signs of drug abuse. Look for personality changes, a drop in grades, a change in attitude, new friends you don't know, or a sudden preference for Dad's place or Mom's place. Your daughter may start staying out too late, oversleeping the next day, and missing school. Your son used to help you work on the car; he used to enjoy shooting baskets with you, and now he won't even look you in the eye. He's always wearing sunglasses, even indoors. Something has changed.

Don't be afraid to invade your child's privacy. If your child *of any age* is living in your home, he has forfeited his right to privacy. His room is not his room. It is *your* room and he keeps his stuff in it. His drawer is not his drawer. It's *your* drawer and he keeps his clothes in it. You have a right and a responsibility to look in his room and make sure nothing illegal is going on in it. You don't hesitate to look around in your two-year-old's room and make sure there is nothing in there that will hurt the baby. You have to do that for your fifteen-year-old too. Don't be afraid to make your kid angry. Nobody has ever died from being angry.

You are looking for burnt pieces of tin foil, joint butts and syringes; a plastic bag with white powder or chunks, or lots of empty zip lock bags. Be suspicious of strange looking pills that don't look like Advil or Tylenol. Look in the toes of the shoes in the bottom of his closet, between the mattress and the box springs, in the pocket of his suit coat, and under the post of his bed. See what's duct-taped to the back of his dresser drawer. You have to pull it clear out and look behind the drawer. He might be using a lot of peroxide to clean out his pipe. Look for charred pieces of tin foil, broken light bulbs, razor blades, glass pipes or straws. You may find a pen taken apart with a burnt yellow color at one end.

Pornography is part of the high, and most addicts have a steady supply of it. Do a history on his computer and see what he's been looking at. Porno sites, cookbook sites, and drug sites abound on the internet. They move around a lot to stay ahead of the law. These sites have suggestions for buying ingredients, manufacturing hints, herbal forms of the drug that are "legal," tips for beating the drug tests, and vivid descriptions of people's highs.

> *Even his most private possessions, his wallet and his car, are not sacred.*

Even their most private possessions, her purse, his wallet and car, are not sacred. Look in the emergency brake crack, the trunk and the glove compartment. See what's taped to the back of the visor on the passenger side, or stuffed into the tracks of the sunroof. You are your kid's parent, not his friend. You serve as his conscience while he is developing his own conscience. You exercise judgment while he is learning good judgment. He doesn't need you to be his friend. He needs you to be his parent. That means looking for sores and needle tracks; a major invasion of privacy. If he's innocent, he won't mind you looking.

I met an addict recently who always kept his foil in his wallet because he knew his mother wouldn't look there. Now he wishes he had been caught while he was living at home. He didn't have strength enough to quit on his own, but if his parents had caught him, he would have been saved the agony of addiction and years of prison time.

Don't be afraid to inspect your older child's room. An "adult" child, over eighteen, still living in your home should not be considered an adult. An adult can support himself and his family. An adult accepts responsibility for himself. If your child is dependent on you for living arrangements and food, he is not an adult. He is functioning as a child and should be treated as a child.

EARLY SIGNS OF A PROBLEM

"I'm seventeen years old and my friend told me a couple days ago he started doing jib [crystal meth] and I'm really scared. He smokes it almost every day, and when I asked him if he was addicted, he said he didn't know, but that he hadn't gone without it the whole time he's been using it. He's been doing it about a month now, and he hasn't been sleeping and he's been not eating and when he does eat he pukes up his food. He's losing weight and he thinks he's fine. I'm so scared 'cause I don't know what to do. I don't know if I should wait until it gets really bad to tell his foster mom or to just let him do what he wants. He said it makes him feel good about himself. I tried to tell him that it was just a high, a fake sense of confidence, but he was high when I was talking to him so he wasn't in a serious mood."

Recognize the early changes associated with methamphetamine abuse. They are all personality changes. A formerly happy and sociable teenager becomes irritable and anxious, suspicious and withdrawn. It is hard to distinguish the earliest changes from normal adolescence. It is a difference of degree. All teens get irritable from time to time. The meth addict is always irritable, and he gets belligerent at times. He will blow up and lose his temper; he may even get violent with you.

The mood swings are rapid and extreme. He comes in after school happy and talkative, he is energetic and focused. He gets a lot of work done very quickly and seems to be in a hurry. A few hours later, he is irritable and aggressive. He gets mad at the microwave for taking so long to cook his hotdog. He blows up at his sister when she doesn't get out of his way fast enough. He can't concentrate, can't sit still; he talks too much and too loud. The next morning, you can't wake him up for school. He's groggy and grouchy. He won't talk to anybody and nothing pleases him. The cycle repeats itself once a week, then twice a week, then every day.

> ## Ignorance is not bliss. Denial kills.

He's gone for three days at a time and then sleeps for three days. He talks too fast; you can't understand him. He forgets what he said and repeats himself a lot. He stays up all night playing music. He grinds his teeth and thrashes in his sleep. He spends hours doing purposeless, repetitive motions, taking his bicycle apart and putting it back together again.

Signs of a problem:

Physical changes
    Blood shot eyes
    Dilated pupils
    Weight loss
    Sudden increase in acne

Change in attitude
    Irritability, wild mood swings
    Fidgety and restless
    Distant look, no conversation
    Loss of interest in former hobbies
    Loss of appetite
    Won't let you in his room
    Doesn't keep clean

Changes in behavior
    Thrashes in his sleep
    Wears sunglasses a lot
    Repetitive motions, drumming fingers
    Twitches and grunts
    Forgets important events
    Stealing and lying
    Talking too much, too fast, too loud

Change in friends
    Late hours
    Lots of phone calls
    New friends you don't know
    Not home when you call from work

Drop in grades
    Calls from teachers, coaches
    Drops out of sports teams
    Loss of interest in school projects
    Last minute scrambles for assignments
    Can't get up for school

This list is not comprehensive and does not describe every addict

Meth users become edgy and jumpy; they can't sit still through a TV show or a ball game. They lose their appetite and lose weight. They don't pay attention to their grooming and cleanliness. If your seventeen-year-old boy does not eat his weight in groceries every day, get that kid to the doctor, something is wrong with him. If your sixteen-year-old girl does not spend twenty minutes in front of a mirror every morning, doesn't even care if her hair is clean or not, something is wrong with that girl. That is not normal behavior for a teenage girl.

She goes through a lot of money and can't account for it. Valuable things come up missing, especially jewelry and guns, things you can pawn. She lies about trivial things and gets in trouble at school. She keeps her door locked and won't let people in. She doesn't want you around when her friends are over and doesn't tell you where she is going. Her grades are dropping and she doesn't seem to care. She has lots of new friends you have never seen before. She gets calls late at night and leaves the house suddenly. Her cell phone bill has skyrocketed.

Ignorance is not bliss. *Denial kills.* While you are busy denying the obvious, your daughter is daily smoking away more and more of her brain. Her attitude changes, her mind slowly disintegrates. It gradually gets more and more out of control. Don't wait until the brain damage is so obvious anybody can see it. It's way too late by then.

You can't go by the stereotypes to know if your kid is at risk. The boy who wears a black rain coat and skull cap to school is no more or less likely to abuse drugs than the normal looking boy who cuts his hair and is popular with the girls. Adolescents are discovering themselves. The one thing they know they are *not* is whatever you are. They know they are *not* the cop's kid, the teacher's kid, the doctor's kid, or the preacher's kid. Teenagers try on different identities to see what works for them. They express themselves with their dress, hair styles, accents, and hobbies. Let them try on lots of different costumes. Share in their excitement as they try on new identities. Pay attention to their attitude, not their wardrobe.

DRUG TESTING

High school cheerleaders use meth, college students use meth, third grade teachers use meth, bank presidents use meth, the mayor's son uses meth, the principal's daughter uses meth. There is no vaccine against drug abuse. It attacks the finest families in this nation just like it does the run-down trailer park neighborhoods and public housing projects. We are all equal in the eyes of methamphetamine.

Employers in most states have the legal right to insist upon a drug test for any employee at any time for any reason, and failure to take or pass that test is grounds for immediate termination. Somebody needs to change the law preventing school systems from doing the same thing. The only students they are allowed to test are the lowest risk ones, the athletes. *It is costing our kids their lives.*

If immediate expulsion were the only possible response, this law would be reasonable. A kid has a right to his education. But that is not the only possible response. Mandated rehabilitation, close supervision, and family counseling are the obvious first step in dealing with our youth who struggle with addiction. There is no reason our high school students should be sheltered from the consequences of their drug use. The day they graduate, they will no longer be sheltered.

The high schools in Marshall County where I live, have adopted a policy whereby students wishing to park their cars on campus must get a permit. In order to obtain a parking permit, they must submit to random drug testing and consent to searches of their cars and school lockers. Parking on campus is a privilege, not a right, and a lot of high school dealers keep their stash in their cars.

> *Behavior like that would not be tolerated by any employer. It should not be tolerated by any school.*

Random drug testing is not as accurate or as effective as directed testing, a test ordered by a teacher in response to a problem; a belligerent attitude in class, tardiness or poor attendance, a drop in grades, a fight with another student, too frequent visits to the rest room or trips outside to get something from his car, obscene words or gestures. All of these things are not in themselves illegal, but they all point to the possibility of a drug problem. Behavior like that would not be tolerated by any employer. It should not be tolerated by any school. The test should be carried out promptly. Even the next day may be too late to detect drug use. Parental permission for drug testing should be obtained on the first day of school from all parents as a condition for student enrollment.

As parents, we can test our kids ourselves. There are urine tests, saliva tests, and hair tests available, most for under $50. Most pharmacies sell a drug test consisting of a cup for the urine and an address to send it to. Some stores carry home tests you can do yourself. These tests are very inexpensive, accurate, and comprehensive. Saliva tests require a cooperative subject, since the person has to retain it in the mouth for several minutes in order to absorb enough moisture to be accurate.

Experienced addicts will game the system and adulterate their urine by adding toilet water, or by the use of diuretics. Most labs test the concentration of the urine to detect dilution. Make him wash his hands first. An addict can get enough powdered bleach under his fingernails to denature the methamphetamine in his urine. The internet abounds with products designed to beat the urine tests.

> *"Hey, my old man gets that hair test on me, and if I come up positive even once, I have to go to boot camp."*

Hair testing is rapidly becoming the gold standard for industry. Unlike urine tests, hair tests cannot be doctored. They are extremely reliable. The best specimen is a small lock of hair cut from the nape of the neck. It does not have to be pulled by the root. A few strands of hair from their brush or comb can be tested without their knowledge or cooperation, but hair testing is more expensive [$60-$80]. Companies offering hair testing can be found on the internet, or you can ask your doctor or pharmacist about them. Some representative websites can be found in Appendix A. Some kids will cut off all their hair and shave their heads to avoid this test. That's okay. Pubic hair will do just fine. A bald patch on his leg won't look very cool with his shorts.

Just the threat of an effective drug test is enough to keep an at-risk teenager clean. If he knows his dad is gong to send a bit of his hair to the lab every three months, he has a good reason to stay away from it. He can tell his friends, "Hey, my old man gets that hair test on me, and if I come up positive even once, I have to go to boot camp."

WHAT HAPPENS WHEN YOU FIND IT

If you find any drug, even 'just pot,' you have my permission to blow your top. Have an absolute explosion. Do not tolerate a little weed. Your daughter will be in denial. "Oh it's just a little pot. I'll never do it again." Don't believe it. Get that girl tested for all drugs that very day. Drag her by the hair to the doctor's office and watch her pee in a cup. She gave up her right to bathroom privacy when you found the pot.

If you find some unknown pills in your son's room, look them up in the PDR at your doctor's office. The PDR has a pictorial directory in the front of it so you can identify any pill made by a pharmaceutical company. Look for pills that look like Xanax, Valium, Klonapin, and Soma. These medications are commonly used to blunt the panic attacks associated with methamphetamine. Narcotics like Dilaudid, Vicodin, and OxyContin are commonly mixed with methamphetamine [speed-balling] to blunt the uncomfortable side effects of methamphetamine and enhance the rush.

When a parent finds methamphetamine in a kid's room, the shock and pain are indescribable. You have to sit down hard, you can't even breathe. "OH MY GOD!" You don't want to believe it. You want it all to be just a big mistake. "Surely that's not crystal in my kid's room!" You take what you found and show it to your sister or your friend, and ask them if it could be crystal. Maybe you get on the internet and try to find out what crystal looks like, what it smells like. What is this charred piece of tin foil?

You confront your son, and he says his friends do that, but he would never do it. "I just tried it once. Honest, Mom, I won't do it again." He means he won't do it again at *your* house, but you know he's going to do it again. You get him tested at the doctor's office, or maybe you send a hair sample to a lab, and it comes back positive. Something inside you dies that day.

BOARD CERTIFIED RATTLESNAKE BITE SPECIALISTS

So you get on the phone and try to get some help. "Somebody, some-where, *help me*. Somebody *do something*. It's like your son got bit by a rattle-snake. You know he's going to die. You call a treatment center and ask to speak to a counselor. The voice on the other end of the line says, "I'm sorry, but all our rattlesnake bite treatment facilities are full at this time, but if you'll give me your name and number, we'll get back with you in two or three months, when a spot opens up."

"Two or three months! My kid might be *dead* in two or three months!" Take him to the emergency room and they just laugh at you. You call a Psy-chiatrist and the receptionist says, "We don't treat rattlesnake bites, you have to go to a Board Certified Rattlesnake Bite Specialist." Your HMO might not cover a Board Certified Rattlesnake Bite Specialist. The mental health care system is daunting when you are sane. It is impossible to deal with when you are in shock.

You find that nobody wants to talk with you about 'Jimmy's little problem.' Drug addiction is one thing we don't talk about in polite company. People are afraid of addicts and they are afraid of addiction. Better to have leprosy than a drug addiction in your family. You find yourself at the end of a ten foot pole. Your sister won't invite you over anymore. She won't let your kids play with hers. The people at church get a strained look on their face and change the subject. Your doctor or your pastor mumbles something about this being a serious problem and he might refer you for counseling, but he makes it clear he does not feel qualified to help you or your child. You've been shown the door.

All you really need at this point is somebody to listen to you. They don't have to solve your problem; you don't expect any miracles. You just need somebody to listen while you talk out your shock and pain. You have to be free to express your anger at your son, your fear for his life, your inevitable sense of guilt that you should have known, you should have prevented it, you should have kept him away from those kids. If you don't express those feelings, you will explode.

What are you looking for?

Joint butts, rolling papers
Small Alligator clip [roach clip]
Baggies and twist ties
Little bits of tin foil wadded up, folded, twisted into tubes
Pills, old pill bottles, candy containers
Charred glass pipes with wire mesh in one end
A hollowed out pen
Candles, lighters, butane torches
Razor blades
Q-tips, pipe cleaners, small wire brush
Scales
Broken bits of light bulb
Large amounts of peroxide
Syringes, needles
Elastic tourniquet or waist band from his underwear
Pipes, bongs
Charcoal looking residue on his towels
Crushed soda cans with slits in the depression
Large amounts of cash
Pornography
Pacifiers, glow sticks
Products designed to beat the drug test
Lots of air-freshener, room deodorant, or Lysol

This list is not comprehensive
Pictures of some representative objects are in the photo spread

---

"WHERE WERE YOU!"

I have always been impressed with Jesus when He came to Bethany and the sisters of Lazarus were so hurt and grief stricken because their brother had died. The story is called the Raising of Lazarus, but it is just as accurately described as the Raising of Martha and Mary. [John 11]

They wanted to know why Jesus didn't come right away and prevent this tragedy. Martha was right out front with Him. "If you had been here, my brother would not have died. But I know that even now, God will give you whatever you ask." There is a tone of scolding, but Martha's faith was strong. "Where were you? You were perfectly capable of preventing this tragedy. Why didn't you?" Can't you see her finger wagging?

Jesus didn't rebuke her for questioning His authority as God. He didn't tell her to shut up and quit whining. He just listened. He let her get it all out. He grieved with her. It really hurt, and He didn't try to tell her it didn't. Jesus' reply complimented her faith and challenged her to believe He was still God and still in control, even though it looked hopeless.

Mary's response sounded the same. She said, "Lord, if you had been here my brother would not have died." But she wasn't scolding. She was aching with pain. She couldn't even hold herself up. She fell sobbing at His feet. The words she couldn't say through her tears were, "But you didn't come. Why? Do you not really love us? Did you not care?" He fell sobbing to the ground with her. "He was deeply moved in spirit and troubled." The words He couldn't say through His tears, "Did you really think I didn't care deeply for you? Did you think I didn't love you?" She felt rejected and abandoned by God and that hurt Him deeply. Jesus wept.

He does the same for you. His heart aches for you. He cries with you. You can let Him have it, you can cry and complain, you can get angry and beat on His chest and say, "Why, God? Why?" If no one else in this universe will listen to you, you know He will. His comfort steals over you, and the pain lessens because it has been shared. You find peace and strength within you, and you can cope.

You know nothing will ever be the same after this. Drug addiction will be a part of your life from now on. Your son will never be what you had hoped he would be. But you don't have to bear it alone. You will build the strongest connection to God you can even imagine. You will realize He is with you through thick and thin, and when it gets really ugly, that's when He is the closest.

God is also faithful to your son. No matter how bad it gets, no matter how far he goes from the life and values you taught him, God is still with your child. When he finally comes to his senses in the far-off land, Jesus will be there to lead him home. So pray for your son. Pray in faith, believing that God really hears you.

PRAYER AND FASTING

A man brought his son to Jesus asking Him to cast out demons from him. The demons would cause the child to throw himself into the fire. [Mark 9: 17–29] Sound familiar? The disciples had been unable to cast it out, and the father pleaded to Jesus. He asked the man if he really believed, and the man answered "Yes, I believe. Help mine unbelief." Help me with my doubts about your power to help, your willingness to help, help mine unbelief. Jesus cast it out with nary a comment. He didn't give the guy a hard time about his doubts; He just cast out the demon. The disciples asked him later why they couldn't get it out, and He answered, *"This kind comes out only by much prayer and fasting."*

"Teacher I brought you my son, who has a mute spirit. And whenever it seizes him, it throws him down, he foams at the mouth, gnashes his teeth, and becomes rigid. So I spoke to your disciples, that they should cast it out, but they could not." . . . *So He asked his father, "How long has this been happening to him?" And he said, "From childhood. And often it has thrown him both into the fire and into the water to destroy him. But if you can do anything, have compassion on us and help us."*

Jesus said to him, "If you can believe, all things are possible to him who believes."

Immediately, the father of the child cried out and said with tears, "Lord, I believe, help my unbelief!"

When Jesus saw that the people came running together, He rebuked the unclean spirit, saying to it, "Deaf and dumb spirit, I command you, come out of him and enter him no more!" Then the spirit cried out, convulsed him greatly, and came out of him. And he became as one dead, so that many said, "He is dead." But Jesus took him by the hand and lifted him up, and he arose.

And when He had come into the house, His disciples asked Him privately, "Why could we not cast it out?" So He said to them, "This kind can come out by nothing but prayer and fasting."

Mark 9: 17–29 NKJ

As you pray for your kid, it looks like things get worse instead of better. He convulses and looks pretty dead for awhile. He gets thrown in jail, he loses his job, he gets kicked out of his apartment, and his wife leaves him. He might be facing life in prison. Everybody says, "He is dead. It is hopeless. So sorry." Jesus takes him by the hand and lifts him up. Prayer and fasting [short fasts that help you focus your prayers, not a hunger strike until God fixes things] are the currency of the spiritual world. Don't give up.

The church offers you vital support and prayer when you are faced with a drug addicted child. You are in way over your head with this problem. Don't try to swim it on your own. Be honest about your problem. Forgive the people who shun you because your child is addicted, and seek out the people who respond with compassion. Join a Bible study or prayer group and be honest about your struggles. Be willing to listen to the other people's struggles. A grief that is shared is not so heavy. You will find comfort.

Behold! I stand at the door and knock. If anyone hears my voice and opens the door, I will come in and sup with him, and he with me. (Rev. 3:20 NKJ)

IMAGES OF ADDICTION.

There are some very graphic and disturbing pictures in this section. Not suitable for all ages.

1 Jim was twenty-two years old when he got hooked on meth. This picture was taken early in his addiction while he was still working. He was enrolled at a Junior College and wanted to be a journalist. His friend was in the Army, and he got sent overseas. This was taken at the party for his friend before he shipped out.

2 This picture was taken at the lake house in Kentucky three weeks before Jim died. He was angry and confused. He didn't talk much, and he had a splitting headache. He would pick at his food and didn't eat very much. Three weeks after this picture was taken, he found a gun at my uncle's house and killed himself.

3,4 "My story is on the mdf friends site. I checked myself into treatment on my own. I was so sick. My health was failing. I'm 5'9" and big boned, a healthy weight for me is 140–145. I weighed 112 when I signed in. After I detoxed, [which took three days] and being in a group for awhile, making friends, I was told that I looked so malnourished and sick that some thought I wouldn't make it. They told me they were scared for me the night I came in. For the longest time my resting heart rate was around 120. They would come in while you were asleep and take your vitals, mine was always so high, even in my sleep. I also have a heart murmur from my years of use. I have aged myself. And I still have cravings–I'm afraid I always will. I hate meth. I will send you my intake photo and a before photo. If you would like to use them in your book I would be honored to be a part of someone's healing process. God bless you and thank you for raising awareness in the public.

5,6 In Memory of Brad "I started noticing changes in Brad a few months after we met. Things like his paranoia, or the way his voice sounded different on the phone. How he would come home and stay up all night long after driving for days.

Trips out west were the worst. He would call me in the middle of the night and tell me to be quiet, not to breathe so loud, I can't hear anything. I would tell him there was nothing to hear, I was alone in bed sleeping when he called. He would not let me off the phone. I knew then he was using again. He was so out of it when he came home, I did not even know who he was. While I was going to the restroom, he picked me up by my neck and threw me into the bathroom wall, broke my glasses and I had bruises all over my arms and back. When he finally crashed about twelve hours later, I snuck out of the house with our baby and went to the police station. Charges were pressed, photographs were taken, the whole nine yards. Brad ran.

The last day I saw my husband alive was at the courthouse at the hearing to make the temporary restraining order permanent. He sent me an e-mail titled "Document of Silence" In it he spoke of his fear, how he failed, how drugs and abuse had ruined his life and said he was ending it. I called the police department and asked them to do a well-being check. They knocked but got no answer. They did not bust in because in the past Brad had been very violent. They did not bust in, but if they had it would have been too late." http//in_memory_of_brad.tripod.com.

1.

.2.

.3

.4.

.5.

.6.

Remembering...

Don't Let This Happen to You.
You don't have to die!
[Images courtesy of www.crackcocaineincamden.co.uk.]

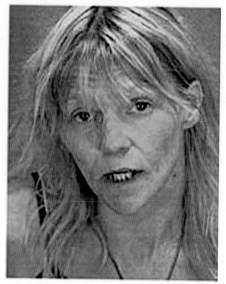

1998   **2002**

This woman gave permission to use her photo in exchange for early release from a long jail sentence on meth charges. She is now successfully rehabilitated and has reclaimed her life and her family. You don't have to die!

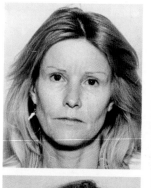
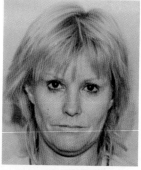
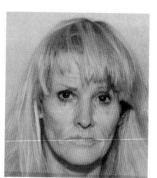

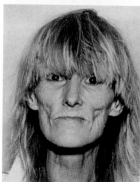
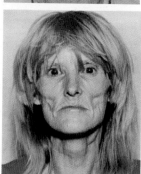
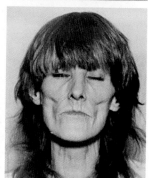

The series one through six is of a woman addicted to cocaine, meth and heroin, speed balling. This deterioration occurred over a ten year span.

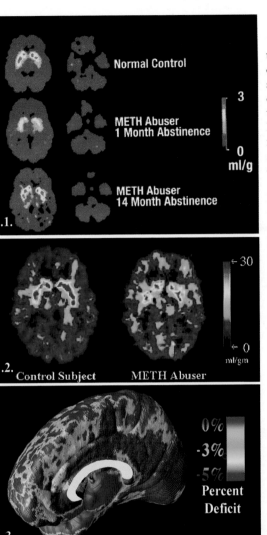

Normal Control

3

0
ml/g

METH Abuser
1 Month Abstinence

METH Abuser
14 Month Abstinence

.1.

← 30

← 0
ml/gm

.2. Control Subject   METH Abuser

0%
-3%
-5%
Percent
Deficit

.3.

1. This brain scan is Fig 11 from page 51. In the top picture, you see areas of red in the middle of the midbrain. That is dopamine transmission controlling mood, reality testing, and self control. In the middle brain, There is no red transmission through the personality centers. In the bottom brain, dopamine transmission is re-established, but there are defects in the substance of the brain. ©2001 Society of Neuroscience, used with permission

2. The second brain scan is Fig 14 from page 64. Compare the right and left scans. There is reduced metabolic activity in the addicted brain. Green areas are those with lower levels of metabolic activity. Those areas are not functioning properly. © 2002, Image Courtesy of Brookhaven National Laboratory

3. This scan is figure 17 on page 79. It shows the widespread damage from chronic exposure to methamphetamine. The red areas are the parts of the brain with the most damage. The frontal lobe, temporal lobe, and hippocampus showed the most severe damage, but evidence of cell death is seen throughout the brain.

4. Cortical areas affected by meth, frontal, [reasoning and learning] temporal, [memory and language] parietal [motor control, sensory cortex] and occipital lobes [visual fields] all show dramatic deficits after ten years of meth exposure. Top brain is meth user; bottom brain is control subject. Images 3 and 4 ©2004, courtesy of Paul Thompson, Kira Hayashi, Eydie London/ UCLA School of Medicine

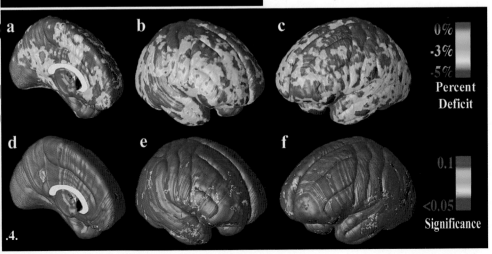

a   b   c

0%
-3%
-5%
Percent
Deficit

d   e   f

0.1

<0.05

Significance

.4.

What Does Meth Look Like?

This is methamphetamine. The small bag is a retail package, and the large one is the dealer's stash. The blue test kit is a field test indicator to identify methamphetamine at the time of an arrest.

Methamphetamine made by the Red P method is often red or pink in coloration.

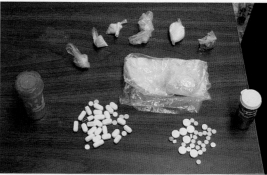

These are mostly pain pills and tranquilizers. Several small bags of crystal are also seen.

left: Here are five packets of ice for reta distribution.
below: This is a single dose of crystal

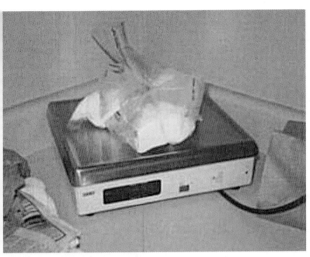

Large stash of meth on a scale

Bag of crystal

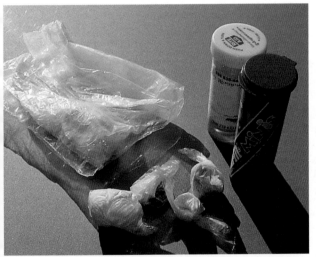

Bags of meth found in small bottles

Meth on the front seat of a car

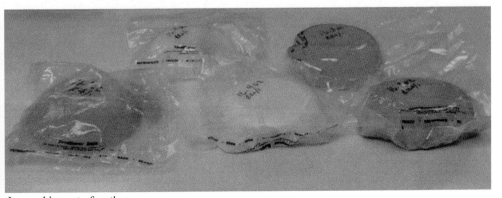

Large shipment of meth

Marijuana Connection

Marijuana is commonly associated with methamphetamine abuse. It eases the symptoms of the crash and reduces the harsh side effects of meth. Most methamphetamine addicts have a steady supply of pot.

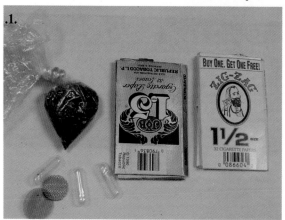

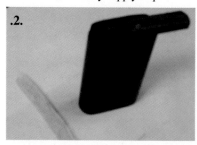

above: Marijuana and rolling papers
top right: Rolled joint and wooden case it is kept in.
bottom right: Glasses case with pot and rolling papers, and a homemade pipe
below: Fresh marijuana left out to dry

1. Wholesale pot 2. Marijuana leaves 3. 'Nickel bags' packs of pot sold for $5 each
4. Nickel bag on the front seat of a car

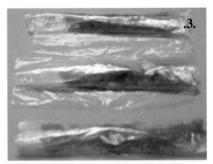

Tools of the Trade

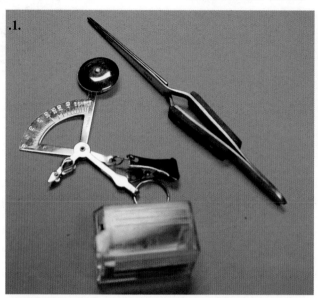

1. Hand scales and tools. Small amounts of drug are measured using these hand scales to get individual doses. The razor blades are used to measure it out in a line for snorting.

2. Charred piece of foil used to smoke meth

3. A bit of crystal is placed on a piece of tin foil, and the lighter is held to the back of it, vaporizing the drug. A black residue remains on the foil.

4. Large collection of foil and straws from a slumber party

5. Glass piping is used to fashion a homemade pipe.

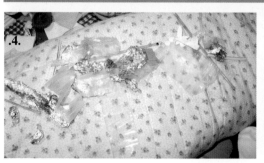

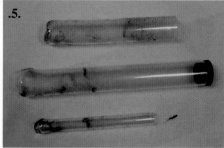

1. The larger lighter here has a "torch-like" effect and is preferred for smoking meth.

2. Collection of foil, small butane torch, film case with meth, and roach clip

3. A pencil torch or a canister of butane can be used instead of a lighter to vaporize the drug.

4. Needle track marks

5. Equipment for IV injection of meth

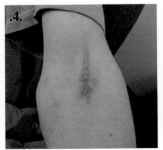

Pipes of All Descriptions

Some pipes are large and ornate, like these to the left standing three feet tall. Note the large torches used to light these pipes.

The other photos on this page show an assortment of homemade pipes

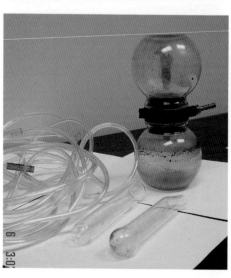

Commercially made pipes and bongs, some of these pictures were taken from a defunct internet headshop shut down by the government

Assortment of Pipes and Bongs

The pipe below closely resembles the child's sippy cup found right next to it. This pipe was found in the living room seen on page 283.

"Geeker Bags"

Geeker bags are innocent looking pencil cases or sacks containing everything you need to get high. Geeker kits have been found in diaper bags, lunch boxes, shaving kits, and brief cases.

1. Scoobie bag with pipe, hand scales, and tools

2. Crown Royal bag with hand scales, pipes and roach clip.

3-4. Large Geeker bag

5. Geeker bags often contain large amounts of money

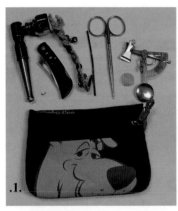

Precursor Ingredients

1. Iodine is used in the Red P method as seen here. A working lab will always have a good set of gloves in it. The chemicals used are caustic and corrosive. They will eat a hole in your hand.

2.-3. Pseudaphed, Actifed, or any pill or liquid medication containing pseudo-ephedrine or ephedrine can be used as a base chemical.

4. Red Devil Lye is the preferred brand of lye.

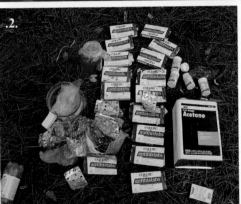

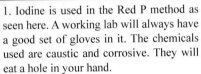

Images courtesy of Marshall County Drug Enforcement Unit

Hazardous Materials

Collections of chemicals for manufacture of methamphetamine *Images courtesy of the Marshall County Drug Enforcement Unit*

Various gasses are used, most of which are flammable.
Image to the left: courtesy University of Missouri Fire and Rescue Training Institute

Large tank of flammable methane stored in a barn right next to welding torches

Fire Hazard

Lithium metal harvested from batteries is a reagent for one reaction.

Lithium is extremely explosive when in contact with water. Cooks generally store it in a bottle of mineral spirits to keep it away from water vapors.

Flash fires are frequent occurrences in a meth lab. The cook knows better than to turn on the stove at certain points in the reaction, but he sometimes forgets about the pilot light on the hot water heater.

Above images courtesy University of Missouri Fire and Rescue Training Institute

These fires are deadly. Often, the fumes will re-accumulate, reignite and explode after the fire is put out.

Laboratories Sites

This barn was the site of a large operation.

Residential neighborhood housing a meth lab.

Interior rooms of a meth house

Images courtesy of the Marhsall County Drug Enforcement Unit

Outdoor and Portable Labs

1. Labs often have a large burn pile nearby with debris from the cooking process

2. This lab was found in the trunk of a car.

3. Portable labs are now common, with each step of the reaction done at a different location.

4. Remote outdoor locations are also found.

Images courtesy of the Marshall County Drug Enforcement Unit

Cooks Are Often Paranoid

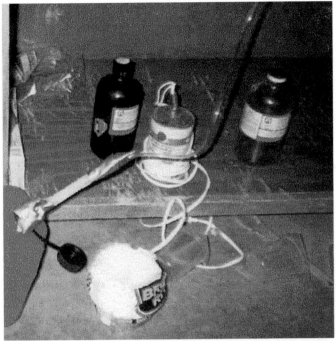

Labs are often protected by boobie traps. This was a motion detector hooked up to explosives. Nearly all labs are protected by an animal, usually a dog.

This lab had a trip wire across a path. Would you be able to see this at two o'clock in the morning?

Cooks monitor police radio frequencies

Courtesy University of Missouri Fire and Rescue Training Institute

Laboratory Contents

A working meth lab is a hazardous waste site. All of the jars and canisters are filled with organic solvents, caustic gasses, reactive metals, strong acids, and corrosive bases.
1. Jars of chemicals in the kitchen
2. Hot plate stove
3. Jar with duct tape lid
4. Crystal forming amid cigarette butts
5. Red Death

Images courtesy of the Marshall County Drug Enforcement Unit

Turkey baster separators

Blender for smashing up pills of pseudoephedrine

Jars of meth settling

Meth and Ammo

A baby was poisoned when his mother mixed his formula in a contaminated mason jar.

Mountain Moonshine

Crystal CD Collection, note separating layers in the jar

Hydrogen gas bubbling through.

Jars of 'mountain moonshine'

Different phases of the reaction
Images courtesy of the Marshall County Drug Enforcement Unit

Waste disposal system

Busting a Lab

1.-2. The sight every meth cook dreads

3. Swat team entry "You don't go into one of those places with anything less than five men. The helicopter allows us to get five guys on the ground really fast."

4. This living room had five adults and three children. All of the adults were armed. One man held a child in one arm and a gun in the other. Note the butane torch on the coffee table. This is the room the sippy cup/bong combo was found in. See page 271.

"The residents of the house have an instant advantage over us. They know where the light switches are, where the bathrooms are, where the boobie traps are, and where the guns are."

--*Rob Savage, Director*
Marshall County
Drug Enforcement Unit

284

"We Are No Longer Out-Gunned"

1.-2. Swat team members are para-military men with high power rifles and sophisticated technology. They wear an apparatus that fits over the vocal cords and has an ear piece, so they can hear each other at only a whisper. "They can't hear us, but we can hear each other."

3.-4. Cooks are heavily armed. They will shoot the police, they will also shoot the firemen, ambulance workers, post office employees, school counselors, social workers, anyone with a uniform or a briefcase is a potential threat. They have been known to throw acid in the face of an intruder if they can't reach their gun.

5. DEU machine guns. "We are no longer out-gunned."

6. DEU crew, Marshall County, Alabama

Images courtesy of Marshall County Drug Enforcement Unit

Clean Up Crew

Clean up of a lab requires protective covering, gas masks, and a lot of training. The cook knows what is in each jar, but nobody else does. The chemicals are noxious, caustic, flammable, and explosive. Most of them are also carcinogens. The OSHA manual for cleaning up a meth lab is 150 pages long. Most communities have a decontamination trailer containing the necessary equipment to safely enter a working lab.

1. Protective clothing used 2. A gas mask prevents lung damage when handling chemicals
3. Releasing the anhydrous ammonia from a tank 4. Toxic clean up 5. Disposing of caustic fluids

Images courtesy of Marshall County Drug Enforcement Unit

Cleaning Up the Mess

Cleaning up a car lab

Caustic fumes

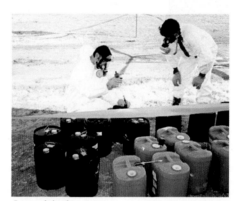

Large lab cleanup

Decontamination trailer. The same men who bust the lab clean up the mess.
Images courtesy of Marshall County Drug Enforcement Unit

Angels in Black

Ronald V Mullins

I sit alone in my room, but I no longer cry
It doesn't seem to matter much to mom and dad
who only care about getting high

I don't go to school much these days,
I'm sick and it's really hard for me to breathe
No one cares about the things I really need

Dad cooks things in my house, but it's not for us to eat
It burns my lungs and my skin and makes it hard for me to see.

Why does no one hear me? Why does no one care?
My mom and dad don't love me back and I don't think that's fair

Then one night I hear the sounds as the door comes crashing down
Mom and dad rush to hide the things I know they don't want found

My mom and dad are on the floor, their hands behind their back
The men all have guns and helmets and they are all dressed in black

They move from room to room as they continue to yell, Police!
I am very frightened as I fall on my knees

Then one of them looks down at me and he can tell I'm a child in need
He puts the gun away as he reaches down to me

He picks me up from the floor that has become my bed
The hand that held the gun now gently holds my head

I can only see his eyes, but they look so very sad
I wonder if he has a BOY like me, I wish he were MY dad

He rushes me from my house to an ambulance on the street
His eyes fill up with tears as he lays me on the seat

I now have good clothes to wear and good food to eat
I can breathe good again and it's not hard for me to see

I know there is a God because when I prayed he sent an answer back
For the men who came to rescue me are really
The Angels in Black

SECTION 4:
THE ADDICT

.14.

IF YOUR CHILD IS THE ADDICT

"I have an appointment to see my son's court appointed attorney on Christmas Eve to see if maybe she can help me know what to do. I have not seen or heard from him in many weeks. I know he was alive on the day after Thanksgiving, as he stopped at my parents house for a few minutes, all the while watching them very closely to make sure they didn't use the phone. He is on the run. He has some drug possession charges, and did not go to court, as he says he CAN'T go to jail, because he will die there. I'm sure it's because he's afraid of being without his best friend, Crystal. He has guns, and I'm afraid he will hurt himself or someone else. No one knows where he is, and of course he has warrants, but if they searched in earnest for everyone with warrants, that's all the police would do. I'm thinking though, that if they know he has guns, and is very paranoid, they might look a little harder. I am praying for him to get busted for something else, so he can get into prison, and then maybe into a rehab in there. I have bought his Christmas presents, and they will be under the tree, but I suspect they will still be there when the tree comes down. This is the hardest, saddest Holiday season I've ever gone through. If I didn't know my Savior, Jesus Christ, it would be SO MUCH worse, I'm not even sure I could make it. This is my only son, and I don't even know whether he is dead or alive. The pain is great, and all I can do is cry and pray. The Bible tells us to pray without ceasing, and that's what I'm doing. It's really hard to hold on. I guess I just needed to type all this stuff out. It's so good to have these places to vent all of this painful stuff. God bless all, and may the Holy Spirit love and comfort all of us who are in pain over our addicts this holiday season. Love Kelly"

You see the child whom you love, the happy healthy young man with a great future ahead of him, a talented athlete, a good student, a budding computer whiz, a generous loving friend, a new father, and he's losing everything to a drug. Every dollar he gets goes to buy drugs and party. He loses his job, his car is repossessed, his house is foreclosed, and his wife leaves him. The grief is unremitting. It's worse than a death. Your formerly happy and generous child is replaced by a selfish, lying, evasive and suspicious monster. He gets violent and abusive toward you, threatens you and steals from you.

He will be in denial. Even with needle tracks up and down his arm, he will deny he is using. The pipe you found belongs to his friend. He uses it to smoke some special tobacco his uncle sent him. Even if you catch him with crystal in his hand, he will deny he is addicted. He will say somebody planted it on him. He just tried it once or twice. He only uses ice on the weekends. It's not doing any harm. He can work better with this stuff; it helps him concentrate. He can drive more safely when he's wide awake. He's just doing it for your own good, so he can make more money, stay up later, or study for finals.

He'll get off of it for a while and 'prove' to you he's not an addict, but he can't stay off for very long. He thinks he can control it. He thinks of it as a tool, a crutch, a hobby, a choice. He uses it as medicine, and it 'works.' He has endless energy, focus and drive. Everything is fun, everything is interesting; it feels so wonderful to be high and alive. Sometimes they know they are dying and they don't care, it feels so good to die!

You can't reason with an addict. Just telling him what meth is doing to his brain won't even slow him down. He thinks he is in control, that's one of the effects of the drug. All that brain damage stuff is about somebody else, not him. All you can do is point out to him what meth is doing to his life *right now*. Today he messed up at work and got fired. Today his wife moved out and filed a restraining order against him for beating her. You are the only reality check your kid has. If you protect him from the results of his drug use, you are not doing your job. You have to force him to *face the consequences* of his drug use.

INTERVENTION

Alcohol counselors have for years recommended an "Intervention" for the alcoholic in denial. It works for meth addicts, too. It goes like this. Your addicted child/ spouse/ employee is making everybody miserable. He thinks nobody knows he's using, it's nobody's business but his, he has a right to do whatever he wants to do, on and on it goes.

You call a meeting, and arrange for a sober friend to bring him to it. His employer, his mother, his wife, his kids' teacher, the next door neighbor, and his friends who don't use, all meet together with him and gently point out to him what he is doing to *their lives.* No condemnation, just information. Have a professional counselor with you at the meeting if at all possible.

Be ready at that point to offer a range of treatments, a program you have already talked to that will accept him more or less immediately, a counselor who can offer outpatient therapy, a doctor, a support group, an internet chat room, a book, a videotape, something concrete he can do today to start to rectify the situation. You are offering help, not punishment. Do *not* involve the law. If you think he might be violent, don't do it. This isn't for everybody.

"My son, who will celebrate his nineteenth birthday at the end of this month, is addicted to meth. We held an intervention for him one week ago and after eleven hours of talking, crying etc, he said he chose meth. He packed his bags and walked out of his family's life. That was our bottom line. Choose the help we offered him or be cut off from the family until he is ready to recover. The interventionist, a former meth addict himself, said that this drug is Satan himself. That is not the first time I've heard this."

Be ready for a denial and refusal to get help. The fact that he refuses you today does not mean this intervention was a failure. He has heard you and needs some time to think about it. An addict has to *want* to get off drugs in order to be successful in rehabilitation. Rehabilitation that is forced on him is doomed to failure in the long run. Every time he goes through forced rehabilitation, he gets more solidified in his determination to use if he wants to. It becomes a control issue, and he will resent your efforts to manipulate him.

MISERABLE

The addict will make your life absolutely miserable. They are brain damaged in a very subtle way. They look normal, but they are self-centered and manipulative. They lie without even thinking about it. Sometimes they honestly believe the lies they are telling you. That's what a delusion is. Addicts are suspicious and paranoid. Every time you get on the phone, they think you are reporting them to the police. They hallucinate and they believe in their hallucinations. They hear voices and 'just know' things that are absolutely ridiculous. They accuse people of bugging their phone or conspiring to destroy them. They accuse their spouse of unfaithfulness, stalk them, and harass them at work.

> *Addicts think they are invincible; they won't get caught.*

They deny the obvious. They don't show up for work and get angry when they get fired. They steal from their boss and get offended when their honesty is questioned. They are too disorganized to steal effectively. They make mistakes and get caught, cover up with lies, forget which lie they told, contradict themselves and get angry when the truth comes out. They actually believe some of the lies they are telling you. They think they are invincible; they won't get caught.

Methamphetamine addicts neglect and abuse their children. They are caught up in their own little world and they don't care that their kids are hungry and tired. They expect a six-year-old girl to take care of a newborn baby. They don't get their daughter up in time for school, so she misses a lot. There are no clean clothes for her to wear, and because the parents are never hungry, they don't buy any food.

Nobody fixes dinner, nobody takes the child to the doctor when she gets an ear infection, nobody changes the babies diaper or gives her a bath. The two-year-old gets into Daddy's stash and dies of a methamphetamine overdose. They fly into a rage when the baby cries and shake her or beat her. There's nothing for Christmas. Nobody remembers her birthday. There's no safe or quiet place for her to sleep. These children have been abandoned, even if they still live with their parents.

They know you love their children, so they ask for money to buy shoes for the kids, or help with the electric bill so the kids won't go without. They need grocery money, rent money, help with the car payment, all the while using the money for more crystal. The children still don't get fed no matter how much money you give them. Your testimony at Child Protective Services will trigger an investigation, and the kids will be removed from that home. CPS doesn't mess around with ice.

"Four-year-old Eve Peterson died of smoke inhalation in a Delmar house fire, her parents face multiple counts of child neglect and endangerment for leaving her and her baby brother alone in a debris littered house with a burning candle. The house was so full of debris that is was difficult to walk and was "unfit for the presence of children." Open containers of garbage, feces, dirty diapers, spoiled food, and broken glass filled the home. There was no access to running water because the sinks were filled with junk. A lock mechanism prevented the escape of the children. The bedroom where she was found had locks installed so that the children could be locked in their rooms. Both parents had used marijuana and methamphetamine on the day of the fire."
Quad City News Mar 4th 2004

Addicts lie, they cheat, they steal, they run off and leave their children at your house. They have a short fuse, and when they get angry, they become violent and punch a hole in the wall. They can't control their temper because of the loss of their mesocorticolimbic tract [cortex talks to limbic emotional centers]. They act on impulse, giving very little thought to the likely consequences of what they do. They are frequently armed, and they pose a real and present danger to their families.

They get paranoid or enraged, and think they have to kill their child. Children are beaten and bruised, arms broken, teeth shattered and ear drums ruptured. A man kills his five-year-old son with an ax. A mother strangles her three-year-old daughter in full view of the neighbors. Children are shot, stabbed, and thrown out of a moving car. A twelve-year-old girl was raped by her daddy's drug buddies in exchange for crystal. These things are horrors, and this is *not* an exaggeration.

To the Teachers

Teachers and school counselors are in a position to help these children. They won't talk about what is going on at home, they've been warned not to tell anybody, but the effects of living in a meth home are impossible to hide.

They come to school in dirty clothes; they are hungry and their homework is not done. The bathtub is full of chemicals, they can't take a bath, so their hair is dirty and they have lice. They fall asleep in class because they can't get any sleep at home. They might be irritable and grouchy; they can't concentrate and focus attention. A significant number of them have ADHD.

They have earaches, and nobody takes them to the doctor. They have rashes and discolorations of the skin from exposure to chemicals. They have a chronic cough and runny nose because of the fumes they are inhaling at home. Their clothes and hair might smell funny, like pot or chemical fumes. They may have headaches and stomach aches, nausea and vomiting, and they get dizzy a lot.

One teacher I know smelled the breath of one of her first graders, and it smelled like dog food. The child had been eating the food the neighbors left out for their dog. In the third grade, these children are just hurting. In the fifth grade, they are getting high with their parents. By the seventh grade, they are already hard core addicts. They are in school dealing the drugs their fathers manufacture, getting high every day, and they think they are smarter than anybody they know. In the ninth grade, they are in juvenile detention on murder charges.

Things like this are reportable to your local Child Protective Services agency. Many labs and drug operations are initially located by child welfare workers, and many of them have a lot of training in this field. You are their eyes and ears.

I HATE WHAT I PUT MY PARENTS THROUGH

The addiction of a child can be very destructive to your marriage. An addicted child knows who the softy is at your house. It's usually mom, but not always. One parent, usually the father, can see right through the lies and manipulation. [He knows because he did the same thing to his mom when he was a kid.] When the father gives up on his son and refuses to bail him out anymore, mom takes over and believes whatever the kid tells her. "It's different now; he just needs a little money to tide him over until he gets paid." "His friends talked him into it; he didn't really want to sell dope." "If we don't give them food they won't have anything to eat!"

When Dad 'abandons his own son' Mom gets angry. If he was abusive toward the boy when he was a child, she feels even more anger at her husband and guilt over what has happened to her son. She will defend her poor little boy no matter what he does. Reverse the roles for daughters. They play 'Daddies little girl' extremely well and keep their fathers wrapped around their fingers.

Eventually, the marriage is fractured beyond repair. The manipulative child will play one parent against the other, accuse the other parent of abuse, and lie about the past to manipulate the sympathetic partner. Trust between spouses is destroyed, communication is broken down, and the kid's only hope for the discipline he needs is gone. Marriage counseling for these parents is essential not just for their survival as a couple, but also for the sake of the addicted child.

"I've been clean for six months now, but I hate what I put my parents through. I can remember cursing at my old grandmother when she wouldn't give me any money. She's eighty years old and I treated her terrible. I remember the mess I left in the house I rented from my parents. They probably had to fumigate the place to get all the chemicals out. The smartest thing they ever did was to throw me in jail. I deserve everything I'm getting now."

Addicts know what buttons to push; they know what to say to make you feel guilty and sympathetic. If they know you are Christian, they use your tendency to forgive against you. They lie and manipulate your compassion, take advantage of your trust and mock your mercy. They tell long sob stories and often have the scars to prove it. They know you love them, and they take advantage of that fact and milk you for all you're worth. They live in your back bedroom. They are gone somewhere getting high for days at a time, and then crash at your place. Every time they decide to quit, they want money for rehabilitation, money for medicine, money for doctors.

They say it's different this time; they are saved now and they have Jesus, so they don't need rehabilitation. A serious addict needs intensive rehabilitation, and follow up care for two years or more. Many addicts will take Jesus as their Savior, and yet have nothing to do with Him as Lord. Jesus said to honor your mother and father. Insist on real professional rehabilitation. If they won't do it, He is not their Lord. They are playing games.

Addicts who are not really ready to quit are wasting their time and your money in rehabilitation. They go through the motions, but they are not really honest about quitting. They play games with the counselors and tell them what they want to hear; they are just putting in their time. They rebel against the rules and get themselves kicked out. They stay a few days and then leave. They have to grow up a little and take responsibility for themselves in order to do a good job at rehabilitation. It's hard work. You can't make them ready to quit, all you can do is respond when they are really ready.

Even the best treatment programs can only boast 50% success at one year. The other 50% relapse even after six months to a year in rehabilitation. Some people use methamphetamine the whole time they are in treatment. Some go through the entire program fully intending to use the day they get out because "they deserve it." Even after all that education, they still think they can use and get by with it. They had no intention of really quitting. It's not the treatment program that failed the patient; it's the patient who failed the treatment program.

"I was down deep in my addiction and my family begged me to stop and we fought constantly and I got put in treatment through the courts. It was outpatient and I still used and then my family got me put into inpatient and I still used and then they pretty much let me go. Finally, I decided that I was so tired of living the life I was and knew I needed help and couldn't quit on my own and so here I am again in outpatient treatment and going to as many meetings as I can but I know that I never would be here today if it wasn't for really wanting to be clean for myself and no one else."

TOUGH LOVE

The deepest grief in the world is watching your child die right before your eyes. He's still alive outside, but he's dead inside. He lies and steals; he manipulates you with promises and then breaks them. He calls every day and accuses you of harassing him and planting bugs in his house. He demands money and threatens you if you don't give it to him. He doesn't care about his children; his heart is dead. Sometimes you wish you could just close the casket and get on with your life.

If you have an addict living in your home, you will eventually have to put him out. You can put it off as long as you want to, but you are not doing him any favors letting him stay high all the time at your place. When you feed him and give a place to stay, you are enabling him to keep using. You are *encouraging* him to use. He will stay high for as long as he can get by with it, every day doing more and more damage to his brain. The kindest thing you can do for your addicted child is to kick him out of the house.

When the prodigal son [Luke 15:11-32] went off to the far country, he didn't come to his senses while there was plenty of money and booze around. He woke up to reality when he was slopping hogs and getting real hungry. The only way you can help your child is by letting him hit bottom sooner, rather than later. Let him hit bottom before he has sustained so much brain damage his life is destroyed. He might have to live there for awhile, but he will eventually get tired of living like that.

> *The kindest thing you can do for your addicted child is to kick him out of the house.*

He will beg and plead and deny he is still using. He'll ask for money, he'll want to use your car, give him just a little more time to 'get on his feet.' You have to cut it all off. Don't lie to his boss, don't give him $100, don't make his car payment for him, and for heaven's sake, don't bail him out of jail. He'll end up living in a dumpster, homeless, hungry, jobless, and alone. I know a man who used crystal for many years, until his mother died. After she died, and nobody was bailing him out of jail anymore, he quit using and went back to his wife and children. He's been clean for two years now.

An addict is not going to quit using until he hits rock bottom. He hits bottom in the county jail, or when his car is repossessed. She hits bottom when her husband leaves and the kids are taken away from her. They hit bottom when they get hungry at the party friend's house and there is nothing to eat and nobody cares. When there's no place to crash, that is the bottom.

Don't let him play games with you. If he won't go to rehabilitation, he has to leave. When he gets out of rehabilitation, make him get a job and go to work. If he wants a car he can pay for it. Let him walk to work. If you give him a ride, make him pay you for it, even if it's only 50 cents. You can give him a safe place to live away from his friends, but if he lives with you, he pays rent [even if it's only $10] and keeps the place clean. If he won't pay the rent you charge, he leaves. If he runs up a big phone bill and won't pay it, he leaves. If he steals from you or assaults you, press charges. Better to sign an arrest warrant than a death certificate. You have to set limits and boundaries, *real* limits and *real* boundaries, *not just for your sake, but for his.*

IT GETS REAL UGLY

It's hard to see your twenty-year-old daughter homeless and on the street. It's hard to leave your son in jail when you know you could bail him out for $75. It hurts you worse than it does them. You have to do it anyway. It is frightening to think your child is going to get killed out there. You know that is a very real possibility. Your child is not really any safer at your house. If you let him stay and keep using, it's a slow death, but nonetheless a real death.

Why? Why does it have to get so ugly? Because it HURTS BAD to get off this drug. The withdrawal is agony, and it lasts for months. Rehabilitation is hard work, and it requires real change. He is not going to do it until it HURTS WORSE to continue using. When it hurts worse to use than it does to quit, he will get some help and make an honest effort to quit. Don't expect him to go through that kind of suffering just because you asked him to.

The withdrawal from ice is agony. It is intense intolerable anxiety and deep depression. It is profound fatigue; you ache all over and have a low grade fever. It is shaky, empty, hungry, craving withdrawal. All he can do is lay there and cry, "Oh God, Oh God, Oh God." It hurts REAL BAD for seven to fourteen days, and the depression lingers for at least six months. And every day of those six months, he knows if he can just get a little more ice, it will all go away and he'll feel great again.

It takes real motivation to get through withdrawal without using again. Most people can't do it unless they are in jail. They are so irrational, they can't make a conscious decision to quit and stick to it. Their brain screams for more ice, and the next thing they know they are high again. In jail, they have the opportunity to quit using. They can get it in jail, but they can stay away from it if they really want to. It is impossible to stay away from it out in the community. The friends and dealers are everywhere. They badger him, tempt him, offer to help him out, and he is hurting so bad, he will use again if he can.

Drug Court

Court ordered rehabilitation is frequently successful, if it is backed up by the credible threat of incarceration. Marshall County Alabama has a Drug Court arrangement where newly arrested addicts are kept in jail for a week or two, and upon pleading guilty to a felony, they are released to intensely supervised drug treatment.

They get a color code assignment, and have to call the drug court every morning for the color of the day. When their color comes up, they have two hours to report to the courthouse annex for a drug test. If they fail that test, or violate any of the other rules, they go back to the county jail immediately, for one week after the first slip, 30 days after the second and third violations, and they serve out their full sentence in jail at the fourth failed drug test. Diluted urine is considered positive.

Drug court participants attend inpatient rehabilitation or outpatient classes at the court's discretion, and receive some individual counseling. They are expected to work fulltime and/or do community service, and pay all fines and restitution. They are required to join a support group, and their attendance is monitored. Over the space of a year or two in drug court, they learn how to live sober. Successful completion of the program results in the felony taken off their record and a nifty diploma, a piece of cake, and a hug from the judge [who knows each one by name].

Many lives have been saved in Marshall County Alabama by the Drug Court. Resources for establishing a drug court are listed in Appendix A

Welfare Drug Testing

There is also a movement afoot to allow drug testing of welfare recipients in order to receive benefits. A positive test results in an offer for counseling or treatment. There is a legal barrier in the 4th Amendment against unreasonable search and seizure, but drug testing of welfare recipients as a condition for benefits has been upheld by at least one Circuit Court. The enormous cost of testing and providing treatment pales in comparison to the even larger cost of leaving these families with small children untreated.

So you have a choice. A serious addict can only get clean in jail. No rehabilitation unit can hold him against his will, without a court order. You can watch him die, or you can have him arrested. Jail or the cemetery, those are your choices. It hurts to put your son in jail. It hurts to have your husband arrested right in front of your children. He will cry and scream and call you an expletive. He'll threaten to burn your house down when he gets out. He tells you it will be different this time. He begs and pleads. He knows what works best on you. Be willing to leave him in there for awhile. He'll hate you for it and curse you every day. That's okay. He's still alive to curse.

Don't Bail Them Out

I've been going to the jails for three years now, and the first time I meet the new girl, she is all beat up, with bloodshot eyes, scratches and cuts from the fight she was in when she got arrested. She can't hear a word I say. This is January. The next time I come, in March, her eyes are clear, and she can hear me. She can't talk yet. She tries to, but she doesn't make any sense. But she listens to what I have to say. By May, she can talk and ask a question. It's an intelligent question, shows she's been thinking about this stuff.

In July, she has a smile on her face, she has gained some weight, and she's looking pretty good. By September, she's been in jail for eight months. She is excited to see me. She shares what's been going on in her life and gives me a poem she wrote. She has dimples when she smiles, she looks like the sweet young college age woman she's always been underneath that crust of meth. These are beautiful people once you chisel them out from under the ice.

But that's how long it took! Eight months in jail to get to where she can think logically, ask questions, control her temper, and follow a conversation. She has her personality back, but it didn't come back very quickly. It takes time for the connections in her brain to heal, time for the cravings to go away, time for her spirit to grow and change. She didn't get sick overnight, and she isn't going to get better overnight.

You are doing the right thing when you let them crash and burn, but they will make you absolutely miserable. When the entire world is crashing in around you, get in the boat where Jesus was sleeping in the back. [Mark 4:37] A storm was raging. All the guys were panicking; they thought the storm was out of control. They didn't know who He was. You do. Crawl in there with Him, under a blanket, close to His heart in prayer. Let the waves crash and the wind blow. There's nothing more you can do about it anyway.

"Not that I don't love her, because I do so much! So much that I know I have to let her go. Do I still think of her? Oh yes! Miss her? You bet!! Worry? Well that's getting better as I have gotten down on my knees and have given her over to God. I do not have the power to change her. I nor her children, or step-dad, or husband has any pull over her, only God will be able to reach her."

SPOUSE AND CHILDREN

"Dear Dr Holley,

My husband was an engineer working for an electronics firm. He made $75,000 per year. We have 3 kids, 12, 10, and 7. I am a 3rd grade teacher. Bob got hooked on methamphetamine 2 years ago, and our life has disintegrated since then. He's gone most of the time; he lies, and we never have any money. He screams at the kids over nothing. He got fired 6 months ago and we're about to lose our home. The kids don't understand. I am so angry I don't know what to do. Why doesn't the government do something about this drug? Is there anything I can do to make him stop?"

The situation for the spouse of the addict is a little different than for the parents. Parents of addicts are tormented by their addicted child, but they still have each other to talk to. Spouses of addicts have the additional pain of being rejected and abandoned by their husband or wife. Even if he doesn't actually leave you, he's not the same person you married. The grief of watching the man you love go slowly insane is indescribable.

This is your husband, the man you love and admire, your friend and partner for life, the father of your children. You remember the good times, the love and joy you shared, the look on his face when your first child was born. You love his quirky way of doing things, the way he says "Hello" when he answers the phone. You see his camping gear and sleeping bag in the garage, and you just want to die it hurts so bad.

He gets enraged at little things and berates the children; he's angry and hostile one minute and happy and loving the next. You never know what to expect. He promises to do things with the kids, and then he doesn't show up. He gets violent, puts his fist through the wall and smashes their toys. You see your children cringe when he walks into the room. If they talk to him, he tells them to shut up. He throws a shoe at the baby and tears up the picture your daughter drew.

Your first responsibility is to your children, not to your husband. You might be willing to tolerate a lot of abuse, but they are too fragile to be subjected to it. You have to protect the children from his violence and abuse, even if that requires leaving him. They are being hurt inside every time he explodes with rage, as we discussed in chapter 11. They can't defend themselves, and they can't get away from him. You have to protect them.

"We would always fight and often in front of my four and five-year-old boys. My husband gets angry about the littlest things. They would always say, "Mom, just don't listen to him" and my four year old would say, 'That's enough!!!'"

The father they love and the husband you married is gone. You now have a violent erratic man who spends all the money for dope, disappears for days at a time, and screams at the children when he is at home. An addicted husband is going to be paranoid and dangerous. He will threaten you, yell at you, harass you at work, and call you all hours of the night demanding money. He will beat you, slap you around, and tell you that you deserved it. He accuses you of infidelity, and yet thinks nothing of his own sleeping around. He wrecks the car and breaks out the windows in the bathroom. He digs up the linoleum looking for listening devices. He fights over stupid things and won't listen to you.

The next day, he says he's sorry and wants to make up. He tells you he'll quit hanging around with those people, he'll get some help, he'll see a counselor. But the next time he gets paid, it starts all over again. Lies and lies and more lies. He'll tell you the car broke down and he spent all the money fixing it. He'll tell you he had to work a double shift, had to go visit his brother in another city, or had to go out of town on business. It all sounds good, you want to believe it, but it's a lie.

> *You are grieved at the loss of your husband and appalled at the monster he has turned into.*

You've been abandoned and abused, rejected and humiliated. You are getting by on $12,000 per year and you have to sell the house. The kids need band uniforms and you can't afford them. You haven't slept in weeks and you are about to lose your job because you can't concentrate. You've lost your insurance and the baby is sick. You might be in trouble with the law because of things your husband has done, or you might have a sexually transmitted disease he gave you. Gee, thanks. He may even have given you AIDS. That is a crushing load.

You are grieved at the loss of your husband and appalled at the monster he has turned into. You are hurt at being rejected and abused, and you are afraid of what he will do next. Your children are frightened and clingy, demanding attention when you are already overwhelmed. You've been kicked out of your apartment, all your furniture is on the sidewalk, your whole life has disintegrated and all you can do is sit in the middle of the kitchen floor and cry.

Eventually, you are going to get tired of it and leave him. Unfortunately, that is not going to solve the problem. If he would just go away, it would be easy, but he won't. You will have custody battles, divorce hearings, restraining orders, fights and accusations. A restraining order will make him even angrier than he was before. You can't enforce it and he knows it. After a while, he will get involved with somebody else and leave you alone, but the torment usually lasts for at least a few months, and sometimes for years.

"Tomorrow I have to appear in court against him for an order of protection. I am so tired of crying from the guilt, degradation, and verbal abuse. I end up feeling worthless. I am scared to death to see him even in court. He blames me for his going to jail. I know that it is not my fault that he uses and I know I should just stay away from him, but I feel like I'm giving up on him just like everyone else has. The other side of him is a wonderful caring person but I have no guarantee that that person will ever come back. He may at first, but then what? Do I take the chance and try to help knowing that it could destroy me again, or do I just get the restraining order in place and never have anything to do with him again and then keep missing him the rest of my life and wondering if it could have gotten better if I'd just kept trying."

The more you reach out to him, sympathize with him, and keep the door open for him, the more he manipulates you. If he knows you still love him, he thinks, "Oh wow, she still wants me back. I can use some more, and she will still be there. She still loves me." He can do one more line, one more gram, and it will be okay. It's sick, but that's how they think. When you change the locks on the door and get a new phone number, make some new friends and a new life *without him,* that's when he knows it's really over and he hits bottom. Addicts usually don't hit bottom until you do.

You can't fix him. As much as you love him, you can't make him go back to what he used to be. It's worse than a death. You can be there for him if and when he finally decides to straighten up, but he has to *prove* it to you before you can let him back in the house with your children. It takes awhile for you to be able to trust him again. He has to *earn* your trust. A couple of negative hair tests would do wonders for your confidence in him. He calls and wants to talk to the kids, and they want their Daddy back. Then, when he uses it again, you just want to scream.

RELAPSE

"While Christmas shopping after a late movie I ran into a friend that was flying, and urges overpowered me. I went home and drank some cough syrup with codeine in it and ended up in an almost dreamlike state and at 2:30 AM four days before Christmas after 3 1/2 months clean I fell off the wagon. I can barely remember it, but I have done it about 6 times since. I've failed myself, my family and all of you that supported me. I am truly a loathsome creature, and my self-loathing runs deep . . . this in fact may be one of my problems."

The frustration of a relapse is sometimes harder to take than the initial addiction. She knew what she was getting into this time. It was a mistake the first time, but this is no mistake. She's been through rehabilitation, a competent and expensive program. She was clean for six or eight months. She had a good job. Her children were so happy to have their Mommy back. She knew what this drug would do to her, and she *chose* to do it again. Your anger is explosive. Your grief is incomprehensible.

Relapse may be triggered by the normal stresses of life, loneliness, depression, normal feelings that she doesn't know how to handle, and she remembers how good it felt to be high. Overwhelming cravings may catch her by surprise; a social situation that puts the pressure on, aggressive dealers, a husband or boyfriend who still uses. Her old friends come around, and they want her to use. They will wave it under her nose, stuff some in her pocket, or use it in front of her.

Even if she tries to avoid it, she wakes up in the night and she can taste it again, smell it again, feel it again, and she gets washed away by the craving. She smells a little pot, sees a piece of tin foil or grandma's insulin syringe, hears her favorite party music on somebody's radio, drives past the convenience store where she used to make her buys, or pulls her license out of her wallet and a flake of it falls out. The triggers are endless and everywhere.

> *If she can't find somebody sober to talk to, she will find her old friends and their stash.*

The depression after the crash is, in some ways, harder to take than the crash. You can steel yourself and plunge into the crash like you would a cold swimming pool, but the depression afterwards lasts for months, and the months get long. Addicts hit a wall along about three months into recovery, and commonly hit another one at six months. These are major depressions with no energy, no ambition, nothing is fun, and everybody gets on her nerves. She can't sleep, but she can't do anything else either. Group support, somebody to talk to, is essential to cope with this depression. Medications take the edge off, but she still has to get through the day, and if she can't find somebody sober to talk to, she will find her old friends and their stash.

In fact, one of the surest signs of a relapse is a sudden dramatic improvement in her depression. It takes at least six months and usually a year for this depression to lift. Abrupt improvement before then is a bad sign. All of the sudden she starts feeling great again, lots of energy, working real hard, talkative and excited. She won't be able to hide it. It will be obvious when she relapses. She'll either suddenly get much 'better' or she'll disappear.

Relapse is not the exception. It is the rule. You can count on it. Think about it, what would happen if every time you had a lustful thought or told a lie it showed up in your urine and your whole life careened out of control? We all struggle with sin and it's our own private matter. With methamphetamine, one false move, one errant thought, one visit to the old neighborhood lands you back in hell again, and you can't keep it private.

Some addicts give up after two or three relapses. She finds herself with a needle in her arm again, and she loses hope she will ever be clean. She resigns herself to a life of crashing and getting arrested, losing jobs and being homeless. Suicide becomes a serious risk, and the suicide rate is high among addicts. Your daughter is just as frustrated with her relapses as you are. She feels like it's not worth trying anymore.

KEEP PRAYING

"Dear God, Please help my cousin Jeremy. He has tooken a drug he shouldn't have tooken. I really love my cousin. Please don't let him die it would break my heart if he does. I'm really trying to take care of him at this time. He's a loving cousin, he really cares about us. I don't want him to die. PS Please take this letter and send me your answer." Wesley, age eight

No matter how ugly it gets, don't quit praying for your child. When you first start praying for your son, you will probably notice it gets worse instead of better. He gets thrown in jail. He loses his job. He's living in his car. Relax. God is answering your prayer. He is taking your kid to a place where there is no one to look to except Him.

Prayer is the most powerful force in this universe. The God who spoke the universe into existence is not standing by helpless to move in your child's life. He will answer your prayer. It may not be very pretty; it may not be what you expected at all. But He knows what He is doing. He's been turning prodigal sons around for a lot of years, and He knows how to really change their hearts, not just their behavior. No paper mache, no band-aids. Your child has a choice in how he responds to God's moves in his life. God has chosen to give us free will. He has so much respect for our free will that He will not force us to respond to Him.

We don't know how long the prodigal's father had to wait for his son to come back home. It might have been years. You feel helpless and discouraged; you want to do something to fix your child. The most powerful thing you can do is pray. It's hard to stay on the porch and watch and pray. It's hard to resist the temptation to go to the far off land and drag him back by the collar. Don't waste your time trying to force him into rehabilitation, spend that time praying. It is much more effective.

> *The only Person who can talk to your*
> *addicted kid is the Holy Spirit.*

You can't talk to your addicted kid. He can't hear a word you say. The only Person who can talk to your addicted kid is the Holy Spirit. When you are praying for your child, it is easy to get discouraged. It doesn't look like anything is happening. Keep praying. The Holy Spirit is on the job, working in your son's spirit. You can't see it, your son is probably not even aware of it consciously, but the Holy Spirit is teaching him, teasing him with the presence of His holy love, speaking God talk into his heart. Keep praying and thanking Him for the mighty work He is doing. This is eternal stuff going on and most of it is invisible to you.

You would like for God to come down on your son with an iron fist. He will not. You would like for Him to work a miracle and magically change your son. He will do so *only* with the full and informed consent of your son. You can't control your child. God knows better than to even try. He has too much respect for your child's free will to try to control him.

It takes incredible courage to quit a drug habit. It takes immense strength of character, brutal honesty, and a real change of heart to escape a drug addiction. He can't do it on his own strength, not even with competent rehabilitation. He no longer has the necessary neurons to stay clean on his own. He can't do it, but Christ in him *can* do it. When Jesus Christ is Lord over somebody's life, He supplies the strength to stay clean.

HOW DOES HE DO IT ?

"My wife came back home last night. One of the first things out of her mouth was, 'Jesus just wouldn't let me live like that anymore.' This morning [Sunday] she wanted to go to church. She wants to go to rehab. Glory to God! He really does answer prayers!"

Most drug addicts are very lonely people. If they weren't lonely before they got addicted, they are now, after they've run everybody off with their temper and their lies. Their drug buddies are just using them. They really need a friend, somebody who understands them and really cares. They need somebody who can see through the lies and won't play games with them, somebody who doesn't condemn them. They are looking for Jesus; they just don't know it consciously.

Every time you pray for your daughter, The Holy Spirit of Jesus speaks into her heart. He will occasionally speak into her mind with overt thoughts, and they can often have a conversation. He is *always* speaking into her heart, deeper than her mind, and she feels it more than she hears it. He speaks peace; He speaks mercy; He speaks love into her heart. No words, not at first. This is Spirit to spirit, Heart to heart. "Lazarus, Come forth!"

> ## "Lazarus, Come on out of there!"

It happens at two o'clock in the morning when she's crashing in the back of somebody's car. It happens when somebody gives her a coat at the Salvation Army. It happens when she hears Christmas music, or somebody smiles at her on the street. Jesus knows when her spirit is open to hearing His voice. His presence is so gentle and so tender, your daughter is drawn to it. She might resist it for a while, but His gentle voice is always there. "Lazarus, Come on out of there!"

As she responds to Him, she understands she's not alone. She draws closer to this Presence, this loving accepting Presence. Jesus understands without being told. He understands your child better than she understands herself. He knows what really motivates her, and what she is really afraid of. He knows what lies she believes, and He exposes the lie and teaches the truth. Your daughter will start praying without even realizing it.

The closer your daughter gets to Jesus, the more like Him she becomes. She slowly takes on the character of Jesus, takes in the Spirit of Jesus. She grows to love Him, respect Him, and draw strength from Him. She feels loved and valued by Him. She heals inside and doesn't need crystal to feel good anymore. She wants to stay in the presence of this God who loves her so very much.

Your addicted kid can't play games with Jesus. She can play games with you, she can play games with her therapist, she can lie to the people in her support group, her boss, and her friends, but the presence of Jesus will not abide with a liar. If she is honestly trying to stay clean, Jesus will continue to work with her, but she can't have her dope and Jesus too.

> *She will love Jesus more than the high.*

Jesus will always hear your daughter's honest cry for help. He doesn't get tired of your child. His mercy is everlasting. But He won't play games with her. If your daughter chooses the drug, the drug is what she'll get; she can't have the presence of Jesus and ice at the same time. Your child will eventually learn to value the presence of Jesus more than the high. Each relapse will be shorter and milder.

Your daughter will learn that Jesus doesn't hang out with her drug friends, doesn't appreciate raunchy music, and finds the porno offensive. She learns that Jesus doesn't mind working with her when she's depressed and tired and feeling down. She learns how to pray and work through frustrations and depressions instead of smoking them away. Jesus helps her grow up. The healing to her personality is lasting and deep. Jesus means for it to last for eternity. Your child will be different. She will become what can only be described as holy. She will have a calmness and peace that doesn't need anybody or anything. When Jesus does something, He does it right.

Your child can't quit on her own strength. She can only quit in the strength of the Spirit of Jesus Christ living in her. Your daughter will go through agony getting off of this drug. She will go through that kind of agony for the sake of the One who went through agony for her.

My sheep listen to my voice; I know them and they follow me. I give them eternal life and they shall never perish; no one can snatch them out of my hand. My Father who has given them to me is greater than all; no one can snatch them out of my Father's hand. I and my Father are one. (John 10:28 NIV)

.15.

THE BLAME GAME

Most parents of addicts go through a stage, sooner or later, of intense guilt over what has happened to their child. The sicker the child gets, the more intense the feeling of guilt. If only I had been a better mother, if only our family had stayed together, if only we hadn't moved so often, if only we'd gone to church more. The guilt surrounding a suicide is increased exponentially. Every word you said, everything you did in the days leading up to a suicide will replay over and over in your mind.

Some addicts will play serious mind games with you. They threaten suicide and you know they are perfectly capable of doing it. They make that threat to get you off their case about their drug use. "Quit badgering me. If you don't back off, I'm going to kill myself." It's a more potent threat than, "I'm going to kill you." You can take steps to protect yourself. There's nothing you can do to protect him from *himself.* You know the horror a suicide would be, especially if there are small children involved. The children will be devastated if Daddy really kills himself.

"We have two children ages fifteen and nineteen. I always told him that one day his children would know about his problem. Now they do. He threatens suicide all the time to them. How can he do that? He blames me for everything. I want to kick him out, but every time I try is when he threatens suicide. Do I go ahead? Will my children blame me if something happens to their daddy? I have no way out! My husband says he will quit . . . but I know he has not. He is in a great mood one day and the next he is angry about everything. What should I do?"

Back up a minute. Who has the problem? You? Or him? Will he commit suicide? He may or he may not. He is using the threat of suicide to get you to continue supporting his drug habit, forcing you to tolerate behavior that is completely unacceptable. Please realize he is sick and irrational. He might very well take his own life, and the lives of you and your children at the same time. A suicidal drug addict is extremely dangerous.

Threats of suicide are grounds for temporary involuntary commitment to a mental institution. Call the police. If he is serious, you have potentially saved his life. If he is just manipulating you, it has backfired in a big way. In either event, after you have him put in the hospital for 72 hours, those threats will vanish. He will know you mean business and you won't tolerate any games.

Suicide is a real possibility. If he does it, please know that *he* did it, not you. You cannot prevent someone from taking his own life. If he is really determined to kill himself, he is going to do it eventually, no matter what you do. If you act, you think it was your fault. If you don't act, you think it was your fault. No matter what you do in the days preceding the suicide death of someone you love, you can always think of something you could have done differently. Unless you sat there and encouraged him to kill himself, told him how much better it would be for everybody if he were dead, you did not kill your husband. He did.

We did everything we knew to do. We begged him to stop using. We pleaded and cried and prayed. We kicked him out, we let him come back home. We put him in rehab, we found him a job. We paid for doctors and medicines and therapists and he still did it. When they closed the casket on Jim, my older brother had to catch me and hold me up. That's when it hit me. The pain was searing. He's not coming back. Our little Jim is gone.

THE LIKELY RESPONSE TO TOUGH LOVE

"I did it. I kicked her out. She was living in the apartment next to my house, and she wasn't paying any rent. She had loud parties, and she wasn't working. When I put her out, she screamed and cussed and called me every name in the book. She knew what to say to really hurt me. She trashed the place before she left. It will take weeks to clean it all out. Piles of dog sh** in the laundry room. I'll have to replace the floor in there. It will cost thousands to get it ready to rent again. And the worst thing is, I don't know where she is."

You did what the book said and you kicked your kid out. Now he blames you for his continuing drug problem. Now he *has* to go live with his drug buddies because you kicked him out. As if that were the only alternative he had. No rehabilitation unit, no sober friend's place, no homeless shelter, there is absolutely nowhere else he could go except to his drug buddy's place. Yeah right.

So now *you* are supposed to solve all his problems. You are supposed to wave a magic wand and get the right rehabilitation center, the right doctor, and the right medicine. After two or three trips through rehabilitation, he has already learned what he needs to know to stay clean. Now it's a matter of *doing* it. Another rehabilitation center is not going to solve anything. The last thing in this world he is willing to do is accept responsibility for himself. That is not your problem. That is his problem.

Your kid will capitalize on your guilt feelings and use them to manipulate you. When he wakes up and realizes what he has done to himself, realizes how serious this is, it is hard for him to accept responsibility for his addiction. That means admitting he was wrong, he made a mistake. He doesn't want to do that. He can't bear to take responsibility for causing the destruction in his life; it's too painful, too shameful. Instead, he'll blame you, your parenting style, your career or lack of one, the neighborhood he grew up in, there is no end to the list of things he can find wrong with you to explain his addiction, and excuse himself from responsibility for his problems.

Don't buy it.

Even if you had been the perfect parent, your kid would find somebody to blame. He would blame the kids at school, his second grade teacher, his high school coach, his wife, his kids, his boss, and his dog. Every parent has made mistakes, every parent has coped with stress, and every parent has had to draw lines and set limits. If you discipline too harshly, it's your fault. If you don't discipline enough, it's your fault.

> *Unless you literally rammed the stuff down his throat, you did not cause his addiction. He did.*

Your kid is responsible for his response to the world around him, including your imperfections and limitations. Everyone has to learn to work with real people, and we all start with our parents. We learn to work with people who are jumpy and nervous. We learn to work with people who are short tempered and irritable. We work with quiet people and people who talk too much. We learn to cope with our friends when they are tired and grumpy, scared and angry, listless and depressed. We learn to do that in a family where everybody can be themselves.

Growing up means learning to negotiate, compromise, and express your needs without throwing a temper tantrum. We learn how to work with difficult people, people we disagree with, and people we just don't like. Most drug addicts are very immature people. They cope with life like a ten-year-old would, refusing to take responsibility for their own actions. They have learned to deal with conflict by escaping it. Have a fight with your wife, go out and get high. Have a problem at work, come home and get high.

Lots of kids grew up in homes like yours and did not become addicted. He's not the only kid who grew up without a father, in a rough neighborhood, with sisters that were prettier than she was, or in a family that never had enough money. Don't let your kid make you feel guilty for things you had no control over, or for things you had no way of knowing about. Even in truly abusive homes, kids make a choice about using drugs.

"You say that most addicts are kids that were battered and abused. WRONG. Any statistics will tell you that is wrong. I was raised in a good home with a good family. I met the wrong guy and wanted to be "bad" for the first time in my life. I was in college going to Campus Crusade and church every Sunday. I got high because I liked to get high. Addicts like the sensation of getting high, not the consequences. If I could have continued getting high without breaking out in jail, handcuffs, DT's, stealing all that stuff I would have. There is not an addict that does not like to get high. You are after all a second hand witness . . . I know you are trying to help, I just think you are going about it all wrong. You are going to end up scaring people who don't need to be scared. You say secular rehabs don't work, wrong again. After eight other rehabs from Christian to state based, I got clean because I wanted to get clean. Until they are ready, they won't. Your parents can lock you up, your spouse, your job, it doesn't matter. Jail systems can keep you until you are detoxed and mandate a rehabilitation program for you. I know that for a fact, that is what I do. I had it done to me. I was court ordered, and no I didn't have drug charges on me. I think you might want to reassess what you are preaching. For someone like me who was in the throes of this and a prisoner to this for six years, it makes me really mad. It is a false representation."

[Am I the only one who hears the hostility in this young woman? Fair warning: If you send me a nasty e-mail, you may see it again, published in a book!]

Some kids are going to rebel no matter what you do as a parent. Your kid is blaming you for his addiction problem, and it's not your fault. Even if you were partly responsible for some serious pain in his life, he chose to respond by escaping, avoiding, and using instead of coping. Unless you literally rammed the stuff down his throat, you did not cause his addiction. He did.

LET'S FACE IT

At the same time, it is important that we look at some of the things we have done as parents and critique ourselves, our lives and our society, and learn from our mistakes. Some of that guilt is appropriate, and approached correctly, it is healing and redemptive. If we see we have made mistakes, we can correct them.

King David's son, Absolom, [2 Sam 15] defied his father and staged a coup against him that very nearly succeeded. David was driven from his palace in disgrace, key aides had joined the rebellion, and Absolom was determined to kill his father. David was distraught. His son, whom he loved, was revolting against him. He went up the Mount of Olives weeping as he went, yet he prayed for the protection of his son. He wanted reconciliation, not revenge. When Absolom was killed [2 Sam 18:32] David grieved mightily.

Absolom's half brother had raped his sister, disgracing her and leaving her desolate. David had absolutely no credibility in punishing his son's crime of rape, his own sin having been made glaringly obvious. Nothing was done for two years after this flagrant violation of the King's daughter, and Absolom was incensed. Absolom killed his half brother and led a coup against his father. David knew he was partly responsible for Absolom's rebellion, and he grieved.

What if you are the parents who emotionally and verbally abused their kids? What if you are the mother who was drunk when her son came home from school, or the father who molested his daughter? What if you had a serious problem with your temper and spanked your kids hard enough to leave bruises? What if you left your family to move in with your girlfriend when the children were young? And now you see the consequences of your actions displayed in their lives.

> *A re-run of the same show*
> *you used to star in.*

You see your adult son acting just as belligerent now as you did when he was a kid. He's verbally abusing his wife just like you did his mother. He tells his son to "shut up," then crawls off in the corner with his newspaper, and won't talk to anybody. He screams at his daughter about her clothes and makeup, reduces her to tears with his tirades. He gets drunk, slaps his little girl around and breaks her arm. You are looking at a re-run of the same show you used to star in.

How do you take responsibility for what you've done? What is the appropriate punishment for what you did to your child? You've seen how deeply your son was wounded by what you did. You've seen how your sexual perversion has damaged your daughter's brain and destroyed her relationships. What does justice demand? Can a holy God accept you? Can you continue to exist in His presence? Only by the cross of Jesus Christ. Close you eyes for a moment. When we come back, we are going to be somewhere very special.

Look at the cross of Jesus Christ. Take a good look. Here is an innocent Man, pure in thought, word, and deed. His face is bruised from the beatings He took. His eye is swollen shut. Again and again they struck him on the head with a staff. He is hardly recognizable. His face drips with blood from the thorns they beat into His skull. The soldiers twisted together a crown of thorns and placed it on His head. All the muscles on His back are gouged out and bleeding, *"I gave my back to those who strike me."* Spasms of pain wrack His body from the flogging He took. *He [Pilate], had Jesus scourged.*

A Roman flogging was a brutal affair. A whip of eight or ten ropes were woven together, each strand of which has a small sharp piece of metal or bone on the end of it. The victim was stripped and received 39 strokes with such a weapon, ripping out large chunks of flesh with each blow. The pain was inconceivable. The blood loss was massive, and wounds of that nature invariably became infected. A man was not expected to survive a flogging. Many of them didn't live long enough to be crucified.

He is nailed to a tree, *"they pierced my hands and feet,"* fully exposed, unable to take a deep breath. He is stripped naked, *dividing up his clothes, they cast lots to see what each would get* humiliated in public, *"they look, they stare at me,"* mocked and derided. *They heaped insult upon him. "All who see me sneer at me."* Church art depicts a loin cloth on the person of Jesus Christ. Roman soldiers had no such scruples. He hangs there naked, unable to cover Himself.

> *No one has ever come down from a Roman cross alive.*

He is thirsty—*"My tongue cleaves to my jaws."* His shoulders are dislocated *all my bones are out of joint* and he hangs forward at an unnatural angle. He is sweating, bleeding, crying, and praying. *Father, forgive them; they know not what they do.* It gets very dark. *Darkness fell over the whole land until the ninth hour.* There is a mist in the air. A cold wind sweeps through, and you get chill bumps. Forsaken by God, He hangs there in agony for hours, gasping for air, and then He dies. No one has ever come down from a Roman cross alive. *[Italics from Isaiah 50, Psalm 22, Matt 27, Mark 15, Luke 23, and John 19]*

The Mel Gibson movie *The Passion of the Christ* depicts the stark reality of the crucifixion of Jesus Christ. The impact of this movie is that it places the cross of Jesus Christ in the realm of this world, a living breathing nightmare suffered by a real Person on a chilly day in early spring. This is not just a story. This is real.

Why do I believe that Christianity is true? Because they are the only ones with a cross, and I, for one, can't live without it. I would have died a long time ago without the mercy of God expressed in the cross of Jesus Christ.

You may resist His cross because you have been taught from the cradle that Jesus is a liar and a blasphemer. And yet all your life, you have loved Him and everything that He is; truth, justice, courage, and compassion. You have always believed in the mercy of God. The mercy of God has a name. His name is Jesus. I am sure you will recognize Him when at last you lay eyes upon Him. I am equally sure He will recognize you, even though you may have worn a turban or a hijab all your life.

No one can stand before our Holy God and live. You come to the Father through mercy and by faith in the atoning death of Jesus Christ. He died for you, too. He died for you, too.

The wrath of God was vented upon Jesus Christ, the Son of God, the Word of God, the incarnation of God, the living representation of all the Holiness of God, the condensation of His character, the exact representation of His eternal and infinite Being. That was God hanging on the tree, absorbing the wrath of God upon Himself, bearing justice in Himself.

He is also the Son of Man, or better translated, the Son of Adam, *Ben-Adam*. Look at His genealogy, a bunch of liars and cheats, prostitutes and thugs, rapists and thieves. He lived in a real human body. He got hungry, He got tired, He grieved, and cried, and laughed, and sang. He loved His mother and got mad at the temple priests. He was most certainly the Son of Man as much as He is the Son of God. *"The Son of Man must suffer many things and be rejected by the elders, chief priests and teachers of the law, and He must be killed and on the third day be raised to life."* [Luke 9:22 NIV] He died as Man and He died as God. What kind of God would *do* something like that? Can you worship a God like that?

> ## *When He took the wrath of God,*
> ## *He took it for you.*

Can you see the love in that cross? He took the humiliation and agony *you* deserve. He suffered the disgust and condemnation of God that was the penalty for your cruelty and selfishness. *"He bore it in His body on the tree so that you can die to sin and live for righteousness; by his stripes we are healed."* [1 Peter 2:24] If anyone else had hung on that cross it wouldn't have done you any good. They just would have suffered the wrath of God for their own sins. Jesus could suffer in your place because He was pure and holy in His human life. When He took the wrath of God, He took it for you.

So you come to the cross of Jesus and say "You died for me, too, Jesus, You died for me, too." Say it out loud. "You died for me, too." Say it again and again. Take it into your heart. Your Creator died for you, too. Unspeakable mercy. Incredible love. He knew what the wrath of God was, and He took it upon Himself. He died for you, too.

Don't think that sacrifice was some sadistic blood-thirsty thing on the part of God. Justice demanded the death of an innocent person, utterly forsaken by a righteous and Holy God. It's called the atonement. You can not atone for what you have done. He knew that, so He did it *for* you. God spoke this universe into existence, knowing full well the price He would pay for beings with a free will, and He did it anyway. He said, *"Let There Be Light."* knowing that He was crucified from the foundation of the world. He didn't have to create and He didn't have to redeem. He chose to create and He chose to redeem. The cross was ugly and obscene. It had to be . . . because God is Holy.

LEVEL WITH HIM

So you level with Him. Tell Him the truth about what really happened. He's not stupid, He's been around a while and He's seen a lot; you can't shock Him. When you come to him with an honest heart, he forgives you. That's what the cross was all about. He died for the right to forgive you. He died for what you've done. He died for what you didn't do. He died for your bad attitudes and imperfections. He died for your immaturity and selfishness. He died for your idolatry. He died for your bad choices. He died for you, too.

He excuses the part that can be excused; he explains the part that can be explained. The part that was somebody else's fault is somebody else's fault, and you're not responsible for it. It's the part left over, the part that says, "I did it, and there's no excuse for it." That's the part He forgives. But He can't forgive it, if you won't admit you did it. You have to come clean with Jesus.

And then it just lifts. The crushing guilt is gone. He has taken it upon Himself "in His body on the tree." The sense of damnation and condemnation is lifted, and your soul has peace and indescribable joy. He died for you, too, and He has forgiven you. When you realize that He, the Holy God, has forgiven you, you will love Him so much you never want to leave His presence. His mercy will fill your heart and breathe life into you. You are not dead anymore. You are raised from the dead in Him. He has reconciled you with your God and Father.

Your heart will ache with gratitude and love for Him, the Lord who bore agony for you. You want to honor Him in everything you say and in everything you do. You want to give Him everything you have and everything you are. You will worship Him and you will obey Him. It follows as naturally as grass follows rain, it wells up within you and spills out all over your life.

This new person starts growing inside of you, a person who loves and cares deeply, a person who sees the pain in the lives of other people. You will love the people who offend you even more than the people who are good to you. You will slowly take on His character, a generous, patient and compassionate character. You will have the heart of Jesus within you; the same gentle heart that spoke this universe into existence will live within you.

YOUR KID HAS HURT YOU TOO

Your addicted kid has caused you immense pain. Your own son, the boy you loved, has turned on you. He had so much going for him, and now he has turned into a thug. He has lied to you, ripped you off, threatened you and assaulted you. He has blamed you for all of his problems and accused you of things you had nothing to do with. He is selfish, lazy, abusive, beligerant and manipulative. He beats his wife and abuses his children. He has rejected every value you ever taught him.

You're angry at what he has done to you, but you're even angrier at what he has done to his family. He has abandoned his children, your grandchildren, and wasted their living on drugs and booze. He has abused his wife and run her off with his threats and violence. He curses and screams at his kids over nothing and they are afraid of him, so they come to your house after school. They are just babies, they don't deserve to be treated like that.

An addict will say and do vicious things as they hit bottom. They destroy your home, they scream and cuss, they know what to do to really hurt you. If you let him make you hate him, you have given him some degree of control over you, over your feelings. You have let him destroy the healthy happy person you used to be. The angrier you are, the more you need the cross of Jesus Christ. You can find peace and justice at the foot of His cross.

All of us have been wounded, by our parents, our spouses, our neighbors and our kids. All of us get insulted on a daily basis. We are ignored, rejected, lied to, humiliated and degraded. It happens every hour of every day. We are misunderstood by our friends and attacked by our enemies, abandoned by our spouse and lied to by our children. We are passed up for promotions and stabbed in the back by co-workers.

All of us have been wounded; some of us have been brutalized. Abusive parents are usually grown up children who have been brutalized themselves. You don't have to live the rest of your life with pain and anger. It's not really living, it's a kind of death that goes on and on. You can take your pain and anger to the cross of Jesus Christ and give it to Him. Justice is met in Him. You know He didn't survive the wrath of God. The penalty was death, and death was what He got. He died on that cross in absolute humiliation and agony.

> *Yes, it really hurts. The pain is real. So is the cross, and the Man who hangs upon it.*

Move around to the side of the cross. Now you can see His side, the side that was pierced. Blood and water are flowing out of His heart. *"One of the soldiers pierced His side with a spear, and immediately there came out blood and water."* [John 19:34] From the side of the cross you can see His broken heart. His heart aches and bleeds for the pain you have suffered. He has taken that, too, in His body on the tree, and by His stripes, you are healed.

He knows the agony you suffered when your wife left you for another man. He knows how bad it hurt when your mother beat you and told you how worthless you are. He knows how angry you were when your son lied and stole from you. He knows the pain and confusion you felt when your father molested you. He felt every stroke of it on that cross.

You can't do it all in one day like you did the forgiveness part. That was instantaneous. When He forgave you, you were forgiven. This is different. Every day you have to come back to His cross, every day vomit out more pain and more anger, get it all out. It might take months or even years. It did for me. Don't be afraid to come back, look at His wounds and bury your face in His shoulder, His Spirit is right there with you at the foot of the cross, holding you up and helping you look. Yes, it really hurts. The pain is real. So is the cross, and the Man who hangs upon it.

JUSTICE

Jesus Christ took the eternal death, the wrath of God for all of His people. But Jesus didn't stay dead. Jesus Christ was pure and holy and He did not stay dead. He is risen from the dead, and so are you. You're not dead anymore either. You don't have to dwell on the injustice of it all, you don't have to relive the insults against you over and over getting more and more resentful. You don't have to hate the people who hurt you. Justice is met in Him. The penalty is paid in full on the cross of Jesus Christ. You can leave your pain and anger there, and you can live again by believing in Him.

Sometimes we even get mad at Jesus! I've seen it several times. It goes like this. "This monster raped me, abused my child, murdered my wife, and Jesus died for him, so now he gets off scot-free. That's not fair. He should have to suffer for what he did to me." And you know, you're right. It's not fair. Jesus died for Pol Pot and Hitler. It's not fair. But no one can argue that His cross was not brutal enough, not enough suffering, not enough humiliation to pay for the sin against them. Nobody can go to His cross and not find justice. Nobody can go to His cross and not find healing. By His stripes we are healed, every last one of us.

The man who stands justified by His cross is the man who came to that same cross on his hands and knees and fell on his face before Jesus. The man forgiven vicious wanton crimes is the man who holds that cross most sacred. You see him as less than human, an animal. Jesus sees a broken person in need of mercy. Don't think he got to play games with Jesus. To be forgiven by Jesus requires true repentance, true contrition, true falling on your face before Him and begging for undeserved mercy. It is not cheap.

> *Of course, you can't forgive them
> by yourself, that's impossible.
> He forgives them in you.*

I think I was probably the only person on the planet who prayed for Tim McVeigh before he was executed. What he did required every stroke of agony Jesus suffered. But can you imagine how one forgiven of such a crime would feel upon realizing the weight of his damnation and being pardoned by a Holy God? Can you imagine the depth of his love for Jesus? Our prisons and death rows are filled with people who love Jesus Christ with every fiber of their being. He who is forgiven much, loves much.

Then you actually start to feel the same way He does about them. You might pity your ex for the smallness of his character; the husband who left you for another woman is a small person indeed. You might ache for the hostility in your sister's soul which destroyed your relationship with her, and which destroys every relationship she has. You will pray for your brother's deliverance from the addiction that has turned him into a vicious animal. You take on His character, His courage and strength, His honesty and humility, and you are a new person.

The church people call it rebirth. You are born into the most incredible joy when you really understand what Jesus did. It is an amazing and powerful thing He did.

When you enter into His death and resurrection, everything changes. You can still remember the horrors you have suffered, but they don't hurt anymore. You can actually forgive the people who hurt you. Of course, you can't forgive them by yourself, that's impossible. He forgives them in you. All you have to do is consent to it. *He does all the heavy lifting.* His Spirit within you forgives them. You can greet them with a smile the next time you see them, and it's a real smile because He has forgiven them in you.

> *Forgiveness is not a thing that you do, but is rather a place where you live.*

Forgiveness is not a thing that you do, but is rather a place where you live. You live in a spirit of forgiveness. People offend you, but you don't get offended. People can reject you, but you don't have to feel rejected. You're feelings get hurt, but you don't harbor resentment because you live in forgiveness. It's a place full of joy and confidence, with no real expectations of the people around you. If they love you that's fine, but if they don't, that's okay too. Forgiveness forms an invisible wall around you, and nobody can hurt you. Jesus calls it meekness, and says that in it, you will inherit the earth.

JESUS ON DIVORCE

Jesus recognized sexual unfaithfulness as grounds for divorce. [Matt 6:31,32 and Mark 10:1–12]. His insight into the situation is profound. He said Moses allowed divorce because of the hardness of our hearts. Moses wasn't sneaking around behind God's back when he said that. A woman married to an unrepentant adulterous or abusive husband is not trapped in that situation. God recognizes the hardness of the heart in such a husband [or wife] and releases spouses from abusive marriages.

But it was not meant to be that way. From the beginning, marriage was supposed to be a life-long growing and nurturing experience for both partners.

His instruction to men was to *"love your wife as Christ loved the church, giving himself up for her."* [Eph 5:25–33] Men are expected to give up their right to peace and quiet and sex on demand for the sake of their wives. Wives are expected to respect their husbands, not insult them or verbally abuse them.

Forgiveness gives 'turn the other cheek' a whole new meaning. It doesn't mean, "Take a lot of abuse and get more and more resentful," but rather, "Stuff happens and it doesn't hurt me anymore. I can love this person anyway." You may or may not remain within shouting distance of the person abusing you. Jesus was not anybody's doormat. He removed himself from situations where He was being verbally abused, [Mark 8:13] and especially when they threatened His physical safety, [John 8:59 among others] but He did not resent and hate His abusers. He *lived in forgiveness.* [Luke 13:34]

Mark 8:11–13 NIV The Pharisses came and began to question Jesus. To test Him they asked for a sign from heaven. He sighed deeply and said, "Why does this generation ask for a miraculous sign? I tell you the truth, so sign will be given to it." Then He left them, got back in the boat and crossed to the other side.

John 8:59 NIV At this they picked up stones to stone Him, but Jesus hid Himself, slipping away from the temple grounds.

Luke 13:34 NIV O Jerusalem, Jerusalem, you who kill the prophets and stone those sent to you, how often I have longed to gather your children together, as a hen gathers her chicks under her wings, but you were not willing.

Luke 23:34 NIV Jesus said, "Father, forgive them, for they do not know what they are doing."

RECONCILIATION

Jesus said, *"If, when you make your offering, you remember that your brother has something against you, go and make up with your brother, and then offer your worship."* [my paraphrase of Matt 5:23] You can't really relate to God while you are living in resentment. It is by the power of the cross of Jesus Christ, His mercy and His forgiveness, that healing and recovery can take place. It starts when somebody says, "I'm sorry." That begins a process through which the Holy Spirit heals and grows and nurtures the spirit of your child, and also your spirit. Both of you come to peace in Him. *"I have come that you may have life, and have it to the full,"* [John 10:10–11 NIV].

No matter what your kid has done to you, no matter what you have done to your kid, it is not too late to seek reconciliation. Children never completely give up hope for a real relationship with their parents. They long for your love, your attention, and your approval. They want to please you. They want to be loved by you, and nobody else will do. When your child hates you and resents you, he is rejecting a part of himself, the part of himself that is you, his parent. He will never be whole in his personality as long as that relationship is broken. He will hate and grieve and continue to be beset with anxiety and depression until he can accept you, understand you, and forgive you.

If you now realize you have hurt your child, you can apologize and seek reconciliation. You can undo a great deal of damage just by admitting to your child that you were wrong, validating his feelings of hurt and disappointment, and saying you are sorry. If we pretend it didn't happen, pretend it didn't matter; neither you nor your child will ever heal.

> *If we pretend it didn't happen, pretend it didn't matter; neither you nor your child will ever heal.*

Find a way to talk to your child. If he's in jail, write him a letter. Tell him you are sorry, and be specific. Tell him the truth and ask him to forgive you. Don't be surprised if he can't at first. He'll mumble something and go away, but in a few days he'll be back. Don't be afraid to talk about it again. Don't make excuses, don't blame anybody else, don't tell him about how bad your family was when you were a kid, he already knows all that. Just tell him you're sorry and ask him to forgive you. Then go on and talk about life, and joy, and the future, as if he has forgiven you, even if you're not sure he really has. Healing takes time.

Lead your child to the cross of Jesus Christ for the healing he needs. Yes, it really happened, and yes, it really hurt. The torment and humiliation hurt, the neglect hurt, the beatings hurt, the rape hurt. We don't have to pretend it didn't really happen. We can take the real pain to the real cross of Jesus Christ. What happened to your child was ugly and obscene. That cross is ugly and obscene.

Even if it's not your fault, you can still be the one who leads him to the Healer. His wife left him for another man, his friend betrayed him, lied to him and ripped him off. Her huband beat her, mocked her, teased her and tormented her for years. Somebody stold your son's car, somebody raped your daughter. The angrier your kid is, the more he needs the cross of Jesus Christ. Justice is met in Him and cannot be found anywhere else. A counselor can listen to his pain and anger. A counselor can sympathize with his pain and anger. A counselor can acknowledge and validate his pain and anger. But a professional counselor cannot *absorb* his pain and anger. Only Jesus can do that. The anger and rage in your child can only be released at the cross of Jesus Christ, no other place will do.

When your child is filled with shame and regret over what he has done, he is unable to face the world with confidence. The shame robs him of the joy in life. He cannot recover from his addiction while still filled with shame. That's why the twelve step programs instruct him to admit his wrongs and make amends, to heal the shame hindering his recovery. A counselor can listen to his shame and guilt. A counselor can acknowledge his shame and guilt. A counselor can even rationalize and explain his shame and guilt. But a professional counselor cannot *absorb* his shame and guilt. Only Jesus Christ can do that.

As your child takes on His character, and grows in strength and courage, honesty and humility, his addiction is easier to handle. He does't need a drug to relieve his anger and depression. He doesn't need methamphetamine to feel good inside. He knows the power of Jesus Christ, so he doesn't feel helpless anymore. Your son cannot defeat this addiction by himself. Jesus does it in him. Your son might never fully recover from his brain damage, he might never be what he could have been had he never gotten addicted, but he doesn't have to live in despair and hopelessless.

See, I will send you the prophet Elijah before that great and deadful day of the Lord comes. He will turn the hearts of the fathers to their children, and the heart of the children to their fathers; or else I will come and strike the land with a curse. [Malachi 4:5 NIV]

.16.

I Have Chains Around My Veins

"I've been using meth for about fifteen years, most heavily the last year. I always considered myself a maintenance user, it was like a medicine to me and I needed it. I started using more heavily and not being careful about it . . . not caring if anyone found out, not caring if it affected my job or my marriage . . . only caring what was happening in my head, and I noticed that my body was giving out on me and that I was out of touch with reality most of the time. I was going crazy."

Some sizable proportion of the readers of this book are addicted to methamphetamine. Many of you consider yourselves 'casual users' and honestly believe you could quit anytime you want. Of course, you have not actually done so, you continue to use it and enjoy it, all the while thinking you have *chosen* to use again. You don't recognize that pull, that urge, that desire to use again as a craving or a compulsion. You can't resist that pull, but you've never really *tried* to resist it.

Many of you use methamphetamine to treat your feelings of inadequacy and depression, or to mask the social anxiety you feel in a group. It removes your inhibitions and you can "party hardy" like everybody else. Some of you started using to improve your work performance, with increased endurance, focus, and energy. The profound fatigue you feel when it wears off just confirms your suspicion, you really *need* this stuff, but you don't see how that qualifies as an addiction. End stage addicts are obviously sick and you recognize that, but you think you are way too smart to ever get *that* out of control.

Low dose addicts are still addicts. You need just a little bit to give you energy. Life without it is so dull and disappointing; you use it as a nerve pill. When it wears off, you feel so bad and grouchy; you think you are doing everybody a favor by using. You don't notice the wild mood swings. You don't see your children flinch when you walk into the room. You don't hear the ranting and raving. You just wish everybody would shut up and leave you alone.

> *You think you are way too smart to ever get that out of control.*

The fact that you don't use it every day does not mean you're not addicted. It is an addiction when it becomes life controlling in any way. When you pursue methamphetamine when you should be doing something else, you are addicted. When you can't stay clean long enough to pass a drug test at work, you are addicted. When you damage your relationships because you are high or in the crash, you are addicted. When you can't concentrate on your job, show up late and make a lot of mistakes, you are addicted, even if you don't use it every day.

You say, "This is the last time. I'm getting off this roller coaster." Then you find another reason why you need just one more gram. If you can't think of one, your friends help you out, you really need just one more gram. You keep using the crash as an excuse to keep using. You need a few days off work for the crash, you need a babysitter for the crash, you don't have time to sleep for a week, you need this stuff to keep working.

Eventually, the reality of it all hits you. You have an explosive temper and you hurt one of your children. You make a lot of mistakes at work and get fired. The thing that used to improve your work performance has just destroyed your work performance. You have a run in with the law, or a fight with your dad. Your supply dries up, and you realize how miserable you are without it. Crystal is always in the back of your mind. Even when you try to think about something else, you are preoccupied by crystal, when you are going to use again, where you are going to hide it, how to get more, buy more, make more, con more.

Got some bad news for you—the *high* is a *lie*.

METHAMPHETAMINE IS A LIE.

Ice promises pleasure, power, and control. It delivers depression, slavery, and insanity. Crystal offers endless energy and delivers death. It gave you a feeling of invincibility. You are not invincible. Meth gave you a hallucination of power and control. You have no power and you are not in control. Ice gave you an illusion of confidence and independence. You are now chained to a chemical. And, by the time you realize it, it's too late. You can't just walk away from it.

The first time you tried to get off, the misery of the crash drove you back into it, and you thought, "I didn't really want to quit anyway. This stuff isn't hurting anything." The second time you tried to quit was when your wife left and moved back in with her mother. You didn't mean to blow up at her like that, and you swore you'd never hit her again, but what does that have to do with ice? The third time was when they threw you in jail for public intoxication when you got lost trying to get home from a party. You were in jail for three days and the crash was unbelievable. You got some more crystal within thirty minutes of your release. Now, maybe, you are ready to admit you have a problem.

"I have chains around my veins." The feeling is like a stab in the pit of your stomach. "Man, I can't just walk away from this stuff. I really am trapped." Now you realize that you are locked into this drug, and it's not funny anymore. You're spending all your money to get high. You've lost your family, and your wife won't talk to you anymore. Nobody believes a thing you say. Where are you going to get some help?

> *Only 6% of addicts who decide to quit methamphetamine can do it on their own.*

You call a rehabilitation center, and they tell you how much it's going to cost. They can get you in their next opening, but the waiting list is six or eight weeks long. You call a counselor and make an appointment. But then, your buddy shows up and offers you some of his stash. "Man, you look awful. Let me help you." If you resist his offer of 'help' he gets offended. "Hey, man, I'm your friend!" Remember, he's high, so he's paranoid. "Man, you a narc? You think you're too good to run with our crowd? You gonna turn on your old friends?" He'll badger you, he'll rub your nose in it, and you are hurting so bad by now that you will cave in and use again. Now you *know* you have a real problem.

It takes enormous courage to quit a drug habit, a lot more courage than most people have in themselves. Only 6% of addicts who decide to quit methamphetamine can do it on their own. You need real help, and you need a lot more help than any book or support group can give you. Professional rehabilitation is important, and you need to learn the skills they teach. It's going to be hard work, the hardest work you've ever done. The more effort you put into it, the more effective it will be. You may need medications for your ADHD, PTSD, depression or hallucinations. By all means take them. God has inspired people like me to make these medications; they are for you.

But you need more than just medications and professional rehabilitation. You also need a real relationship with Jesus Christ. Not just lip service, slogans, songs or ceremonies, but a *real* relationship. You need somebody with you 24 hours a day, 7 days a week when you wake up in the night and you can taste it again. You need somebody to help you think straight when those obsessive thoughts crowd in on you. There is no one on this planet who can do that for you except Jesus Christ.

You've been listening as your parents found the cross of Jesus Christ, and maybe you found Him too. You believe He died for you, and you believe He lives again. You've seen His power and felt His Spirit. You can't get this far in this book without having an experience of His grace. Come with me.

"Lord Jesus, I believe you died for me, and I believe you live again. I believe you have forgiven me and I believe you can help me with this addiction. Come into my life and fill me with your Spirit. Give me your courage, your wisdom, and your strength one day at a time."

SO NOW WHAT?

Now you are a Christian and you are an addict. Does Jesus make the brain damage go away instantly? Nope. No magic wands here, that's just not how He does things. This is a healing process, not a magical event, and healing takes time. He heals you from the inside out, your heart first, your fear and anger; then your mind, your thoughts and attitudes; and a change of behavior is frequently the last thing that happens. That's why your mother gets so frustrated. She's praying for you and she's not seeing any results.

Jesus knows what you are up against. He knows what happened to your fasciculus retroflexus and all that brain stuff. He knows how strong the craving is when you see a piece of tin foil and a cigarette lighter. He knows who your friends are and where they hang out. He knows how miserable the crash is and how bad you want to do it again. He knows all that stuff.

Jesus knows all that brain stuff. And it doesn't scare Him at all.

And you know what? It doesn't scare Him at all. He looks at you with the same mercy and compassion He has for everybody else. He knows He can get you free of methamphetamine and give you a happy, healthy life. He's got this big grin on His face because He knows how happy you are going to be when you come with Him.

It takes incredible courage and strength of character to quit a drug habit. You have to change your whole way of life. You can't hang around with your old friends anymore and you can't think the same old way anymore.

When you get close enough to Jesus, you don't *want* to hang out with those people, and you can't even remember how to think that way anymore. He gives you a new identity, actually it is your real identity given back to you. He restores you to be the person He created you to be.

Let's look at the way Jesus handled temptation. He faced the fiercest temptation any person has ever faced in the garden of Gethsemane. Think about it. He's in this garden overlooking the city and He can see the torch lights coming out of the city. He knows Judas is a traitor, and He knows He has just infuriated a whole bunch of priests last Sunday by turning over their tables and calling them hypocrites and extortionists.

Matt 21:12,13 NEB

Jesus then went into the temple and drove out all who were buying and selling in the temple precincts; he upset the tales of the money changers and the seats of the dealers in pigeons; and said to them, "Scripture says, 'My house shall be called a house of prayer.' But you are making it a den of thieves."

The priests had quite a racket going, selling 'acceptable sacrifices' for ten times the real value of the animals. Extortion in the name of God is especially despised by Him.

Jesus was not stupid. He didn't have to be the Son of God to know what they were going to do to Him. It was dark. He knew the roads. He had friends who would have sheltered Him. He could have run like a jack-rabbit and gotten out of there in plenty of time.

He also knew He was the Son of God. He knew He didn't deserve that cross. He had lived a pure and holy life, and He did not deserve to be tortured, humiliated and killed. *"Don't you know I could call down twelve legions of angels and get myself out of this jam? I don't have to do this! I've never done anything to deserve this! But then, how could I bear the wrath of God against all of my people? How could the demands of justice and righteousness be met?"* [My paraphrase of Matt 26:53–54] And so He stepped forward and said, *"Here I am. I'm the one you're looking for. Take me."* That took guts. That took immense courage, enormous strength of character and self discipline. *"No one takes my life from me. I lay it down of my own accord."*

> Matt 26:53 NIV Do you think I cannot call upon my Father, and he will at once put at my disposal more than twelve legions of angels? But how than would the scriptures be fulfilled that say it must happen in this way?
>
> Gen 3:15 NIV And I will put enmity between you [Satan] and the woman, and between your offspring and hers, and he will crush your head, and you will strike his heal.

How did He defeat the temptation to bail out on that cross thing? Three ways:

- First, He resisted by the power of prayer; intense anguished prayer, and this Man knew how to pray. He was on His face before God, pouring His heart out and praying for strength.
- Second, by sheer force of will to obey the God whom He loved.
- Third, by deep understanding of the Scriptures, the Bible.

LEARN HOW TO PRAY

Everyone prays during the crash. Even the most virulent atheist prays during the crash. It's the months *after* the crash that separate the men from the boys. The boys go back and use again. The men pray. They pray with power and with faith. They pray with all their hearts and with all their minds. They pray when they feel good, and they pray even harder when they feel bad.

Jesus will teach you how to pray, and the more it hurts, the better you will pray. This demands real prayer, not some scripted performance prayer. You can scream and cry and agonize with Him. You can pour it all out and fall on your face. You can pray all night and you can pray all day. You can get mad and cuss and He still stays with you. The more you pray, the closer He gets, and the more power you feel surging up within you.

Then, a few hours later, you say, "Look! I did it! I stayed out of that mess! See? I did it!" You didn't do it in your own strength. You did it in His strength. You stay tuned in to His strength by staying connected with Him. This is a relationship and it requires communication. Communication with God is called prayer. Get good at it. Practice, practice, practice.

> *He enjoys your company. He likes it when you talk to Him.*

And the next day, you pray for strength again. He gives you each day enough courage for that day. You can't stuff enough in your pocket to last a few days. It doesn't work that way. He gives you enough for one day. He's not being stingy; it's just that you can't carry that much courage and strength around with you. You have to come back every day to get more. Give us this day our daily bread.

Besides, He enjoys your company. He likes it when you talk to Him, even if it's mostly cussing and complaining. If He gave you enough strength and courage to last a week, you'd be gone for a week. He wants you to come back every day for more strength, more courage, and more wisdom. He wants you to be real with Him. He doesn't enjoy phony prayers. Gradually your prayers will change from, "OH, HELP ME GOD" to "Wow, God, you are really cool! Thank you!" That's what the church people call "praise and thanksgiving."

You will grow closer and closer to your *real* Daddy, the One who created you and loves you with abandon. He understands your struggles, He knows whether you really love Him or not, and even if you fail, He recognizes the intentions of your heart. *In Him we live and move and have our being.* Your spirit will feel the presence of His Spirit, and this strength wells up within you that you know comes from Him. The experience of His undeserved love changes you, it melts your heart.

REAL PRAYER

When you focus your mind on Him, you will admire Him; you can't help it, He is so awesome and beautiful. Tell Him what you think of Him. Remember the glory of the day He said, "Let There Be Light," and appreciate His power. His mercy captivates you. His courage and strength win your admiration. His precision and intelligence amaze you. His gentleness and compassion are stunning in their power to transform your life. He is so beautiful, you can't take your eyes off of Him. The church people call that *"praise."* When they say, "Praise the Lord!" that's what they are talking about.

As you focus and meditate more and more on His power and mercy, you will feel love for Him welling up within you, and you run out of words. Your heart is about to explode with love for this God who died for you and cares so deeply about you. There *are* no words for what you are expressing to Him. That is *"worship."* Let it flow out of you, heart lifted up, wordless worship. Just enjoy it. Stay in it for as long as you want to.

What I have just taught you to do is called *"contemplative prayer,"* your spirit joined with His Spirit in prayer. I did this for years before I knew it had a name. I wasn't thinking about *it,* I was only thinking about Him, His mercy, His glory, His power, His tenderness, His courage, His strength, his holiness . . . I could praise Him all day long and never use the same words twice. And He was filling me with His comfort, His love, His confidence and His joy. It never ends. He doesn't run out and He never gets tired of giving it to you.

Once you've had that kind of experience with Him, you really don't want it to end. You find yourself praying in the back of your mind all day, instead of craving in the back of your mind all day. You find you can get up and go to work, and still be just as near to Him as you are in deep prayer. What started out as a life-line you clung to in deep water, turns into a cord you keep under your shirt. You don't ever completely let go of it. As you follow Him deeper into prayer, as He draws you deeper into Himself, you will find a world of power, confidence, intelligence, endurance, and control. Sounds familiar, only now they are real, not an illusion. Now they are the truth, not a lie.

THE GOD THAT YOU LOVE

As you realize what Jesus has done, you will love Him so much, you will want to honor Him in everything you do and in every word you say. That gives you the second way to resist temptation, sheer force of will to obey the God whom you love. You don't want to do anything that would offend Him or disappoint Him. You don't want to slap His Holy face. You want to draw ever closer to Him. Anything that draws you away from Him is repulsive to you. Doing the thing that honors Him the most is called obedience, and that is *"high worship."*

You learn to know and trust the presence of Jesus continually, sharing every thought and observation with Him, being His friend. Then one day, when your thoughts stray in the wrong direction, you realize the presence of Jesus is not there anymore. It is like a cold draft through your soul. You will know it immediately. It doesn't take you long to learn that if you guard your mind and heart, you stay in the presence of Jesus, in the love and mercy of Jesus. All kinds of thoughts will enter your head. You decide whether they stay or not.

I'm going to get kind of personal here to help you understand how this works. [This is really embarrassing, but I love you enough to tell you about it.] One day, I was driving down the road and I had this thought, an evil lustful thought. And as I drove down the road enjoying this thought, I realized Jesus wasn't there. It was like a cold draft through my soul. He wasn't there. The warmth of His presence I was so accustomed to was gone. Then it hit me, "Oh, my God, I'm worshipping Baal!" I was allowing my imagination to dwell on an immoral thought. Of course, Jesus was not in a thought like that. He hadn't left me. I'd left Him.

I ran back to Him in my thoughts. Part of me didn't want to go back. It felt good! I had to mentally grab myself by the wrist and say, "This is our

Saviour we're talking about. Now get over here!" I dragged myself by the hair back to Jesus and said, "I am so sorry, Lord, but part of me wants to go back. *Can you help me with this?*" and the thought vanished. I couldn't even remember exactly what it was, it was gone, and I was back in the warmth of His love and mercy. The whole episode lasted two or three miles.

"If you love me, you will obey what I command, and I will ask the Father and He will give you another counselor to be with you forever–the Spirit of Peace." [John 14:15 NIV] The gift of the Holy Spirit empowers you, encourages you, enlightens you, and instructs you, not from some place out there somewhere, not even from the words of a pastor or friend, but from within. *He is in you.* You don't have to look for Him or make an appointment with Him, He is already there. He knows what you need before you ask.

> *Whatever hell-hole you are in,*
> *He's in it with you.*

After the resurrection, Jesus could have said, "Okay, I paid the price. They're redeemed. I'm out of here." He could be the disinterested King up on His throne, having grapes dropped into His mouth by adoring angels. God knows He deserves to be, but He isn't. Where is He? Right here. With me. With you. He comes in His Spirit so He can continue to be with us as we struggle with the results of our sin. He's in jail. He's in the gutter. Whatever hell-hole you are in, He's in it with you. What incredible love!

> If anyone loves me he will obey my teaching. My father will love him, and we will come to him and make our home with him. He who does not love me will not obey my teaching.
>
> John 14:23 NIV

"If anyone loves me, he will obey my teaching." It follows naturally and you don't really have to think about it. You obedience does not have to be perfect. He died so you wouldn't have to be perfect. But when you love Him, it is sheer *joy* to please Him, honor Him and obey Him. The natural consequence of that kind of love and obedience is this: *"My Father will love him and we will come to him and make our home with him."* [John 14:23 NIV]

USE YOUR BIBLE

Love for Him will naturally lead you to the third way to resist temptation. A deep understanding of the Bible will sustain you when the days get long and the nights get even longer. It is the long letter He wrote to you, teaching you how to live and love, how to understand yourself, other people, and the world around you.

You have to retrain your brain. Obsessive thoughts, resentments, and fears will continue to torment you. The Bible will always break the power of those old thought patterns. Just open it up and read. It's impossible to rehearse your old negative thoughts about your resentments and your failures while reading the Bible. It forces you to look up at God instead of down at yourself.

> *You are not dead anymore, and you don't have to think dead men's thoughts.*

In time, you train your brain in new thought patterns. *"Do not conform any longer to the pattern of this world, but be transformed by the renewing of your mind."* [Romans 12:2 NIV] That's not just spirit talk. That is brain talk. A new way of thinking is hard at first; you are using neural connections and tracts that are not accustomed to any traffic. As you practice new thought habits, they become more natural to you. It takes some work, but you can do it.

If you concentrate on His love and forgiveness, you can resist selfish and destructive thoughts. The old thought patterns will reassert themselves in your head, but you don't have to listen to that stuff anymore. Jesus has called you out of the grave. "Hey Lazarus, come on out of there." You are not dead anymore, and you don't have to think dead men's thoughts.

Spend a lot of time with your Bible reading it slowly, thoughtfully, and prayerfully. Meditate on it, you might spend an hour on one verse, *"A Father to the fatherless, a defender of widows is God in His holy dwelling."* [Psalm 68:5 NIV] I could spend three days meditating on that one verse. Psalm 23 is a world of meditation on the Lord who is a faithful Shepherd. Get into it. Live it and breathe it. It belongs to you.

Don't just read the Psalms, experience the Psalms. They are all about you. Pray them in your own words. Addiction is captivity and bondage. Cravings and temptations are the enemy trying to kill you. Depression and despair are the trap set for you. The house of the Lord is His presence within you. The temple is prayer and praise and worship. Write your prayers out as you are praying, it helps you focus. Pray like David did. When David was angry, God heard about it. When David was scared, God heard about it. And when David was joyfully singing in victory, God heard about it. Every time David laid his fears and doubts before Him, they evaporated and gave way to praise. Try it. This stuff is *real*.

Psalm 23 NKJ

The Lord is my shepherd, I shall not want. He makes me lie down in green pastures, he leads me beside the still waters, he restores my soul. He guides me in the paths of righteousness for His name's sake. Yea, though I walk through the valley of the shadow of death, I will fear no evil, for you are with me. Your rod and your staff, they comfort me.

You prepare a table before me in the presence of my enemies. You anoint my head with oil; my cup runs over. Surely goodness and mercy shall follow me all the days of my life, and I shall dwell in the house of the Lord forever.

The war stories in the Old Testament are for you, too. We don't fight against flesh and blood [other people] but against temptation, despair, cravings, depression, obsessions and compulsions. Those Old Testament stories teach us to trust God for deliverance, and not be frightened at seemingly insurmountable obstacles. They teach us that we can beat the odds, even overwhelming odds, when He is on our side.

Study the character of God as it is revealed in the Bible. Understand the personality of your Father, His mercy and His righteousness, His glory and His power, His faithfulness and His love. He will listen to you all night long. He does not tell you to shut up. When things get rough, He comes in all the closer. He does not abandon you. He is not like your dad, so get all those images of the Big Guy with the Stick out of your head.

A NEW PERSON IN CHRIST

As you grow closer to Jesus, you start taking on His character. Don't we all tend to act like the people we hang around with? You need courage to resist temptation. You need strength of character, honesty, integrity, humility, wisdom, and perseverance to defeat an addiction. Where do you get that kind of stuff? You get it from Him. Those are all the things He is. When He comes into your life, He unloads His suitcase, puts His things in your drawers, and now *you* have courage, *you* have strength of character, *you* have honesty and humility. Now you can walk away from your drug buddies and stand tall like a man [even if you are a woman].

You have become a new person in this relationship with Jesus. You are no longer a lonely depressed drug addict; you have a new spirit, a new personality, and a new attitude. Your relationships will also change. Your friends will notice the change in you, and many of them will not like it. You are more independent now, you can think for yourself. You don't follow the old crowd.

Some of your relationships will adjust and some will not. Some of the people around you have been using you, and they will resent the changes in you. These people don't really love you. They just *use* you for drugs or for sex. They are trying to manipulate you, but you don't respond the way you used to. Some relationships will end for this reason. It hurts to realize these people never really loved you after all, they were just using you. Grieve it and go on.

Some relationships will end because you choose not to hang around with those people anymore. You don't have to be a rocket scientist to figure out that some of your old friends are bad news. They are addicts; they are still using and justifying their drug use. They have attitudes about crystal you no longer share. That doesn't mean you don't love them anymore, you most certainly do. If means you love them enough to stay away from them. If they love you, they will come where you are; they will come clean. Many of your old friends will reject you and choose ice over you. It hurts, but you can't compromise. Somebody had to be sane in order for you to see the light; your friend needs that too. Look back over the sections in Chapter 14.

> *Look around, see who hates you. Make*
> *sure they are the right people.*

When you stand up for what you believe, you can be sure some people will not like it. They will mock you and insult you. They will be suspicious of you and they may get violent. The dealers will hate you and call you a narc. When they get arrested, they will accuse you of snitching. The self-centered party people will hate you. No matter what you do, somebody is going to hate you. Look around, see who hates you. Make sure they are the right people.

Some relationships will end simply because the people, places, or surroundings trigger cravings in you that you know you can't handle. You have to avoid those people, even if that means breaking off family relationships. You may never see your brother again because he cooks and uses, pulls you back into old ways of thinking, listens to the wrong kind of music, or smells like pot. You know you are going to end up in jail again if you go back to your brother's place. It hurts, but you have to make a clean break with people who use, even if they are family.

You have to make some changes in the way you do things. You have to get rid of your cell phone and pager. Destroy your list of contacts and their numbers. Make it HARD for yourself to get more crystal in a moment of weakness. You may have to move to another town or get a new job.

You can't compromise and expect to get by with it. You can't smoke a little pot, enjoy a little porno, tell jokes about drugs, or think about getting high. When God told the children of Israel to take over Canaan, He told them to kill every man, woman, and child, and He meant it. You can't tolerate a little bitty baby sin in your life, not even a fantasy about sin. If you are aware that it is a sin, you have to eliminate it immediately. If you don't, you can be sure it will not stay an innocent looking baby sin. It will grow up, and it will grow up fast. It will turn in to a 250 pound linebacker sin, and destroy your life.

RECOVERY GROUP

You're going to need to establish new relationships with people who help you stay clean, friends who know how to have fun without getting smashed, people who are sensitive to your problems. You need mentors, people who inspire you, encourage you, and genuinely like you. You meet those people at church, at support groups like NA, (Narcotics Anonymous), and at Bible studies like Overcomers Outreach and Alcoholics for Christ.

Call a local church and ask if they have a program for recovery from addiction. If they don't, they may know a church that does. Don't give up, keep calling until you find one. You need a community of people around you who share your love for Jesus Christ and understand the challenges you face. You are extremely fragile in your recovery for *two to three years* after getting off ice. Be careful who and what you expose yourself to while your brain is healing.

HONOR YOUR MOTHER AND FATHER

Make a real effort to heal the relationship with your parents. That may not be possible; they may be in even worse shape than you are. In that case pray for them. But if it is possible, make peace with them. Reconciliation heals something deep inside you, something you can't describe or explain, but something very real. They might treat you like a child for quite some time, but let's face it; you've been acting like a child. As you prove yourself, you will earn their trust and respect.

Honor your mother and father, the first command with a promise, that it may go well with you. [Eph 6:2] Honoring your mother and father usually involves forgiving them. They hurt your feelings. That was their job. Remember, your parents had the unenviable job of breaking the bad news to you that **you are not the center of the universe**, and you didn't want to hear it. Nobody wants to hear it. My kids are struggling with that one right now. Some day they will have to forgive me. I hope they can do it.

You have to forgive your parents for the indignities you suffered as you learned to . . . share your toys [most of us still don't know how to do that], wait your turn [anybody pulled out in front of you recently?], be nice to your brother [we don't have that one down yet either], tell the truth [still working on that], talk nice [no comment], and clean up your room [how does your garage look?].

> *Even if you never see them again, you give them honor by praying for them.*

But even if your parents brutalized you, abandoned you, or raped you, you can still forgive them and honor them, respect them and take care of them financially. You take your pain and anger to the cross of Jesus Christ, and you can honor your mother and father. Even if you never see them again, you give them honor by praying for them. You are the one they brutalized. When you pray for your parents, all of heaven responds.

Remember the right side of the cross, where the blood and water flowed from His heart? His heart was broken for the pain you suffered. You are His precious child and you have been brutalized. He aches for you. He bleeds for you. His love and His blood, they heal you. By his stripes you are healed. You don't have to dwell on it, reliving all the hurt and rejection, the love you didn't get from your father and mother. You don't have to feel unloved and unlovable. You don't have to feel dirty and unworthy, stupid and inadequate. As you live in His presence you absorb His love and His acceptance, and you heal. You re-wire your brain to *think* of love and acceptance, re-program your heart to *feel* loved and accepted. You gradually become confident and joyful as you realize your Daddy loves you with all His heart.

DAVID AND SAUL

The story of David and Saul [1 Sam 16–31] is the story of a father and a son. David was the son of Jesse, and you may remember that David and Jesse didn't have much of a relationship. When Samuel came to anoint one of the sons of Jesse to be King of Israel, Jesse didn't even bring David in from the field. He was the youngest, insignificant, not even counted as a son. His brothers despised and insulted him when he brought them provisions. He lived in rejection.

David went to battle, killed Goliath, and was taken in by Saul and treated as a son by him. 1 Sam 16:21–23 is the scriptural account. David received admiration, approval, and attention at the hand of Saul. David had been invited to Saul's table and given his daughter's hand in marriage. David sang for him on the battlefield when Saul had a migraine headache—songs like the 23rd Psalm. David was very close to God, and he led Saul to be closer to God. Saul was David's daddy. Jesse was his father, but Saul was his daddy.

Then Saul turned on David in a jealous rage and did his best to kill him. David was a threat to his throne, his authority, his ego, and Saul wanted him dead. He chased David throughout the countryside for years. He was viscious and relentless. He was irrational in his rage, and went out of his way to abuse David.

David had several chances to kill Saul, but he wouldn't do it. David teased him, even mocked him, but refused to kill him. David loved Saul. He wanted peace with his daddy. I Sam 26 is the account of how David got his interview with Saul. When Saul acknowleged him and blessed him, David went on his way in peace. He avoided Saul after that, but he had the blessing of his daddy. When Saul was killed in battle David mourned him and gave him a decent burial. The dirge he sang was the dirge of a bereaved son. He never had a true reconciliation with his daddy. He knew his daddy didn't really care about him, but he still loved Saul and grieved his death. [2 Sam 1]

Many of us never get a reconciliated with our father. I have met many people who do not even know who their father is. They grieve the loss of a daddy they never knew. There will never be a reconciliation. They have to have the funeral and bury their daddy and accept the fact that he is not coming back. He is dead to them, even if he is still living.

Then, after the funeral, you get to know your real Daddy, the Father whom Jesus gave you when He rose from death and returned to, *"My God and your God, My Father and your Father."* [John 20:17] You know Him in prayer, real heartfelt honest crying out to Him in prayer. You do it with much time spent alone with Him, working with Him, open Bible in hand so you can hear what He says to you.

Leave your shame outside the door.
You won't need it in here.

You've been adopted by God. The very God who spoke this universe into existance wants to be your Daddy. Can you imagine a kid who has been adopted coming into his father's house for the first time. He's not real sure about this. "This guy says he loves me, but I don't really believe it." He's real cautious. If he makes a mistake, he flinches. He doesn't really trust Him because he's never learned how to trust.

When I first came to grips with the Father I was afraid of Him. I felt uncomfortable, I was pretty sure He was going to slap me up the side of the head. I would stare at the ground and wait for it to be over. I honestly didn't think He cared anything about me. I still struggle with that. It takes time to heal the wound in your heart. God is very patient.

Jesus said, "*All that the Father gives me will come to me, and whoever comes to me I will never drive away. . . . No one can come to me unless the Father who sent me draws him, and I will raise him up at the last day.*" [John 10:28] You are here because Almighty God *wanted* you to be here. You don't have to sneak into His presence and hide behind the curtains, hide behind a chair. You are here because He wanted you here, and He welcomes you. Leave your shame outside the door. You won't need it in here.

Can you picture God doing and saying the things you've always wished your father would say? Experience Jesus coming to your ballgame and being proud of you. Let Him listen to you, He won't tell you to shut up. Experience gentle affection, kind words, and loving provision. Let Him tell you that you are smart and beautiful. Let Him tell you that He loves you. The feel good thing in your brain is broken, but the feel good thing in your heart still works. Let Him love you. It feels good. It's better than any high.

The best thing about it is, He's portable. God is transcendent, He is equally everwhere. His Spirit is within you, and you are within His Spirit. You can get up and go to work and He is just as near to you as He is in deep prayer. He is not confined to gender roles either. If you need a mother, He can love and nurture you more tenderly and gently than any woman. Go to Him in prayer every day and feed your spirit on His love. Meditate on His love, concentrate on His mercy, focus on His compassion, live in the shadow of His wing.

Over the months and years, as you realize He isn't going to leave you, get mad at you, or tell you to "shut up," you gain condfidence in His love. He doesn't expect you to be perfect, He died so you wouldn't have to be perfect. He is the spring of living water within you, and it doesn't matter who attacks you, rejects you, ignores you, or despises you, you are still loved by the only One who matters, *even when you can't feel it.*

WHAT ABOUT RELAPSE

How you handle a relapse is crucial to your long term survival. You are going to have struggles. You will probably fail at least once, even if it's only in your mind. The critical thing is how you handle it when it happens. Say you screw up and get high once. That doesn't mean you have to spend the next six weeks tweaking and destroy your life again.

> ## *"Man, I thought I was a Christian, and here I am doing it again!"*

Relapse happens in your mind a long time before you actually reach for the drug. You *want* it before you go out looking for it. For as long as you live you will never forget how good it felt; you have to decide you don't *want* it even though you know how good it feels. It's a kind of death. You die to your desire for the high because your love for Him is so great. No one takes it from you, you lay it down of your own accord.

Jesus had a lot of friends, and one day a bunch of his friends were trying to row across the lake. These guys were big strong fisherman and they knew how to run a boat, but they weren't getting anywhere because the wind was against them. It was getting late. It was getting dark. It was two o'clock in the morning and they still weren't there. They were getting scared. You know the feeling. "Will it *always* be this way? Will I always have to live like this, getting busted, thrown in jail, losing everything? Will I always be a slave to this addiction? Man, am I *lost* out here?"

Jesus knew exactly where they were. They didn't have to find Him. He found them. Jesus came out to them, walking on the water, doing the impossible, and Peter called out, *"Lord, if that is really you, let me come out and walk on water with you. Let me do the impossible."* [My paraphrase of Matt 14:22–31] Jesus said, *"Come!"* He was pleased and surprised that Peter would be so daring. Peter got down out of the boat. That took some serious courage. He walked toward Jesus and everything was fine until he looked at the wind and the waves. Then he started to sink.

You stepped up to the challenge and quit using. You walked along just fine for a while, doing the impossible. As long as your thoughts were focused on Jesus, you could do it with minimal effort. You did it in His strength, not yours. But then, you looked away for just a little while. You let yourself daydream about getting high, and then one thing led to another. You went to your old friend's house. You met a good looking girl, and she offered you some; or you just got real bad depressed and didn't go back to Him for your daily bread. You're sinking. "Man, I thought I was a Christian, and here I am doing it again!"

What did Peter do when he started sinking? Did he try to swim it on his own strength? Did he give up and say, "Well, I guess I was stupid trying to walk on water. I'll just give up and drown." Did he get all embarrassed and not ask Jesus to help him because he was ashamed? No! He prayed, *"LORD, SAVE ME!"*

What did Jesus do when Peter started sinking? Did He say, "Peter should have known better than to look at that stuff; I've had just about enough of him."? Did He say, "Well, I always knew Peter was really just a loser. It's just as well he drowned."? No! *Immediately* Jesus reached out His hand and caught him. He pulled him back in the boat. No judgment, no condemnation, just mercy and some dry clothes.

And then there were the eleven other guys in the boat ready to dry him off and cheer him on. When you get Jesus, you get a community, all His other friends, and they are all on your side. They pray with you and for you. They encourage you and inspire you. They understand how bad it hurts and how hard it is, and they speak the words of Jesus to you when you need it. Don't try to swim it alone.

> *As long as you really love Him, He will always pull you back into the boat.*

Jesus pulls you back up out of relapse the same way he pulled you out of addiction in the first place, with prayer. Be honest with yourself and be honest with Jesus. Did you fall out of the boat, or did you *jump* out of the boat? Don't try to play games with Him. He's not stupid. He knows what you did. You knew what would happen if you went to see your old friends, and sure enough it happened. Don't try to pass it off as an innocent mistake. He knows better.

'Fess up and come clean, let Him forgive you and keep walking. Each relapse will be shorter and milder, sometimes only in your mind, and you will get stronger in your relationship with Him. The strength of your prayer life is the strength of your recovery. Keep your heart focused on Him, even when your attention is on your job or your kids or your driving. Keep Him in the back of your mind all the time, remembering His mercy, His cross, His power, and His love.

A man once told me, "This is my third time through rehab. He can't possibly forgive me again." Oh, yes, He can! Don't try to tell Jesus whom He can and cannot forgive. He told us to forgive seventy times seven times. Do you think He's not willing to do the same? He's not surprised when you mess up. He knows you are human, and He knows you are a sinner. You are going to fail sometimes, and He loves you anyway. Jesus loves sinners! Even you! You are precious to Him. He's not going to let you drown any more than I would let my four-year-old daughter drown.

I've been a Christian for many years. Do I screw up from time to time? You bet I do. Do I still love Jesus? With all my heart. Does He forgive me? Absolutely.

You might get discouraged, but don't despair. You raise your hand, admit what you did, and He pulls you back in the boat. You never lose hope because He never stops loving you. He doesn't care how wet He gets. As long as you really love Him, He will always pull you back into the boat.

THIS IS NOT A BOY SCOUT WE'RE UP AGAINST

You need to be aware that you have an enemy. When you joined yourself with Jesus Christ, you removed yourself from Satan, and believe me, he noticed. He will fill your head with doubts, fears, and resentments. He will badger you, mock you, and try to weaken you. Our battle is not against flesh and blood [other people], but rather against spiritual forces we cannot see.

When the Bible teaches about doing battle with the forces of evil, it prefaces the discussion with instructions for the important relationships in life. [Ephesians 5:15 through 6:9] Those relationships have to be right before any effective spiritual warfare can take place. The most important relationship you need to heal is the one with your parents, as we discussed above. Your marriage is also important and your children need attention. Those relationships must be healed, even if they cannot be completely reconciled, before you go to war against evil spirits. Your wife may have moved on and married someone else. If so, you cannot expect her to come back to you. But you can apologize to her, ask her to forgive you, and become a positive influence in her life and in the lives of your children. [Remember, you represent God to your children.]

Satan knows which temptations would be most effective in getting you to sin and separate yourself from God. He tempts you with the perverse pleasure of anger and resentment, being the 'wounded one.' You can meditate on your resentment, your hurt, your disappointment, and your anger, or you can meditate on His love, His cross, His power, and His grace. When you forgive the people who hurt you and renounce the obsessive, depressing, and resentful thoughts, you take the dagger out of Satan's hand. He can't stab you in the heart anymore. Reliving old offences keeps them alive in your mind; Jesus came to nail them to His cross.

Satan knows each one of us intimately. He knows our weaknesses. He knows what buttons to push. He knows when you harbor anger and resentment against the people who hurt you. He knows when you have an unmet "father-need" that leaves you selfish and needy, demanding and controlling, or seductive and promiscuous. He knows when you have unconfessed sin, things you won't even admit to yourself. He uses those things against you, tormenting you with doubt, fear, and anger.

> ## *You've believed a lot of lies for a long time.*

Satan knows when you have ideas about yourself that are not true, like believing you are stupid or worthless. You've believed a lot of lies for a long time. You need an honest assessment of yourself. Accept yourself as a beautiful and valuable person, the precious and beloved child whom God created. Yes, you have made some mistakes. You have done some very ugly things. He didn't love you because you were beautiful. You are beautiful because He loves you. All of your ugliness is either sin which has been forgiven or a lie which you no longer believe.

He also knows when you have ideas about God that are not true, like the "Teddy Bear in the Sky," or the "Big Guy with the Stick." Satan tells you that you've been treated unjustly by God, to make you angry at God. Every one can point to times in their lives when God let them down. Why would a good God allow a three-year-old girl to be raped by her own father? Yes, there is evil in this world. There is also a cross. He did not let us down.

Satan has been defeated by Jesus Christ. He can torment us, but he cannot destroy us. He can tempt us, but he cannot make us sin. He can lie to us, but we do not have to believe his lies. Satan tells you that you are worthless, useless, and hopeless. Jesus came to tell you that you are a priceless treasure to Him. Satan tells you God is too busy and important to mess with you. Jesus came to tell you He has the very hairs on your head numbered. He knows all your thoughts, all your hurts, and all your feelings, and He loves you.

Satan tries to tell you that God is disgusted with you, tired of you. The Holy Spirit of Jesus came to show you that He never takes his loving eyes off of you. Satan tells you that you've gone too far, you've committed the "unforgivable sin." Jesus came to show you that His cross is big enough for everyone. The only sin He can't forgive is the one you won't confess. The Holy Spirit came to convict the world of sin, righteousness, and judgment. [John 16:8] The sin against the Holy Spirit is to *refuse* to be convicted, *refuse* to admit that what you are doing is wrong. That is the "unforgivable sin" . . . it has nothing to do with sex or violence.

Satan will tell you to go ahead and do it one more time. You're been clean for six months, one year, two years, you deserve a little reward. Just once won't hurt anything. He reminds you of how good it felt, not how sick you got.

This is not a boy scout we're up against. Satan fights dirty. Get your armor on, the armor of God from Ephesians 6. It is detailed in the next chapter. Take it seriously and pray for protection. You know you'll be under attack; get other people to pray with you.

You don't have to put up with the lies and the torment from the evil spirits hanging around. You are in Jesus Christ and He is in you. You don't have to be afraid of evil spirits. They are *creatures*. They are subject to His power. You can evict them in His Name if you are His disciple. It goes like this.

Jesus, I belong to You. I am being tormented by doubts, fears, lies, and temptations. I have been cursed by people who hate me. In Your Holy Name I renounce these spirits and curses. I repent of the actions in my life that enabled them to have a hold on me. Cleanse me and fill me with Your Spirit. Jesus, my Savior, thank You for Your cross, Your blood, and Your suffering on my behalf. Glorify Your Name in my life.

You don't have to defeat Satan, Jesus has already done that. Your job is to stay in Him, and you do that by persistent focused prayer, Bible study, and obedience. The battle is the Lord's.

POWERFUL CHRISTIAN

When after some days he returned to Capernum, the news went around that he was at home; and such a crowd collected that the space in front of the door was not big enough to hold them. And while he was proclaiming the message to them, a man was brought who was paralyzed. Four men were carrying him, but because of the crowd they could not get him near. So they opened up the roof over the place where Jesus was, and when they had broken through they lowered the stretcher on which the paralyzed man was lying. When Jesus saw their faith, he said to the paralyzed man, "My son, your sins are forgiven."

Now some lawyers were there and they thought to themselves, "Why does this fellow talk like that? This is blasphemy! Who but God can forgive sins?" Jesus knew in his own mind that this was what they were thinking, and said to them, "Why do you harbor thoughts like these? Is it easier to say to this paralyzed man, "Your sins are forgiven," or to say, "Stand up and take you bed and walk?" But to convince you that the Son of Man has the right on earth to forgive sins, he turned to the paralyzed man and said, "I say to you, stand up, take your bed, and go home." And he stood up, and at once took his stretcher and went out in full view of them all.

Mark 2:1 NEB

So now I have chipped away the roof and made a hole to lower you, my precious friend, into the presence of Jesus, and He has forgiven you. [Mark 2:1] Now it's time to get up and walk. You are not paralyzed anymore. As a recovered addict, you will become an extremely powerful Christian. The enemy knows it. That's why the battle has been so fierce. The strength of your spirit is the strength of your prayer connection with Jesus.

You will love Him more than the average Christian. You will be much stronger than someone who has never faced addiction and never had to struggle. You are unlikely to fall into pride and arrogance, because you will always remember where you came from.

When Jesus called His original twelve disciples, they had already been listening to Him for quite some time. They had heard Him talk about the kingdom of God, the mercy and holiness of God, about humility and courage and how they are two parts of the same thing, about the love of God and the love of other people and how they are two parts of the same thing. They had heard all this and they loved Him. Then, when He asked them to follow Him, they jumped up from what they were doing and ran. "He picked me! I get to go with Him! Today's my lucky day, He picked me!" Well, honey, He has picked you. You get to go with Him. Today is your lucky day. He picked you.

Matt 4:18–22 NEB

Jesus was walking by the sea of Galilee when he saw two brothers, Simon, called Peter, and his brother Andrew, casting a net into the lake, for they were fishermen. Jesus said to them, "Come with me, and I will make you fishers of men." And at once they left their nets and followed him.

He went on and saw another pair of brothers, James, son of Zebedee and his brother John; they were in the boat with their father Zebedee, overhauling their nets. He called them, and at once they left the boat and their father, and followed him.

Use your strength in your church to teach others how to pray and reach people with His mercy. You know Him in a way few other people do. Pray aggressively for the people around you, especially those you know are addicted. Pray yourself deeper and deeper into His character, and then do what He gives you to do. His character is loving and giving. Give of your time and experience to the people around you. Don't think the brain damage you have impairs your work for Him. It rather empowers it. You are more able to do the spiritual work He calls you to do, the compassion, listening, caring, and praying that are so powerful in the spiritual world. If you are in jail, use your spiritual power in jail. You are a priceless treasure to Him exactly the way you are.

Life is made meaningful by the long term goals and purpose in life. You can get clean and yet not be truly sober if you do not realize your value to God and to the world around you. Your recovery becomes complete when you assume your new identity in Christ and fulfill your role in His kingdom. You are not an accident–no matter what your birth history. You were deliberately made by Him, redeemed by Him, and healed by Him. He had a purpose in your creation.

And the God of all grace, who called you to His eternal glory in Christ after you have suffered a little while, will Himself restore you and make you strong, firm and steadfast. [1 Peter 5:10 NIV]

Testimony of a child of God

Hi my name is Jackson. I am twenty-three and I was a meth addict for three years. Till the intervention of Jesus Christ in my life. I used to use on a daily basis till Sept 28th 2003. That is the day I will never forget because that is the day God stepped in my life and said, "Follow me."

When I first started meth I don't think I could be classified as a weekend user because we just started doing it all the time. I had a job where I could buy as much as I wanted, and when I wanted, and had a dealer were it was always there any time I had the urge. I started out just being a user well I thought I was helping my dealer by selling some for him. Then I found myself what ever I bought if I didn't have it sold before I got home I would do it all my self.

So I spent three years of my life in HELL. Growing up, I always thought there was a God, but never acted on trying to find Him.

But the awesome thing is God is always with you. We are all in God's hands and that is so awesome to think about. Even though I was doing drugs, God had a plan for my salvation and he has a plan for everyone's salvation and He offers it freely.

Well, Sept 28, 2003 I was driving around and I had just bought a half gram of meth. Then a cop started following me so I ate the ½ gram in a panic. Well the cop ends up turning down the road and so I decided I better go to a friend's house. Well when I got to there house they were in bed I wake them up and tell them what was going on and they said if I had any problems to wake them up. So I was sitting there in there house. They have this dog and this dog will bark at anything that comes there in there house. I was sitting there and this dog started barking well I was like someone is here. I stand up to look out the window and found no one was there. So I looked up stairs and this dog walks to the edge of the stairway and starts looking at something I couldn't see falling in the room, and I started toward the dog and something stopped me in my tracks and I started swaying back and forth and it didn't seem like anything seemed to matter.

I came back to and I remember yelling for help and no one got up. So I make it up the stairs and wake everyone up and tell them I'm feeling a bit funny. About that time it felt like I was pushed against a wall and the room was spinning. I can remember they was asking if I was alright and I get up again and convince myself I was alright walk back downstairs. So we are all standing downstairs and this dog is going nuts. The funny thing is this dog knows me and always came to me. Only thing I remember concentrating on was this dog. This is the honest truth this dog goes to the glass door and looks out it. Then turns around and looks at me as if it was telling me to go. Dog turns back to the door looks out and looks back at me and stares at me. I sat there I was like well maybe this dog is trying to tell me to leave and I sat there for a second and said, if that dog does this again I am going to the hospital that dog did it again.

So on the way to the hospital I can remember how cold it was the person driving me had the heater cranked and the flashers on. I couldn't hardly see the road because my vision was blurring in and out. But I remember hearing these voices telling me your not going to make it. At one point they told me to look at the speedometer and I looked at it and it said we was going 45 mph when I knew we was flying down a two lane with the flashers on.

Finally we get to the hospital it was about two o'clock in the morning. I'll never forget this there was two or three cop cars there. I still have no reason why these cops was there. I knew some of them. One of them was asking me questions and telling me he know I was doing meth and all that. But all of the sudden I was back to were nothing mattered and I found my self praying the sinner prayer for I asked God for forgiveness and a second chance to right my wrongs. I'll be totally honest that night if I hadn't made my vow with the Lord I wouldn't be here today because I know in my heart if I hadn't prayed that prayer at that time He was going to take me out.

So that night my friends that was there with me said when I started stabilizing I started flipping out. I turned to them and said that dragon in the corner and in revelation the dragon is referred to as the devil. So when I came to I was like, I have to go to church somewhere and I was like, where will I go and at that time my mom called and asked me to come live with her and they had this awesome church for me to go to. That next Sunday I was sitting in church getting saved in the church, the Lord was ready for me. I have been clean for ten months and I have given my life to the missionary for addictions and I came across this awesome material you have here. I pray God blesses *you with what you are doing it is so awesome knowing that we have people that care.*

―――――――

Hi. My name is Herb. Funny name for an addict, isn't it.

My journey began in Phoenix, Arizona, where crystal abounds. I served the enemy on the streets and on all the highways and byways for six or seven years. I was a main line user, advancing right on the effects of heroin. At a low point I decided suicide was the only way I could be free. That vow was made looking out a hole I cut out of a refrigerator box that was my bedroom for the night behind a grocery store, looking up at the moon with two stars.

Upon coming to the next morning, after a three day drug binge, starving and penniless, I went to a 7–11 store and panhandled enough money for a cup of coffee. As I'm pacing outside remembering my vow, a van full of men pulled up and started setting up for a car wash. One of the men approached me and stated sharing Jesus with me, and the more he spoke to me, the more comfort I felt.

I eventually went back to the Christian Discipleship men's home from Victory Outreach that evening with the men. It was while in the men's Home that I first spoke the sinner's prayer, and received Jesus Christ into my life.

At a later date, I backslid and got myself in trouble with the law, violated probation, and was facing a 10–25 year prison term. God dealt with me heavy and I ended up in jail and then right back at the Men's home. It was at that time that God really revealed himself to me and I took heed as to what He really wanted me to do with my life.

I regret the things that I got involved in, my lifestyle, and the torture I put my family through, But in another way, I'm glad because the relationship I have now, not only with the Lord, I've been blessed with a God fearing woman and a wonderful life free of probation and drugs.

[Author's note: I still hear from Herb from time to time. He is clean and happy and doing the Lord's work.]

―――――――

My run with drugs started in high school during 1975. Smoking pot was just for fun. My life was always on the up and go. There wasn't no fear of anything. It seems I was never in trouble and I seemed to have the right answer for everything. As life went further I saw crack cocaine around 1980, but I just didn't care for it, plus the expense was too much.

About 1999 I was self-employed and the cash flow was great. The brief exposure to meth was around and I started using it and before long I was at a gram or two a day. My self personality was different but I would not face the fact. Finally one day in August 2001, my wife found the box of meth, pot, and stuff and the world stopped. You see I knew the Lord, and with a family of four, I knew better. I do believe God works in all ways. At this point my expenses in business and home were a mess. The meth gets to you to sell your soul, just like the devil. I had fallen into this by my self. After two run ins with the I.C.U. at the hospital I clearly asked the Lord into my life.

The meth gets you thinking three things. You have a fear of life, fear of success, and fear of self. When this happened I seemed to not have the will to go and ask for help. The detox the next two months was hell. I would eat some onions on a salad and this would trigger a high. This would go away in time but the weakness of not having trust in food or self took some time. Today I can say to meth addicts that there is hope.

Through Jesus Christ, He will and did heal me and my family. The travel each day is real. You take it one day at a time. You can't worry about others until first you rework yourself and the help is from Christ. From the dealers to the demons, Jesus is bigger than all that. Today I am clean and when that little look back shows up, Jesus reminds me who is first.

Decolores.

———————

At first I was a weekend user, then it turned into a few days a week. Soon it took over my lie. Nothing else mattered to me, but doing crystal meth seven days a week. I couldn't go to work without it. I would stay up days at a time. It had total control over my life. I would do anywhere from two grams to an eight ball a day. I would smoke it, snort it, or eat it. I was taking about an eight ball a day to work to sell and a couple ounces of pot. I didn't care about anyone or anything except my drugs. It got so bad, I would come home from work, lock the door, close the shades and just do my dope until it was time to go to work again and I did it over and over, day after day.

Then a man stopped one day and told me that Jesus loved me. That got me to thinking. So the next day I asked him to prove it to me. He showed me in the Bible that it really was so. The Lord got to dealing with my heart. I was so miserable for the next few days. When I lay down in bed, it felt like a cold hard slab of concrete. The man asked me to come to church on a Wednesday night and I did. That night I was saved by the grace of God. I realized that this man called Jesus really did love me and died for me.

He was and still is loving me and protecting me today. I've been clean eight years now. I honestly believe that if it weren't for the grace of God, I would be dead today.

Jason

———————

I'm a former meth addict. I've been clean for almost a year. Thanks to Jesus who turned my life around then I got arrested over in Honolulu last June. I was on a collision course of self destruction and it ended abruptly when I landed in federal prison for three months leaving three small children behind in California. I did the unthinkable, the unforgivable, the worst thing I could do to my children . . . I abandoned them. For that I am making a living amends—one day at a time.

What was I thinking? Well I wasn't. I was spun out, torn up, dragged down and worn out. And I thought this was all good! I was deep into the cycle of addiction and denial and I was as far away from God as I could ever get. But God knew exactly what it would take to save me from myself. He never gave up on me. I owe Him my life and intend to spend the rest of my days making a difference for Him and for all our children, including mine.

I have a fourteen-year-old named Cassie and she is severely autistic. Her father died seven years ago from a drug overdose. It was at this time I began using meth. My life since then has been a steady downward spiral until my arrest and subsequent incarceration last summer.

I have two more children ages three and five. While their father is gone somewhere on meth, I continually praise God for my salvation and recovery. I can testify to using meth and having my life evolve into sheer devastation and destruction. The good news is I'm back and living out what God has for me—a plan and a purpose . . to serve in whatever way I can.

SECTION 5: THE RESPONSE

.17.

THIS IS NOT A BOY SCOUT WE'RE UP AGAINST

SUPERNATURAL EVIL

The following is an excerpt from Uncle Fester's book *Secrets of Methamphetamine Manufacture Including Recipes for MDA, Ecstasy, and Other Psychedelic Amphetamines*- Revised and Expanded Sixth edition 2002 p 25.

"The first thing he [a good underground chemist] does is test the chemicals . . . within a few seconds they should mix together entirely. At this point, he may offer a prayer to the chemical god, praising his limitless chemical power and asking that some of this power be allowed to flow through him, the god's High Priest. He may also ask to be delivered from the red tar that can be the result of this reaction."
Used with permission Loompanics Unlimited, Inc

At the risk of being branded an extremist, I have to point out the reality of an evil force in this universe; a force the Bible calls Satan. Anyone involved with methamphetamine in any real way, realizes the evil spiritual power of this drug. This stuff came straight from the bowels of hell.

The rituals associated with drug use, the symbols and liturgy, are frankly spiritual and are directed toward Satan. There are chants and incantations used in the ceremonies associated with its preparation and use, incense and candle light, raucous music, secrecy and code words all contribute to the ambience of a drug party. I hesitate to call it a party, though most users do call it that, because there is almost no social interaction going on. The people there usually do not even know each other. They didn't come to socialize. They came to use.

Many users admit and celebrate this association with the occult. They say "I have some 'god' in my pocket." They say, "Let us worship," as they smoke or shoot. When asked, they will say it is all just a joke. It is not a joke. It is thinly veiled sorcery. The magic potion bubbles and boils. Cooks and dealers are admired and revered like high priests of the faith, and they get a rush from that feeling of control over other people. The users become objects in the eyes of the cooks. They refer to them as boys, dogs, or slaves.

The liturgy is openly erotic. Women throw their bodies at men in exchange for meth, becoming sex slaves to their dealer or cook. Methamphetamine creates an insatiable desire for sex leading to violent crimes against women and children. Daughters are raped and held out for others to rape. Wives and children are offered to the dealer in exchange for drugs. Pornography and indiscriminant sex are part of the high, part of the ritual associated with drug use.

> *They can see through the walls and they can read your mind.*

Steve Box is a recovered methamphetamine addict who has written an insightful book about the spiritual nature of addiction, *Meth = Sorcery* [published by Above All Ministries]. He gives a first hand description of the hallucinations and distortions caused by methamphetamine. The hallucinations associated with meth are typically demonic and violent in nature. They are fed by paranoia, and include commands to kill other people or kill yourself. You see a gang of thugs, but they disappear as you approach, you see disembodied heads cursing and taunting you. You panic and run, wreck your car, get out and run some more, run into barbed wire and get all cut up running away from your hallucinations. They can see through the walls and read your mind.

You see messages written in blood on the mirror with the date you are going to die. You see people moving slowly toward you with knives and guns, and no matter how far you run, they are always right behind you. Your children's crayon drawings turn into violent threats or obscene phallic symbols. These are evil hallucinations and evil delusions, different in character and content from the hallucinations and delusions seen in natural schizophrenia.

You act on these hallucinations and delusions. You accuse your wife of sleeping around; you assault your dad for mocking you. Every car driving by is a narc or a cop. You think people are talking about you, plotting against you, planning to torture you and kill you. If you really believe you are being threatened, you will take action, and since you are never very far away from a gun, that action is frequently lethal.

What kind of evil leads a father to murder his five-year-old son with an ax? What kind of evil causes a mother to set fire to her baby in his crib? This is not natural evil, the kind we can explain by appeals to human selfishness and lust. This is *supernatural* evil, irrational mindless evil. Supernatural evil is not a normal part of our human nature distorted and twisted against us. It is an evil from outside our human nature. It is supernatural, demonic, satanic evil.

There is evil in the results of addiction, there is also evil in the precipitating causes of addiction. Why do fathers abandon their wives and children to move in with their girlfriends? Why does any child suffer from child abuse or incest? We are all sons of Adam, we are all fallen creatures, and we are all fundamentally selfish. We were not created to be like that.

Know Your Enemy

When God spoke us into existence, He said, "It is very very good." He expressed Himself in His creation. He made us in His image, joyful and confident, generous and loving. We were meant to express all of His goodness in our lives. He also made us creatures with a free will, capable of effortless control over our desires; freedom to choose to obey, choose to love, choose to worship, and it was very very good. We were capable of truly loving Him because we were capable of choosing not to love Him.

Satan was once a powerful angel of great beauty, and he was very close to God. He saw that God had created beings with a will, the capacity to choose, and that meant they could choose to love God. They were capable of worship. He also saw that they had been given an eternal spirit, an identity which would not just pass away and dissipate. They could worship Him forever, in timeless eternity. Let's use our imaginations for a minute. What do *you* suppose the conversation sounded like?

Here these smelly little animals with animal brains have been given the capacity to appreciate the glory of the eternal and infinite God. They have a will, they can choose and initiate, not just respond like an animal. They can worship with the work of their hands, their choices and priorities, the highest form of worship. Satan was incensed. "How *could* you? They are animals! See? They eat, they defecate, they copulate; they are animals! How could you give such lowly creatures the capacity to worship eternally like a real spirit? Why, the spirit you have given them is almost as great as the spirit I have! They can see and adore you in eternal timelessness just like a real spirit!"

Who knows, perhaps the spirit we have is even superior in quality to the spirits of angels. After all, we have suffered, and to our knowledge, angels have never truly suffered. We can know God in ways they cannot, and choose to obey him under circumstances they have never faced. The capabilities of our spirits, to adore God in the face of suffering, was latent in our natures until the fall, but was nonetheless there.

We can worship God in the face of wrenching pain. We can lose a child and still worship the eternal and infinite God. We can be mocked by our business associates and still serve and desire God. We can obey Him in the face of fierce temptation. We can worship Him through our tears when we are rejected and despised by other people. We can sacrifice things of great value to honor Him.

> ## *"Ye shall be as gods, knowing right from wrong."*

Satan was determined to destroy these creatures God had made in some small way superior to him. How better to do it than turn them back into animals, distort their free will and turn it into self will? "Ye shall be as gods, knowing right from wrong." [Gen 3:5] Satan told us we were capable of deciding for ourselves what is right and what is wrong. He could tempt us to sin, to exalt our desires over the desires of God and act on those desires. We could use our minds to justify and rationalize all manner of sin, things our conscience does not hesitate to condemn. That's what eating of the fruit of the tree of knowledge of good and evil was all about. We are all still chewing on that fruit. We sinned before there was a Bible. His laws were written on our hearts from the moment of our creation, and still are.

Satan knew God would have to destroy us. God could never tolerate the presence of something so arrogant and insolent in His universe. Here is a human, a mere creature, and he has made himself to be his own god, doing his own will, pursuing his own pleasure, exalting it above the demands of truth, righteousness, justice, goodness, above the demands of God. Such a thing could never be tolerated by a Holy God.

THE DEMANDS OF JUSTICE

Satan knew what the demands of justice would be. Satan didn't think He would do it. Satan thought the Son of God would balk at being humiliated for the sake of some fleshy worms on an insignificant planet, but then He, the Holy One, Ancient of Days, consented to being born into the world He had created, in a human body, to an unwed teenager, in a stable. You can be sure nobody believed Mary's story about an angel and an immaculate conception. They went to Bethlehem, the town of Joseph's family, and you'd think his relatives would have helped them out. You'd make room for your sister-in-law, wouldn't you? She can have her baby out in the barn with all the rest of the animals.

No relatives, no midwife, no baby shower, no blue balloons. No universal acclamation, no splitting of the skies, none of the pomp and honor you would expect for the birth of the Jewish Messiah. Jesus was born into abject humiliation. Mary wasn't acclaimed a virgin by the religious powers. She held her head low and said quietly, "*But I have never known a man. How can this be?*" [Luke 1:34] If they were going to make up a dramatic birth story for Jesus, don't you think they would have done a better job than *that?*

The virgin birth was predicted long before the much disputed passage in Isaiah 7:14, "*Behold a virgin shall conceive and bear a son, and they shall call his name Immanuel.*" Immediately after the fall, in Genesis 3, redemption was promised in the 'seed of the woman.' *I will put enmity between you [Satan] and the woman, and between your offspring [evil and lies] and hers [the Christ]; He will crush your head, and you will strike his heel.*" [Gen 3:15 NIV] Salvation was not in the seed of the man, but in the seed of the woman.

Satan thought Jesus would balk at relinquishing His divine power and keep for Himself the power to provide His own sustenance [turn the stones into loaves]. He thought Jesus would exalt himself [throw Himself off the pinnacle of the temple in a dramatic display of deity]. [Matt 4:1–11] He thought Jesus would exert His will above God's will and refuse the humiliation and torture of the cross. He certainly expended a great deal of time and effort tempting Him to do just that in the Agony of Gethsemane. He counted on His human nature, His possession of a free will, separate from God's will, which could be set at odds with God's will.

> ## "Not my will, but thine be done."

Well, it backfired. Jesus prevailed. "*Not my will, but thine be done.*" He submitted His will perfectly to the will of God. He suffered an atoning death for us as sons of Adam. He suffered the wrath of God, the condemnation we deserved, and He did it willingly. We are His *creatures,* and He suffered and died in order for us to live. Now we can know God in even greater ways than we could before our fall. We can know His mercy, the incredible depth of His love expressed in His Son taking the wrath of God for us.

"*In the day that you eat of it, you will surely die.*" [Gen 2:17] We died to the constant fellowship of God, the life and love of God, the indwelling Spirit of God, when we exalted our will above His. Jesus submitted His will to the will of God, and in so doing, broke the curse on our behalf. The rebellion was quelled. The atonement had been offered.

> *Sacrifice and offering you did not desire, but a body you prepared for me; with burnt offerings and sin offerings you were not pleased. Then I said, "Here I am—it is written about me on the scroll—I have come to do your will O God. You law is written on my heart.*
>
> Heb. 10:6 and Psalm 40:6 NIV

Satan underestimated the love of God. After all, He had never been called upon to extend mercy before. Mercy and forgiveness were latent in God's nature and had never been expressed before the fall of mankind. We were tempted and deceived. We had sinned, but we could call upon the mercy of God, where Satan could not. The fall of mankind was no surprise to God, and He could have prevented our sin, but only by taking our free will away from us, something He is not willing to do. We were given a will at our creation, the power to choose, initiate, and express our selves. He made us to be persons, not objects, created in His image. Our freedom to *choose* to worship Him, adore Him, serve Him, and obey Him is so priceless to Him it was worth dying for.

> Alas! No man can ever ransom himself, nor pay God the price of that release; his ransom would cost too much, forever beyond his ability to pay, the ransom that would let him live on always and never see the pit of death.
>
> Psalm 49:7 NEB

The mercy of God is expressed in the selfless sacrifice of Jesus Christ, the Son of Adam and the Son of God. Perfect justice is met in Him. The demands of righteousness, truth, and holiness are met in the suffering and death of Jesus Christ, the Lamb of God. And when we partake of His sacrifice, eat His body and drink His blood, when we say from the heart, "You died for me, too," we are reconciled with the Holy God who spoke us into existence, and His Holy Spirit is restored to us.

And yes, physical life and death still go on, as they have for centuries, but spiritual life, eternal life is restored to us. *"And this is eternal life, that they may know you, the only true God, and Jesus Christ, whom you have sent."* [John 17:3 NIV] His Holy Spirit is restored to us, His creatures. The great mercy of God would never have had its full expression without the sin of mankind. No one would ever have known how deeply God could love, how completely He could forgive, if we had never sinned.

> *For the joy set before Him*
> *He endured the cross.*

He is the Joyful Giver, this One who died for us. When you give a gift to your child, you don't even think about the monetary value of the gift. The only thing concerning you is whether she will like it or not. Your joy is in the child's acceptance of the gift, the squeal when she rips the paper off, her gratitude for it, and the joy she has playing with it or using it. The more she plays with your gift, the better you like it. When she takes it to bed with her, you *sing* inside. It is your delight to see her enjoy what you have given her.

Jesus takes delight in seeing your life and love and healing at the foot of His cross. When you accept His love, it pleases Him immensely and gives Him much glory. When your life is transformed by His mercy, His heart is filled with joy. The great cost of the gift is forgotten in the pleasure of giving it. *". . . for the joy that was set before Him, [He] endured the cross. . ."* [Heb 12:2 KJ]

ANIMALS

Satan still hates us with a vicious, murderous hatred. He still wants to destroy us, destroy our capacity to relate to God, and turn us into animals instead of persons. Nothing does that better or faster than methamphetamine. The addict is reduced to a craving, irrational, irresponsible animal, answering only to his own desires, totally without honor, and oblivious to God. He worships a substance instead of his Creator. He sacrifices everything he has and everything he is, to worship his god.

> *If Satan is unable to turn us into animals,*
> *he'll settle for second best and make us*
> *think we're just animals.*

If Satan is unable to turn us into animals, he'll settle for second best and make us *think* we're just animals. Evolution is taught in my daughter's fifth grade science book as if it were an established fact when it is nothing of the sort. The evidence just isn't there. Anyone who challenges the assumptions of these learned professors is ridiculed and excluded. Their work doesn't even get published. The height of scientific insult is to call someone a creationist. It's paramount to calling him an idiot; he obviously believes in the Easter

Bunny. Our children are raised to believe they are just animals, is it any wonder they act like animals, addicted, promiscuous hedonists.

Our children are in a trance, marching off the edge of a cliff. They are worshipping drugs and pleasure and money. They see no reason not to go for it, "party hardy," live it up and "fly high." No one is watching, so it doesn't really matter what they do. They are driven by their impulses, lusts, and desires, unwilling or unable to see the truth about what they are doing. People in our culture believe they are descended from a monkey, with no spiritual significance, accidents of nature in an uncaring cosmos that neither knows nor cares what they do. When I go into a jail or rehabilitation center and start teaching about the worship of God, invariably somebody says, "You don't actually believe that stuff, do you?" The implication is that intelligent educated people couldn't possibly believe in God.

The academic atheists accuse me of closed-minded intolerance when I teach about the authority of God and the validity of the Bible. They tell me that I am exalting my beliefs above the obvious facts of the universe. Who among them can prove that this universe is just an accident of nature? The evidence for an Intelligent Agent responsible for this universe is pervasive in both cosmology and biology. Atheists categorically deny the entire realm of spiritual reality, and then have the audacity to call *me* 'narrow-minded.' They have exalted *their* belief system which denies God, and then they accuse *me* of bigotry! Excuse me, but who is guilty of bigotry here?

Atheists disbelieve in the spiritual world and mock anyone who claims to have experienced it, discounting their testimony as obvious insanity. We have eyes because there is something to see. We have ears because there is something to hear. We have the capacity to experience the spiritual world because there is a vast spiritual world to be experienced by those who choose to do so. If I declare that Europe does not exist, and then someone points out to me that they have *been* to Europe and *know* it to exist, I would be remiss if I then declared that person insane because everybody knows there is no Europe. And then I refuse to go to Europe and see for myself because I don't want to admit that I have been wrong about this Europe thing all along.

Atheists teach *their* religion of disbelief in the schools with impunity while denying that it is a religion. The scientific evidence for the existence of God is overwhelming and persuasive. *Someone* created this universe, and Whoever did it - is God. To refuse to teach Intelligent Design in the schools is a failure of the first order, and it makes the failure of society inevitable. We are basing our lives upon a LIE. (See Appendix C for more on this issue.)

SELF-ACTUALIZATION

The pinnacle of maturity is called 'self actualization,' a form of hedonism that exalts the individual will. We are 'psychologically healthy' when we engage all of the passions and lusts we find in ourselves, express our deepest longings and desires, irrespective of their morality. We have been taught to look to ourselves as the final authority as to what we should do, think, and say. Anyone looking to an external authority, and especially to God, is considered immature or brainwashed. We don't consider ourselves *anybody's* creature.

We live in a society that believes nothing is wrong and nothing is right. It's all relative. If it feels right to you, then it must be right. We even go through 'therapy' to get rid of that Annoying Voice, the one who insists on telling us that what we are doing is wrong. There is no absolute, no standard of right and wrong. We each decide for ourselves what is right and wrong. We will not be confined by somebody else's ethical or sexual moral code.

> ## *We don't consider ourselves*
> ## ***anybody's*** *creature.*

We value 'free thinking,' independence of thought, freedom of speech, and honest debate, but only if it *does not* involve the person of Jesus Christ. We are forbidden the study of His life and character, even as a historical figure, in the schools and public places. Any morality claiming an origin in God is dismissed out of hand as irrelevant, backward and oppressive. Any culture's religion is more valid than the Judeo-Christian one, and the fewer moral demands it makes, the better. We enjoy 'spirituality' as long as it makes no claims upon our behavior. The natural result of this kind of thinking is chaos—abandoned children, humiliated wives, angry people who have been insulted and wronged.

We all know lies, murder, and adultery are wrong; we don't need anyone to tell us that. The shame and guilt we feel is evidence enough of that truth. When God spoke this universe in to existence, the first thing He did was to separate light from darkness, right from wrong, truth from a lie, good from evil. Morning and evening, the first day. It is written into reality just as surely as is gravity. Those moral principles we call foundational to human society were not written by cave men seeking to promote the survival of the tribe. They were written by God upon every human heart. No human society has ever actually *lived* by those principles, but we all know that they are right, true and good.

IMPULSES

Our children see no reason to suppress the impulses coming out of their animal natures; after all, these impulses are legitimized by a society that condones almost anything, provided it feels natural. Consciously suppressing those impulses is what society frowns upon. Controlling our sex drive is considered "frigidity," managing our impulses is regarded as confining, suppressing our desires is called "brainwashing." Our kids are mocked for maintaining virginity until marriage. Marriage is mocked if it includes people of opposite gender. You're not cool unless you are deviant in some way.

Deviant sexuality is celebrated in the drug culture, and the high itself is a source of intense arousal. The crystal community encourages promiscuity and exalts extreme expressions of sexuality, the wilder the better. They mark themselves by piercing tongues, nipples, and genitalia. Pornography is a prominent part of the drug experience; porno enhances the high by contributing to the arousal component. Deviant impulses are encouraged and shared with a group of like-minded and creative people who are also highly aroused. Nothing is forbidden.

Those deviant impulses become wired into the brain as thought patterns and fantasies. When fantasies are entertained, dwelled upon, talked about, and accepted by like-minded people, they become engrained in the brain *neurochemically*. Once acted upon, they become established as habits, lifestyles, and eventually compulsions. A society which rewards deviant behavior encourages this process in the name of tolerance and liberation. Our brains adjust to the patterns of activity required of them, with structural changes in the neural tracts mediating impulse control. Instead of controlling our impulses we allow our impulses to control us, our urges and drives and cravings control us, we are little more than animals and *that* is considered 'mature and self-actualized.'

> *Not all of our impulses are right and good.*
> *Most of what comes natural to us is wrong.*

The sexually deviant feel compelled to justify their behavior because they know in their spirit it is wrong. I call it the "Fig Leaf Effect." No one has to justify doing what they know is right. I don't have to explain why I am faithful to my husband. Sure, he's really a nice guy and I know all those other guys are nice too, but I'm kind of partial to the man I married, and you just have to understand, I know I *should* just hop in bed with whoever comes along, but I really prefer my husband. We don't feel compelled to justify doing what's right, even when it's unpopular or socially unacceptable to do what is right.

It's socially unacceptable to quit your high octane job to spend more time with the kids, but you don't feel obligated to justify that action. Explain it, maybe, but not justify it.

Our children act out of their impulses; anger impulses, sexual impulses, adventure impulses, and if it feels right to them, they rationalize that it must be right to do whatever comes into their heads. Not all of our impulses are right and good. Most of what comes natural to us is wrong; selfishness, adultery, greed, rage, lies, and cowardice, they all come natural to us. If it comes naturally, that's a pretty good clue it is *wrong*. We are given the Word of God to know what's right and good, not our sexual and carnal impulses!

THE WORD OF GOD DENIED

The Word of God is under constant attack. Academic theologians go through the Bible and take a vote on what is historically true, and what is the pious daydream of the devoted and deluded followers of this little Jewish sect under constant attack by various power brokers. Early Christians were defending themselves against the Romans, and so they made Pilate look like an altar boy to get the Romans off their backs. They injected fulfillments of prophesy into every corner of the Gospels. The birth story of Jesus is said to be obvious fantasy deliberately concocted to glorify the story these poor psychotic people had staked their lives on.

> *A story about a dying God would not have been manufactured by a Jewish culture.*

If the Gospels were fantasy, wouldn't they have made their homemade Messiah a powerful glorious Being, unencumbered with hunger and thirst, appearing and disappearing at will? Instead, He was a hungry tired Man asleep in the back of a boat, walking miles of dusty roads, keeping company with lepers and tax collectors, treating women with respect, and holding squirmy children on His knee [at a time when women and children were considered much less than human]. The children are our best evidence for the veracity of the Gospels. Kids can see right through a phony. Can you imagine a child sitting on the lap of Chiaphas, the stuffed shirt high priest? Can you imagine a bunch of deluded hero worshippers telling a story about *children* [read 'dog turds'] sitting on the lap of their Messiah?

And then, at the climax of the story, their Messiah dies in agony on a tree. If we were going to make up a story, you can be sure the cross would not be in it. The suffering servant passages of Isaiah 53 predicting it were not considered Messianic prophesy by anybody in first century Judaism. They liked the stuff in Daniel much better. Christians were even accused of making up the Isaiah passages until they were found intact in the Dead Sea Scrolls. A story about a dying God would not have been manufactured by a Jewish culture.

> It wasn't the Jewish people who called for the crucifixion of Jesus. They loved Him and wept for Him along the trail to the cross. It was a collection of arrogant priests and scholars [the one's with overturned tables last Sunday] who arrested him in the middle of the night, tried Him in an illegal trial, and pushed for His execution. Too cowardly to arrest him openly, they did it in the dark of night and had the whole deed done by midmorning the next day. *"Every day I was with you in the temple courts, and you did not lay a hand on me. But this is your hour, when darkness reigns."* Luke 22:53 NIV The Jewish people were shocked and dismayed by His execution, and *thousands* of them believed on Him after His resurrection.

But no part of the Bible undergoes as much ridicule and disdain as the story of the resurrection of Jesus Christ. After all, if this story is true, all of our fine theories about 'relative morality' and 'equally valid religions' are reduced to ashes. If Jesus really rose from the dead, then He is God, and His claims are validated by the One who spoke this universe in existence. And so eyewitness accounts of His resurrection are dismissed as the ravings of a few lunatics. The fact that these people died for the veracity of their story is attributed to the same religious fanaticism that makes suicide bombers die for the cause of Islam. People don't die for something they know is a lie. Those Islamic terrorists are dying for something that *they* believe is the truth. The eyewitnesses of the resurrection of Christ died horrible deaths rather than recant their testimony that Jesus rose from the dead. Nobody dies for something they know to be false.

The testimony of the early church as to the resurrection of Christ began immediately after the event, with written documents arising within ten years. It was not a gradually developing accretion embellished by each subsequent generation [as the miracle stories of Muhammad are]. There were many eye-witnesses to the risen Christ, not just the few whose writings survive the centuries. Paul reported that the risen Christ appeared first to His friends and followers, but also to a group of 500 people at one setting, most of whom were still living at the time of his writing and could be easily consulted as to the veracity of these claims [1Cor 15:6.] It would be pretty ribald of Paul to make a claim like that if he were not able to produce the 500 people and demonstrate their testimony. As Paul stated to Festus, "These things were not done in a corner!" [Acts 26:26]. The same mentality that seeks to deny the Holocaust [even within the lifetime of the survivors] tries to discredit the eye-witnesses to the resurrection. The testimony of these men is just as valid as the testimony of the survivors of Ravensbruk.

If we can just make the resurrection go away, we can run our own lives without any interference from these 'moralists.' And so a first hand historical document, written by eyewitnesses in good Greek, the likes of which is unparalleled in ancient times is judged unreliable by a few critics seeking fame and fortune on the cover of Newsweek. And we fall for that. We throw out the most valuable record of any person's life ever written. All because these supernatural miracles can't possibly be true, in a culture that disbelieves the spirit world because it has never *seen* it. If it were visible to our physical eyes, it wouldn't be a spirit world, would it? The spirit world is sensible to the spirit, and those who live in their spirit can appreciate its beauty without the slightest doubt as to its reality.

THE WORD OF GOD DISTORTED

The Word of God is distorted by homosexual special interest groups within the church. Bishops and Elders are determined to legitimize their impulses turned lifestyle, behavior which is roundly condemned by the Bible beginning on page one. Most of these people are badly wounded, some of them since infancy, but when healing is offered to them, they reject it, preferring to slander the Word of God rather than leave their sexual appetite unindulged. Drug users similarly want to legitimize their use of pot as an herb and a gift from God. They, too, can site Scripture out of context and distort it to further their own political agenda.

> *Satan knows the Scripture better than most of us church going Christians do.*

Before the gay community trips over its shoe laces trying to get to its e-mail to bash me, let me clarify my position on homosexuality.

Our bodies were created by God to relate in a heterosexual way. That is obvious in both the scriptures and in the natural world. Our anatomy speaks for itself. The Being who spoke this universe into existence made our sexuality to be heterosexuality. Those who claim to believe in the authority of the Bible have more than just Leviticus and Romans to contend with. Heterosexual marriage is upheld by God throughout the Bible beginning on page one. Sex outside of marriage is condemned by the Bible with no exceptions.

God has a goal for you to experience sexuality the way He made it. He wants every man to know the joy of being loved by a woman. He wants every woman to know the joy of being loved by a man. He wants healing for homosexual people, and He knows how to accomplish that healing in your life. When Jesus set about to heal someone, He started by forgiving them. When they caught the woman in the act of adultery and lined up to stone her, Jesus put a stop to their judgmental arrogance. "Neither do I condemn you. Go and sin no more." [John 8:1–11]

All of us have been wounded, but many of us who were sexually wounded have unmet needs for the affection of a same-sex parent. We may have deep seated fears of our opposite sex-parent. Many of us have intense anger towards our abuser, and to some extent are still controlled by him or her.

All people, even heterosexuals, have at least occasional minimal homosexual impulses. You experience those impulses and immediately dismiss them. You don't have any deep longings, unmet needs, or overwhelming fears, and so you can easily dismiss your homosexual impulses, indeed barely recognize them. Those of us who are wounded have a lot more trouble with those impulses. But then, the Lord says, "Go and sin no more." In Him, we don't *have* to sin anymore. In Him, we can find healing for our wounds and love to fulfill our needs. In Him, it is possible to leave a life of sin.

I have been judged and condemned by people, both in the church and out of it, on many occasions. I know what it is to be harshly judged by people who have absolutely no idea what is in my heart. People who struggle with homosexuality have issues in their hearts that no one but God can see. Only God has the right to condemn them, and He chose to die for them instead. He does not want a bunch of judgmental Christians to hate and condemn their neighbors whom they do not understand and probably never will understand. We drive people away from the mercy of Jesus Christ when we condemn those we don't understand.

THIS IS WAR

All the power of hell has been unleashed on this planet in preparation for the end. This is Satan's last chance to deceive as many as he can. Millions of people are not going to get a death bed experience, one last chance to consider the mercy of Jesus Christ. There was a beginning, and there will be an end. Like a thief in the night He will come, and each one of us will live with the choices we have made. We are eternal beings, and eternal decisions are being made every day, each time we exalt our own will above that of our Creator.

No one will be able to stand before Him and say, "I never knew." Every person on this planet has an opportunity to choose to love and worship God. They make that choice now, not someday. Satan knows that, and is determined to alienate as many as possible from God, separate them from their only hope, faith in the blood of Jesus Christ. If we don't claim Jesus and His atonement, we get to face the wrath of God all by ourselves. It will not be pretty.

Hell is not some sadistic punishment thing God dreamed up to torment His enemies. Some of the same people who object to God because there is evil in this world react with shock that God would sentence some people to hell. What kind of tyrant is this God of yours? Hell is the natural result of the separation of good from evil, truth from a lie, right from wrong. Evil will finally be separated from good when its purpose has been served, namely to give us a real choice. If we refuse to separate ourselves from evil, refuse to repent of the evil things we do, we will be separated from God along with evil itself. That is hell. If people who cherish their lies and hatred were allowed into heaven, it wouldn't be heaven.

This is war, and we have been drafted. We are on the front lines in a spiritual battle, not against flesh and blood [other people] but against spiritual forces, powers and principalities, big guys that know what they're doing. This is not a boy scout we're up against. This is Satan, and he's playing for keeps. Our children are being dragged by the hair straight into hell by the millions. This is not a game. This is war.

Some of you are getting dizzy now. You didn't even believe in God when you picked up this book, and now you find yourself in His army, getting shot at no less. Some of the most heroic moves in a war are made by rookies, but they need a little training. The Bible is your field operations manual, and you need to take it seriously. Get some help from a church, listen to the pros, and dedicate some quality time to it. That probably means turning off the TV.

GET YOUR ARMOR ON

Remember the armor of God [Ephesians 6] and get it all on:

The **belt of truth** is honesty, be honest with yourself, be honest with your kid, be honest with God. Honesty is usually humbling if not humiliating. We shy away from it because it hurts. Reconciliation with your child is impossible without it. He is not going to believe a word you say about Jesus until he hears you say, "I'm sorry."

The belt of truth is also *knowing* the truth. The truth about God, the truth about yourself, the truth about the Bible, and the truth about prayer. When you find yourself believing a lie, renounce it and learn the truth.

The **breastplate of righteousness** is obedience. You know what's right and you know what's wrong. Do what you know is right. Live the life you profess, honor God with your decisions and priorities, be faithful to your spouse, generous with people in need, kind to people who are irritating, honest when it is embarrassing to tell the truth, and patient in traffic. That kind of life speaks volumes about the true nature of God. Without it, God is held up to public ridicule.

The **preparation of the gospel of peace** is standing ready to bring your child to Christ. Know enough about the Bible to be able to teach your child what it says. If you are solid in your faith and persistent in prayer, you will exude a peace that doesn't make any sense [passes all understanding]. Your peace and confidence in God will do more to bring your child back to Him than anything you can say.

The **shield of faith** is your assurance that God is real, God is powerful, and God is able and willing to save your child. Doubts will harass you as you grow in faith. Put up your shield and remember the glory of God in creation and His power displayed in the laws of nature. Meditate on His righteousness and truth. Nourish yourself on His Word. Draw close to God, and He will draw close to you. Resist the doubts, and they will flee from you.

The **helmet of salvation** is knowing His love and the power of His redemption. The lies of Satan will fall on deaf ears when you are immersed in the truth of His love and mercy. Meditate on His love for you, focus on it, get it into your heart and let it feel good. Accept His joy and confidence. Believe this Holy God really loves you. Come back to the cross again and again and remember how Jesus took the wrath of God for your salvation.

The Bible is a powerful book.

Provide your child with a Bible, the **sword of the Spirit**, at your first opportunity. He may sneer at you, but he will look at it when nobody is around. He knows it offers him hope, and he will not forget it. I remember the first time I taught at juvenile probation, I had one kid who would not look me in the eye. He was hostile and angry, rude to the lady running the classes. About two thirds of the way through my class, I passed out Life Recovery Bibles to all the students. He still wouldn't look me in the eye, but he took the shrink wrap off his Bible; he wanted to see what was in there. A few months later, I saw him again, in a church youth group, where he was recognized as a leader among their youth, helping other kids get off drugs. The Bible is a powerful book.

Pray in the Spirit. All of us are involved in this war, not just the addict. As your daughter's parent, you have some authority over the evil spirits harassing your child. They take advantage of the biochemical weaknesses in her brain and use them to torment her. The brain damage is real, but so are the spirits that nag her, tempt her, and lie to her. Even if your child has invited them in and desires their presence, you have authority over your child *and your spouse* [remember the 'one flesh' part] in the spirit world. It goes like this.

Jesus, my Lord, I am your disciple. My child is in the grip of evil spirits. She is tormented with temptation, lies, fears, and doubts. In Your Holy Name I renounce the spirits that are tormenting my child. Take my daughter to your cross for healing and forgiveness. Draw her into your heart and heal her. Glorify your Name in her life.

I do not speak directly to evil spirits. They are in rebellion against God and I will not give them the dignity of a conversation between equals. They are not my equal. I am in Christ and these spirits are subject to Him.

POWER IN PRAYER

As family members of addicts, we need to be aggressive in prayer. *"This kind comes out only by much prayer and fasting," [Matt 17:21].* You know it is not God's will for your child to be destroyed by this drug, so get on your knees and duke it out with Him. Pray like you mean it. Be persistent and faithful with your prayers, confident that God is answering them in ways you will never know about. You can't hear the conversations going on in your child's heart between her and God. Just keep praying.

Prayer is a powerful spiritual force. It is the 'strong nuclear force' of the spiritual world, and when it is used, the result is a nuclear explosion. He will not interfere with anyone's free will, but He will move in hearts and minds, arrange circumstances, enable willing people to do wonders, equip His servants with the necessary resources, and protect them with powerful angelic presences. He is not unconcerned about your child or helpless to do anything about it. You can go to Him with confidence that the God who spoke this universe into existence hears you, and He will act.

> *An addict is not healed in a day.*

Jesus teaches persistence in prayer on many occasions. He doesn't mean you have to nag Him to get Him to do what is right and just. He means that many requests are needed, because many answers are given. An addict is not healed in a day. The addict is broken on many levels, believes many lies, and needs the touch of Jesus many times. Every one of those prayers is needed, and every one of them is answered, most of them deep in the heart of the addict. He has chosen us, His creatures, to mobilize His power with our prayers. Remember it's a relationship He's after—a relationship with you, and a relationship with your child.

Don't get discouraged when your child relapses. The only sin He can't forgive is the one your child won't confess. Relapse is an opportunity for both of you to grow even stronger in faith. God is likely to be a little rougher with your kid when he relapses. Remember, He disciplines every son whom He receives. [Hebrews 12:6] God knows how to discipline your kid, strengthen him, and encourage him. Don't be surprised when your relapsing child gets into a lot of trouble. God knows just how loud He has to speak in order to get your child's attention.

So when you pray for your child, watch out, things are going to get worse . . . a lot worse. She'll get thrown in jail or she'll end up living in her car. Trust that God knows what He's doing. Your child is far more precious to God than she is to you. He has made your child to be an eternal spirit, and He knows how important this is. He loves your daughter so much that He became incarnate in a smelly messy human body, surrounded by smelly messy vicious people to redeem her.

But what about the guy I met in prison today. His mother is dead, she can't pray for him. His wife left him because he beat her, she certainly isn't praying for him. Who's going to pray for this guy? He's too sick to pray for himself, he needs somebody to pray *for* him. Well, I will. I'll pray for him. Will you join me? That makes two. But hey, there are a whole lot of you out there. That makes an army. That makes a Church.

Satan came only to steal kill and destroy, but I have come that they may have life and have it to the full. [John 10:10 NIV]

.18.

CHALLENGE TO THE CHURCH

We think drug abuse is a social problem having nothing to do with the church. Methamphetamine is *primarily* a spiritual problem. That's why secular society is so helpless against it. No spiritual battle is ever going to be won by law enforcement or education. It's not their job. It is our job.

Methamphetamine is not something rammed down our kid's throats by foreign cartels. Ice is homemade and it is driven by demand, not supply. Interdiction will never solve the problem of methamphetamine. Even if ephedrine, the parent compound, were eliminated from the planet tomorrow, we would still have a problem with ice. The drug chemists can make their own ephedrine. It takes some work, but they can do it.

Government will never solve the methamphetamine problem until and unless it recognizes the spiritual poverty of this nation, the rank idolatry resulting from the wholesale campaign to eliminate and discredit religion in this nation. The government most certainly has established a religion, and that religion is atheism.

Evolution is a philosophy dressed up to look like science and presented in the schools as an established fact. Creation is presented as a quaint old story only the ignorant believe. Vast numbers of people believe God is a myth, and since no one really worships God, we have to find something else to worship. Our kids have a God shaped hole in their hearts and they are trying to find peace and wholeness in drugs, in sex, in fashion, in possessions, and in belonging to the crowd.

As a church, we are losing ground daily. Why is it our kids graduate from church the day they graduate from high school? Why is it the general population thinks God is a fairytale? Why do people treat Him like a convenience, a vending machine, or a security blanket? Why is there no *reverence* for God in our society? Maybe it has something to do with the teachings of the church.

We avoid talking about Creation because we fear the conflict with hard line literalists who insist that anyone who believes in a 14 billion year natural history is denying the veracity of the Bible. Nothing could be further from the truth. Genesis describes the creation of *this* world, not some fantasy world that cannot be described by science.

> *Six literal 24 hour solar days of creation is an **interpretation** of scripture, and a very weak one at that.*

When we shy away from this issue, we are worshipping the approval of men, and it is costing many people their souls. Large numbers of people cannot swallow the Six Day Creation thing, and so they reject the whole church. Six literal 24 hour solar days is an *interpretation* of Scripture, and a very weak one at that. It is not internally consistent with the text itself, and it is used to exclude thinking intelligent people from the church. Do we let millions of people, including our own children, be alienated from God rather than risk offending this small group of people? Are we really that spineless? Church people can be vicious, but some things are worth standing up for.

To say that raw scientific data, dinosaurs and light years for example, are fraudulent is insulting to the many people who report the truth to their honest and best ability. To insist that there is no value in radio isotope dating, no validity to geological strata, [except when it suits our arguments] and no authenticity to the fossil record is ludicrous and arrogant. When we claim God just made the world to look old to deceive certain types of people, we make Him out to be a liar and a tyrant.

> *People of real faith are not afraid of facts.*

When we just avoid the subject and refuse to talk about Creation science, what the average citizen understands is that this Bible thing is unsupportable by any kind of real logic, and can only be supported by blind faith, brainwashing, and dogma. Any interpretation of Scripture which cannot account for the natural history God created calls the whole Bible into question. People of faith are derided as emotional fanatics relying on guilt trips, fire and brimstone for converts. Converts to fear, perhaps, but not converts to faith.

People of real faith are not afraid of facts. People of real faith embrace real science as reflecting the glory of God. *"For since the creation of the world*

His invisible qualities, His eternal power and divine nature have been clearly seen, being understood through what has been made, so that men are without excuse," [Romans 1:20 NIV]. God created natural history, and His Word accurately describes it.

There is nothing any scientist can find or prove that will ever disprove the existence and sovereignty God. We have nothing to be afraid of. God made the cosmic background radiation field and the red shift. God made the genetic code and mitochondrial DNA. God made the fossil record and the vast variety of life forms. We don't have to be embarrassed of Genesis. We can celebrate Genesis, because it is the truth.

When we shrink from meaningful dialogue about scientific matters, we announce to the world that our faith is fragile and cannot stand any kind of close scrutiny. And now we want people to stake their lives on this faith, give up their favorite lusts and addictions for this faith, humble themselves before God based on a faith that refuses to learn a little physics for fear it might be destroyed?

Many people cherish the Six Day Creation story. It is like a comfortable old blanket, and it makes them feel safe and secure. It is fine to believe that in your heart of hearts. It is not fine to destroy somebody else's faith by insisting they throw out all of natural history in order to embrace their God and Creator. The Scripture does not demand a 24 solar day interpretation of the creation account, and I believe God is far more concerned with how we treat the people with whom we disagree, than He is with how we interpret the word "Day" in Genesis.

I found Jesus because I first believed the Bible. He is on every page, Old Testament and New. I believe this book, the Bible, is true because I first believed Genesis is true. It describes creation accurately and beautifully. Don't try to tell me that my interpretation of the word "Day" in any way compromises or corrupts my faith. It *empowers* my faith and empowers my evangelism.

THE CHURCH HAS A JOB TO DO

Twenty years ago, when I was in medical school, crack cocaine swept through the inner city areas of Houston, Texas where I was training. I worked in the ER and every day we saw five or six young kids come in dead on arrival or in full cardiac arrest from crack cocaine. On the surgical side, we saw the carnage from the nightly activities of the knife and gun club. It wasn't only the addicts getting killed, but also their wives and children caught in the crossfire.

Law enforcement was helpless against crack cocaine. Even in the city, where there was one cop for every 150 people, the police couldn't keep up with it. The schools were overwhelmed with the social problems, abused and abandoned children, truant kids, violent teenagers in the schools, and armed and dangerous drug dealers ruling the playgrounds.

The inner city black churches stood up and said, "We will not tolerate this." They preached against it, educated against it, took in the orphan children, and set up support groups and Bible studies both for families and for addicts, and they prayed a mighty prayer. Crack cocaine use has dropped dramatically as a result of their efforts. The average teenager in the inner city won't touch a rock of cocaine with a ten foot pole. They saw what it did to their parents and they don't want any part of it.

We can do the same thing with methamphetamine. As a community of faith we can stand up and say "We will not tolerate this."

Methamphetamine has historically been an urban problem in the Western states, though that is changing. It now thrives in remote areas where it can be made easily without anyone smelling the fumes. In rural counties, there might be one cop for every 10,000 people. Small Midwestern and Southern communities are inundated with methamphetamine. That means small rural churches are being called to battle against big city forces of evil. Fortunately, God hears the prayers of little old ladies who storm heaven on behalf of grandchildren, even in small churches on unpaved roads. A spiritual battle is won by large spirits, not large buildings or large budgets or even large congregations. One praying person can make a difference against this drug.

> *Prayer is powerful because*
> *God is powerful.*

We underestimate the power of prayer because we underestimate the power of God. When we pray, we are talking to the God who said, "Let There Be Light." Prayer is powerful because God is powerful. When we pray, in faith believing, spiritual forces are mobilized. These are powerful supernatural beings operating on a different level than we are used to seeing.

Opportunities are opened up that no amount of human finagling could ever manage. Human hearts are no mystery to the God who created them. He can open a person's heart to be receptive to the offer of grace and mercy of Jesus Christ, and then *you* get to speak the words that touch this heart. You get to see that person's face as he realizes he is not helpless against addiction. You get to see his body relax as he realizes he is loved by his Creator. It strengthens your faith when you see these things happen, but you won't see them happen if you don't take the risk and ask the question and listen and talk. It was the servants who filled the water pots at the wedding at Caana; they *knew* what Jesus had done.

Don't think your pastor can do it all because he can't. You have opportunities to reach people that he can only dream about. The guy who fixes your air conditioner, the family next door, the lady who does your hair, all of them have a loved one on crystal. Sure it takes some guts to approach those people, but if you express even the tiniest bit of interest in them and their problem, they will talk to you and listen to you. Don't worry about what to say, love them and say what you know is true. We win this war one soul at a time.

THE LADY AT THE LAUNDROMAT

Let's go back to the story of the lady at the well in John Chapter 4 for a minute. I'd like to update that story a little. Allow me some license here. A woman pulls up to the laundromat in her '75 Ford Pinto with the tail pipe falling off, and unloads five kids worth of dirty clothes. She weighs about ninty-five pounds, her hair is pulled back with a rubber band, her fingernails are chewed down to the quick, and she has a cigarette hanging out of her mouth.

Jesus is in the laundromat drying His clothes, and He bums a quarter from her to finish His dryer out. He winces when He sees a baby size t-shirt fall out of the pillowcase as she carries it all in. They start talking. Right away, she realizes He knows too much. He knows all five kids have a different father. He knows the first one beat her and she had to leave. He knows she left the second one because she had a thing for the third one, but he beat her too. He knows her fourth husband is in jail for twenty years, and her fifth husband was old enough to be her father and he died. He knows the man she's with now won't marry her. Her heart has been broken many times.

She'd always longed for a world of truth and justice, a place where she would be loved and respected. She'd always heard that one day God would come into this world and bring peace and victory over evil. She had studied the Bible and she knew she didn't measure up to the standards it set, but she hoped for a day when she could know God somehow. And now this Man knows all about her without being told, He accepts her and talks to her. He *knows* all that and yet He loves her. How can this be? By the time He got done with her, she was an evangelist.

We are called to be the man in the laundromat. It is our job to see the broken people around us with eyes of compassion, not judgment. If anyone had a right to judge this woman it was Jesus, and He chose to accept her instead. He didn't just look *at* her, He felt *with* her. Big difference. When people have been rejected a lot they, put up a pretty tough exterior. You have to look past that to see the hurting person inside. You don't have to get people to admit they are using in order to help them. Just show them the love of Jesus and let Him take it from there. "He died for you, too."

Isn't it good to know that somebody out there is loving your addicted child?

THE BODY OF CHRIST

This battle needs to be joined by the whole church in a meaningful and organized way. We are the body of Christ and we need to take that seriously. Jesus Christ is not helpless against methamphetamine, and we don't have to think we are helpless against methamphetamine. *"Having a form of Godliness but denying its power"* applies to many churches today.

Real worship is more than singing songs and reciting the Lord's Prayer at church. Real worship is expressing His character in this world, living out His Spirit in everyday life. Real worship is communing so closely with Him that His gentleness pervades your actions, His compassion guides your decisions, His truth directs your speech, His righteousness infects your home-life with your spouse and children, His integrity lives in your workplace. It's His righteousness, not yours, and it lives in you, flows through you. You consent to it, but you do not generate it. He does.

Real prayer is not scripted, and real prayer usually does not sound very 'nice.' It is heartfelt groaning and agony before God. It expresses the full range of human experience, and it gets pretty ugly at times. Real prayer gets angry sometimes. Real prayer grieves and mourns. Real prayer speaks loudly from the heart; it cries and pleads. And real prayer gets answered. It gets up rejoicing and praising, knowing it has been heard in heaven. When we pray in faith believing, God hears, and we know it.

Prayerless churches pray prayerless prayers, oratory for an audience that does not usually include God. "Let us pray" is a code word for let us not pray, let us continue preaching, let us stab each other in the back, or let us get in the last word in an argument. We're not fooling God. When a church really prays, it really moves into the kingdom of God.

> *Real prayer moves and*
> *real churches move.*

Real prayer does more than just talk. It is not passive, waiting for a bolt of lightning from on high. Real prayer has hands and feet. Real prayer listens and cares. Real prayer teaches and instructs. Real prayer goes into the jail and the welfare office. Real prayer moves and real churches move. Jesus didn't look the other way when He saw suffering. He doesn't expect us to look the other way either.

I have to tell you a story that makes me sad and angry at the same time. I was at my church one Saturday with my daughter, three years old, and as we were walking out, she got sick and vomited in the foyer. Two ladies were in the foyer arranging flowers in a large vase about three feet from where my daughter was getting sick. She was crying and vomiting, there is no way those ladies did not know what was happening. They never even looked up. I had to clean up the mess on the floor, so I needed paper towels. I couldn't take her back into the church because she might vomit again on the carpet. I couldn't leave her alone out there in the foyer because she was three years old and crying. The ladies with the flowers pretended I wasn't there.

Do we, the Body of Christ, really want to be the ladies with the flowers?

THE CHURCH IN ACTION

Church is not the thing that comes before the country club brunch on Sunday. It is not just a social event. Church is the voice and hands of Jesus Christ, and He didn't hang out with the country club set. We deliberately separate ourselves from the sinners in our community by our attitude and dress, and Jesus would have none of it. He ate with sinners, and they obviously felt comfortable around Him.

Changing the dress code at church would do wonders for outreach to addicts and their families. If we want to reach out to people who don't even own a suit or a dress, we might have to give up our suits and dresses. They are not going to feel comfortable around us if they know they won't fit in. We make them feel like they fit in when we dress within reach of the poorest and lowliest of the poor and lowly. Our choice of music, building, location, time of meeting, and language all separate us from the people we need to serve. 'Be ye separate' refers to our lifestyles of sobriety, faithfulness to our spouses, our commitment to integrity, and our values on the used car lots of life. We do not need to be so separate in our attitudes that we exclude the very people He has sent us to serve.

We have to model Christian charity within our congregations. If we allow back biting, gossip and conflict within church committees to spill out into harsh words, hurtful boycotts, snubs and insults between 'Christian' church members, how can we convince people that Jesus Christ has anything to offer them for their addiction? We tolerate rank idolatry within the church and then wonder why people have no respect for God. People on the outside know right from wrong. They know they are sinners, but they also know holiness when they see it. They are longing for the truth and for real morality displayed in the lives of believers. When they see Christians divorcing their wives and ripping people off, they are disgusted and disappointed.

> *People on the outside know*
> *right from wrong.*

We have pastors afraid to speak out against sin because they might offend the wrong people and get fired. They are afraid to preach the truth because of the threat of division, conflict, dissention, and upheaval. So they say what the people want to hear and avoid the sensitive issues. The prophets of old spent their spare time in pits and dungeons. Do we really expect to be treated any better?

When churches focus their energy and resources on buildings and decorations, fountains and gazebos instead of ministry to hurting people, the kingdom of God, people see that and get nauseated. We invest our money in parking lots and building projects, but cannot afford to buy even inexpensive paperback Bibles for the county jail. We have two hour meetings about the color of the paint and carpet, but no one is interested in mentoring an addict just released from prison or teaching a Bible study at the county jail. The church is worshipping status and appearance, attendance numbers and amenities instead of worshipping God. People see that and reject it. If that's all God is, then they're not interested.

Solomon built a temple exactly as he had been instructed by God. It was a worthy structure; it met the needs of the worshippers. Years later, in the time of Jesus, Herod built on to the old temple and made a gold plated monstrosity, patterned after the pagan temples nearby. Was that a monument to God, or a monument to Herod?

Outreach to the community is the primary mission of every church. If we really take this seriously, we can make a real difference in our nation, and not just with the drug problem. One of the major risk factors for drug abuse is a dysfunctional family which fails to meet the needs of the children. The church is in a position to support the family in meaningful ways, with marriage counseling and enrichment seminars, preaching that isn't afraid to address sexual and relationship issues, one on one support for those in troubled marriages, and mentoring relationships with successful couples. A healthy marriage makes for a healthy family environment.

Our ministry to the poor has to be more than once a year at Christmas time loading them up with clothes and toys. The church has the power and authority to bring real healing to broken people with divorce care classes, anger management classes, charity medical clinics, job training, financial planning, GED classes, English as a second language classes, parenting classes, and single parent support groups. The opportunities are endless and the need is real. No one church can do all this, but a community of churches most certainly can, if they are willing to cooperate, share the burden and share the glory, even with churches of *other denominations.* Gasp!!

[You can talk to the guy from the church across the street; just wash your hands real good when you're done.]

MEN'S MINISTRY

There is a growing recognition in the American church that we are not meeting the needs of the men in our congregations. Our church culture devalues masculine qualities, even though both men and women have them. Aggressiveness, persistence, courage, and honor are less valued than compassion, empathy, listening, and caring. Men feel like they are forced into a box, castrated in a way. No wonder men are under-represented in the church.

Nobody was more of a Man than Jesus Christ was when He walked upon this earth. Nobody showed more courage and strength of character than He did in the Garden of Gethsemane. Jesus is a whole person; both feminine and masculine qualities are at their zenith in Him. Both are necessary and important to the Kingdom of God and to the mission of the church.

Our culture in general emasculates men, and we are making a big mistake. We need strong men just like we need strong women. There are important roles for men in the church, not just in the pastorate, but also in teaching and leadership, courageous words and actions in the workplace and community, perseverance in the face of opposition, honorable actions in the family, and the example we set for our children.

Young men growing up are faced with a world of adult men who take no responsibility for themselves and their community. They are mocked and derided by the feminists on TV, and have abdicated their leadership positions. They are demoralized. The one thing they have to offer, their masculinity, is not appreciated and valued by the world they offer it to. Even if nobody else wants these courageous and powerful men, the church can sure use them. Men need to step up to the plate and be counted, and we need to welcome them and their ideas, their vision, and their courage.

SPIRITUAL AUTHORITY

Many of our churches compromise on the Word of God when they elect Bishops and leaders who are not ordained by God. God decided that men, the husband of one wife, should have that authority, and it's not open to discussion or vote. Women clearly have a role in the church, but Bishop is not one of them. Says who? Says God [1 Tim 2:12]. If we are going to claim to be His church, then it rather behooves us to do it His way. When we compromise on this issue, we leave ourselves open to compromise on many other issues, and we relinquish the authority God gave us as a church.

Feminist and homosexual Bishops who declare homosexuality a gift from God are corrupting the church and teaching our youth that their homosexual impulses are good and right. They teach that those who act on those impulses, in blatant disregard of the Word of God, are to be respected and obeyed, fit to be ministers of God. Why should our youth make the effort to exert control over *their* sexual fantasies when recognized spiritual authorities have failed to control their own sexual fantasies? Adolescent boys, struggling with their insecurities about girls, are being told, not just by society, but also *by religious authorities* that they don't have to go the trouble and discomfort of learning how to relate to women. They can get their satisfaction among the guys.

God has chosen to exert His authority over His church through men, the *husband of one wife.* That is His prerogative. He's God and He's not up for re-election anytime soon. Spiritual gifts are given to women in abundance. Spiritual authority is not. We can't make God in our own image, and we can't make His church in our own image either.

Joel 2:28

Therefore the day will come when I will pour out my spirit on all mankind; your sons and your daughters will prophesy, your old men dream dreams and your younger men shall see visions; I will pour out my spirit in those days even upon slaves and slave girls.

Leadership and authority are not the same thing. Female ministers are not in positions of authority. Just ask any minister and he [or she] will tell you, he has absolutely no authority. He answers to everybody from the Bishop to the cleaning lady. A minister is a servant, and the good ones realize that. Daughters will prophesy, but men are held responsible for guiding, instructing, encouraging and supporting those daughters. And He will pour out His Spirit when they do it.

YOUTH MINISTRY

To make a real difference in the problem of methamphetamine, we need to take youth ministry seriously. Any church can minister to the community youth like the Mount Zion Church of God in Sardis, Alabama does. This is a very small rural church with less than seventy-five people in attendance on Sunday, but youth ministry is a real priority at this church and they invest some resources in it. They fund a youth minister and provide him with program materials, a state of the art sound system, and an old barn to meet in where they can make plenty of noise.

They send out busses every Wednesday night and fetch about eighty kids, feed the kids [for free], and let them play basketball and listen to loud Christian music. Then, they teach them about the mercy and character of Jesus Christ so they have the courage to stand up to the dealers at school and tell them to get lost. These are not just the children of their members. These are the 'stray kittens,' otherwise unchurched, and they have to go out looking for these kids. They send the bus out into rough neighborhoods, pick up kids who are considered trouble makers, and offer them a meal and some fun. Even trouble-maker kids need to feel welcome and accepted, and they will respond to your welcome and acceptance.

> *Youth groups are not just a social event*
> *for our children.*

If we keep our youth groups pure, just for the children of our members, they will never be the voice of Jesus Christ to the nation's youth. We need to take our responsibility seriously, not just to our own children, but also to the children of the town drunk and the trailer trash, even the teenagers who get kicked out of school and put on juvenile probation. Youth groups are not just a social event for our children. They are an essential outreach to the community.

The mere presence of these sinner kids is frightening to most parents. Isn't that why we take our children to church, so they won't be exposed to that element? Our teens' purity will only be threatened by the presence of these sinner teens if we don't have competent youth leadership. They are going to be exposed to these kids every day, whether we like it or not. Our children need to see the transforming power of Jesus Christ in the lives of the kids they go to high school with, people who would otherwise be lost.

Jesus didn't keep His disciples cloistered away from the sinners. He had all twelve of them at the tax collector's house as well as at the Pharisee's place. They got into a lot more trouble at the Pharisee's place, where they ridiculed the woman's gift of priceless ointment for Jesus, [Luke 7:36] than they did at Zaccheus' house where they witnessed real repentance. [Luke 19:5] If anybody was a bad influence on them, it was the hypocrite.

> *When the church offers them the one thing they need most in this world, a Daddy, they will respond.*

When we do bring these 'sinner kids' into our churches, we had better have something meaningful to offer them. You can't talk to them about their loving Heavenly Father unless you are willing to listen to their feelings toward their abusive or absent human father, and deal with it in a meaningful way. When the church offers them the one thing they need most in this world, a Daddy, they will respond.

We had also better be ready to discuss the problems they are facing in their daily lives. Drug education is a legitimate function of the church youth group. Obviously, whatever the public schools are doing is not adequate. They lack the resources and moral authority to have any meaningful impact on drug abuse in our youth. Seventy-five percent of drug addicts start using as teenagers, twenty-five percent of them by age fifteen. We have to reach them at age ten in order to have any impact.

> *Seventy-five percent of drug addicts start using as teenagers, twenty-five percent of them by age fifteen.*

Don't think the 'good kids' in your church youth group are immune to drug abuse. I was teaching one night in a Baptist church, and the youth group was seated on the front three rows. I made eye contact with one of those kids as I was saying, "You used it once, and within one week you used it again." His eyes got as big as dollars. "You thought you just chose to use again. You felt a *desire* to use again, and you couldn't control that desire. You didn't choose it. It chose you." That kid, a fifteen-year-old boy, started crying. His friends sitting next to him started crying too. When we gave the altar call inviting people to come forward and pray after my talk, that kid and three of his friends came barreling out of their seats and fell on the altar and sobbed and prayed and cried. All four of them had been using ice 'casually' and all four of them had a problem.

I can't count the number of times inmates have told me, "Yeah, Doctor, I know all that Jesus stuff; I went to church when I was a kid." If that kid has received meaningful instruction in his grade school church experience, he might not be in jail now. Some of the kids in your Sunday school class are going to end up in jail, addicted to drugs, homosexual, having abortions, or committing suicide if you are not willing to tackle the tough issues. Every kid has these impulses, and every kid is being told by society that it is okay to indulge these impulses. Nobody at school is going to teach them right from wrong. If you don't do it, nobody will.

FAMILY PRAYER GROUPS

We can minister to families of addicts like the Church of the Rock in Piedmont, Alabama does. This is another tiny church with an average attendance of twenty-five people. They have a Tuesday night prayer group for parents and family members of addicts. Remember, the families of addicts often feel isolated and ostracized by the rest of the community, like it was their fault their child got hooked on crystal. Even if it *was* their fault, we can still minister to them and help them cope with the horror of having an addicted child.

The addiction of a child can and should be the lever pushing the whole family into the arms of Jesus. Now, perhaps for the first time in their lives, they are up against something they cannot handle by themselves. They will either turn to Him, or the family will disintegrate. Our openness to them can spell the difference between a life changing challenge and a social disaster.

A family support group must be, first and foremost, a prayer group. We can share our pain and swap stories and advice, but that will only go so far. If we don't pray together and teach the new people how to pray from the heart, we are wasting our time and the group will fail. When people come in and find real power and real hope, that prayer group can change people's lives.

Where two or more are gathered in the name of Jesus, there is real power in prayer. A prayer group gives support and instruction to people who don't really know how to pray. The guidance of a good book on intercessory prayer gives structure to the group and keeps it focused on prayer. Some good examples are Stormie Omartian's series, especially *The Power of a Praying Parent, Praying Prodigals Home* by Quinn Sherer and *When Mothers Pray* by Cheri Fuller. [See Appendix A]

Prayer groups should not limit their focus to drug addiction. Most parents of addicts either don't know, or won't admit, their kid is addicted to drugs. They know he has dropped out of school, he is in trouble with the law, and he can't keep a job. He's angry, belligerent and violent, he's stealing from them and from the neighbors, but they don't see the connection between his behavior and the drugs he's using. He says it's nothing, and they believe him. The prayer group should focus on the behavior, and teach parents about the drug. Don't focus on the drug until they have coped with the behavior.

Your prayer group should welcome all parents of all ages having problems with their children of all ages, whether drug related or not. The elderly parents of the adult addict face problems of enormous proportions. They have no more control over their child than you do over your next door neighbor, and yet they have to deal with the lies and manipulation every day, take care of the grandchildren, and pay for rehab, lawyers, groceries, and doctors. They are seventy years old and they are completely overwhelmed. Prayer support for these people is essential to their survival.

OUTREACH TO ADDICTS

Outreach to addicts starts, unfortunately, at the county or city jail. A serious addict is deluded. He believes crystal is the best thing in the world. It makes him feel powerful and confident, intelligent, and invincible. He doesn't even want any help with his addiction until it starts causing him pain. That usually happens in the county jail, mental ward, or homeless shelter. Jail and prison ministry is essential to reaching these people. They can't hear a word you say to them until they've been in jail for at least a week. It takes that long to live through the crash and be able to think again. These people are usually not hardened criminals. They are kids like yours who made a bad decision and got in trouble, and once they realize how serious this is, they are usually willing to get some help.

There is a network of jail ministers, most of whom are lay people with a heart for the inmate. They are working people, equipped only with a Bible, and they go into jails all over this nation in their spare time with the good news of Jesus Christ. Most of them have no resources, no curriculum materials, and no money to buy those things. They need the support of sponsoring churches to give them Bibles, hymnals, and Bible study materials. They don't have to be expensive Bibles; a box of 100 $2 New Testaments would keep these people in business for weeks.

When Jesus raised Lazarus to life, He told the people around him, the bystanders and the relatives, to take the grave clothes off of him. He assumed Lazarus could not do that for himself. He assigns that task to us, the people who have just witnessed a resurrection. We don't just stand there with our mouths hanging open; we get in there and take the smelly grave clothes off of our Lazarus.

Once they are released from jail, we can welcome recovering addicts to our churches with Bible studies geared and staffed for their needs. We have a ministry like this in little Marshall County, Alabama, where a group of churches have cooperated in establishing Christian recovery groups meeting at a different church every night of the week. No matter what day it is, you can find a recovery Bible study in Marshall County, and every pastor in the county refers people to them.

> *Nothing offers them more hope than the flesh and blood presence of someone who's 'been there, done that' and really understands the struggle they face.*

That might mean hiring a professional counselor to meet with these people for group support. Churches willing to make a financial sacrifice can provide a service like that. But even if all your church has is one or two recovered addicts in it, you are fully qualified to make a recovery ministry. All it really takes is a Christlike attitude and a few folding chairs.

There are not enough rehabilitation services to meet the needs in the community. Waiting lists are long even for the expensive programs. A family without significant financial resources faces a real problem. Even when an addict does get a place in a rehab program, he gets twenty-eight days of treatment and then he's 'done.' That is not sufficient for an addiction like methamphetamine.

Twenty-eight days is just the beginning. It takes two to three *years* for an addict to fully recover from the effects of ice. They are vulnerable to relapse for the rest of their lives. They need continuing encouragement, support and fellowship with people who really understand and care. They need to meet people who have been through the hell of withdrawal and craving and have come out on the other side. Nothing offers them more hope than the flesh and blood presence of someone who's 'been there, done that' and really understands the struggle they face.

Your church-based recovery program should be led by a mature Christian who is himself a recovered addict or alcoholic with a minimum of two years sobriety. Those with less time in recovery are often eager to lead these groups but they *should not do so alone.* They need to be ministered to and listened to, and they cannot be the guy everybody looks to for all the answers. Some incredibly needy and manipulative people will come to these meetings, and the leadership must be mature. In Marshall County, we have a Christian Counseling Center providing training for recovery group leaders.

There are many twelve step programs available, including the classic **Alcoholics Anonymous** or **Narcotics Anonymous** curriculum which has been in use for many years. In recent years, AA and NA have been watered down in their approach to God. The Bible is not 'approved AA literature,' and some chapters are almost New Age in their theology. That's why the leadership has to be mature in their Christianity. An AA or NA program that prays to the real God and goes to the real cross of Jesus Christ is a very powerful thing.

I take a lot of abuse from members of the AA and NA communities. I am accused of bigotry because I insist that faith in Jesus Christ is essential to real healing. What about all the atheists who want to get clean from drugs and alcohol? Doesn't my insistence upon the gospel of Jesus Christ alienate these people? Generic spirituality may be enough to get you clean from drugs, but it is not enough to get you clean before our Holy God. In the name of tolerance, we allow people to stumble around trying to relate to the 'God of their understanding.'

We're not taking about just physical death or brain damage. We are talking about eternal death, timeless eternity spent in hell, separated from truth, goodness and life. If we really believe that the cross of Jesus Christ reconciles us to our Creator, and that we are subject to the wrath of God if we don't avail ourselves of His mercy, then we are guilty of gross negligence when we fail to reveal the God who *created us,* and His Christ. Sure, some people are going to reject Jesus. He told us that from the beginning. That doesn't mean its okay to stop telling them about Him. We do a serious injustice to these people when we allow them to think that any old spirituality is good enough, and do not even offer them the opportunity to know Jesus Christ.

There are many excellent Bible centered twelve step programs including: **Celebrate Recovery,** which has workbook, audiotape and videotape resources for Christian recovery available from Zondervan, and **Overcomers Outreach**, a twelve step Bible study which is very flexible and open ended. **Alcoholics for Christ** and **Overcomers In Christ** have lesson plans and a workbook for twelve step recovery. **Alcoholics Victorious** is another Christian twelve step program for substance abuse recovery. Contact information for each of these organizations is listed in Appendix A. Your church should also be willing to provide **Life Recovery Bibles** to participants, a twelve step Bible I have used in counseling for several years.

The *addict* is not the enemy. The *drug* is the enemy. The addict needs our encouragement and support. We need to welcome them into our Bible studies and Sunday schools, make an effort to reach out to them and understand them, just like we reach out to the recently divorced woman in our neighborhood and invite her to church. We have to hold them accountable, but also extend them a caring hand.

Nobody gets up one morning and says, "Gee, I think I'll become a junky and lose my mind on methamphetamine." These people want help. They want to get out of this hell called addiction. If they think you care about them, they will listen to you. If you really offer help and encouragement instead of judgment and condemnation, they will come to you, because then you look a lot like Jesus.

SPECIAL EVENTS

Everyone knows we are up against a serious evil in methamphetamine. The kids call it ice. It is not ice. Methamphetamine is *fire*. It is burning down our homes and communities. It is destroying our families, schools, and neighborhoods. It is taking out multiple generations and people from all walks of life. We have a common enemy to unite against, and the wall between church and state is going to have to come down if we want to fight this fire.

Community outreach is the responsibility of the church. As citizens in our communities, we have a lot to offer the general public in the way of information and public awareness. The whole community is burdened by addiction, not just the families directly involved. Everyone loses when parents abandon their children and our workforce is in jail.

We can take our personal testimonies into public schools, and, to the extent the law will allow, share with the kids both the heart ache of the loss of our child and the victory of the ones who found God and escaped addiction. Public school officials realize they are up against a serious evil in methamphetamine. They are receptive to your efforts to reach these kids with the truth about drugs.

The government may not allow us to speak at *their* events, but we are allowed to have government people speak at *our* events. We can sponsor drug education rallies in our churches, ask for the help of the Sheriff, the Police Chief, or the Drug Enforcement Unit. Ask them to bring their helicopter and rappelling team on a Saturday afternoon. They can bring samples of drugs and paraphernalia so families know what to look for. Civil authorities will be glad to cooperate. They are eager to reach out to the public with information and resources.

Invite physicians, Christian counselors, and rehabilitation professionals to speak, or set up a booth, describing their program or ministry. The emergency room doctor can describe the early signs of addiction, health risks and complications. Child Protective Services can describe the child abuse and neglect they see every day. Your pastor should prepare a message of hope and encouragement for addicts in the audience, and an invitation to know Jesus as Lord and Savior.

The local press can contribute to an awareness event sponsored by your church. Ask them to cover it as a news story, get all the free publicity you can, but don't be afraid to use paid advertisements. List the people and professionals you have coming to help generate interest. These events have a real impact on people. They see a church that cares about the issues concerning them. They find in the Body of Christ real power over a force much too strong for them. People who have never set foot in a church before will come and meet the God who cares about the problems they face. People who have never prayed before will find the power of the One who spoke the universe into existence.

The inner city black churches took a stand against cocaine in their neighborhoods twenty years ago, and now the average inner city teenager in Houston, Texas won't touch a rock of cocaine with a ten foot pole. Only losers use crack. We can do the same thing with methamphetamine all over this nation. When the average kid in the average school says to a dealer, "Man, are you using ice? What are you? Stupid?" we will see an end to this fire.

I received a call from a minister in Hawaii, where methamphetamine has been a problem for twenty years. They are on the verge of a social collapse because of crystal. There are not enough foster homes to take in all the abandoned children. "The twenty- year-old is high, her forty-five-year old mother is high, and the seventy-five-year old great-grandmother is in the nursing home. She can't take care of the kids. We're running out of grandmothers, and there's nobody to take care of the babies."

The inner city churches in Houston, Texas are proud of what they have done about cocaine in their neighborhoods. Things have turned things around since 1983, when I lived there. We can take a page from their playbook and do the same with methamphetamine. If we don't, twenty years from now *this entire nation* will be running out of grandmothers.

If my people which are called by my name will humble themselves and pray and seek my face and turn from their wicked ways, then I will hear from heaven, will forgive their sin, and will heal their land. [2 Chronicles 7:14 NIV]

Afterword:

Mothers Against Meth-Amphetamine

I have equipped the Body of Christ with a collection of tools to fight methamphetamine addiction. I have founded an outreach effort called **Mothers Against Meth-Amphetamine** and we have chapters all over the nation. Our mission is to glorify God by providing competent and compassionate drug education and rehabilitation resources that reflect the mercy of Jesus Christ for the addict, his family, and the community.

We are a 501-C 3 corporation based in Arab, Alabama that has been in operation since 2002. We started in November 2001 as a private effort on my part to educate my community about methamphetamine. I wrote a guest editorial for my local newspaper about the personal impact of methamphetamine in my family. The editor of the Arab Tribune is a friend of the family, and he printed it. People started calling my medical office asking questions, and if I didn't know the answer, I looked it up. I taught my community the basic biochemistry of methamphetamine on the editorial page of the Arab Tribune.

All of my editorials contained a significant spiritual message of hope in the power of Jesus Christ to defeat addiction. The tone was authoritative and yet loving, much like the tone of this book. Families and addicts flocked to me for more information, asking me to pray for them or for their loved one. I started teaching in the city and county jails at the invitation of the County Sheriff who is now on our Board of Directors. Juvenile Probation and Mental Health invited me to teach in their facilities as well.

I started getting calls about other drugs. "My kid takes ecstasy. What is that going to do to his brain?" The result was another guest editorial for the newspaper. I learned about cocaine, inhalants, marijuana, alcohol, GHB, LSD, and heroin, and each one was dutifully printed by my friends at the Arab Tribune and at the Sand Mountain Reporter, the Albertville local newspaper.

PAMPHLETS

The editorials I wrote for the newspaper were refined and finished as a series of pamphlets I distribute to Christian ministries all over the nation and all over the world. I wrote booklets for prisons and youth that are also distributed nationally. Each one includes an invitation to know the power of Jesus Christ over addiction.

I opened the **Mothers Against Meth-Amphetamine** office in January 2003 in a small office across the street from the post office in Albertville, Alabama to facilitate distribution of this work. We relocated to larger offices in Arab, AL in 2004. We have a website, **www.mamasite.net**, that we advertise nationally, and about fifty Mothers' chapters are using our literature to minister to their communities, schools, and jails.

Mothers' chapters distribute this literature door to door, in police stations, truck stops, convenience stores, pawn shops and thrift shops. Doctor's offices, hospital emergency rooms, and mental health centers display our literature. Bail bondsmen, parole offices, police stations, and county jails have racks of pamphlets. County courthouses, Child Protective Services and welfare offices usually welcome our literature. They are displayed at community fairs and drug awareness events, church events, and school events. Our Mothers' chapters are very creative in their community outreach.

PUBLIC SCHOOLS

I seldom teach in a school because I still work full time in my medical practice, but I have written a booklet and a powerful little pamphlet for public schools featuring the brain scans from page 261. These materials are not evangelical, and can be safely used in any school. The booklet, called **"Meth Death"** is $1 per copy and the pamphlet, **"The High is a Lie"** is $10 per 50 count. Our local schools use these materials extensively, assigning them as part of the health curriculum. Occasionally, a student will send me a copy of the writing assignment he did based on my booklets.

I have recently completed **"The High is a Lie"** videotape for use in the public schools and other settings where the gospel of Jesus Christ is not welcome. This video is available for $30 through our web site at www.mamasite. net. It is forty minutes long and includes a teacher's guide and study materials appropriate for students in the sixth through twelfth grades. This videotape is also used by businesses for drug education of their employees.

THE POWER OVER ADDICTION VIDEOTAPE

As I learned more, I taught more, and the drug course grew to be over two hours long. I would set up my power-point projector on a cell block and talk to fifty or sixty inmates at a time. Since there weren't enough chairs to sit on, they would stand for that whole two hours and listen to me. I gave them my heart, and the heart of Jesus, and I could see the peace come over their faces. Every time I walked into a store, some big burly tattoo looking guy would come up to me and give me the biggest bear hug and tell me how I saved his life. Things like that will keep you going when the going gets tough.

I was teaching twice a week at jails, rehab centers, and homeless shelters, and also keeping up a full time Obstetrics practice. Realizing that many people needed to hear this message, I made a videotape, live, as I was teaching for the clients at a rehabilitation center. That videotape, and the study guide that goes with it, is called **"Power Over Addiction."**

The videotape and study guide are used by prison chaplains and jail ministers all over the nation as well. We ship study guides by the hundreds to chaplains and prisons at no cost. I don't even charge for the shipping if they cannot pay. We get twenty-five or so letters each day from inmates requesting a copy of **Power Over Addiction**, and each copy we send is read by multiple people. The letters I get are powerful testimonies about how Jesus Christ has freed these people from a lifetime of slavery to addictive drugs.

Pastors, counselors, and rehabilitation professionals who counsel adult drug addicts also use our videotape and workbook, and they are used by church support groups, and drug court meetings nationally. Individual pastors faced with large numbers of addicts use our material for one on one counseling with excellent results.

T-SHIRTS AND POSTERS

I do not charge for the pamphlets and booklets that proclaim the good news about Jesus Christ. We request a donation, and occasionally we receive some funding from church groups or individuals who have been helped by our work. Thus far, 90% of the funds that have financed this effort have come from my husband and me. It is our passion to fight this evil and to bring glory to our Savior.

We have a line of t-shirts and posters we sell to help us raise money. They were designed by an inmate I spoke to the first time I taught in the county jail. He showed me his work when I was there, and a few weeks later, when he got out of jail, he hitch hiked up to my office and gave me the pictures he had drawn, and signed over the copyrights to me. He also illustrated my booklets which were under construction at the time.

The t-shirt and posters have not sold well. They are vivid and rather distasteful to the average church going Christian. But they speak to the audience for whom they were intended, the junior high and high school youth being tempted by the drug culture to use methamphetamine. The graphics feature disembodied heads with horns concocting chemical potions guaranteed to destroy your brain with just one try. But we also have graphics intended for the elementary school set, featuring multicolor slugs and an anti-drug message.

We welcome donations to help with the costs of providing this material, especially the large volumes we are shipping to jails and prisons. Most prison ministries have tiny budgets for curriculum materials, and county jail ministries often have no resources at all. Our goal is to empower these ministers as they bring the mercy of Jesus Christ to broken people behind bars.

MOTHERS AGAINST METH-AMPHETAMINE CHAPTERS

Mothers Against Meth-Amphetamine chapters are springing up all over the nation in small towns and large cities. You don't have to be a mother to start a Mothers' chapter. Many of our chapters are headed by men. We are an equal opportunity group, despite our name. Most chapters are church based, some are not. Some even involve secular police departments and probation offices.

Information on membership or forming a Mothers' chapter is available on line at **www.mamasite.net**. Or by phone **1–256-498-6262.** We can be reached by mail at:

Mothers Against Meth-Amphetamine
P O Box 8
Arab AL 35016

A Mothers' chapter is, first and foremost, a prayer group. We feel strongly that prayer should be the basis of any endeavor taken up by a Mothers' chapter. Some Mothers' groups are vocal and aggressive, some are quiet and unobtrusive; some focus on the schools, others on the jails. Some go to community fairs and craft shows, shopping malls and grocery stores, with a display of our literature. Some chapters do a lot of public speaking in schools, jails, and churches. Many of the people heading our chapters have riveting testimonies in their own right.

I am willing to provide training to people who would like to learn how to teach this material in their community. Obviously, I can not speak in every community that needs to hear this message. As much as I enjoy teaching this material, I can't do it all. I can provide you with slides, pictures, diagrams, and graphs, to which you can add your own story and your own personality. If you would like to receive this training, please contact me at mholley@mamasite. net.

The Board of Directors for Mothers Against Meth-Amphetamine includes only one clergy person. Other board members include the Marshall

County Sheriff; Marshall County District Attorney; Arab City School Superintendent; Director of a Christian twelve month residential rehabilitation center; Director of a secular twenty-eight day rehabilitation facility; and the mother of a recovered addict. All of us are dedicated servants of the Lord Jesus Christ. We welcome you to join us as we spread the word about the power of Jesus Christ over addiction.

Lord, your forgiveness, your mercy, is a mighty, mighty power. With it you hold your lambs, your broken addicted lambs close to your heart. And you lead the weak and the vulnerable and the brain damaged into the holy presence of a Father who loves them. All glory and honor and power are yours, Almighty God, forever and ever. Amen.

Decolores.

APPENDIX A:
RESOURCES

INFORMATION RESOURCES

National Institute on Drug Abuse has comprehensive information on all drugs of abuse at www.nida.nih.gov.

National Clearinghouse for Alcohol and Drug Information sponsored by U.S. Dept of Health and Human Services has an abundance of educational materials at www.health.org.

Healthfinder is sponsored by the U.S. Dept of Health and Human Services and summarized scientific information about methamphetamine at www.healthfinder.gov.

WebMDHealth offers an abundance of understandable information on methamphetamine at my.webmd.com.

Institute for Intergovernmental Research/ Center for Task Force Training has excellent information under the CTFT banner at www.iir.com.

Above All Ministries Steve Box P O Box 122 Pierce City MO 65723

Parentshelpingparents.info an Oklahoma group with resources for recovery

REHABILITATION RESOURCES

SAMHSA National database of government approved substance abuse treatment facilities organized by state and zip code. www.findtreatment.samhsa.gov

Teen Challenge is a national association of Christian rehabilitation centers that serves both teen and adult addicts in six to twelve month programs usually in rural settings. www.teenchallenge.com or P O Box 1015 Springfield MO 65801 1-417-862-6969

Addiction Resource Treatment Guide gives information about drug treatment centers at www.addictionresourceguide.com or P O Box 8612 Tarrytown NY 10591 1-914-725-5151

Association of Gospel Rescue Missions has a directory of Christian missions, many of which operate drug rehabilitation programs. www.agrm.org

click on the directory of member missions to get a worldwide map and directory. 1045 Swift St Kansas City MO 64116–4127 phone 1–816–471–8020

RECOVERY GROUP RESOURCES

Most Excellent Way International, a Biblically centered One Step program with recovery groups nationaly. 1177 Pacificia Pl Encinitas, CA 92024 1-800-548-8854 www.mostexcellentway.org.

Overcomers Outreach, a Bible Study for recovery, has meetings across the nation with a national directory at www.overcomersoutreach.org. 1–800–310–3001

Alcoholics for Christ also has a national presence with meetings listed on their web site. They are at www.alcoholicsforchrist.com. 1-800- 441–7877

Overcomers In Christ has a listing of meetings on their site. They are at www.overcomersinchrist.org. 1–402–573–0966

Alcoholics Victorious has groups all across the nation. A national database of meetings is available at www.alcoholicsvictorious.org. 1–816–471–8020

Narcotics Anonymous has a national database of recovery groups. A sponsor is needed to join their groups. P.O. Box 9999 Van Nuys CA 91409 www.na.org 1–818–773–9999

Crystal Meth Anonymous [CMA] Patterned after narcotics Anonymous but specializing in methamphetamine addiction. 8205 Santa Monica Blvd PMB 1-114 West Hollywood, CA 90046-5977 www.crystalmeth.org 213-488-4455

Life Recovery Bible Tyndale Press A New Living Translation of the Bible, available in both the entire Bible and the New Testament Psalms and Proverbs only. Footnotes and sidebars are correlated with the twelve steps of recovery.

PRISON MINISTRY RESOURCES

Bibles at Cost has inexpensive Bibles, both full text and New Testament, at wholesale prices in bulk, and very reasonable prices for single copies. 7455 Aberdeen Ct. Gilroy CA 95020 1–800–778–8865 www.biblesatcost.com

Reentry Ministries, a web based resource listing of prison ministries nationwide, including prison Bible studies, half way houses, support groups for recently released inmates and their families. www.reentry.org

Prison Fellowship is a national prison ministry founded by Chuck Colson, has Bible study resources, an inmate magazine, support groups and resources for family members, pen pals, and resources for local prison ministries. 1-877-478-0100 www.pfm.org

Kairos Prison ministry has three day retreats in the prisons with followup after care and family support groups. 1-407-629-4998 www.kairosprisonministry.org

International Network of Prison Ministries has information about many local and national ministries to inmates and families. hppt://prisonministry.net

INTERNET SUPPORT GROUPS

Christians in Recovery operates a chat room and discussion board for recovering addicts www.christians-in-recovery.com

Crystal Recovery Discussion board and chat room for recovering addicts and their families. This site is not officially Christian, but is populated by many faithful people who pray and struggle together. www.crystalrecovery.com

KCI at www.kci.org [formerly the Koch Crime Institute] has an abundance of information and also links to the same discussion board with crystalrecovery.com

These discussion boards are financed by donations. Please consider helping them.

PRAYER GROUP RESOURCES

Stormie Omartian *The Power of a Praying Parent,* Harvest House Publishers

Quinn Sherer *Praying Prodigals Home* Regal Books

Cheri Fuller *When Mothers Pray: Bringing God's Power and Blessing to Your Children's Lives* Multnomah Publishers

Richard Burr *Praying Your Prodigal Home: Unleashing God's Power to Set Your Loved Ones Free* Christian Publications

Joyce Meyer *The Joy of Believing in Prayer: Deepen Your Friendship With God* Warner Books

Cynthia Head *Becoming a Woman of Prayer* Navpress

Germaine Copeland *Prayers That Avail Much* Harrison House

Dutch Sheets *Intercessory Prayer: How God Can Use Your Prayers to Move Heaven and Earth* Regal Books

Richard J. Foster *Prayer: Finding the Heart's True Home* HarperSanFrancisco. This is the classic work on prayer. Highly recommended.

Buddy Scott *Relief for Hurting Parents* Allon Publishing

Pauline Neff *Tough Love: How Parents can Deal With Drug Abuse* Abingdon Press

Brandon O'Rourke, DeEtte Sauer *Hope of a Homecoming: Entrusting Your Prodigal to a Sovereign God* Navpress

Phil Waldrop, Pat Springle, David Jeremiah *Parenting Prodigals: Six Principles for Bringing Your Son or Daughter Back to God* Baxter Press

Ruth Bell Graham *Prodigals and Those Who Love Them* Baker Books

John White *Parents in Pain Overcoming the Hurt and Frustration of Problem Children.* InterVarsity Press

DRUG TESTING RESOURCES

Current federal guidelines for schools from the Office of National Drug Control Policy www.whitehousedrugpolicy.gov/publications/drug_testing or 1-800-666-3332 P O Box 6000 Rockville MD 20849–6000

American Screening Corporation www.american-medical.net 1–866–526-2873

Mistral Security Inc. Has a spray chemical that can detect traces of methamphetamine and other drugs on clothing, backpacks, dashboards, any surface material. Very inexpensive and accurate. Used in schools and by parents. 1-800-9MISTRAL or www.mistralgroup.com.

Psychemedics www.psychemedics.com 1–800–628–8073

Tests Shop www.tests-shop.com 1–800–801–8378

ALTERNATIVE SENTENCING/ DRUG COURT

National Association of Drug Court Professionals, NADCP www.nadcp.org 1–703–575–9400 or by mail 4900 Seminary Rd. Suite 320 Alexandria VA 22311

School of Public Affairs, American University, Justice Programs Office www.american.edu/justice 1–202–885–2875

National Criminal Justice Reference Service www.ncjrs.org has thousands of documents on establishing a local drug court system. 1-800-851-3420

INTELLIGENT DESIGN RESOURCES

Michael Behe *Darwin's Black Box* The Free Press

Michael Denton *Evolution: A Theory in Crisis* Adler and Alder

William A Dembski *Mere Creation* Intervarsity Press

William L Craig *Reasonable Faith* Crossway

Phillip E Johnson *Darwin on Trial* Intervarsity Press

Phillip E Johnson *The Wedge of Truth* Intervarsity Press

J P Moreland *The Creation Hyposthesis* Intervarsity Press

Gerald L Schroeder *The Science of God* The Free Press

Jonathon Wells *Icons of Evolution* Regenery

Larry Wiltham *By Design: Science and the Search for God* Encounter Books

APPENDIX B

A Peek into Pandora's Box: The Medical Excuse Marijuana Controversy

Eric A Voth MD FACP
Used with permission Dr. Eric A Voth and Haworth Press

Abstract: The smoking of marijuana for medicinal application is a volatile and difficult issue for the medical and regulatory communities which has reached the forefront of discussions of public policy.

Any consideration of this issue must take into account the substantial toxicity, impurity, and morbidity associated with marijuana use. Several states have passed ballot initiatives of legislation that allow a medical excuse for possession of marijuana. These initiatives bypass the Food and Drug Administration process of proving safely and efficacy, and they have created serious regulatory dilemmas for state regulatory boards. Several examinations of the issue have consistently drawn question to the validity of smoking an impure substance while voicing concern for the well being of patients in need. The historical, social, medical, and legal issues are examined.

HISTORY

In 1972, the Department of Justice Drug Enforcement Administration DEA was petitioned to reschedule marijuana from a Schedule I drug [unable to be prescribed, high potential for abuse, not currently acceptable for medicinal use, and lack of safety of the drug] to a Schedule II drug [high potential for abuse, currently accepted for medical use, but able to be prescribed].

This rescheduling petition was initiated by the National Organization for the Reform of Marijuana Laws [NORML], Alliance for Cannabis Therapeutics [ACT] and the Cannabis Corporation of America. It is significant that these organizations lobby for the legalization of marijuana and have neither a medical base, nor do they represent any accredited or respected medical entity.

Because of continued controversy surrounding the rescheduling of marijuana, Administrative Law Judge Francis Young was retained by the DEA in 1988 to rule on the merits of rescheduling marijuana to Schedule II. Judge Young ruled that marijuana should be rescheduled to Schedule II for nausea associated with cancer chemotherapy and spasticity. He concluded, however, that insufficient evidence existed to warrant use of crude marijuana for glaucoma or other applications.

The administrator of the DEA ultimately denied the petition to reschedule. In the face of extensive expert testimony provided to the DEA which opposed the rescheduling of marijuana, the marijuana lobby only produced evidence consisting of anecdotes and testimony of a handful of physicians with limited or no clinical experience with the medical areas in question. During the rescheduling hearings it became clear that crude, especially smoked, marijuana had not been accepted as a medicine by any reputable medical entity.

The denial of the rescheduling petition by the DEA resulted in an appeal by marijuana advocates to the United States Court of Appeals for the District of Columbia. In a decision handed down in February 1994 the Court set forth the guidelines that only rigorous scientific proof can satisfy the requirement of "currently acceptable medical use" [Table 1]. Crude marijuana does not meet these guidelines.

TABLE 1
Criteria for Designation for a Drug to be considered a Medicine

1. The drug's chemistry must be known and reproducible.
2. There must be adequate safety studies.
3. There must be adequate and well controlled studies proving efficacy.
4. The drug must be accepted by qualified experts.
5. The scientific evidence must be widely available.

Several voter initiatives have been undertaken by marijuana advocates to circumvent the FDA process and the DEA scheduling rules. While not actually legalizing marijuana for medical use, the initiatives create a "defense to possession" for those possessing a medical recommendation to use marijuana. The ballot initiatives were heavily financed by individuals and organizations who seek the legalization of marijuana and other drugs [Table 2]. The funding bought media consultants, airtime, and legal expertise. While initiatives were promoted as being 'compassionate' for suffering patients, they also created legal protection to those claiming medical ailments as justification for possession and personal use.

TABLE 2
Examples of Funding for the State Marijuana Ballot Initiatives

Prop 215 California		Arizona 2000 HB 2516	
George Soros	$550,000	George Soros	$105,000
Peter Lewis	$500,000	Peter Lewis	$105,000
John Sperling	$200,000	John Sperling	$105,000
George Zimmer	$100,000		
Life AIDS Lobby	$344,750	Massachusetts Initiative	
TEAMSTERS	$195,000	Peter Lewis	$122,500
Total	$1,889750	George Soros	$122,500
		John Sperling	$122,500
Prop 36 California			
George Soros	$983,080	Arizona 2002 Prop 203	
Peter Lewis	$1,026,337	Soros	$406,467
John Sperling	$1,066,337	Sperling	$590,383
Prop 200 Arizona		Ohio Drug Treatment Init 2000	
George Soros	$430,000	Soros	$271,276
Drug Policy		Sperling	$271,276
Foundation	$200,000	Lewis	$271,276
Peter Lewis	$330,000		
John Sperling	$430,000		
Social Policy			
Reform	$100,000		

The danger of such ballot initiatives is that they create an atmosphere of "medicine by popular vote" rather than the rigorous processes required by federal law that all medicines must undergo. There also exists great concern that the movement to accept marijuana for medicinal applications is having the secondary effect of softening public attitudes on marijuana use. In the 2002 election cycle, initiatives in Florida, Michigan, and Ohio ostensibly sought to require treatment for drug-related arrests. Underlying what would be perceived as a positive change, however, were no controls on what drugs nor what criminal acts would be eligible for treatment. Furthermore, the definitions of "treatment" were generally quite loose. Even literacy or vocational training could have qualified for hard core felons with long standing drug problems. The Florida and Michigan propositions did not require drug abstinence even during treatment. All three created a situation where criminal addicts would have statutory preference for treatment over non-criminals and were deemed unconstitutional.

This year, proposals in San Francisco and San Deigo would require the cities to provide marijuana to individuals with medical excuses. This type of action puts the cities in the difficult situation of assessing the validity of the excuses, the purity of the marijuana, and the potency of the marijuana. It also raises the question as to what legal risks the cities would be exposed to if complications such as accidents, infections, or other problems which might arise from the marijuana provided.

Recently, the Justice department filed an injunction in United States District Court against the Oakland Cannabis Buyers Cooperative in an attempt to close down the apparent open dealing of marijuana. This injunction was overturned upon appeal. A subsequent appeal to the United States Supreme Court has set the legal tone for the medicinal marijuana issue. The Supreme Court ruled on May 14, 2001 that the Controlled Substances Act may not be violated by the sale of marijuana for medicinal purposes, and that there is no medical necessity exception to the Controlled Substances Act's prohibition on manufacturing and distributing marijuana. The Supreme Court decision will likely have a chilling effect of future legislation and litigation regarding the use of marijuana for medical purposes.

Serious regulatory questions have also been raised regarding the standard of care that have not been adequately dealt with by ballot initiatives [Table 3]. These questions may serve as a template for regulatory boards who are faced with the medical excuse marijuana issue. Unfortunately, regulatory agencies have also been handed a difficult situation to assess.

MEDICINAL APPLICATION OF THC OR MARIJAUNA

Several medical surveys have examined physician attitudes regarding the use of marijuana for medicinal purposes. Kleiman and Doblin reported that 48% of the respondents would prescribe marijuana if rescheduled for legal prescription. Upon closer review, the survey had a low response rate of approximately 40%. Respondents only accounted for 9% of practicing oncologists. Sixteen percent of those surveyed felt that marijuana was effective in 50% or more of patients. Unfortunately, inaccurate interpretations of this survey were widely released, widely publicized in the media, and incorrectly gave the impression that about half of oncologists generally want smoked marijuana available as a medicine.

The author of this study, Rick Doblin, was a student at Harvard at that time. He is also the President of the Multidisciplinary Association for Psychedelic Studies [MAPS]. MAPS specializes in trying to gain legal access and status for psychedelic substances and marijuana. Doblin has openly admitted that the study was initiated so the results could be used in the marijuana rescheduling suit against the DEA.

TABLE 3
Standards to Consider Before Recommending Marijuana

- Is there documentation that the patient has had failure of all other conventional medications to treat his or her ailment? Have you counseled the patient [documented by the patient's signed informed consent] regarding the medical risks of the use of marijuana–at a minimum to include infection, pulmonary complications, suppression of immunity, impairment of driving skills, and habituation?
- Has the patient misused marijuana or other psychoactive drugs?
- Is Do you periodically provide drug testing of the patient who has been prescribed marijuana, and have patients been excluded from being prescribed marijuana who are found to be using other illicit drugs? Who does the drug testing and by what means?
- Is the use of smoked marijuana part of a study and/or will the monitoring of that use be under the supervision of an investigational review board?
- Have you carefully reviewed exactly which patients should be allowed to use this drug medicinally and for how long?
- Do you carefully examine and consistently follow up patients who use smoked marijuana as a medical treatment, including pulmonary function testing, evaluation of immune status, and the presence of any superinfection?
- Have you exercised due care in assuring the standardization of the tetrahydocannabinol potency content of the marijuana to be considered for medicinal use and whether it is free of microbial contaminants?
- Because marijuana is a federally controlled substance, has a system been established in the state to track all patients and their source of marijuana, as with other controlled substances? Are you complying with such requirements?
- Will you be required to be licensed by the state or federal government?
- Have you shown knowledge, training, of certification in addiction medicine? Do you have demonstrable knowledge of the physiologic effects of marijuana, the side effects, and its interaction with other drugs before prescribing it?

[Author's note: These are all standard requirements for the prescription of any drug, and especially a drug of abuse potential.] MH

Concurrent with Doblin and Kleiman, Schwartz surveyed oncologists in the Washington DC area and determined that pure THC in pill form ranked ninth in preference for the treatment of mild nausea and sixth for the treatment of severe nausea. It is important to recognize that this form of THC is not smoked marijuana.

Only 12% had recommended THC [by prescription or illegally] for more than 50% of patients. It was felt that nausea was relieved in only 50% of patients and that 25% had adverse effects.

Because of the exclusion of newer antiemetics from the two earlier surveys, Schwartz and Voth surveyed 1500 clinical adult oncologists in 1994 with a 75% response rate. Over 88% of respondents had never recommended crude marijuana to patients. Twelve percent had ever recommended a marijuana cigarette, and 1% of the respondents estimated that they had recommended crude marijuana more than five times per year. Only 9% said that they would prescribe crude marijuana more than ten times per year. In contrast, the median annual use of antiemetics ondansetron [Zofran] and granisetron [Kytril] was 250 prescriptions. Furthermore, the support of making crude marijuana available to patients was strongest among physicians who also supported the concept of general legalization of marijuana for recreational use.

In 1993, Grinspoon published a compilation of anecdotes which now serves as the bible of the "medical excuse marijuana" movement. He suggests that marijuana would be used for the nausea associated with cancer chemotherapy, glaucoma, wasting in AIDS, depression, menstrual cramps, pain, and miscellaneous ailments. His anecdotes contained no controls, no standardization of dose, no quality control, and no independent medical evaluation for efficacy or toxicity.

The discussion of historical uses of marijuana cited in Grinspoon's book include such cultures as India, Asia, the Middle East, South Africa, and South America and are considered by the medical excuse marijuana movement as evidence of appropriate medical uses of the drug. The Chinese allegedly used marijuana "to quicken the mind, induce sleep, cure dysentery, stimulate appetite, relieve headaches, and cure venereal disease." One of Grinspoon's references from 1860 states marijuana provided beneficial effects "without interfering with the actions of the internal organs." Such folk medicine applications of marijuana from the 1700s and 1800s are referenced by the authors as evidence justifying the modern medical applications.

The field of medicine in those earlier years was fraught with potions and herbal remedies. Many of those were absolutely useless, or conversely were harmful to unsuspecting subjects. This situation gave rise to the development and evolution of our current Food and Drug Administration and drug scheduling processes.

Advocates of marijuana contend that the smoking of marijuana has the advantage of providing a rapidly absorbed, titratable dose of THC. While rapid absorption could be an advantage in some areas, neither anecdotal nor controlled studies have delineated whether antiemetic qualities appear before, after, or concurrent to the intoxicating effects. Indeed, the therapeutic end point for successful administration of smoked marijuana has not been established.

Research on the utility of THC has demonstrated some effectiveness of the purified drug in treating nausea associated with cancer chemotherapy or appetite stimulation, but even researchers are cautious about using smoked substances. Tranner evaluated the state of the research on cannabinoids and concluded that in selected patients they may be useful as mood enhancing agents, but serious side effects will likely limit their usefulness.

They also stated, "These results should make us think hard about the ethics of clinical trials of cannabinoids when safe and effective alternatives are known to exist and when efficacy of cannabinoids in known to be marginal."

An example of the therapeutic benefits of cannabinoids for nausea was work by Sallan et al. who dealt with pure THC in the treatment of chemotherapy associated nausea, not smoked marijuana. Chang tested THC and then followed treatment failures with marijuana, thus conclusions regarding effectiveness cannot be readily attributed to either THC or crude marijuana. Levitt actually determined that purified THC was more effective that smoked marijuana.

Vinciguerra et al. found that smoked marijuana had some beneficial effect for nausea in patients who had failed other conventional forms of antiemetic therapy. Responders tended to have had prior marijuana experience. This study was uncontrolled and patients' self-evaluated results. Smokers were required to inhale deeply, hold the smoke for ten seconds, and then smoke four cigarettes completely each day of chemotherapy. Twenty-five percent refused to smoke the marijuana. Over 20% of the remaining subjects dropped out of the smoking group prior to the end of the study, and 22% of the remaining subjects reported no benefit from smoking marijuana. Dosing was also variable because of the fact that the dose was rounded to the nearest one-fourth marijuana cigarette and no THC levels were checked for consistency of dose response.

Mattes et al. evaluated oral and rectal suppository preparations of THC in comparison to smoked marijuana for appetite stimulation. All of the study participants were experienced marijuana users thus accounting for a relatively high drug acceptance. Smoked marijuana was no more effective than suppository THC in stimulating appetite as measured by caloric energy intake. Rectal suppositories and oral THC were dosed at 2.5 mg. twice daily. Smoking marijuana required the subjects to inhale over 3 seconds, hold the smoke deeply in their lungs for 12 seconds, and then continue the process until the cigarette was smoked to the stub. The plasma THC levels peaked more quickly with the inhaled THC, but also fell more quickly, whereas the suppository THC maintained a more sustained level.

Several comprehensive reviews have been undertaken to assess the potential medical uses for marijuana. Voth and Schwartz extensively reviewed available therapies for chemotherapy associated nausea, glaucoma, multiple sclerosis, and appetite stimulation and concluded that no compelling need exists to make crude marijuana available as a medicine for physicians to prescribe. They recommended that the most appropriate direction for cannabinoid research is to research specific cannabinoids or synthetic analogs rather than pursuing the smoking of marijuana as a way to deliver THC.

Former Assistant Secretary of Health Lee at the request of the Congress solicited opinions from investigators at the National Institute on Allergy and Infectious Diseases, who commented on the AIDS wasting syndrome; the National Cancer Institute which commented on the use of marijuana as an antiemetic in cancer chemotherapy; the National Eye Institute which commented on marijuana's use in glaucoma; and the National Institute for Neurological Disorders and Stroke which commented on marijuana's role as an antispasticity drug in multiple sclerosis.

The summary opinion stated: This evaluation indicates that sound scientific studies supporting these claims are lacking despite anecdotal claims that smoked marijuana is beneficial. Scientists at the National Institutes of Health indicate that after carefully examining the existing preclinical and human data, there is no evidence to suggest that smoked marijuana might be superior to currently available therapies for glaucoma, weight loss associated with AIDS, nausea and vomiting associated with cancer chemotherapy, muscle spasticity associated with multiple sclerosis, or intractable pain.

The National Institutes of Health reconsidered this issue in 1997 and has called for further research into alternate delivery systems for pure THC as well as research into the comparative efficacy of marijuana with newer available medicines that have added heightened efficacy to medication regimens. The summary also expressed concern over pulmonary, neuro, and immunotoxicity of cannabis.

In 1997 the White House Office of National Drug Control Policy commissioned the National Academy of Science, Institute of Medicine [IOM] to evaluate the utility of marijuana for medicinal applications. The study concluded [Table 4] that the challenge for future research will be to find cannabinoids which enhance therapeutic benefits while minimizing side effects such as intoxication and dysphoria. Useful delivery systems for isolated or synthetic cannabinoids could include nasal sprays, metered dose inhalers, transdermal patches, and suppositories. The future for medicinal applications of cannabinoids and whether cannabinoids are equal or superior to existing medicines remains to be determined, but the IOM evaluation is particularly clear on the smoking of marijuana:

If there is any future for marijuana as a medicine, it lies in its isolated components, the cannabinoids and their synthetic derivatives. Isolated cannabinoids will provide more reliable effects than crude plant mixtures. Therefore, the purpose of clinical trials of smoked marijuana would not be to develop marijuana as a licensed drug, but such trials could be a first step towards the development of rapid onset, non-smoked cannabinoid delivery systems.

TABLE 4
Institute of Medicine Recommendations

1. Research should continue into the physiological effects of synthetic and plant derived cannabinoids and the natural function of cannabinoids found in the body. Because different cannabinoids appear to he different effects, cannabinoid research should include, but not be restricted to, effects attributable to THC alone. Scientific data indicate the potential therapeutic value of cannabinoid drugs for pain relief, control of nausea and vomiting, and appetite stimulation. This value would be enhanced by a rapid onset of drug effect.

2. Clinical trials of cannabinoid drugs for symptom management should be conducted with the goal of developing rapid onset, reliable, and safe delivery systems. The psychological effects of cannabinoids are probably important determinations of the potential therapeutic value. They can influence symptoms indirectly which could create false impressions of the drug effect or be beneficial as a form of adjunctive therapy.

3. Psychological effects of cannabinoids such as anxiety reduction and sedation, which can influence perceived medical benefits, should be evaluated in clinical trials. Numerous studies suggest that marijuana smoke is an important risk factor in the development of respiratory diseases, but the data that could conclusively establish or refute this suspected link have not been collected.

4. Studies to define the individual health risks of smoking marijuana should be conducted, particularly among populations in which marijuana use is prevalent. Because marijuana is a crude THC delivery system that also delivers harmful substances, smoked marijuana should generally not be rec-

ommended for medical use. Nonetheless, marijuana is widely used by certain patient groups, which raises both safety and efficacy issues.

5. Clinical trials of marijuana use for medical purposes should be conducted under the following limited circumstances: trials should involve only short term marijuana use [less than six months]; be conducted in patients for which there is reasonable expectation of efficacy; be approved by institutional review boards; and collect data about efficacy.

If there is any future for marijuana as a medicine, it lies in its isolated components, the cannabinoids and their synthetic derivatives. Isolated cannabinoids will provide more reliable effects than crude plant mixtures. Therefore, the purpose of clinical trials of smoked marijuana would not be to develop marijuana as a licensed drug, but such trials could be a first step towards the development of rapid onset, non-smoked cannabinoid delivery systems.

6. Short term use of smoked marijuana [less than six months] for patients with debilitating symptoms [such as intractable pain or vomiting] must meet the following conditions:

- Failure of all approved medications to provide relief has been documented;
- The symptoms can reasonably be expected to be relieved by rapid onset cannabinoid drugs;
- Such treatment is administered under medical supervision in a manner that allows for assessment of treatment effectiveness;
- and involves an oversight strategy comparable to an institutional review board process that could provide guidance within 24 hours of a submission by a physician to provide marijuana a to a patient for a specified use.

[Author's note: These recommendations are consistent with widely accepted procedures for evaluating any proposed drug or therapeutic intervention.] MH

The advocates of marijuana would have the public and policy makers incorrectly believe that crude marijuana is the only treatment alternative for large populations of patients who are inadequately treated for the nausea associated with chemotherapy, glaucoma, multiple sclerosis, and other ailments. Numerous effective medications are however currently available for conditions such as nausea. To date no compelling data substantiates the existence of significant numbers of marginally treated or untreated patients for the maladies for which marijuana is advanced.

MEDICAL COMPLCATIONS OF MARIJUANA USE

Marijuana continues to be widely used in our society. While its use declined in the late 1980s and early 1990s, a trend toward increasing use has recently been seen in high school students. The chronic use of marijuana has now been demonstrated to be associated with higher utilization of the health care system and associated cost, a long suspected phenomenon.

TABLE 5
Drug Use Rates–Marijuana
PERCENT OF HIGH SCHOOL SENIORS USE OF MARIJUANA

	1978	1986	1987	1988	1991	1992	1993	1994	1995	2000
Last 12 Mo	50.2	39	36	33.1	23.9	21.9	26	30.7	35	36.5
Last 30 days	37	23	21	18	13.8	11.9	15.5	19	21.2	21.6
Daily	10.7	4.0	3.3	2.7	2.0	1.9	2.4	3.6	4.6	5.0

The negative side effect profile of marijuana far exceeds most other effective agents available. In the studies performed to examine THC for chemotherapy associated nausea, elderly patients would not tolerate the drug well. Chronic, daily doses of the drug would be necessary to treat many of the proposed medical conditions. This would unnecessarily exposed patients to the toxic effects.

Mental, affective, and behavioral effects are the most easily recognized consequences of acute and chronic marijuana use. Concentration, motor coordination, and memory are all adversely impacted.

The ability to perform complex tasks, such as flying is impaired even 24 hours after the acute intoxication phase. The association of marijuana use with trauma and intoxicated motor vehicle operation is also well established. Evaluations of the effect of marijuana on driving have determined that the combination of blood alcohol concentrations [BAC] of 0.07 and marijuana at 100 mcg/kg gave effects similar to BAC alone of 0.09. Blood alcohol concentrations of 0.07 and marijuana levels of 200 mcg/kg demonstrated effects similar to a BAC alone of 0.14 when measuring reaction time, on road performance, and vehicle following. The study concluded, "Under marijuana's influence, drivers have reduced capacity to avoid collisions if confronted with sudden need for evasive action." A second related study found that BAC of 0.05 combined with moderate marijuana had a significant drop in the visual search frequency. This is of central importance in an ambulatory environment where patients may smoke marijuana and then drive automobiles.

Several biochemical models have demonstrated abnormal changes in brain cells, brain blood flow, and evidence of brain wave changes. Pathologic behavior such as psychosis is also associated with marijuana use. Solowij et al, reported that the ability to focus attention and filter out irrelevant information was progressively impaired with the number of years of use, but was not related to the frequency of use. Solowij also demonstrated in a separate report that even among ex-cannabis smokers, the inability to reject complex irrelevant information persisted despite a mean abstinence of two years from marijuana use.

In an examination of college students, daily use of marijuana was associated with impairment of "executive functions" such as learning of lists, perseverations, and attention. In that study, heavy use was defined as use only 29 of the last 30 days which could have actually been as little as one time daily.

Positron scanning of subjects whose mean use of marijuana was 17 times per week for the last two years found lower blood flow in a large region of the posterior cerebellum. Not only does this have implications of motor coordination and function, but also cognition, timing, processing sensory information, and attention.

Despite arguments from marijuana advocates to he contrary, marijuana is a dependence producing drug. Strangely, in the course of the DEA rescheduling hearings, the petitioners admitted that "marijuana has a high potential for abuse and that abuse of the marijuana plant may lead to severe psychological or physical dependence." This dependence and associated "addictive" behaviors have been well described in the marijuana literature. Marijuana dependence consists of both a physical dependence [tolerance and subsequent withdrawal] and a psychological dependence. Withdrawal form marijuana has been demonstrated in both animals and humans.

The gateway effect of marijuana along with tobacco and alcohol is also well established in research. The use of cocaine and heroin is virtually always preceded by marijuana. Kandel and co-workers have pioneered research in this area and continue to find clear evidence of a gateway phenomenon. Golub and Johnson contends that the importance of marijuana as a gateway drug has actually increased in recent years.

While the dependence producing properties of marijuana are probably a minimal issue for chemotherapy associated nausea when treatment is required short term or sporadically, it is a major issue for the chronic daily use necessary for glaucoma, AIDS wasting syndrome, and other alleged chronic applications.

The respiratory difficulties associated with marijuana use preclude the inhaled route of administration as a medicine. Smoking marijuana is associated with higher concentrations of tar, carbon monoxide, and carcinogens than are found in cigarette smoking. Marijuana adversely impairs some aspects of lung function and causes abnormalities on the respiratory cell lines from large airways to the alveoli. Marijuana smoke causes inflammatory changes in the airways of young people that are similar to the effects of tobacco. In addiction to these cellular abnormalities and consequences, contaminants of marijuana smoke are known to include various pathogenic bacteria and fungi. Those with impaired immunity are at particular risk for the development of disease and infection when these substances are inhaled.

[Author's note: The primary targets for the 'legitimate' use of marijuana are cancer patients on chemotherapy and AIDS patients with wasting. Neither patient group should be exposed to these pathogens.] MH

The effects of marijuana on the unborn were long suspected after original studies in Rhesus monkeys demonstrating spontaneous abortion. While these are insignificant issues for terminal cancer patients, they are serious issues for young women potentially using marijuana for migraines or dysmenorrhea.

Exposure to marijuana during pregnancy is associated with changes in size, weight, and neurologic abnormalities in the newborn. A very alarming association also exists between maternal marijuana use and the development of non-lymphocytic leukemia in offspring. Additionally, hormonal function in both males and females is disrupted. The potential for hormonal abnormalities in the unborn is undetermined, but real. Day et al identified a negative effect on intelligence parameters among three year olds when mothers used marijuana during the first and second trimesters of pregnancy. Dahl et al have discovered sleep disruption among three year olds when exposed during pregnancy. Consistent with the reports of delayed performance, Fried reported the children exposed in utero demonstrate increased behavioral problems, language comprehension, sustained attention, and memory at age four.

One of the earliest findings in marijuana research was the effect on various immune functions, which is now evidenced by an inability to fight herpes infections and the discovery of a blunted response to therapy for genital warts during cannabis consumption. Abnormal immune function is, of course, the cornerstone of problems associated with HIV. The use of chronic THC in the smoked form for AIDS wasting not only exposes the patient to unnecessary pathogens, but also risks further immune suppression. Evaluation of the effect of THC on NK-kB has suggested a possible effect on the HIV genome. In chronic use or use in populations at high risk for infection and immune suppression, the risks are unacceptable.

LOOKING TOWARD THE FUTURE

Bypassing the usual safety and efficacy process of the FDA is a dangerous and unnecessary precedent which widely enhances the availability and acceptance of marijuana. Smoking an impure and toxic substance is of questionable value in the modern medical armamentarium. It is no more reasonable to consider crude marijuana a medical treatment than it is to consider tobacco as medicine.

If marijuana is to be examined for medicinal applications, rigorous research protocols should be focused on pure THC and other cannabinoids rather than crude forms of marijuana. Examples could include the formulation of rectal suppositories or aerosol forms, nasal inhalers, or transdermal delivery systems of dronabinol. An exciting new arena of THC analogues and synthetic cannabinoids may yet produce cannabinoid like substances which enhance efficacy while having minimal or no toxicity. Naturally occurring substances with medicinal value are well known to medicine. Substances like digitalis are found in foxglove plant, but modern medicine either purifies or synthesizes such substances to create pure and reliable medicine. The same can be done for the therapeutically beneficial cannabinoids found in marijuana.

While recognizing that there may exist a small group of inadequately treated patients for whom isolated or synthetic cannabinoids may be beneficial, the general use of crude or leaf marijuana for medicinal purposes cannot be supported except in highly circumscribed, controlled, research settings.

Regulatory agencies have a critically important role in the examination of the use of marijuana. They have, unfortunately, been handed a difficult problem to monitor, which has emerged from an atmosphere of "medicine by popular vote." The use of marijuana in states who allow it needs to be tempered by careful patient selection and monitoring. Unless marijuana were approved as a safe and effective treatment by the FDA, allowing it to be used as a medicine is a step backward to the times of potions and herbal remedies.

References and Appendixes omitted.

Voth EA A Peek into Pandora's box: the medical excuse marijuana controversy. J Addict Dis 2003 22:27–46

APPENDIX C

INTELLIGENT DESIGN IN PUBLIC SCHOOL SCIENCE CURRICULA–A LEGAL GUIDEBOOK

David K. DeWolf, Stephen C. Meyer,
and Mark E. DeForrest
Used with Permission by The Foundation for Thought and Ethics

1. INTRODUCTION

Public schools face a dilemma when they address the subject of biological origins. From the Scopes "Monkey Trial" (1925) to the Supreme Court's opinion in *Edwards v. Aguillard* (1987), the teaching of biological origins has put the public schools in the awkward role of resolving a controversy that divides scientists, educators, and the courts. While the experts debate the issues, and the media sometimes inflame the controversy, school boards, administrators, and teachers must still answer the question, What should we teach our students about how living organisms arose on earth?

For many scientists, educators, and activists, the answer is clear: Teach only Darwinian and related evolutionary theories that explain the origin and development of life as the result of undirected natural processes. Despite the vehemence with which many scientific authorities express this view, many Americans remain unconvinced and seek an alternative approach.

In the 1970s and early 1980s an approach known as scientific creationism (or creation science) was proposed. Scientific creationism sought to defend the biblical account of creation in *Genesis* as scientifically accurate.1 Advocates of this approach persuaded the State of Louisiana to enact a statute requiring teachers to give scientific creationism "equal time" if they taught Darwinian evolution.2 But the effort proved unsuccessful; the United States Supreme Court decided that scientific creationism advanced a religious view in the guise of science and therefore violated the Establishment Clause of the Constitution. Many proponents of Darwinian evolution greeted the *Edwards* decision as officially endorsing neo-Darwinism as the undisputed orthodoxy in public school science curricula.

Yet the Supreme Court's decision was more careful than that. While finding that the Louisiana statute failed to comply with the Establishment Clause of the First Amendment, the Court encouraged "teaching a variety of scientific theories about the origins of humankind to school children . . . with the clear secular intent of enhancing the effectiveness of science instruction."3

Within the last decade or so, just such an alternative theory has emerged. Darwinian theorists have long acknowledged that biological organisms "appear" to be designed. Oxford zoologist Richard Dawkins, a leading Darwinian spokesman, has admitted: "Biology is the study of complicated things that give the appearance of having been designed for a purpose."4 Statements like this echo throughout the biological literature. Francis Crick, Nobel laureate and co-discoverer of the structure of DNA, writes, "Biologists must constantly keep in mind that what they see was not designed, but rather evolved."5 Nevertheless, Darwinists insist that this appearance of design is illusory since the mechanism of natural selection entirely suffices to explain the observed complexity of living things.

Over the last forty years, however, even many evolutionary biologists have acknowledged fundamental problems with the Darwinian explanation for apparent design. As a result, an increasing number of scientists have begun to argue that organisms appear to be designed because they really are designed. These scientists (known as design theorists) see evidence of actual intelligent design in biological systems. They argue that, contrary to neo-Darwinian orthodoxy, nature displays abundant evidence of real, not just apparent, design. As their numbers have grown, their work has sparked a spirited scientific controversy over this central issue.

The purpose of this guidebook is to help teachers, school boards, and school administrators to negotiate the difficult scientific, legal, and pedagogical issues that arise from the origins controversy. At present many groups advise educators and administrators to ignore the controversy over design and to continue to teach a single theoretical viewpoint, ignoring scientific dissent and parental concerns about dogmatism and intellectual intolerance. In short, their approach is to suppress the controversy. We believe there is a better way. We suggest that public schools teach the controversy over biological origins in a way that faithfully reflects the debate that is actually happening among scientists.

Several benefits will accrue from a more open discussion of biological origins in the science classroom. First, this approach will do a better job of teaching the issue itself, both because it presents more accurate information about the state of scientific thinking and evidence, and because it presents the subject in a more lively and less dogmatic way. Second, this approach gives students greater appreciation for how science is actually practiced. Science necessarily involves the interpretation of data; yet scientists often disagree about how to interpret their data. By presenting this scientific controversy realistically, students will learn how to evaluate competing interpretations in light of evidence-a skill they will need as citizens, whether they choose careers in science or other fields. Third, this approach will model for students how to address differences of opinion through reasoned discussion within the context of a pluralistic society. Finally, as we will demonstrate, constitutional precedent now provides ample legal latitude for adopting just such an open approach.

This book addresses three basic questions: (1) Science: Does the discussion of evidence for intelligent design in biology belong in the science classroom? (2) Law: Does the law permit the discussion of such evidence in a public school setting, even if it may have larger philosophical implications? (3) Education: Does teaching the origins controversy in a more open way constitute good pedagogy and educational policy?

2. A Brief Overview of Design Theory

How did the astonishing diversity and complexity of life on earth come about? Could a designing intelligence have had anything to do with the origin of biological organisms? Darwinian evolutionary biologists say No. They contend that life arose and diversified by entirely naturalistic processes like random variation and natural selection. While they admit that many of the complex features of living systems manifest the "appearance of design," neo-Darwinists insist that the mechanism of natural selection entirely suffices to explain this appearance without invoking an actual designing intelligence.

But if evidence can count against a theory, it must be possible for evidence also to count for that same theory. Scientific refutation is a double-edged sword. For a claim to be scientifically refutable, it must have the possibility of being true. Further, because scientific theories never claim to be the final truth, new evidence can always challenge a currently dominant theory and provide new support for a previously discarded one.

Since the 1980s, a growing number of scientists have argued that precisely such evidences have come to light in the origins controversy. They argue that, contrary to neo-Darwinian orthodoxy, nature displays abundant evidence of design by an intelligent agent. These scientists, known as design theorists, advocate an alternative theory of biological origins known as design theory or the theory of intelligent design (sometimes abbreviated simply design or intelligent design). They have developed design theory in scientific and scholarly journals as well as in such books as *Darwin's Black Box, The Mystery of Life's Origin, Mere Creation, The Design Inference,* and the supplemental high school textbook *Of Pandas and People.*6 Design theory holds that intelligent causes rather than undirected natural causes best explain many features of living systems. During recent years design theorists have developed both a general theory for detecting design and many specific empirical arguments to support their views.

A THEORY OF INTELLIGENT DESIGN

Developments in the information sciences have recently made possible the articulation of criteria by which intelligently designed systems can be identified by the kinds of patterns they exhibit. In a recent book titled *The Design Inference,* published by Cambridge University Press, Baylor University probability theorist William Dembski shows how rational agents often infer or detect the prior activity of other designing minds by the character of the effects they leave behind. Archaeologists assume, for example, that rational agents produced the inscriptions on the Rosetta Stone. Insurance fraud investigators detect certain "cheating patterns" that suggest intentional manipulation of circumstances rather than "natural" disasters. Cryptographers distinguish between random signals and those that carry encoded messages. Dembski's work shows that recognizing the activity of intelligent agents constitutes a common and fully rational mode of inference.7

More importantly, Dembski's work explicates the criteria by which rational agents recognize the effects of other rational agents and distinguish them from the effects of natural causes. Dembski argues that systems that manifest the joint properties of "high complexity"8 (or low probability) and "specification"9 invariably result from intelligent causes rather than from chance or physical-chemical laws. These criteria are equivalent (or isomorphic) to what information theorists call specified information or information content. Dembski's work demonstrates that "high information content" reliably signals prior intelligent activity.

This theoretical insight agrees with common, as well as scientific, experience. For example, no one would attribute hieroglyphic inscriptions to natural forces such as wind or erosion; instead, one immediately recognizes the activity of intelligent agents. Dembski's work shows why: Our reasoning involves a comparative evaluation process that he represents with a device he calls the explanatory filter.10 The filter outlines the method that scientists (as well as ordinary people) use to decide among three types of causal explanations-chance, necessity, and design. His explanatory filter constitutes, in effect, a scientific method for detecting the effects of intelligence.

DESIGN THEORY: AN EMPIRICAL BASIS?

Along with their formal theory articulating the criteria by which intelligent causes can be detected in the "echo of their effects," design theorists point to specific empirical evidence of design, both in biology and physics. They argue that biological organisms in particular display distinctive features of intelligently designed systems. Indeed, a growing number of scientists are now willing to consider alternatives to strictly naturalistic origins theories. Many now see especially striking evidence of design in biology, even if much of it is still reported by scientists and journals that presuppose a neo-Darwinian perspective.

For example, in 1998 the premier biology journal *Cell* featured a special issue on "Macromolecular Machines." All cells use complex molecular machines to process information, build proteins, and move materials back and forth across their membranes. Bruce Alberts, president of the National Academy of Sciences, introduced this issue with an article titled "The Cell as a Collection of Protein Machines." In it he stated that

We have always underestimated cells. . . . The entire cell can be viewed as a factory that contains an elaborate network of interlocking assembly lines, each of which is composed of a set of large protein machines. . . . Why do we call the large protein assemblies that underlie cell function protein machines? Precisely because, like machines invented by humans to deal efficiently with the macroscopic world, these protein assemblies contain highly coordinated moving parts.11

Alberts notes that molecular machines strongly resemble machines designed by human engineers. Nevertheless, as an orthodox neo-Darwinist, he denies any role for actual, as opposed to apparent, design in the origin of these systems.

In recent years, however, some scientists have presented a formidable challenge to the neo-Darwinian view. For example, in *Darwin's Black Box* Lehigh University biochemist Michael Behe shows that neo-Darwinists have failed to explain the origin of complex molecular machines in living systems.12 Behe examines the acid powered rotary engines that turn the whip-like flagella of certain bacteria. He shows that the intricate machinery in this molecular motor-including a rotor, a stator, O-rings, bushings, and a drive shaft-requires the coordinated interaction of some forty complex protein parts. Yet the absence of any one of these proteins would result in the complete loss of motor function.13 To assert that such an irreducibly complex engine emerged gradually in a Darwinian fashion strains credulity. Natural selection selects functionally advantageous systems. Yet motor function only ensues after all necessary parts have independently self-assembled, an astronomically improbable event.

Thus, Behe insists that Darwinian mechanisms cannot account for the origin of molecular motors and other such irreducibly complex systems that require the coordinated interaction of multiple independent protein parts. To emphasize his point, Behe has conducted a literature search of relevant technical journals.14 He has found a complete absence of gradualistic Darwinian explanations for the origin of the systems and motors that he discusses. Behe concludes that neo-Darwinists have not explained or, in most cases, even attempted to explain, how the appearance of design in irreducibly complex systems arose naturalistically.

Instead, he notes that we know of only one cause sufficient to produce functionally integrated, irreducibly complex systems, namely, intelligent design. Whenever we encounter irreducibly complex systems and we know how they arose, invariably a designer played a causal role. Thus, Behe concludes on the basis of our knowledge of present cause-and-effect relationships (that is, in accord with the standard uniformitarian method employed in the historical sciences), that the molecular machines and complex systems we observe in cells must have also had an intelligent cause.15 In brief, molecular motors appear designed because they were designed.

Behe's book, published in 1996, has received international acclaim and critique in over eighty book reviews. Generally, critics have conceded the scientific accuracy of Behe's claims (including his literature search showing the complete absence of neo-Darwinian explanations for many of the irreducibly complex systems that he examines). Instead, they have objected to his argument on philosophical and methodological grounds. Behe's critics claim that to infer an intelligent cause for the origin of these complex systems, as Behe does, "goes beyond science." (We discuss this objection in section 3 below.)

Even so, Behe is not alone in his conclusions. Consider the case of Dean Kenyon, a biologist at San Francisco State University.16 For nearly twenty years Professor Kenyon was a leading evolutionary theorist who specialized in origin-of-life biology. While at UC Berkeley in 1969 he wrote a book, *Biochemical Predestination,* that defined evolutionary thinking on the origin-of-life for over a decade.17 Kenyon's theory attempted to show how complex biomolecules such as proteins and DNA might have "self-organized" via strictly chemical forces.

Yet as Kenyon reflected more on the recent discoveries in molecular biology about the complexity of living things, he began to wonder whether undirected chemistry could really produce the information-rich molecules found in even the simplest of cells. Studies of the genetic molecule DNA revealed that it functions in much the same way as computer software or alphabetic text in a book. As Richard Dawkins notes, "The machine code of the genes is uncannily computer-like."18 Or, as software innovator Bill Gates notes, "DNA is like a computer program, but far, far more advanced than any software we've ever created."19

Indeed, studies in molecular biology and the information sciences have shown that the assembly instructions inscribed along the spine of DNA display the characteristic hallmarks of intelligently encoded information-indeed, both the complexity and specificity of function that, according to Dembski's theory, indicates intelligent design.20 As a result of this evidence, Kenyon and many other scientists (notably Charles Thaxton, Walter Bradley, and Roger Olsen) have concluded that the specified complexity or high information content of DNA-like the information in a computer program, an ancient scroll, or in this very book-had an intelligent source.21

In recent years the fossil record has also provided new support for design. Fossil studies reveal a "biological big bang" near the beginning of the Cambrian period 530 million years ago. At that time roughly fifty separate major groups of organisms or "phyla" (including most all the basic body plans of modern animals) emerged suddenly without evident precursors. Although neo-Darwinian theory requires vast periods of time for the step-by-step development of new biological organs and body plans, fossil finds have repeatedly confirmed a pattern of explosive appearance followed by prolonged stability of living forms. Moreover, the fossil record shows a "top-down" hierarchical pattern of appearance in which major structural themes or body plans emerge before minor variations on those themes.22 Not only does this pattern directly contradict the "bottom-up" pattern predicted by neo-Darwinism, but as University of San Francisco marine paleobiologist Paul Chien and several colleagues have argued,23 it also strongly resembles the pattern evident in the history of human technological design, again suggesting actual (i.e., intelligent) design as the best explanation for the data.

Other scientists now see evidence of design in the information processing systems of the cell, the signal transduction circuitry of the cell, the complexity and specificity of proteins, the end-directed embryological processes of organismal development, the complexity of the human brain, and even the phenomenon known as homology (evidence previously thought to provide unequivocal support for a neo-Darwinian perspective).24 Design theorists have begun to marshal an impressive array of empirical evidence in support of their perspective, thus challenging standard evolutionary theories for the origin and development of life across a variety of subdisciplines within biology.

Of course, the legal and educational point at issue is not whether design theorists are right in their scientific claims, but whether their work should be discussed in public school science classrooms. Assuming it is legally permissible (we consider this issue in due course), should students be told that there are well-credentialed scientists (like Behe, Kenyon, Thaxton, Chien, and Dembski) who are publishing articles and books that explicitly challenge the neo-Darwinian denial of (actual) design in biology?

The preceding discussion demonstrates that, right or wrong, the work of such scientists is clearly germane to the topic of biological origins. It is noteworthy that Darwin's theory attempted to explain the appearance of design in biology without reference to an actual designer. Thus, it is misleading to suggest, as many do, that Darwinism and design address two fundamentally different topics, the one scientific and the other religious. Rather, both Darwinism and design represent competing answers to the very same question: How did living forms (with their appearance of design) arise and diversify on earth? At present, many biology texts routinely recapitulate Darwinian arguments against intelligent design and for the sufficiency of an undirected mechanism of evolutionary change. Clearly, good science education requires that students learn and understand the evidence and arguments for a neo-Darwinian interpretation of the history of life. But shouldn't students also know the arguments against the sufficiency of the neo-Darwinian mechanism and for design, especially now that many well-credentialed contemporary scientists are making these arguments in print?

Of course, design theory is relatively new, and teachers may require some time to adjust their teaching, especially given that few textbooks address the subject (a notable exception being *Of Pandas and People*). But the relative novelty of design does not justify its exclusion, either on legal or pedagogical grounds. Indeed, quite the reverse is the case. Good teachers know that exposing students to new (and even controversial) ideas can stimulate student engagement and interest in a subject and lead to greater subject mastery. Thus, one must ask: Why wouldn't teachers, school boards, and parents want their students exposed to competing interpretations of the scientific evidence relevant to the origins controversy?

3. Is Design Theory Science? - Darwinism, Design, and Demarcation

Critics of design theory generally do not dispute the data (as opposed to the interpretation) that design theorists marshal in support of their view, nor do they disagree that some evidences might be interpreted to support the idea of intelligent design. They argue instead that the very idea of intelligent design is inherently unscientific-that design theory does not qualify as science according to established definitions of the term. To justify this claim, critics cite various definitional or "demarcation" criteria that purport to define science and distinguish it (or provide demarcation) from pseudo-science, metaphysics, and religion. These kinds of arguments have previously played an important role in framing the scientific and therefore legal status of creation science (or scientific creationism). Moreover, many continue to use these arguments to cast doubt on the scientific status of other alternatives to strictly naturalistic origins theories, including design theory.[25]

MCLEAN V. ARKANSAS AND THE DEFINITION OF SCIENCE

In 1982 a federal judge adopted a five-point definition of science as part of his finding that a law requiring Arkansas public schools to teach creation science alongside standard neo-Darwinian theory was unconstitutional.[26] While there are decisive differences between design theory and creation science (as detailed in section 6 below) critics of design theory often rely on the *McLean* criteria to establish definitional or methodological norms.

In *McLean,* Judge William Overton ruled that an Arkansas law requiring the teaching of creation science in public schools violated the First Amendment's Establishment Clause.[27] The judge based his decision not only on the Establishment Clause, but on a finding that so-called creation science does not qualify as science.[28] Moreover, he reasoned that because creation science does not qualify as science, it constitutes religion. In making its determination, the court relied upon the expert testimony of the Darwinian philosopher of science Michael Ruse. In his testimony, Ruse asserted a five-point definition of science that provided allegedly normative criteria for determining whether a theory qualifies as scientific.[29] Any theory, according to Ruse, which failed to meet these five criteria could not qualify as scientific.[30]

According to Ruse, for a theory to achieve scientific status it must be:
+ guided by natural law,
+ explanatory by natural law,
+ testable against the empirical world,
+ tentative, and
+ falsifiable.[31]

Ruse further testified that scientific creationism-in part because it invoked the singular action of a creator as the cause of certain events in the history of life-could never meet these criteria. Thus, he concluded that creationism might be true, but it could never qualify as science. Judge Overton ultimately agreed, adopting Ruse's five demarcation criteria as part of his opinion.

Although this case was in some ways superseded by the subsequent ruling of the United States Supreme Court in *Edwards v. Aguillard,*32 (discussed below in section 5), the *McLean* case, and the philosophy of science that underwrites it, pose an implied challenge to the scientific status of all theories of origins (including design theory) that invoke singular, intelligent causes as opposed to strictly material causes. If design theory does not qualify as science, as Ruse testified and the court ruled concerning creation science, then at least as a pedagogical matter design theory does not belong in the science classroom.

THE DEMISE OF DEMARCATION ARGUMENTS

Notwithstanding the favorable reception that Michael Ruse's arguments enjoyed in Judge Overton's courtroom, many prominent philosophers of science including Larry Laudan and Philip Quinn,33 (neither of whom supported creation science's empirical claims), soon repudiated Ruse's testimony on the grounds that, as Laudan argued, it "canoniz[ed] a false stereotype of what science is and how it works."34 These philosophers of science insisted that Ruse's testimony egregiously misrepresented contemporary thinking in the philosophy of science about the status of the demarcation problem. Indeed, it now seems clear for several reasons that the philosophy of science provides no grounds for disqualifying non-materialistic alternatives to Darwinism as inherently "unscientific."

First, as Laudan noted, philosophers of science have generally abandoned attempts to define science by reference to abstract demarcation criteria. Indeed, they have found it notoriously difficult to define science generally via the kind of methodological criteria that Ruse and the court promulgated in the *McLean* case-in part because proposed demarcation criteria have inevitably fallen prey to death by counterexample. Well-established scientific theories often lack some of the presumably necessary features of true science (e.g., falsifiability, observability, repeatability, and use of law-like explanation), while many poorly supported, disreputable or "crank" ideas often meet some of these same criteria.

Consider, for instance, the criteria of falsifiability and tentativeness, two key and related litmus tests in the 1981 trial.35 Contrary to Ruse's assertion that all truly scientific theories are held tentatively by their proponents and are readily falsifiable by contradictory evidence, the history of science tells a very different story. As Imre Lakatos, one of the premier historians and philosophers of science of the twentieth century, showed in the 1970s, some of the most powerful scientific theories have been constructed by those who stubbornly refused to reject their theories in the face of anomalous data.36 For example, on the basis of his theory of universal gravitation, Isaac Newton

made a number of predictions about the position of planets that did not mate-
rialize. Nevertheless, rather than rejecting the notion of universal gravitation,
he refined his auxiliary assumptions (e.g., the assumption that planets are perfectly spherical and influenced only by gravitational force) and left his core
theory in place. As Lakatos showed, the explanatory flexibility of Newton's
theory in the face of apparently falsifying evidence turned out to be one of
its greatest strengths. Such flexibility emphatically did not compromise the
scientific status of universal gravitation, as Ruse's definition of science would
imply.37

On the other hand, the history of science is littered with the remains of
failed theories that have been falsified, not by the air-tight disproof of a single
anomaly, but by the judgment of the scientific community concerning the pre-
ponderance of data. Are such falsified, and therefore falsifiable, theories (e.g.,
the flat earth, phlogiston, geocentricism, and flood geology) more scientific
than successful theories (such as Newton's was in, say, 1750) that possess
wide-ranging explanatory power?

As a result of such contradictions, most contemporary philosophers
of science have come to regard the question "what distinguishes science from
non-science" as both intractable and uninteresting. Instead, philosophers of
science have increasingly realized that the real issue is not whether a theory
is "scientific" according to some abstract definition, but whether a theory is
true or warranted by the evidence. As Laudan puts it, "If we could stand up on
the side of reason, we ought to drop terms like 'pseudo-science' . . . they do
only emotive work for us."38 Martin Eger offers this summary: "Demarcation
arguments have collapsed. Philosophers of science don't hold them anymore.
They may still enjoy acceptance in the popular world, but that's a different
world."39

There is a second flaw in the contention that design is (in principle)
unscientific: Even if we assume for the sake of argument that criteria could be
found to demarcate science in general from non-science in general, the specific
demarcation criteria used in the McLean case have proven utterly incapable
of discriminating the scientific status of materialistic and non-materialistic
origins theories.40 Laudan noted, for example, that Judge Overton's opinion
made much of creation science's inability to be tested or falsified. Yet as Laudan argues, the claim that

[To claim that] creationism is neither falsifiable or testable is to assert
that creationism makes no empirical assertions whatever. That is surely false.
Creationists make a wide range of testable assertions about matters of fact.
Thus, as Judge Overton himself grants (apparently without seeing the implications) creationists say that the earth is of very recent origin . . . ; they argue that
most of the geological features of the earth's surface are diluvial in character

. . . ; they assert the limited variability of species. They are committed to the view that since animals and man were created at the same time, the human fossil record must be paleontologically co-extensive with the record of lower animals.41

Laudan notes that, although creation scientists "are committed to a large number of factual claims," available evidence contradicts their empirical claims. As he explains,

No one has shown how to reconcile such claims with the available evidence-evidence which speaks persuasively to a long earth history, among other things. In brief, these claims are testable, they have been tested, and they have failed those tests.42

Yet, Laudan notes, if creationist arguments have been shown false by empirical evidence (as Ruse and other expert witnesses at the Arkansas trial no doubt believed), then creation science must be falsifiable. But if it is falsifiable, then by Ruse's own criterion, it must qualify as scientific.

Similar problems have afflicted Ruse's other demarcation criteria. For example, insofar as both creationist and evolutionary theories make historical claims about past causal events, both theories offer causal explanations that do not explain by natural law. The theory of common descent, a central thesis of Darwin's *Origin of Species,* does not explain by natural law. Common descent explains by postulating hypothetical historical events (and a pattern of events) which, if actual, would explain a variety of presently observed data.43 The theory of common descent makes claims about what happened in the past-namely, that unobserved transitional organisms existed forming a genealogical bridge between presently existing life forms. Thus, on the theory of common descent, a postulated pattern of events, not a law, does the main explanatory work.

Similarly, as Laudan notes, scientists often make existence claims about past events or present processes without knowing the natural laws on which they depend. As he notes, "Darwin took himself to have established the existence of [the mechanism of] natural selection almost a half century before geneticists were able to lay out the laws of heredity on which natural selection depended."44 Thus, Ruse's second demarcation criterion would require, if applied consistently, classifying both creation science and classical Darwinism (as well as much of neo-Darwinism) as unscientific. As Laudan notes,

If we took the *McLean* opinion seriously, we should have to say that . . . Darwin [was] unscientific; and, to take an example from our own time, it would follow that plate tectonics is unscientific because we have not yet identified the laws of physics and chemistry which account for the dynamics of crustal motion.45

Finally, several analyses of the demarcation problem have suggested that naturalistic and non-naturalistic origins theories (including both Darwinism and design theory) are methodologically equivalent, both in their ability to meet various demarcation criteria and as historical theories of origins. As noted earlier, Laudan's critique suggests that when the specific demarcation criteria promulgated in *McLean* are applied rigidly, they disqualify both Darwinism and various non-materialistic alternatives. Yet, as his discussion of falsification suggests, if certain criteria are applied more liberally, then both theories may qualify as scientific.

More recent studies in the philosophy of science have confirmed and amplified Laudan's analysis.46 They suggest that philosophically neutral criteria do not exist that can define science narrowly enough to disqualify theories of creation or design without also disqualifying Darwinism and other materialistic evolutionary theories on identical grounds. Either science will be defined so narrowly as to disqualify both types of theory, or science must be defined more broadly and the initial reasons for excluding opposing theories evaporate. Thus, materialistic and non-materialistic origins theories appear to be methodologically equivalent with respect to a wide range of demarcation criteria-that is, both appear equally scientific or equally unscientific provided the same criteria are used to adjudicate their scientific status (and provided philosophically neutral criteria are used to make such assessments).

Indeed, recent work on the historical sciences has suggested that the methodological and logical similarity between various origins theories runs quite deep. Philosopher of biology Elliott Sober has argued that both classical design arguments and the Darwinian argument for descent with modification constitute attempts to make "inferences to the best explanation."47 Other work in the philosophy of science has shown that both Darwinism and design theory attempt to answer characteristically historical questions; both may have metaphysical implications or overtones; both employ characteristically historical forms of inference, explanation, and testing; and, finally, both are subject to similar epistemological limitations.48

Accordingly, even many of those who previously wielded demarcation arguments as a way of protecting the Darwinist hegemony in public education, including the most prominent advocates of these arguments, have either abandoned or repudiated them.49 For example, Eugenie Scott of the National Center for Science Education (an advocacy group for an exclusively Darwinist curriculum) no longer seeks to dismiss creation science as pseudoscience or unscientific; instead she argues that it constitutes "bad science."50 Scott no longer repudiates design theory as inherently "unscientific," as she did as recently as 1994; she now argues that it constitutes a minority viewpoint within science.51 Similarly, during a talk to the American Association for the Advancement of Science (AAAS) in 1993, Michael Ruse himself repudiated his previous support for the demarcation principle by admitting that Darwinism (like creationism) "depends upon certain unprovable metaphysical assumptions."52 In his more recent scholarship Ruse has openly argued that evolutionary theory has often functioned as a kind of "secular religion."53

SUMMARY

The demise of demarcation arguments within the philosophy of science has made it difficult for critics to label design theory as unscientific in principle. As Laudan and others have argued, the status and merit of competing origins theories must be decided on the basis of empirical evidence and argument, not on abstract philosophical or methodological litmus tests. Yet as we have seen, design theorists in particular make extensive appeals to such empirical evidence and argument. Moreover, their arguments are now informed by an empirically based and mathematically sophisticated theory for detecting design. If design theory has both theoretical and evidential support, and if it meets abstract definitional criteria of scientific status equally well as its main theoretical rivals, then it is natural to ask, On what grounds can design theory be excluded from the public school science curriculum?

4. THE LEGAL PARAMETERS: IS IT RELIGION?

Rather than argue that design theory lacks scientific merit, many critics claim that it should be excluded because the courts have determined that it constitutes an unconstitutional intrusion of religion into the science curriculum. Thus, even though Edwards v. Aguillard encourages the teaching of other scientific theories, and even though design theory might qualify as being scientific, these critics have argued that design theory is nonetheless a religious view and must therefore be excluded from the public school science curriculum.

For instance, in reviewing the intelligent design textbook *Of Pandas and People,*54 Jay Wexler concedes that design theory could, for the sake of argument, be classified as science.55 Nevertheless, he argues that teaching design theory would offend the Establishment Clause of the First Amendment:56 "The First Amendment forbids the government from establishing religion; it does not require it to teach science."57 Consequently, if design theory is both a scientific theory and a religious doctrine, the same limitations will apply to it that apply to teaching traditional religions like Christianity, Judaism, or Buddhism.58

But design theory does not fit the dictionary definition of religion, or the specific test for religion adopted by the Ninth Circuit in its recent cases concerning the establishment of religion. Consider, for example, *Peloza v. Capist-*

*rano Unified School District.*59 Peloza sued the Capistrano school district in which he was a teacher. He claimed that by forcing him to teach "evolutionism" and "secular humanism," the school district had created an "establishment of religion."60 The court rejected this claim, finding that neither "evolutionism [nor] secular humanism are 'religions' for Establishment Clause purposes."61 The court's finding was based on both the "dictionary definition of religion and the clear weight of the case law," thereby contradicting Peloza's claim.62 The court also cited the recommendation by Harvard law professor Laurence Tribe that "anything 'arguably non-religious' should not be considered religious in applying the Establishment Clause."63

Similarly, in *Alvarado v. City of San Jose*64 a group of citizens brought suit against the city of San Jose, alleging that the city's installation of a sculpture of the Aztec god Quetzalcoatl violated the Establishment Clause.65 The court ruled that the sculpture was not religious.66 In making its ruling, the court relied on a three-part test to define religion:67

First, a religion addresses fundamental and ultimate questions having to do with deep and imponderable matters. Second, a religion is comprehensive in nature; it consists of a belief-system as opposed to an isolated teaching. Third, a religion often can be recognized by the presence of certain formal and external signs.68

The court further clarified this test by noting that "formal and external signs" include "formal services, ceremonial functions, the existence of clergy, structure and organization, efforts at propagation, observance of holidays and other similar manifestations associated with the traditional religions."69 Taken together, the Ninth Circuit cases of *Peloza* and *Alvarado* provide a broad definition of religion for Establishment Clause purposes.

Clearly, design theory does not satisfy this three-part test. Take the first part. Design theory does not attempt to address "fundamental and ultimate questions" concerning "deep and imponderable matters."70 On the contrary, design theory seeks to answer a question raised by Darwin as well as contemporary biologists: How did biological organisms acquire their appearance of design? Design theory, unlike neo-Darwinism, attributes this appearance to a designing intelligence, but it does not address the characteristics or identity of the designing intelligence. To be sure, design theory is consistent with theism and adds plausibility to the classical design arguments for the existence of God.71 But this compatibility does not make it a religious belief. As Justice Powell wrote in his concurrence to Edwards v. Aguillard: "A decision respecting the subject matter to be taught in public schools does not violate the Establishment Clause simply because the material to be taught 'happens to coincide or harmonize with the tenets of some or all religions.'"72 According to Powell, interference by the federal courts in the decisions of local and state educational officials is justified "only when the purpose for their decisions is clearly religious."73

The second part of the test identifies religion with a comprehensive belief system "as opposed to an isolated teaching."74 Design theory does not offer a theory of morality or metaphysics, or an opinion on the prospects for an afterlife. It requires neither a belief in divine revelation nor a code of conduct; nor does it purport to uncover the underlying meaning of the universe or to confer inviolable knowledge on its adherents. It is simply a theory about the source of the appearance of design in living organisms. It is a clear example of an "isolated teaching," one that has no necessary connections to any spiritual dogma or church institution. Design theory has no religious pretensions. It simply tries to apply a well-established scientific method to the analysis of biological phenomena.

The third part of the test concerns the "presence of certain formal and external signs."75 The court provided a list of such signs, including liturgy, clergy, and observance of holidays. Obviously, design theory has none of these-no sacred texts; no ordained ministers, priests, or religious teachers; no "design theory liturgies"; no holidays; and no institutional structures like those of religious groups. Design theorists have formed organizations and institutes, but these resemble other academic or professional associations rather than churches or religious institutions.76

According to the court's three-part test, design theory should not be classified as religion. To say that, however, is not to suggest that it has no religious implications. Design theory argues that a designing intelligence is responsible for the complex, information-rich structures of biology. Students who believe in God as creator may therefore find support for their faith from design theory and identify the designing intelligence responsible for biological complexity with the God of their religious belief. Alternatively, students with no religious convictions may find that design theory leads them to ask theological questions and to inquire into the identity of the designing intelligence responsible for biological complexity.

This potential for religious extrapolation, however, does not make design theory a religious doctrine. Nor is this potential unique to design theory. It applies equally to Darwinism. Darwinism, which holds that life originated and evolved via an undirected natural process, implies that common religious beliefs about the origin and purpose of human life are, if not false, then implausible. Indeed, a host of prominent neo-Darwinian scientists and social thinkers-from Douglas Futuyma to William Provine to Stephen Jay Gould-have insisted that Darwinism has made traditional beliefs about God and humanity untenable. Consider the following statements by Gould:

"Biology took away our status as paragons created in the image of God. . . ."77

"Before Darwin, we thought that a benevolent God had created us."78

"Why do humans exist? . . . I do not think that any 'higher' answer can be given. . . . We are the offspring of history, and must establish our own paths in this most diverse and interesting of conceivable universes-one indifferent to our suffering, and therefore offering us maximal freedom to thrive, or to fail, in our own chosen way."79

Contrary to the popular "just-the-facts" stereotype of science, many scientific theories have larger ideological and religious implications. Origins theories in particular have unavoidable philosophical and religious overtones. Theories about where the universe, life, and humanity came from invariably affect our perspectives about human nature, morality, and beliefs about ultimate reality. As many prominent evolutionary biologists have made clear, neo-Darwinian evolutionary theory does not maintain strict neutrality on such questions.

Darwinism (in both its classical and contemporary versions) insists that living systems organized themselves into increasingly complex structures without assistance from a guiding intelligence. Chemical evolutionary theorists likewise insist that the first life arose from brute chemistry. The Oxford zoologist Richard Dawkins has dubbed this the "blind watchmaker" thesis. He and other leading evolutionary theorists claim that biological evidence overwhelmingly supports this purposeless and fully materialistic account of creation. Thus George Gaylord Simpson, the leading neo-Darwinist a generation back, could claim: "Man is the result of a purposeless and natural process that did not have him in mind. He was not planned."80

Accordingly, many major biology texts present evolution as a process in which a purposeful intelligence (such as God) plays no detectable role. As Miller and Levine put it, evolution process is "random and undirected" and occurs "without plan or purpose."81 Some texts even state that Darwin's theory has profoundly negative implications for theism, and especially for its belief in the purposeful design of nature. As Douglas Futuyma's biology text puts it: "By coupling the undirected, purposeless variations to the blind, uncaring process of natural selection, Darwin made the theological or spiritual explanations of the life processes superfluous."82

The content of a scientific theory, and not its implications, determines its legal status in public school science classrooms. Otherwise, the anti-theistic implications of neo-Darwinism (as articulated by some of its chief advocates) would disqualify it from inclusion in the curriculum. Obviously, such an outcome is unthinkable. Yet, if the implications, rather than the specific content, of neo-Darwinism and design theory were at issue, then arguably neither theory could pass constitutional muster. This result would not only undercut science education, but also violate constitutional precedents. One of the few fixed points in Establishment Clause jurisprudence during the last half-century has been that incidental harmonies with religious practices and beliefs do not disqualify secular concepts under the First Amendment.83

5. *EDWARDS V. AGUILLARD*

The U.S. Supreme Court has ruled that educators and school officials may include non-Darwinian scientific theories alongside Darwinism in the science curriculum of public schools. The principal case in which the Court addressed the teaching of origins in the public schools is *Edwards v. Aguillard.* The background of this case is as follows. In the early 1980s creationists in Louisiana sought to introduce scientific creationism into the Louisiana public school system. As a result, the Louisiana legislature passed a law titled the "Balanced Treatment for Creation-Science and Evolution-Science in Public School Instruction Act."84 The Act did not require teaching either creationism or evolution, but did require that when one theory was taught, the other theory had to be taught as well.85

Several parents and concerned citizens challenged the constitutionality of the Act in Federal Court.86 They argued that the Act violated the First Amendment's Establishment Clause, which prohibits the government from officially endorsing a religious belief.87 The State responded that the Act did not violate the First Amendment because it had the legitimate secular purpose of strengthening and broadening the academic freedom of teachers.88 The district court and the Court of Appeals for the Fifth Circuit, however, found that the State's actual purpose was to promote the religious doctrine of scientific creationism (known also as creation science).89 The Supreme Court granted certiorari and heard arguments by both sides.90 On June 19, 1987 the Court issued its ruling in the case.91

The Court, in a majority opinion written by Justice Brennan, ruled that the Act constituted an unconstitutional infringement on the Establishment Clause of the First Amendment,92 based on the Lemon test.93 This test, which was first enunciated by the Court in *Lemon v. Kurtzman,*94 consists of three prongs:

- ◆ The government's action must not promote a particular religion or religious view;
- ◆ The government's action must not have the primary effect of either advancing or inhibiting religion; and

- The government's action must not result in an "excessive entanglement" of the government and religion.95

If any of these three prongs is violated, the government's action is deemed unconstitutional under the Establishment Clause.96 The first of these prongs has become known as the "purpose prong." The Court found that the Act violated the purpose prong and was therefore unconstitutional.97 The Court did not consider whether the second and third prongs were also violated.

The Court ruled that government intention to promote religion is clear "when the State enacts a law to serve a religious purpose."98 Since the legislative history of the Act constantly referenced the religious views of the legislators, the Court became suspicious of the State's claim that the Act supported academic freedom.99 The Court found that the intent of the legislator who drafted the Act was to narrow the science curriculum in order to favor a particular religious belief (i.e., scientific creationism).100 In support of this finding the Court noted that the Act's sponsor actually preferred that "neither [creationism nor evolution] be taught."101 The Court therefore concluded that the Act undermined both academic freedom and science education.102

The Court also found that the Act did not grant teachers any new flexibility in teaching science that they did not already possess.103 The Court noted that no Louisiana law barred the teaching of any scientific theory about biological origins.104 Thus, since teachers were already free to teach scientific alternatives to Darwinian evolution, the Court reasoned that the Act did not expand the academic freedom already enjoyed by teachers in Louisiana.105

Having rejected the State's reason for the Act, the Court then uncovered what it regarded as the true intent of the Louisiana law: the promotion of a particular religious view. The Court found that the Act had a "discriminatory preference" for the teaching of creationism because it required the production of curriculum guides for creationism.106 Further, it found that only creationism was protected by certain sections of the Act, and that the Act undercut truly comprehensive science instruction by limiting the theories of origins to be taught to only two: evolution and creationism.107 To sum up, the Act directed public resources to the teaching of a religious doctrine (creationism) in the science curriculum of public schools; at the same time, the Act discriminated against other scientific theories of biological origins.

In deciding against the Act, the Court was careful to point out that its decision in nowise excluded the teaching of other theories about biological origins. Likewise, the Court left the door open to scientific critiques of evolution.108 In an illuminating section of the majority opinion, the Court even stated that teaching a variety of scientific theories about origins "might be validly done with the clear secular intent of enhancing the effectiveness of science instruction."109 This intent, however, was not present in the Act because the primary purpose of the State's action was to promote a particular religious doctrine, thereby violating the Establishment Clause.

The Court even went so far as to assert that academic freedom requires that alternative theories about origins be permitted in public school science classrooms.110 In particular, academic freedom includes a science teacher's right to teach scientific alternatives to the dominant Darwinian approach to biological origins.111 As a legitimate scientific theory about biological origins and development, design theory passes every test set by the Court for inclusion in public school science curricula.

Nothing in the Supreme Court's decision in Edwards forces local school districts, the states, or the federal government to bar teaching about design theory.112 The Court explicitly stated in *Edwards* that it is constitutionally lawful for teachers and school boards to expose students to the scientific problems with current Darwinian theory as well as to any scientific alternatives.113 In *Edwards v. Aguillard,* far from placing its *imprimatur* on Darwinism, the Supreme Court actually defended the principle of openness in science education.114

6. DESIGN AND SCIENTIFIC CREATIONISM

Against the clear precedent of *Edwards v. Aguillard,* some critics of design theory cite *Edwards* to support the exclusion of design from public schools. They charge that design theory is indistinguishable from scientific creationism-that it is just another name for scientific creationism. And since (as we've just seen) the Supreme Court's decision in *Edwards* disallows scientific creationism in the public school science classroom, they argue that design theory must be excluded as well.

On the contrary, design theory and scientific creationism differ in propositional content, method of inquiry, and, thus, in legal status. Recall that in *Edwards* the Court decided against the legality of scientific creationism because it constituted an advancement of religion. The court reached this decision in large part because the propositional content of scientific creationism closely mirrors the creation narrative in the book of *Genesis.*115 While philosophers of science now agree that the scientific status of an idea does not depend upon its source, the Court has held that the legal status of an idea-and therefore the legal status of any curriculum based on that idea-does depend on its source. Thus, given the court's reasoning in *Edwards,* the teaching of scientific creationism remains legally problematic.

Nevertheless, the court's decision does not apply to design theory because design theory is not based on a religious text or doctrine. Design theory begins with the data that scientists observe in the laboratory and nature, and attempts to explain them based on what we know about the patterns that generally indicate intelligent causes. For design theorists, the conclusion of design constitutes an inference from biological data, not a deduction from religious authority.

Furthermore, the propositional content of design theory differs significantly from that of scientific creationism. Scientific creationism is committed to the following propositions:116

- There was a sudden creation of the universe, energy, and life from nothing.
- Mutations and natural selection are insufficient to bring about the development of all living kinds from a single organism.
- Changes of the originally created kinds of plants and animals occur only within fixed limits.
- There is a separate ancestry for humans and apes.
- The earth's geology can be explained via catastrophism, primarily by the occurrence of a worldwide flood.
- The earth and living kinds had a relatively recent inception (on the order of ten thousand years).

These six tenets taken jointly define scientific creationism for legal purposes. The Court in *Edwards* ruled that taken jointly this group of propositions may not be taught in public school science classrooms. (Nevertheless, the Court left the door open to some of these tenets being discussed individually.117)

Design theory, on the other hand, asserts the following:

- High information content (or specified complexity) and irreducible complexity constitute strong indicators or hallmarks of past intelligent design.
- Biological systems have a high information content (or specified complexity) and utilize subsystems that manifest irreducible complexity.
- Naturalistic mechanisms or undirected causes do not suffice to explain the origin of information (specified complexity) or irreducible complexity.
- Therefore, intelligent design constitutes the best explanation for the origin of information and irreducible complexity in biological systems.

A comparison of these two lists demonstrates clearly that design theory and scientific creationism differ markedly in content. Clearly, then, they do not derive from the same source. Thus, the Court's ruling in *Edwards* does not apply to design theory and can provide no grounds for excluding discussion of design from the public school science curriculum.

7. VIEWPOINT DISCRIMINATION

Often school board members privately support teaching alternatives to Darwinism, whether because they themselves entertain doubts about Darwinism or because parents urge them to permit alternative theories. As soon as they publicly support exposing students to the scientific challenges to Darwinism, however, these same school board members are often intimidated by the threat of lawsuit. Maintaining the status quo by leaving Darwinism unchallenged therefore appears to them the safest course, even if it undercuts the science curriculum. Nevertheless, as public officials have learned from Lamb's Chape1118 and Rosenberger,119 discrimination from a misplaced fear over the Establishment Clause can be even more risky than permitting a diversity of viewpoints.

The Supreme Court has ruled that the First Amendment prohibits the government from regulating speech based on "its substantive content or the message it conveys."120 Accordingly, it is unconstitutional under the Free Speech Clause of the First Amendment to exclude ideas from a public forum simply because of the content of those ideas. The Court has strongly affirmed this principle in several opinions,121 addressing issues as diverse as civil rights meetings,122 the funding of a religiously-based student publication at a public university,123 and the use of a public school auditorium by a religious group to show a film.124

In its most recent case on viewpoint discrimination-*Rosenberger v. Rector and Visitors of the University of Virginia*125-the Supreme Court held that unduly restricting others out of a misplaced fear of violating the Establishment Clause is itself unconstitutiona1.126 Rosenberger, a student at a state university, objected to the university's refusal to grant his organization's newspaper the same financial subsidy that had been granted to other campus organizations.127 The university defended its policy by citing the newspaper's evangelical Protestant perspective. The university held that any funding of the paper would constitute an endorsement of religion and thus be unconstitutiona1.128 The Supreme Court rejected this argument, holding that if a public institution opens a forum for free speech, it cannot then censor the forum based solely on the content of the speech expressed.129

The Court noted that viewpoint discrimination is rightly "presumed to be unconstitutional."130 Nevertheless, when the government itself targets speech simply because of its content, "the violation of the First Amendment is all the more blatant."131 Consequently, the Court found that the government must "abstain" from content-based speech restrictions when the "ideology or the opinion or perspective of the speaker is the rationale for the restriction."132 The Court affirmed that the government must abstain from content-based suppression of speech even when the public forum where the speech occurs was created by the government in the first place.133

The Court's position on viewpoint discrimination allows two exceptions. First, the government may control access to a non-public forum based "on subject matter and speaker identity" if the government's action is reasonable given the forum's purpose and if the action is viewpoint neutral.134 This means that the government can suppress speech in a non-public forum if the speaker wants to discuss "a topic not encompassed within the purpose of the forum,"135 or the speaker is outside of the special class for whom the forum was created.136 Second, if the government is charged with viewpoint discrimination, it can clear itself of that charge by showing that to permit the speech in question would violate the Establishment Clause.137

Neither of these exceptions applies to the teaching of design theory. The overwhelming majority of public schools address the subject of biological origins in their science curricula. Thus, for public schools or other governmental agencies to bar the teaching of design theory-which clearly addresses that topic-undermines the right to free speech.138 While it is true that the courts have limited the free speech rights of teachers in the public school context,139 the Constitution's free speech provisions still apply behind school doors.140 When public schools censor a scientific theory like design theory, they discriminate against both students and teachers by unfairly depriving them of the opportunity to examine the full range of scientific theories about biological origins.

The First Amendment prohibits the government from interfering with people's right to free speech.141 Teachers have the right to present material that is appropriate to the subject they are teaching. Likewise, students have the right to be exposed to material that is appropriate to the subject they are studying.142 Further, the Supreme Court has found that teachers, students, and parents have a "liberty interest" under the Fourteenth Amendment's Due Process Clause not to be prohibited from studying certain subjects.143 A critical aspect of this liberty interest is academic freedom. Academic freedom allows teachers to present appropriate material to their students without fear of censorship or retribution from the government. Academic freedom is essential not only for teachers to teach effectively, but also for students to explore and develop new ideas. Without academic freedom, education becomes indoctrination.

The Supreme Court recognized this fundamental right to academic freedom in *Epperson v. Arkansas.*144 In that case, the court struck down an Arkansas statute that restricted the teaching of biological origins.145 The statute prohibited, with criminal sanction, the teaching of evolution in the public schools of that state.146 It was challenged by a teacher who claimed that the statute violated her academic freedom.147 The Supreme Court, in rejecting the Arkansas law as unconstitutional, strongly upheld the academic freedom of teachers in public schools.148

The Court found that the First Amendment's guarantees apply to our school systems, where it is "essential to safeguard the fundamental values of freedom of speech and inquiry and of belief."149 Quoting *Keyishian v. Board of Regents,* the Court made clear that "the First Amendment 'does not tolerate laws that cast a pall of orthodoxy over the classroom.'"150 Most significantly, the Court found that the government's power to determine school curricula does not give it the power to prevent "the teaching of a scientific theory or doctrine where the prohibition is based upon reasons that violate the First Amendment."151 The same freedoms that apply to teaching students about Darwinian evolution apply with equal force to teaching them about design theory.

8. THE AUTHORITY OF THE LOCAL SCHOOL BOARD

Until recently, Darwinian evolution has monopolized the teaching of biological origins in public schools. Yet with the accumulation of increasingly persuasive evidence for design theory, as well as a more careful reflection on the nature of science itself, the basis for excluding alternative theories has evaporated. Thus, when science teachers seek to present design theory to their students to provide a more thorough treatment of biological origins, school officials need to make every effort not only to encourage them but also to assure that they are not subjected to unwarranted legal or social intimidation. Indeed, the exclusion of design theory from public school science curricula may constitute a form of viewpoint discrimination that not only undermines academic freedom but also violates the First Amendment's Free Speech Clause.152

Traditionally, local school boards have exercised broad discretion in deciding what subjects and materials are appropriate for inclusion within the curriculum of public schools. This discretion extends to the origins issue. The Supreme Court has repeatedly upheld the freedom of school boards to exercise discretion in the selection of curriculum materials.153 For instance, Justice Powell, in his concurrence to *Edwards,* stressed that the Court's decision in no way restricted the traditional rights of school boards and other local public education officials to set the curriculum:

[N]othing in the Court's opinion diminishes the traditionally broad discretion accorded state and local school officials in the selection of the public school curriculum.154

The freedom of school boards to determine what can be included in their curricula is a long-established prerogative. No Supreme Court decision about biological origins has questioned this freedom. In fact, the Court has upheld the principle that a school board has the right to decide what subjects will be taught in its schools, and within broad limits, how those subjects are to be taught. This is not to say there are no limits to the local school boards' discretion. Those limits, however, are designed to prevent the discriminatory exclusion of viewpoints-not to inhibit the teaching of a full range of scientific theories. Thus, the question is not whether school boards have the freedom to include design theory in the science curriculum of the public schools, but whether there is a valid reason to exclude it.

The Supreme Court has ruled that school boards do not enjoy unlimited power to exclude ideas from the classroom and school libraries. In *Board of Education, Island Trees Union Free School District v. Pico*155 a local school board had removed several books from its public school library system.156 When this exclusion was challenged, Justice Brennan, writing for the Court, stated that local school boards cannot remove books from the public school library merely because the school board disagrees with the ideological content of those books. Brennan wrote:

[J]ust as access to ideas makes it possible for citizens generally to exercise their rights to free speech and press in a meaningful manner, such access prepares students for active participation in the pluralistic, often contentious society in which they will soon be adult members.157

Schools cannot, by removing material from their libraries, enforce an orthodoxy prescribing the ideas that can and cannot be presented to students.158 The students' unimpeded access to ideas is critical if they are to succeed in an open society where ideas are discussed and disputed.159 If a school board fails to provide students with reasonable access to ideas, it fails to perform one of its most crucial functions. The Court distinctly denies school boards the right to suppress ideas.

To summarize, the safest course is one in which a school board permits a biology teacher to teach the full range of scientific theories about origins. In doing so, the board would be following the specific guidance issued in *Edwards v. Aguillard,* as well as upholding the more general efforts of the Court to avoid viewpoint discrimination. On the other hand, a school board that rejects a teacher's effort to teach the full range of scientific theories would place the board on a collision course with the First Amendment. Such a board sets itself the impossible task of specifying precisely what the teacher would be forbidden to teach: Is it only the theory of intelligent design, or does the prohibition also include the evidence upon which the theory is based? May the teacher introduce evidence that contradicts Darwinian expectations? In a misguided effort to avoid litigation, a school board might very well create its own minefield of illogical and unenforceable guidelines. Instead, we suggest, the school board should encourage the biology teacher to teach the controversy. This approach not only helps a science curriculum fulfill its scientific objectives, but also provides it with the soundest footing from a legal standpoint.

9. CONCLUSION

Local school boards and state education officials are frequently pressured to avoid teaching the controversy regarding biological origins. Indeed, many groups, such as the National Academy of Sciences, go so far as to deny the existence of any genuine scientific controversy about the issue.160 Nevertheless, teachers should be reassured that they have the right to expose their students to the problems as well as the appeal of Darwinian theory. Moreover, as the previous discussion demonstrates, school boards have the authority to permit, and even encourage, teaching about design theory as an alternative to Darwinian evolution-and this includes the use of textbooks such as *Of Pandas and People* that present evidence for the theory of intelligent design.

The controlling legal authority, the Supreme Court's decision in *Edwards v. Aguillard,* explicitly permits the inclusion of alternatives to Darwinian evolution so long as those alternatives are based on scientific evidence and not motivated by strictly religious concerns. Since design theory is based on scientific evidence rather than religious assumptions, it clearly meets this test. Including discussions of design in the science curriculum thus serves an important goal of making education inclusive, rather than exclusionary. In addition, it provides students with an important demonstration of the best way for them as future scientists and citizens to resolve scientific controversies-by a careful and fair-minded examination of the evidence.

References and Appendix omitted

Appendix D: References

The following is a list of the references used in the construction of this book. Sources cited in multiple chapters are listed only once. Where there are multiple authors, I have listed the first two. Citations in boldface refer to the figures used in the text. Please forgive any misspellings or omissions.

Scope of the Problem

Baker Col SL Drug abuse in the United States Army. Bulletin NY Accad Med 1971 47:541–9

Berk E Black J et al Traumatogenicity: effects of self reported noncombat trauma on MMPIs of male Vietnam combat and noncombat veterans treated for substance abuse. J Clin Psychol 1989 45:704–8

Brown Capt D, Belland Cdr KM Performance Maintenance During Continuous Flight Operations, a guide for flight surgeons. Naval Strike and Air Warfare Center 1 Jan 2000

Cook RF Hostetter RS Patterns of illicit drug use in the Army. AM J Psychiatry 1975 132:1013–17

Couper FJ Pemberton M et al Prevalence of drug use in commercial interstate tractor trailer drivers. J Forensic Sci 2002 47:562–7

Cunningham JK, Liu LM Impact of federal ephedrine and pseudoephedrine regulations on methamphetamine related hospital admissions. Addiction 2003 98:1177–9

Davidson JR Kudler HS et al Symptom and comorbidity patterns in World War II and Vietnam veterans with post traumatic stress disorder. Compr. Psychiatry 1990 31:162–70

Drummer OH Gerostamoulos J et al The incidence of drugs in drivers killed in Australian road traffic crashes. Forensic Sci. Int. 2003 134:154–62

Emonson DL Vanderbeek RD The use of amphetamines in the U.S. Air Force tactical operations during Desert Shield and Storm. Aviation Space and Environmental Med 1995 66:260–3

Giam GC Effects of sleep deprivation with reference to military operations. 1997 Ann Acad Med 26:88–93

Gibson DR Leamon MH et al Epidemiology and public health consequences of methamphetamine use in California's Central Valley. J Psychoactive Drugs 2002 34:313–9

Gonzalez CF Barrington EH et al Cocaine and methamphetamine: differential addiction rates. Psychol Addict Behav 2000 14:390–6

Heston L, Heston R *The Medical Case Book of Adolph Hitler* Stein and Day 1980

Hyar L Leach P et al Hidden PTSD in substance abuse inpatients among Vietnam veterans. J Subst Abuse Treat 1991 8:213

Jenlinek JM Williams T Post traumatic stress disorder and substance abuse in Vietnam combat veterans: treatment problems, strategies and recommendations. J Subst Abuse Treat 1984 1:87–97

Johnson DR Fontana A Long term course of treatment seeking Vietnam veterans with post traumatic stress disorder: mortality, clinical condition, and life satisfaction. J Nerv Ment Dis 2004 192:35–41

Johnson LD, O'Malley PM et al 2002 Monitoring the Future national results on adolescent drug use: an overview of key findings 2001. National Institute of Drug Abuse, Bethesda MD [NIH Pub No. 02–5105]

Keane TM Gerardi RJ et al The interrelationship of substance abuse and posttraumatic stress disorder: epidemiologic and clinical considerations. Recent Dev Alcohol 1988 6:27–48

McFall ME, Mackay PW et al Combat-related posttraumatic stress disorder and severity of substance abuse in Vietnam veterans. J Stud Alcohol 1992:53:357–63

O'Brien CP Nace EP et al Follow up of Vietnam veterans. I Relapse to drug use after Vietnam service. Drug Alcohol Depend 1980 5:333–40

Price RK Risk NK et al Remission from drug abuse over a 25 year period: patterns of remission and treatment use. Am J Public Health 2001 91:1107–13

Redlich F *Hitler: Diagnosis of a Destructive Prophet* Oxford University Press 1998

Robbins LN Davis HD et al Drug use by US Army enlisted men in Vietnam: a followup on their return home. Am J Epidemiology 1974 99:235–49

Robbins LN Helzer JE et al Narcotic use in Southeast Asia and afterward: an interview study of 898 Vietnam returnees. Arch Gen Psychiatry 1975 32:955–61

Sommers I Baskin D *The Social Consequences of Methamphetamine Use* Edwin Mellel Press 2004

Stanton MD Drugs, Vietnam, and the Vietnam veteran: an overview. Am J Drug and Alcohol Abuse 1976 3:557–70

Yager T Laufer R et al Some problems associated with war experience in men of the Vietnam generation. Arch Gen Psychiatry 1984 41:327–33

Yudko E, Hall HV *Methamphetamine Use: Clinical and Forensic Aspects* CRC Press 2002

ANATOMY

Cardinal RN Pennicott DR et al Impulsive choice induced in rats by lesions of the nucleus accumbens core. Science 2001 292:2499–501

Christoff GR Leonzio RJ Wilcox KS Stimulation of the lateral habenula inhibits dopamine containing neurons in the substantia nigra and ventral tegmental area of the rat. Journal Neuroscience 6:613–619 1986

Cooper JR Bloom FE *The Biochemical Basis of Neuropharmacology* [Eighth Edition] Oxford University Press 2003

Ellison G. Continuous Amphetamine and Cocaine Have Similar Neurotoxic Effects in Lateral Habenular Nucleus and Fasciculus Retroflexus. Brain Research 1992 598:353–356.

Felton TM Linton L First and second order maternal behavior related afferents of the lateral habenula. Neuroreport 1999 10:883–7

Felton TM Linton L Intact neurons of the lateral habenular nucleus are necessary for the hormonal, pup mediated display of maternal behavior in sensitized virgin female rats. Behav Neurosci 1998 112:1458–65

Kalivas PW and Duffy P J Dopamine D1 receptors modulate glutamate transmission in the ventral tegmental area. Neurosci 1995 15:5379–88

Lett BT Repeated exposures intensify rather than diminish the rewarding effects of amphetamine, morphine, and cocaine. Psychopharmacology 1989 98:357–62

Nestler E J Hyman SE, and Malenka R C *Molecular Neuropharmacology A foundation for clinical neuroscience* McGraw-Hill 2001

Nudo RJ Plautz EJ Frost SB Role of adaptive plasticity in recovery of function after damage to motor cortex. Muscle Nerve 2001 24:1000–9

Pirot S Godbout R Inhibitory effects of ventral tegmental area stimulation on the activity of prefrontal cortical neurons: evidence for the involvement of both dopaminergic and GABAergic components. 1992 Neuroscience 49: 857–65

Von Bohlen und Halbach O Dermietzel R *Neurotransmitters and Neuromodulators Handbook of Receptors and Biological Effects* Wiley-VCH 2002

METH

Acikgoz O The effects of a single dose of methamphetamine on lipid peroxidation levels in the rat striatum and prefrontal cortex. Euro Neuropsychopharmacol 2000 10 [5] 415–8

Akiyama K, Suemaru J Effect of acute and chronic administration of methamphetamine calcium-calmodulin dependent protein kinase II activity in the rat brain. Ann N Y Accad Sci 2000 914:263–74

Amano T Matsubayashi H, et al Repeated administration of methamphetamine causes hypersensitivity of D2 receptor in rat ventral tegmental area. Neuroscience Letters 347 [2003] 89–92

Baptista T Teneud L et al Effects of acute and chronic lithium treatment on amphetamine induced dopamine increases in the nucleus accumbens and prefrontal cortex in rats as studied by microdialysis. J Neural Transm Gen Sect 1993 94:75–89

Battaglia G, Fornai F, Letizia Busceti C Alpha IB adrenergic receptor knockout mice are protected against methamphetamine toxicity. J Neurochemistry [2003] 86:413–421

Baumann MH Phillips JM Preclinical evaluation of GBR12909 decanoate as a long acting medication for methamphetamine dependence. Ann N Y Acad Sci 2002 965:92–108

Bittner SE, Wagner GC et al Effects of a high-dose treatment of methamphetamine on caudate dopamine and anorexia in rats. Pharmocol Biochem Behav.1981 14:481–86

Cadet JL, Jayanthi S et al Temporal profiling of methamphetamine induced changes in gene expression in the mouse brain: evidence from cDNA array. Synapse 2001 412:40–8

Chen CK Lin SK et al Premorbid characteristics and co-morbidity of methamphetamine users with and without psychosis. J Psychol Med 2003 33:1407–14

Conant K St Hillaire C et al HIV virus type 1 Tat and methamphetamine affect the release and activation of matrix-degrading proteinases. J Neurovirol 2004 10:21–8

Cubells JF Raypot S et al Meth neurotoxicity involves vacuolization of endocytic organelles and dopamine dependent intracellular oxidative stress. J Neuroscience 1994 14:2260–71

Deng X, Jayanthi S et al Mice with partial deficiency of Jun show attenuation of meth induced neuronal apoptosis. Mol Pharmacol 2002 62:993–1000

Dwoskin LP Crooks PA A novel mechanism of action and potential use for lobeline as a treatment for psychostimulant abuse. Biochem Pharmacol 2002 63:89–98

Ernst T Chang L et al Evidence for long term neurotoxicity associated with methamphetamine abuse: a 1H MRS study. Neurology 2000 54[6] 1344–9

Flora G Lee YW et al Methamphetamine induced TNF alpha gene expression and activation of AP-1 in discrete regions of mouse brain: potential role of reactive oxygen intermediates and lipid peroxidation. Neuromolecular Med 2002 2:71–85

Fornai F Lazzeri G et al Amphetamines induce ubiquitin positive inclusions within striatal cells. Neurol Sci 2003 24:182–3

Fornai F, Lenzi P et al Methamphetamine produces neuronal inclusions on the nigrostriatal system and in PC12 cells. J Neurochem 2004 88:114–123

Goldberg JF Garno JL A history of substance abuse complicates remission from acute mania in bipolar disorder. J Clin Psychiatry 1999 60:733–40

Goldstein RZ and Volkow ND The orbitofrontal cortex in methamphetamine addiction: involvement in fear. Neuroreport 2002 13:2253–7

Gough B, Imam S Comparative effects of substituted amphetamines on monoamines in rat caudate a microdialysis study. Ann NY Acad Sci 2002 965:410–20

Guilarte TR Is meth abuse a risk factor for Parkinsonism? Neurotoxicology 2001 22:725–731

Guilarte TR Nihei MK et al Methamphetamine induced deficits of brain monoaminergic neuronal markers: distal axotomy or neuronal plasticity. Neuroscience 2003 122:499–513

Halasz AS Palfi M et al Altered nitric oxide production in mouse brain after administration of 1 methyl 4 phenyl- 1236 tretrahydro-pyridin or methamphetamine. Neurochem Int 2004 44:641–6

Itzhak Y Gandia C et al Resistance of neuronal nitric oxide synthetase deficient mice to meth induced dopaminergic neurotoxicity. J Pharmacol Exp Ther 1998 284:1040–1047

Iyo M Namba H Abnormal cerebral perfusion in chronic methamphetamine abusers: a study using 99MTc-HMPAO and SPECT. Prog Neuropsychopharmacol Biol Psychiatry 1997 21:789–96

Jovanovski D Zakzanis KK Donepezil in a chronic drug user—a potential treatment? Hum Psychopharmacol 2003 18:561–4

Kantac KM Vaccines against drugs of abuse: a viable treatment option? Drugs 2003 63:341–52

Kita T Wagner GC Nakashima T Current research on methamphetamine induced neurotoxicity: animal models of monoamine disruption. J Pharmacol Sci 2003 92:178–95

Kita T Wagner G, Naklashima T J Current research of methamphetamine induced neurotoxicity. Pharmacol. Sci 2003 92:178–195 2003

Kita T Matsunari Y et al Meth induced striatal dopamine release, behavioral changes and neurotoxicity in BALB/c mice. Int J Dev Neurosci 2000 18:521–530

Lansia AJ Williams EA et al Vulnerabilities of ventral mesencephalic neurons projecting to the nucleus accumbens following infusions of 6 hydroxydopamine into the medial forebrain bundle in the rat. Brain Res 2004 997:119–27

LaVoie MJ Hastings TG Peroxynitrite and nitrate induced oxidation of dopamine: implications for nitric oxide in dopaminergic cell loss. J of Neurochem 1999 73:2546–54

Lee Y Hamamura T et al The effect of lithium on methamphetamine induced regional Fos protein expression in the rat brain. Neuroreport 1999 10:895–900

Lee Y Hamamura T et al Carbamazepine suppresses methamphetamine induced Fos expression in a regionally specific manner in the rat brain. Possible neural substrates responsible for antimanic effects of mood stabilizers. Neuropsychopharmacol 2000 22:530–7

Levi MS Borne RF A review of chemical agents in the pharmacotherapy of addiction. Curr Med Chem 2002 9:1807–18

London ED Simon SL et al Mood disturbances and regional cerebral metabolic abnormalities in recently abstinent methamphetamine abusers. Arch Gen Psychiatry 2004 61:73–84

Matsuzaki H Namikawa K et al Brain derived neurotrophic factor rescues neuronal death induced by methamphetamine. Biol Psychiatry 2004 55:52–60

Matuszewich L Yamamoto BK Chronic stress augments the long term and acute effects of methamphetamine. Neuroscience 2004 124:637–46

McCabe RT Hanson GR et al Meth induced reduction on D1 and D2 dopamine receptors as evidenced by autoradiography comparison with tyrosine hydroxylase activity. Neuroscience 1987 23:253–61

McCann U Ricuarte GA Amphetamine neurotoxicity: accomplishments and remaining challenges. Neuroscience and Behavioral Reviews 2004 27:821–26

McQuade R Sharp T Release of cerebral 5 hydroxytryptamine evoked by electrical stimulation of the dorsal and median raphe nuclei: effect of a neurotoxic amphetamine. Neuroscience 1995 68:1079–88

Melega WP Larean AF et al Ethological and 6-fluro L dopa pet profiles of long term vulnerability to chronic amphetamine. Brain Res 1997 84:259–68

Namima M Sugihara K et al Quantitative analysis of the effects of lithium on the reverse tolerance and the c-Fos expression induced by methamphetamine in mice. Brain Res PRotoc 1999 4:11–18

Newton TF Kalechstein AD et al Association between quantitative EEG and neuro recognition in methamphetamine dependent volunteers. Clin Neurophysiology 2004 115:194–8

Nordahl TE, Salo R et al Low N-acetyl aspartate and high choline in the anterior cingulum of recently abstinent methamphetamine dependent subjects: a preliminary proton MRS study. Psychiatry Rees 2002 116:43–52

Park SU and Ferrer JV et al Peroxynitrite inactivates the human dopamine transporter by modification of cysteine 342: potential mechanism of neurotoxicity in dopamine neurons. J Neuroscience 2002 22:4399–405

Paulus MP Hozack NE et al Behavioral and functional neuroimaging evidence for prefrontal dysfunction on methamphetamine dependent subjects. Neuropsychopharmacology 2002 26:52–63

Paulus MP Hozack N Decision making by methamphetamine dependent subjects is associated with error rate independent decrease in prefrontal and parietal activation. Biol Psychiatry 2003 53:65–74

Piasecki MP Steinagel GM et al An exploratory study: the use of paroxentine for methamphetamine craving. J Psychoactive Drugs 2002 34:301–4

Pennypacker KR, Yang X et al Long term induction of Fos related antigen 2 after methamphetamine, methylenedioxymethamphetamine, 1 methyl 4 phenyl 1,2,3, 6 tertahydropyridine and trimethyltin induced brain injury. Neuroscience 2000 101:913–9

Prince JA Oreland L Mitochondrial activity in the mapping of functional brain changes in schizophrenia. Restor Neurol Neurosci 1998 12:185–93

Sabol KE Roach JT et al Long term effects of a high dose methamphetamine regimen on subsequent methamphetamine induced dopamine release in vivo. Brain Res 2001 892:122–9

Salo R Nordahl TE Preliminary evidence of reduced cognitive inhibition in methamphetamine dependent individuals. Psychiatry Res 2002 111:65–74

Schroder N O'Dell SJ et al Neurotoxic methamphetamine regimen severely impairs recognition memory in rats. Synapse 2003 49:89–96

Segal DS Kuczenski R An escalating dose "binge" model of amphetamine psychosis: behavioral and neurochemical characteristics. J Neurosci 1997 17:2551–66

Seiden LS Oglesby MW Catecholamines and drug behavior interactions. Fed Proc 1975 43:1823–31,

Seiden LS, Vosner G Formation of 6-hydroxydopamine in caudate nucleus of the rat brain after a single large dose of methylamphetamine. Pharmocol Biochem Behav. 1984 21:29–31

Sekine Y Iyo M et al Methamphetamine related psychiatric symptoms and reduced brain dopamine transporters studied with PET. AM J Psychiatry 2001 158:1206–14

Sekine Y Minabe Y Association of dopamine transporter loss in the orbitofrontal and dorsolateral prefrontal cortices with methamphetamine related psychiatric symptoms. Am J Psychiatry 2003 160: 1699–701

Shoblock JR and Maisonneuve IM Glick SD Differences between d-methamphetamine and d-amphetamine in rats: working memory, tolerance, and extinction. Psychopharmacology 2003 170:150–6

Simon SL Dacey J et al The effect of relapse on cognition in abstinent methamphetamine abusers. J Subst Abuse Treat 2004 27:59–66

Soderstrom H Hultin L et al Reduced frontotemporal perfusion in psychopathic personality. Psychiatry Res 2002 114:81–94

Sokolov BP Schindler CW et al Chronic methamphetamine increases fighting in mice. Pharmaocol Biochem Behav 2004 77:319–26

Smith DF Central and peripheral effects of lithium on amphetamine induced hyperactivity in rats. Pharmacol Biochem Behav 1981 14:439–42

Stefanski R Justinova Z et al Sigma 1 receptor upregulation after chronic methamphetamine self administration in rats: a study with yoked controls. Psychopharmacol 2004 173: Mar 17 e-pub

Suemaru J Akiyama K et al Methamphetamine decreases calcium calmodulin dependent protein kinase II activity in discrete brain regions. Synapse 2000 36[3] 155–66

Switzer EG Dissimilar patterns of degeneration in brain following four different addictive stimulants. Neuroreport 1993 5:17–20

Thompson PM Hayashi KM et al Structural abnormalities in the brains of human subjects who use methamphetamine. J Neurosci 2004 24:6028–36

Ugarte YV Rau KS et al Methamphetamine rapidly decreases mouse vesicular dopamine uptake: role of hyperthermia and dopamine D2 receptors. Eur J Pharmacology 2003 472:165–71

Ujike H Takaki M et al Gene expression related to synaptogenesis, neuritogenesis, and MAP Kinase in behavioral sensitization to psychostimulants. Ann NY Acad Sci 2002 965:55–67

Valjakka A Vartiainem J et al The fasciculus retroflexus controls the integrity of REM sleep by supporting the generation of hippocampal theta rhythm and rapid eye movements in rats. Brain Res Bull 1998 47:171–84

Vizi ES Palkovits M et al Distinct temperature dependent dopamine releasing effect of drugs of abuse in the olfactory bulb. Neurochem Int 2004 45:63–71

Volkow ND Chang L et al Association of dopamine transporter reduction with psychomotor impairment in meth abusers. Am J Psychiatry 2001 158:377–82.

Volkow ND Chang L et al Higher cortical and lower subcortical metabolism in detoxified methamphetamine abusers. Am J Psychiatry 2001 158:383–9

Volkow ND, Chang L et al Low levels of brain dopamine D2 receptors in methamphetamine abusers: association with metabolism in the orbitofrontal cortex. AM J Psychiatry 158:2015–21

Wang HD Reciprocal information flow between prefrontal cortex and ventral tegmental area in an animal model of schizophrenia. Neuroreport 2000 11:[9] 2007–11

Wang HD Takigawa M et al A Shift in information flow between prefrontal cortex and the ventral tegmental area in methamphetamine sensitized rats. Int J Psychophysiology 2002 44: 251–9

Wang GJ Volkow ND et al Regional brain metabolic activation during craving elicited by recall of previous drug experiences. Life Sci 1999 64:775–84

Wang GJ Volkow ND et al Partial recovery of brain metabolism in methamphetamine abusers after protracted abstinence. Am J Psychiatry 2004 161:242–8

Watanebe T Morimoto K et al Kindling of the ventral tegmental area induces supersensitivity in the central dopamine system. Brain Res 2004 1003:194–8

Wilson JM Kalasinski KS, et al Striatal dopamine nerve terminal markers in human chronic methamphetamine abusers. Nature Med 1996 2:699–703

Woolverton WL, Ricuarte GA et al Long term effects of chronic methamphetamine administration in rhesus monkeys. Brain Res 1989 486:73–78

Yui K Ishaguro T Studies of amphetamine and methamphetamine psychosis: relation of methamphetamine psychosis to schizophrenia. Ann NY Acc Sci 2000 914:1–12

Yui K Ishaguro T Susceptibility of subsequent episodes in spontaneous recurrence of methamphetamine psychosis. Ann NY Acc Sci 2000 914:292–302

Zhou F C and Bledsoe S Serotonin transporters are located on the axons beyond the synaptic junction: anatomical and functional evidence. Brain Research 1998 805:241–254

Zhou FC and Bledsoe S Methamphetamine causes rapid varicosis perforation and definitive degeneration of serotonin fibers: an immunocytochemical study of serotonin transporter. 1996 Neuroscience Net V1 article 10009 Oct 28ᵗʰ 1996 http://www.neuroscience.com/.

MEDICAL

Chan P Chen JH et al Fatal and non-fatal methamphetamine intoxication in the intensive care unit. J Toxicol Clin 1994 32: 147–55

Chuck RS Williams JM et al Recurrent corneal ulcerations associated with smokable methamphetamine abuse. AM J Opthalmol 1996 121:571–2

Coco TJ Klasner AE Drug induced rhabdomyolysis Curr Opin Pediatrics 2004 16:206–10

Flora G Lee YW et al Methamphetamine potentiates HIV-1 Tat protein mediated activation of the redox sensitive pathways in discrete regions of the brain. Exp Neurol 2003 179:60–70

He SY, and Matoba R et al Cardiac muscle lesions associated with chronic administration of methamphetamine in rats. Am J Forensic Med Pathol 1996 17:155–62

Ishigami A Yokunaga I Immunohistochemical study of myoglobin and oxidative injury related markers in the kidney of methamphetamine abusers. Leg Med 2003 5:42–8

Ito Y Jono H and Shojo H A Histopathological study of pancreatic lesions after chronic administration of methamphetamine to rats. Kurume Med J 1997 44:209–15

Karch SB Green GS et al Myocardial hypertrophy and coronary artery disease in male cocaine users. J Forensic Sci 1995 40:591–5

Kendrick WC, Hull AR, Knockel JP Rhabdomyolysis and shock after intravenous amphetamine administration. Ann Inter Med 1977 86:381–7

Maruta T Nihira M Histopathological study on acute poisoning of methamphetamine morphine or cocaine. Nihon Arukoryu Yakabutsu 1997 32:122–138

Matoba R Cardiac lesions on methamphetamine abusers. Nippon Hoigaku Zasshi 2001 55:321–30

Nakahara Y Kikura R et al Hair analysis for drug abuse XIV Identification of substances causing acute poisoning using the hair root: I Methamphetamine. Forensic Sci Int 1997 84:157–64

Nath A Hauser KF et al Molecular basis for interactions of HIV and drugs of abuse. J Acquired Immune Defic Syndr 2002 31 S2 62–9

Richards JR Johnson EB et al Methamphetamine abuse and rhabdomyolysis in the ED: a 5 year study. Am J Emerg Med 1999 17:681–5

Rippeth JD Heaton RK et al Methamphetamine dependence increases risk of neurophysiological impairment in HIV infected persons. J Int Neuropsychol Soc 2004 10:1–14

Roth MD, Whittaker K et al Mechanism for impaired effector function in alveolar macrophages from marijuana and cocaine smokers. J Immunology 2004 147:82–6

Shibata S Mori K Subarachnoid and intracerebral hemorrhage associated with necrotizing angiitis due to methamphetamine abuse- an autopsy case. Neurol Med Chir 1991 31:49–52

Wijetunga M Seto T et al Crystal methamphetamine associated cardiomyopathy: tip of the iceberg? J Toxicol Clin Toxic 2003 41:892–6

NEONATAL

Acuff-Smith KD Schilling MA et al Stage–specific effects of prenatal d-methamphetamine exposure of behavioral and eye development in rats. Neurotoxicol Teratol 1996 18:199–215

Bandresta ES Vogel AL et al Severity of prenatal cocaine exposure and child language functioning through age seven years: a longitudinal latent growth curve analysis. Subst Use Misuse 2004 39:25–59

Dixon SD Bejar R Echoencephalographic findings in neonates associated with maternal cocaine and methamphetamine use: incidence and clinical correlates. J Pediatrics 1989 115:770–8

Gomes-da-Silva J, Perez-Rosado A et al Prenatal exposure to methamphetamine in the rat: ontogeny of tyrosine hydroxylase mRNA expression in mesencephalic dopaminergic neurons. Ann N Y Acad Sci 2002 965:68–77

Heller A, Burbula N Gender dependent enhanced adult neurotoxic response to methamphetamine following fetal exposure to the drug. J Pharmacol Exp Ther 2001 298:769–79

Inoue H Nakatome M et al Maternal methamphetamine administration during pregnancy influences on fetal heart development Life Sci 2004 74:3053

Little BB Snell LM et al Patterns of multiple substance abuse during pregnancy: implications for mother and fetus. South Med J 1990 83:507–9

Neddens J Lesting J et al An early methamphetamine challenge suppresses the maturation of dopamine fibers in the nucleus accumbens of gerbils: on the significance of rearing conditions. J Neural Tranm. 2002 109:141–55

Noailles PA Becker KG et al Methamphetamine induced gene expression profiles in the striatum of male rat pups exposed to the drug in utero. Brain Res Dev Brain Res 2003 147:153–62

Smith LM and Chang L et al Brain proton magnetic resonance spectroscopy in children exposed to methamphetamine in utero. Neurology 2001 57:255–60

Smith L Yonekura ML et al Effects of prenatal methamphetamine exposure in fetal growth in infants born at term. J Dev. Behav Pediatrics 2003 24:17–23

Weissman AD Caldecott-Hazard S In utero methamphetamine effects I. Behavior and monoamine uptake sites in adult offspring. Synapse 1003 13:241–50

Weissman AD Caldecott-Hazard S Developmental neurotoxicity to methamphetamine. Clin Exp Pharmacol Physiol 1995 22:372–4

Williams MT Brown RW et al Neonatal methamphetamine administration induces region specific long term neuronal morphological changes in the rat hippocampus, nucleus accumbens, and parietal cortex. Eur J Neurosci 2003 19:3165–70

Won L Bubula N et al Methamphetamine concentration in fetal and maternal brain following prenatal exposure. Neurotoxicol Teratol 2001 23: 349–54

Won L Bubula N Heller A fatal exposure to methamphetamine in utero stimulated development of serotonergic neurons in three dimensional reaggregate tissue culture. Synapse 2002 43:139–44

Yamamoto Y, Yamamoto K et al Teratogenic effects of methamphetamine in mice. Nippon Hoigaky Zasshi 1992 46:126–31

Zimmerman EF Substance abuse in pregnancy: teratogenesis. Pediatr Ann 1991 20:541–7

NICOTINE

Carlson J Armstrong B Selective Neurotoxic effects of nicotine on axons in fasciculus retroflexus; further supporting evidence that this is a weak link in the brain across multiple drugs of abuse. Neuropharmacology 2000 39:2792–98

Carlson J Noguchi K Ellison G Nicotine produces selective degeneration in the medial habenula and fasciculus retroflexus. Brain Res 2001 906:127–34

Gerasimov MR Ashby CR et al Gamma vinyl GABA inhibits methamphetamine, heroin, or ethanol induced increases in nucleus accumbens dopamine. Synapse 1999 34:11–19

Glick SD Maisonneuve IM Dickinson HA 18-MC reduces methamphetamine and nicotine self administration in rats. Neuroreport 2000 11:2013–15

Kuribara H Does nicotine modify the psychotoxic effects of methamphetamine? Assessment in terms of locomotor sensitization in mice. J Toxicol Sci 1999 24:55–62

London ED, Connoly RJ et al Effects of nicotine on local cerebral glucose utilization in the rat. J Neurosci 1088 8:3920–8

Miyata H Ando K, and Yanagita T Comparison of the effects of nicotine and methamphetamine on extracellular dopamine in the nucleus accumbens of behaviorally sensitized rats. Nihon Shinkei Seiahin Y Z 1996 26:41–47

Maggio R Riva M et al Striatal increase of neurotrophic factors as a mechanism of nicotine protection in experimental Parkinsonism. J Neural Trans 1997 :1113–23

Maggio R Riva M et al Nicotine prevents experimental Parkinsonism in rodents and induces striatal increase of neurotrophic factors. J Neurochem 1998 71:2439–46

Suemaru K Gomita Y et al Chronic nicotine treatment potentiates behavioral responses to dopaminergic drugs in rats. Pharmacol Biochem Behav 1993:46:135–9

Takaki T Chronic treatment with nicotine enhances the sensitivity of dopamine autoreceptors that modulate dopamine release from the rat striatum. Nihon Shinkei Seishin Y Z 1995 15:335–344

Walker DD Venner K et al A comparison of alcohol and drug disorders: is there evidence for a developmental sequence of drug abuse? Addict Behav 2004 29:817–23

Wilens TE Biederman J Spencer TJ et al Pilot controlled clinical trial of ABT 418, a cholinergic agonist in the treatment of adults with attention deficit hyperactivity disorder Am J Psychiatry 1999 156:1931–37

INHALANTS

Garriott J Petty CS Death from inhalant abuse: Toxicological and pathological evaluation of 34 cases. Clin Toxicol 1980 16:305–15

Gerasimov MR Ferrieri RA et al Study of brain uptake and biodistribution of C11 toleune in non human primates and mice. Life Sciences 2002 70:2811–28

Hans JJ Bernsen A et al Magnetic resonance studies on brain dysfunction induced by organic solvents. Acta Neurol Belg 1992 92:207–14

Kucuk NO Kilic EO et al Brain SPECT findings in long term inhalant abuse. Nuclear Medicine Comm 2000 21:769–73

Morrow LA Robin N etal Assessment of attention and memory eficiency in persons with solvent neurotoxicity. Neuropsychologia 1992 30:911–22

Reigel AC French ED An electrophysiological analysis of rat ventral tegmental dopamine nueronal activity during acute toluene exposure. 1999 85:37–43

Riegel AC French ED Abused inhalants and central reward pathways: electrophysiological and behavioral studies in the rat. Ann NY Acad Sci 2002 965:281–91

Rosenberg N.R. and Grigsby J. Neuropsychological Impairment and MRI Abnormalities Associated With Chronic Solvent Abuse. Journal of Clinical Toxicology 2002;40:21–34.

Tenenbein M Pillay N Sensory evoked potentials in inhalant [volatile solvent] abuse. J Paediatric Child Health 1993 29:206–8

ALCOHOL

Brumenfeld R Truran D Effects of heavy drinking, binge drinking, and family history of alcoholism on regional brain metabolites Alcohol Clin Exper Res 2004 28:4

Chen CK Lin SK et al Pre-morbid characteristics and co-morbidity in methamphetamine users with and without psychosis. Psychol Med 2003 33:1407–14

Dougherty DM Mathias CW et al Age at first drink relates to behavioral measures of impulsivity: the immediate and delayed memory task. Alcohol Clin and Exp Res 2004 28:408–414

Hunt WA Nixon SJ *Alcohol-Induced Brain Damage* NIAA Monograph No 22 1993

Lawton-Craddock A Nixon SJ et al Cognitive efficiency in stimulant abusers with and without alcohol dependence. Alcohol Clin Exp Res 2003 27:457–64

Nishiguchi M Kinoshita H et al Effects of chronic alcohol administration on changes of extracellular dopamine and serotonin concentration induced by methamphetamine–comparison of two different alcohol preferring rat lines. Nihon Arukoryu YIZ 2002 37:555–76

Theilen RJ Engleman EA et al Ethanol drinking and deprivation alter dopaminergic and serotonergic function in the nucleus accumbens of alcohol preferring rats. J Pharmacol Exp Ther 2004 Jan 12

POT

Ameri A The Effects of cannabinoids on the brain. Prog Neurobiol 1999 58:315–48

Azad SC Eder M Activation of Cannabinoid receptor type 1 decreases glutaminergic and GABAergic synaptic transmission in the lateral amygdala of the mouse. Learn. Mem 2003 10:116–128

Brown TL Flory K et al Comparing the developmental trajectories of marijuana use of African American and Caucasian adolescents: patterns, antecedents, and consequences. Exp Clin Psychopharmacol 2004 12:47–56

Cheer JF Marsden CA et al Lack of response suppression follows repeated cannabinoid administration: an in vitro electrophysiological study. Neuroscience 2000 99:661–7

Cheer JF Wassum KM et al Cannabinoids enhance subsecond dopamine release in the nucleus accumbens of awake rats. J Neurosci 2004 24:4393–400

De Vries TJ Shaham Y et al A Cannabinoid mechanism in relapse to cocaine seeking. Nat Med 2001 7:1151–4

Diana M Melis M et al Mesolimbic dopaminergic decline after cannabinoid withdrawal. Proc Natl Acad Sci USA 1998 95:10269–73

Diana M Melis M et al Increase in meso-prefrontal dopaminergic activity after stimulation of CB1 receptors by cannabinoids. Eur J Neurosci 1998 10:2825–30

Fried P Watkinson B Current and former marijuana use: a longitudinal study of effects on IQ in young adults. Can Med Assoc J 2002 166:887–91

Ganzalez S Fernandez-Ruiz J et al; Chronic exposure to morphine, cocaine, or ethanol in rats produced different effects in brain cannabinoid CB1 receptor binding and mRNA levels. Drug Alcohol Depend 2002 66:77–84

Gardner EL Addictive potential of cannabinoids: the underlying neurobiology. Chem Phys Lipids 2002 121:267–90

Gessa GL, Melis M et al Cannabinoids activate mesolimbic dopamine neurons by an action on cannabinoid CB1 receptors. Eur J Pharmacol 1998 341:39–44

Hanley M and Ward AS Abstinence symptoms following smoked marijuana in humans. Psychopharmacology 1999 141:395–404

Heath RG Fitzjarrell AT Cannabis Sativa effects on brain function and ultrastructure in Rhesus monkeys. Biol Psych 1980 15:657–90

Hoffman AF and Lupica CR Direct action of cannabinoids on synaptic transmission in the nucleus accumbens: a comparison with opiates. J Neurophysiology 2001 85:72–83

Hoffman AF Oz M et al Functional tolerance and blockade of long term depression at synapses in the nucleus accumbens after chronic cannabinoid exposure. J Neurosci 2003 23:4815–20

Huang YC, Wang SJ et al Mediation of amphetamine induced long term depression of synaptic transmission by CB1 cannabinoid receptors in the rat amygdala. J Neurosci 2003 23:10311–20

Ilan AB Smith ME et al Effects of marijuana on neurophysiological signals of working and episodic memory. Psychopharmacology 2004 May 7

Jentsch JD Andrusiak E et al Delta 9 tetrahydrocannabinol increases prefrontal cortical catecholaminergic utilization and impairs spatial working memory in the rat: blockade of dopaminergic effects with HA966. Neuropsychopharmacology 1997 16:426–32

Jentsh JD Verrico CD et al Repeated exposure to delta 9 tetrahydrocannabinol reduces prefrontal dopamine metabolism in the rat. Neurosci Lett 1998 246:169–72

Katona I Rancz EA et al Distribution of CB1 cannabinoid receptors in the amygdala and their role in the control of GABAergic transmission. J Neurosci 2001 21:0506–1

Kaminer Y Burleson JA Psychotherapies for adolescent substance abusers: 15 month follow up of pilot study. AM J Addict 1999 8:114–119

Kelley BG, Thayer SA Delta tetrahydrocannabinol antagonizes Endocannabinoid modulation of synaptic transmission between hippocampal neurons in culture. Neuropharmacology 2003 46:709–15

Kim D Thayer SA Activation of CB1 cannabinoid receptors inhibits neurotransmitter release from identified synaptic sites in rat hippocampal cultures. Brain Res 2000 852:398–405

Kim D Thayer SA Cannabinoids inhibit the formation of new synapses between hippocampal neurons in culture. Journal of Neuroscience 2001 21:RC 146

Manzoni OJ Bockaert J Cannabinoids inhibit GABAergic synaptic transmission in mice nucleus accumbens. Eur J Pharmacol 2001 412: R3–5

McDonald AJ Mascagni F Localization of the CB1 type cannabinoid receptor in the rat basolateral amygdala: High concentrations in a subpopulation of cholecystokinin containing interneurons. Neuroscience 2001 107:641–52

Morales M, Wang CD et al Cannabinoid CB1 receptor and serotonin 3 subunit A are co expressed in GABA neurons in the rat telencephalon. J Comp Neurol 2004 468:205–16

Pistis M Ferraro L et al Delta 9 tetrahydrocannabinol decreases extracellular GABA and increases extracellular glutamate and dopamine levels in the rat prefrontal cortex: an in vivo microdialysis study. Brain Res 2002 948:155–8

Pistis M Muntoni AL et al Cannabinoids inhibit excitatory inputs to neurons in the shell of the nucleus accumbens an in vivo electrophysiological study. Eur J Neurosci 2002 15:1795–802

Pistis M Perra S et al Cannabinoids modulate neuronal firing in the rat basolateral amygdala: evidence for CB1 and non CB1 mediated actions. Neuropharmacology 2004 46:115–25

Pope HG Turgelun-Todd D Residual cognitive effects of heavy marijuana use in college students. JAMA 191996 275:521–27

Ramaekers JG, Berghaus G Dose related risk of motor vehicle crashes after cannabis use. Drug Alcohol Depend. 2004 73:109–19

Riegel, AC French ED Abused inhalants and central reward pathways: electrophysiological and behavioral studies in the rat. Ann NY Acad Sci 2002 965:281–91

Szabo B Siemes S et al Inhibition of GABAergic neurotransmission in the ventral tegmental area by cannabinoids. Eur J Neurosci 2002 15:2057–61

Tzavara ET Davis RJ et al The CB1 receptor antagonist SR141716A selectively increases monoaminergic neurotransmission in the medial prefrontal cortex: implications for therapeutic actions. Br J Pharmacol 2003 138:544–53.

Valjent E Mitchell JM et al Behavioral and biochemical evidence for interactions between Delta 9 tetrahydrocannabinol and nicotine. Br J Pharmacol 2002 135:564–78 pot nicotine interaction

Verrico CD, Jentsch JD, Roth RH Persistent and anatomically selective reduction in prefrontal cortical dopamine metabolism after repeated intermittent cannabinoid administration to rats. Synapse 2003 49:61–66

Voruganti LN Slomka P et al Cannabis induced dopamine release: an in vivo SPECT study. Psychiatry Res 2001 107:173–7

Voth EA A Peek into Pandora's box: the medical excuse marijuana controversy. J Addict Dis 2003 22:27–46

Walter, L., Franklin A et al Nonpsychotropic cannabinoid receptors regulate microglial cell migration. J Neurosci 2003 23:1398–405

ECSTASY

Alting Von Geusau N Stalenhoef P et al impaired executive function in male MDMA users. Psychopharmacol 2004 Mar 18 e-pub ahead of print

Battaglia G et al 3,4 methylenedioxymethamphetamine destroy serotonin terminals in rat brain: qualifications of neurodegeneration by measurement of [3H] paroxentine-labeled serotonin uptake sites. J Pharmacol Exp Ther, 1987 242:911–6

Battaglia G Yeh SY De Souza EB MDMA induced neurotoxicity: Parameters of degeneration and recovery of brain serotonin neurons. Pharmacol Biochem Behav 1988 29:269–274

Becker J Neis P et al A fatal paramethoxymethamphetamine intoxication. Leg Med 2003 5s :138–41

Beirdsley PM Balster RL Evaluation of discriminative stimulus and reinforcing effects of GHB Psychopharmacology. 1996:127:315–322

Broening HW Morford LL et al MDMA induced learning and memory impairments depend on the age of exposure during early development. J Neurosci 2001 21:3228–35

Camarero J Sanchez V et al Studies using in vivo microdialysis on the effect of the dopamine uptake inhibitor GBR 12909 on MDMA induced dopamine release and free radial formation in the mouse striatum. J Neurochem 2002 81:961–72

Carvalho M Remiao F Metabolism is required for the expression of ecstasy induced cardiotoxicity in vitro. Chem Res Toxicol 2004 17:623–32

Clemens KJ Van Nieuwenhuyzen PS et al MDMA, methamphetamine and their combination: long term changes in social interaction and neurochemistry in the rat. Psychopharmacol 2004 173:318–25

Colado MI Camerero J et al A Study of the mechanisms involved in the neurotoxic action of MDMA on dopamine neurons in mouse brain. Br J Pharmacol 2001 134:1711–23

Colado MI O'Shea E et al Acute and long term effects of MDMA on cerebral dopamine biochemistry and function Psychopharmacol 2004 173:249–63

Cowan RI L Yoo IK et al Reduced cortical grey matter density in human MDMA users: a voxel based morphometry study. Drug Alcohol Depend 2003 72:225–35

Daniela E Brennan K et al Effect of SCH 233990 and MDMA hyperactivity and self administration in rats. Pharmacol Biochem Behav 2004 77:745–50

Dafters RI and Biello SM The effect of MDMA on Serotonergic regulation of the mammalian circadian clock mechanism on rats: the role of dopamine and hyperthermia. Neurosci Lett 2003 350:117–21

Daws LC Irvine RJ et al Differential behavioral and neurochemical effects of para methoxyamphetamine and MDMA in the rat. Prog Neuropsychopharmacol Biol Psychiatry 2000 24:955–77

De Win MM Reneman L et al Mood disorders and serotonin transporter density in ecstasy users–the influence of long term abstention, dose, and gender Psychopharmacology 2004 173:376–82

Easton N Fry J et al Synthesis in vitro formation and behavioral effects if glutathione regioisomers of alpha methyldopamine with relevance to MDA and MDMA. Brain Res 2003 987:144–54

Farnai F Gesi M et al Striatal postsynaptic ultrastructural alterations following MDMA administration. Ann NY Acad Sci 2002 965:381–98

Fletcher PJ Robinson SR Pre-exposure to MDMA facilitates acquisition of intravenous cocaine self administration in rats. Neuropsychopharmacology 2001 25:195–203

Fornai F Lenzi P et al DNA damage and ubiquitinated neuronal inclusions in the substantia nigra and striatum of mice following MDMA. Psychopharmacology 2004 173:353–63

Frei E Gamma A et al Localization of MDMA induced brain activity in healthy volunteers using low resolution brain electromagnetic tomography. LORETA Hum Brain Mapp 2001 14:152–165

Green AR Machan AO et al The Pharmacology and clinical pharmacology of MDMA. Pharmacol Rev 2003 55:463–508

Gudelsky GA and Yamamoto BK Neuropharmacology and neurotoxicity of 3,4 methylenedioxymethamphetamine Methods in molecular medicine. 2003 79: 55–73

Hatzidimitriou G Mc Cann UD Altered serotonin innervation patterns in the forebrain of monkeys treated with MDMA seven years previously factors influencing abnormal recovery. J Neurosci 1999 19:5096–5107

Hanson KL Luciana M Neurocognitive function in users of MDMA: the importance of clinically significant patterns of use. Psychol Med 2004 34:229–46

Hegadoren KM Baker GB et al 3,4,methylenedioxy analogues of amphetamine: defining the risks to humans. Neurosci and Biobehavioral Review 1999 23:539–553

Iravani MM Asari D et al Direct effects of MDMA on serotonin or dopamine release and uptake in the caudate, putamen, nucleus accumbens, substantia nigra pars reticulate, and the dorsal raphe nucleus slices. Synapse 2000 36:275–85

Itzhak Y Ali SF et al Relevance of MDMA induced neurotoxicity to long lasting psychomotor stimulation in mice. Psychopharmacology 2003 166:241–8

Jacobsen LK Mencl WE et al Preliminary evidence of hippocampal dysfunction in adolescent MDMA users: possible relationship to neurotoxic effects. Psychopharmacology 2004 173:383–90

Kalant K The pharmacology and toxicology of ecstasy and related drugs Can Med Assoc J 2001 165:917–28

Kish SJ, Furakawa Y et al Striatal serotonin is depleted in brain of a human MDMA user. Neurology 2000 55:294–6

Koprich JB Chen EY et al Prenatal MDMA alters exploratory behavior, reduces monoamine metabolism, and increases forebrain tyrosine hydroxylase fiber density of juvenile rats. Neurotoxicol Teratol 2003 25:509–17

Liechti ME Baumann C et al Acute psychological effects of MDMA are attenuated by the serotonin uptake inhibitor citalopram. Neuropsychopharmacology 2000 22:513–21

Liechti ME Vollenweider FX Acute psychological and physiological effects of MDMA after haloperidol pretreatment in healthy humans. Eur Neuropsychopharmacol 2000 10:289–95

Liechti ME Vollenweider FX Which neurotransmitters mediate the subjective effects of MDMA in humans? A summary of mechanistic studies. Hum Psychopharmacol 2001 16:589–98

Maitre M Mampandry C Gammahydroxybutyric acid as a signaling molecule in the brain. Alcohol 2000 20:277–83

Mayerhofer A Kovar KA Schmidt WJ Changes in serotonin dopamine and noradrenalin levels in striatum and nucleus accumbens after repeated administration of the abused drug MDMA in rats. Neurosci Lett 2001 308 : 99–102

McCann UD et al Serotonin neurotoxicity after ecstasy: a controlled study in humans. Neuropharmacology 1994:10, 129–38

McCann UD Mertle M et al Cognitive performance in 34 MDMA users: a controlled study. Psychopharmacol 1999 143:417–25

McCann UD Wong Z et al PET evidence of toxic effect of MDMA on brain serotonin neurons in human beings. Lancet 1998 352:1433–1437

McCardle K Luebbers S et al Chronic MDMA use, cognition and mood. Psychopharmacol 2004 173:434–9

McGregor IS, Gurtman CG et al Increased anxiety and "depressive" symptoms months after MDMA in rats: drug induced hyperthermia does not predict long term outcomes. Psychopharmacology 2003 168:465–74

Meyer JS Ali SF Serotonergic neurotoxicity of MDMA in the developing rat brain. Ann NY Acad Sci 2002 965:373–80

Miotto K Darakjian J GHB Patterns of use, effects, and withdrawal. Am J Addiction 2001 10:232–41

Montiel-Duarte C Ansorena E et al Role of reactive oxygen species glutathione and NF kappa B in apoptosis induced by MDMA on hepatic stellate cells. Biochem Pharmacol 2004 67:1025–33

Navarro JF Rivera A et al Anxiolytic like activity of MDMA in the social interaction test is accompanied by an increase of c-fos expression in mice amygdala. Prog Neuropsychopharmacology Biol Psychiatry 2004 28:249–54

O'Cain PA Hletko SB et al Cardiovascular and sympathetic responses and reflex changes elicited by MDMA. Physiol Behav 2000 70:141–8

Parrott AC Human Research on MDMA neurotoxicity: cognitive and behavioral indices of change. Neuropsychobiology 2000 42:17–42

Parrott AC Recreational ecstasy MDMA the serotonin syndrome and serotonergic neurotoxicity. Pharmacol Biochem Behav 2002 71:837–44

Parrott AC Is ecstasy MDMA? A review of the proportions of ecstasy tablets containing MDMA, their dosage levels, and the changing perceptions of purity. Psychopharmacology 2004 173:234–41

Quednow BB Kuhn KU et al Prepulse inhibition and habituation of acoustic startle response in male MDMA users, cannabis users, and healthy controls. Neuropsychopharmacology 2004 29:982–90.

Rememen L Majoie CBLM et al Prefrontal N acetylaspartate is strongly associated with memory performance in abstinent ecstasy users: preliminary report. Biol Psychiatry 2001 50:550–554

Schifano F, Di Furia L et al MDMA consumption in the context of polydrug abuse: a report on 150 patients. Drug Alcohol 1998 52:85–90

Semple DM, Ebeimer K P et al Reduced in vivo binding to the serotonin transporter in the cerebral cortex of MDMA ecstasy users. Br J Psychiatry 1999 175:193–9

Semple SJ Patterson TL et al The context of sexual risk behavior among heterosexual methamphetamine users. Addict Behav 2004 29:807–10

Simantov R Peng W MDMA ecstasy controls in concert a group of genes involved in GABA neurotransmission. FEBS Lett 2004 563:3–6

Stephenson CP Hunt GE et al The distribution of MDMA induced c-fos expression in the rat brain. Neuroscience 1999 92:1011–23

Thompson MR Li KM et al Chronic fluoxdetine treatment partly attenuates the long term anxiety and depressive symptoms induced by MDMA in rats. Neuropsychopharmacology 2004 29:694–704

COCAINE

Bolla KI Eldreth DA et al Orbitofrontal cortex dysfunction in abstinent cocaine abusers performing a decision making task. Neuroimage 2003 19:1085–94

Ciccopioppo R, Sanna RD Cocaine predictive stimulus induces drug seeking behavior and neural activation in limbic brain regions after multiple months of abstinence: reversal by D1 antagonists. Proc National Accad Sci 98:1976–81

Ellison G Continuous amphetamine and cocaine have similar neurotoxic effects in lateral habenular nucleus and fasciculus retroflexus. Brain Res 1992 598:353–356

Kilts CD, Schweitzer JB et al Neural Activity related to drug craving in cocaine addiction. Arch Gen Psychiatry 2001 58:334–341

Lim KO Choi SJ et al Reduced frontal white matter integrity in cocaine dependence: a controlled diffusion tensor imaging study. Biol Psychiatry 2002 51:890–5

Matochik JA London ED et al Frontal cortical tissue composition in abstinent cocaine abusers: magnetic resonance imaging study. Neuroimage 2003 19:1095–102

Ross BM Moszczynska A et al Decreased activity of brain phospholipids metabolic enzymes in human users of cocaine and methamphetamine. Drug and Alcohol Dependency 2002 67:73–9

HEROIN

Gerasimov MR Ashby CR et al Gamma-vinyl GABA inhibits methamphetamine, heroin, or ethanol–induced increases in nucleus accumbens dopamine. Synapse 1999 34:11–9

McLeman ER Warsh JJ et al The human nucleus accumbens is highly susceptible to G protein down regulation by methamphetamine and heroin. J Neurochem 2000 74:2120–6

Ranaldi R Wise RA Intravenous self administration of methamphetamine-heroin [speedball] combinations under a progressive ratio schedule of reinforcement in rats. Neuroreport 2000 21:2621–3

Platt DM Rowlett JK et al Discriminative effects of intravenous heroin and its metabolites in rhesus monkeys: opioid and dopaminergic mechanisms. J Pharmacol Exp Ther 2001 299:760–7

Taylor DA Flemming WW Unifying perspectives on the mechanism underlying the development of tolerance and physical dependence to opioids. J Pharmacol Exp Ther 2001 1:11–18

ADHD

Adler LA Chua HC Management of ADHD in Adults. J Clin Psychiatry 2002 63 29–35

Akhondzadeh S Tavakolian R et al Selegiline in the treatment of attention deficit hyperactivity disorder in children: a double blind and randomized trail. Prog Neuropsychopharmacol Biol Psychiatry 2003 27:841–5

Barkley RA Fischer M et al Young adult followup of hyperactive children: antisocial activities and drug use. J Child Psychol Psychiatry 2004 45:195–211

Blum K Sheridan PJ et al Dopamine D2 receptor gene variants: association and linkage studies in impulsive addictive compulsive behavior. Pharmacogenetics 1995 5:121–141

Bush G Frazier JA et al Anterior Cingulate cortex dysfunction in attention deficit hyperactivity disorder revealed by fMRI and the Counting Stroop Test. Biol Psychiatry 1999 45:1542–52

Bussing R Grudnick J et al ADHD and conduct disorder: a MRI study in a community sample. World J Biol Psychiatry 2002 3:216–20

Castellanos FX Sharp WS Anatomic brain abnormalities in monozygotic twins discordant for attention deficit hyperactivity disorder. Am J Psychiatry 2003 160:1693–6

Castaneda R Sussman N et al A treatment algorithm for attention deficit hyperactivity disorder on cocaine dependent adults: one year private practice study with long acting stimulants, fluoxdetine and buproprion. Subst Abuse 1999 20:59–71

Cheon KA Ryu YH et al Dopamine transporter density in the basal ganglia assessed with [123I] IPT SPET in children with attention deficit hyperactivity disorder. Eur J Nucl Med Mol Imaging 2003 30:306–311

Choong KC Shen RY Methylphenidate restores VTA dopamine neuron activity in prenatal ethanol exposed rats by augmenting dopamine neurotransmission. J Pharmacol Exp Ther 2004 Jan 14

Cocores JA Davies RK et al Cocaine abuse and adult attention deficit disorder. J Clin Psychiatry 1987 48:376–7

Conners CK Levil ED et al Nicotine and attention in adult attention deficit hyperactivity disorder. Psychopharmacol Bull 1996 32:67–73

Dimitri CA Zimmerman FJ Early television exposure and subsequent attentional problems in children. Pediatrics 2004 113:708–713

Faraone SV Biederman SV et al Dopamine D4 gene 7 repeat allele and attention deficit hyperactivity disorder. AM J Psychiatry 1999 156:768–770

Itami S Uno H Orbitofrontal cortex dysfunction in attention deficit hyperactivity disorder revealed by reversal and extinction tasks. Neuroreport 2002 13:2453–7

Kaya GC Pekcanlar A et al Technetium 99m HMPAO brain SPECT in children with attention deficit hyperactivity disorder. Ann Nucl Med 2002 16:527–31

Kim BN Lee JS et al Regional cerebral perfusion abnormalities in attention deficit hyperactivity disorder statistical parametric mapping analysis. Eur Arch Psychiatry Clin Neurosci 2002 252:219–25

Kuczenski R Segal DS Exposure of adolescent rats to oral methylphenidate: preferential effects on norepinephrine and absence of sensitization and cross-sensitization to methamphetamine. J Neurosci 2002 22:7264–71

Lanan F Zenner MT et al Epinephrine and norepinephrine act as potent agonists at the recombinant human dopamine D4 receptor. J Neurochemistry 1997 68:804–812

Lichter JB, Barr CI et al A hypervariable segment in the human dopamine receptor D4 [DRD4] gene. Hum Mol Genet 1993 2:767–773

NIH consensus Statement Diagnosis and treatment of attention deficit hyperactivity disorder Nov 16–18 1998 16[2]:1–37

Mac Master FP Carrey N et al Proton spectroscopy in medication free pediatric attention deficit hyperactivity disorder. Biol Psychiatry 2003 53:184–7

Michelson D Faries D et al Atomoxetine in the treatment of children and adolescents with attention deficit hyperactivity disorder a randomized placebo controlled dose response study. Pediatrics 2001 108:E83

The MTA Cooperative Group A 14 month randomized clinical trial of treatment strategies for attention deficit hyperactivity disorder. Arch Gen Psychiatry 1999 56:1073–86

Schubiner H Tzelepis A et al Prevalence of attention deficit hyperactivity disorder and conduct disorder among substance abusers. J Clin Psychiatry 2000 61:244–51

Sim T Simon SL et al Cognitive deficits among methamphetamine users with attention deficit hyperactivity disorder symptomatology. J Addict Dis 2002 21:75–89

Spencer TJ Biederman J et al Overview and neurobiology of attention deficit hyperactivity disorder. J Clin Psychiatry 2002 63 [suppl 12] 3–9

Volkow ND Fowler JS et al Role of dopamine in the therapeutic and reinforcing effects of methylphenidate in humans: results from imaging studies. Eur Neuropsychopharmacology 2002 12:557–66

Willens TE et al Does stimulant therapy of attention deficit hyperactivity disorder beget later substance abuse? A meta analytic review of the literature. Pediatrics 2003 111:179–185.

Zametkin A J Nordahl TE Cerebral glucose metabolism in adults with hyperactivity of childhood onset. NEJM 1990 323:1413–1415 and

Zametkin A J Liebenauer L L at al Brain metabolism in teenagers with attention deficit hyperactivity disorder. Arch Gen Psychiatry 2003 50: 333–40

Zhuang X Oosting RS et al Hyperactivity and impaired response habituation in hyperdopaminergic mice. Proc Natl Acad Sci 2001 98:1982–7

PTSD

Anderson CM Teicher MH et al Abnormal T2 relaxation time in the cerebellar vermis of adults sexually abused in childhood: potential role of the vermis in stress enhanced risk for drug abuse. Psychoneuroendocrinology 2002 27:231–244

Bremmer JD Randall P et al MRI Based measurement of hippocampal volume in patients with combat related posttraumatic stress disorder. AM J Psychiatry 1995 152:973–81

Bremner JD Vythilingam M et al Cortisone response to a cognitive stress challenge in posttraumatic stress disorder [PTSD] related to childhood abuse. Psychoneuroendocrinology 2003 28:733–50

Bremner JD, Vythilingam M wet al MRI and PET study of deficits in hippocampal structure and function in women with childhood sexual abuse and posttraumatic stress disorder. Am J Psychiatry 2003 160:924–32

Celada P Puig MV et al Control of the Serotonergic system by the medial prefrontal cortex: potential role in the etiology of PTSD and depressive disorders. Neurotox Res 2002 4:409–419

Comings DE Muhleman D et al Dopamine D2 receptor DRD2 gene and susceptibility to posttraumatic stress disorder: a study and replication. Biol Psychiatry 1996 40:368–72

Elzinga BM Schmahl CG et al Higher cortisol levels following exposure to traumatic reminders in abuse related PTSD. Neuropsychopharmacology 2003 28:1656–65

Fredrickson M Furmark T Amygdaloid regional cerebral blood flow and subjective fear during symptom provocation in anxiety disorders. Ann NY Acad Sci 2003 985 341 -7

Hall CW, Webster RE Traumatic symptomatology characteristics of adult children of alcoholics. J Drug Educ 2002 32:195–211

Harvey BH Naciti C Endocrine, cognitive and Hippocampal/cortical 5HT 1A/2A receptor changes evoked by a time dependent sensitization [TDS] stress model in rats. Brain Res 2003 983:97–107

Hendler T Rotshtein P et al Sensing the Invisible: differential sensitivity of visual cortex and amygdala to traumatic context. Neuroimage 2003 19:587–600

Hedges DW Allen S et al Reduced hippocampal volume in alcohol and substance naïve Vietnam combat veterans with posttraumatic stress disorder. Cogn Behav Neurol 2003 16:219–24

Langeland W, Draijer N et al Psychiatric comorbidity in treatment seeking alcoholics: the role of childhood trauma and perceived parental dysfunction. Alcohol Clin and Exper Res 2004 28:441–447

Lanius RA Williamson PC et al Recall of emotional states in posttraumatic stress disorder: an fMRI investigation. Biol Psychiatry 2003 53:204–10

Mc Ewen BS The neurobiology and neuroendocrinology of stress. Implication for post traumatic stress disorder from a basic science perspective. Psychiatric Clinics North America 2002 25:469–94

Nunes EV Levin FR Treatment of depression in patients with alcohol or other drug dependence: a meta analysis. JAMA 2004 291:1887–96

Nutt DJ Malizia AL Structural and functional brain changes in post traumatic stress disorder. J Clin Psychiatry 2004 65:S1 11–17

Ouimette P. Moos RH Finney JW PTSD treatment and 5 year remission among patients with substance abuse and posttraumatic stress disorders. J Consult Clin Psychol 2003 71:410–4

Pavic L Gregurek R et al Alterations in brain activation in posttraumatic stress disorder patients with severe hyperarousal symptoms and impulsive aggressiveness. Eur Arch Psychiatry Clin Neurosci 2003 253:80–3

Rauch SL Shin LM et al Selectively reduced regional cortical volumes in post traumatic stress disorder. Neuroreport 2003 14:913–6

Semple W E, Goyer P F et al Higher brain blood flow at amygdala and lower frontal cortex blood flow in PTSD patients with comorbid cocaine and alcohol abuse compared with normals. Psychiatry 2000 63:65–74

Teicher MH Andersen SL et al Developmental neurobiology of childhood stress and trauma. Psychiatric Clinics North America 2002 25:397–426

Vermetten E, Vythilingham M et al Long term treatment with paroxentine increases verbal declarative memory and hippocampal volume in posttraumatic stress disorder. Biol Psychiatry 2003 54:693–702

ALCOHOLIC HOME

Neil Swan, Early Childhood behavior and temperament predict later substance use. NIDA Notes Jan 1995 10:1

Andrews J.A. Hops H, Parental influence in early adolescent substance use: specific and nonspecific effects. J Early Adolescence 1993 13:285–310

Gerrra G Angioni L et al Substance abuse among high school students: relationship with temperament, personality traits, and parental care perception. Subst Use Misuse 2004 39:345–67

Hops H. Tildesley E. et al Parent-adolescent problem solving interactions and drug use. Am J Drug and Alcohol Abuse 1990 16:239–58

National Center on Addiction and Substance Abuse at Columbia University, *So Help Me God Substance Abuse, Religion and Spirituality* A CASA White Paper Nov. 2001

Neil Swan, Early Childhood behavior and temperament predict later substance use. NIDA Notes Jan 1995 10:1

Prinstein MJ La Greca AM Childhood peer rejection and aggression as predictors of adolescent girl's externalizing and health risk behaviors: a 6 year longitudinal study. J Consult Clin Psychol. 2004 72:103–12

Ritt-Olson A Milam J et al The protective effect of spirituality and "Health as a Value" against monthly substance abuse among adolescents varying in risk. J Adolesc Health 2004 34:192–9

Roberts TA Auinger P et al Body piercing and high risk behavior in adolescents. J Adolesc Health 2004 34:224–9

Wallace JM Jr Brown TN et al The influence of race and religion on abstinence from alcohol, cigarettes and marijuana among adolescents. J Stud Alcohol. 2003 64:843–8

INDEX

Contact Dr. Mary F. Holley
or order more copies of this book at

TATE PUBLISHING, LLC

127 East Trade Center Terrace
Mustang, Oklahoma 73064

(888) 361 - 9473

Tate Publishing, LLC

www.tatepublishing.com